Hensley Henson

Apostolic Christianity

Notes and Inferences Mainly Based on S. Paul's Epistles to the Corinthians

Hensley Henson

Apostolic Christianity
Notes and Inferences Mainly Based on S. Paul's Epistles to the Corinthians

ISBN/EAN: 9783337022730

Printed in Europe, USA, Canada, Australia, Japan

Cover: Foto ©Lupo / pixelio.de

More available books at **www.hansebooks.com**

APOSTOLIC CHRISTIANITY

NOTES AND INFERENCES MAINLY
BASED ON S. PAUL'S EPISTLES
TO THE CORINTHIANS

BY

H. HENSLEY HENSON, B.D.

FELLOW OF ALL SOULS' COLLEGE, OXFORD
INCUMBENT OF S. MARY'S HOSPITAL, ILFORD
CHAPLAIN TO THE LORD BISHOP OF S. ALBAN'S
RURAL DEAN OF SOUTH BARKING

METHUEN & CO.
36 ESSEX STREET, STRAND
LONDON
1898

PREFACE

THE charm of Apostolic Christianity is unique, and its importance supreme. Partly, it may not be questioned, the natural but irrational disposition to exalt the past at the expense of the present explains the lofty estimate of the earliest Church which most modern Christians have formed, and an actual study of the extant memorials of the first century will, to this extent, chasten and modify that estimate. Chiefly, however, the interest of thoughtful men in the first beginnings of the Divine Society arises from a just conviction of the solemn importance of the subject. It is felt on all hands that the Christianity of history, and especially the Christianity of contemporary history, is a very different thing from the Christianity of the Apostles: there is an uncomfortable suspicion in many minds that the proportions of the Faith have been deranged, that the intrinsically greater things have fallen into the background, and the intrinsically lesser things have usurped their prominence. The Church, the Ministry, the Sacraments, the Creeds—these have, in many minds, seemed to crowd out of view more ultimate and august realities; and so powerful is the vague, almost unconscious, resentment of the human conscience, that a wide and ever-widening breach has silently discovered itself between religious men and organized religion. On all hands it is observable that Christian men are quietly withdrawing themselves from all formal religious observances. They neither attend public worship nor receive the Blessed Sacrament, nor outwardly concern themselves with religious affairs. It would be a grave error to suppose that these people are in any definite way opposed to Christianity. Most of them have a real respect and admiration for Jesus Christ, and a vague but confident belief that if only religion were what He intended it to be, if only the Church were again what it was in the Apostles' times, they would eagerly profess themselves disciples. During the years that I have lived in East London and "London over the Border" I have often heard vehement denunciations of the Church, of the clergy, of the Sacraments, and of the Bible, but I can only recall a single instance in which the stream of invective was directed against the Founder of Christianity, and then it provoked very manifest repugnance. Largely, it must be admitted, this attitude is reflected and, by an inevitable reaction, stimulated by the so-called religious romance of the day. Scarcely anybody reads the New Testament: the current notions about the Gospel and the Apostolic age are largely based on the productions of Marie Corelli, Mr. Hall Caine, and writers of that type. Religious sentiment and emotion are developed by a thousand devices, while the prevailing conception of contemporary Christianity is often a strange and various product of ignorance, prejudice, and delusion. Yet I cannot escape the conviction that there is a more legitimate foundation for the deliberate and sustained alienation of so vast a multitude than mere sentiment on the one hand and mere mistake on the other.

The causes of this quiet repudiation of definite external religious observance are not altogether obscure. Probably few realize the gravity of the fact that, through the rapid growth of the cities, the main stream of the national life is now running, with an ever increasing volume, in urban channels. Life in a great city affects powerfully and distinctively the development of character. I am far, indeed, from suggesting that the urban influence is necessarily or even generally bad; but I am very sure that in certain directions that influence is hostile to religion. The passion for amusement pathetically testifies to the deep weariness of routine, which the city-worker chained from day to day to his office-stool, or penned behind his counter, feels so acutely. Even the religiously-minded men feel this revulsion against restraint: the mass, consciously or unconsciously, are swept along by it. The services of Religion are found too long and too dull. Only on the condition that they become "bright," "popular," above all, short, will they be attended. The result is disastrous on the public worship and on the preaching. I am convinced that an unconscious effort to match the tastes of the giddy and emotional urban folk, far more than any real religious conviction or any innate bent towards anarchy, lies at the root of the ritual eccentricity which now distresses many sober-minded Churchmen, and perplexes the Bishops. It is melancholy to observe that Religion, which should grapple with and bring under discipline that frivolity which is the inevitable effect of urban life, rather aspires to conciliate and use it.

The Decline of the Pulpit is not less serious. Here, no doubt, special causes have contributed. The Oxford Movement was very largely a reaction against the arid and tyrannous Evangelicalism which oppressed the national conscience at the beginning of this century. As the Pulpit had been unduly magnified by the earlier movement, so it was unduly minimized in the later. Moreover, the Tractarians widened the area of clerical interests. Church History was no longer eschewed, though its study was severely conditioned by ecclesiastical presuppositions. Ritualism opened a new and delightful world to the weaker members of the Anglo-Catholic party. The Sermon was habitually depreciated. It was made to symbolize human self-assertion as against Divine Grace : it stood for "Protestantism" as against the "Catholic Church." It is still the fashion in "High Church" circles to affect a great contempt for preaching : <u>and commonly the Sermon in "advanced" Churches faithfully reflects the humble theory which may be supposed to have governed its composition.</u> It may be held for certain that an excessive care for religious ceremony is incompatible with a high standard of preaching. The human mind cannot with impunity multiply its interests. A close and affectionate study of Ritual will leave little margin of time or mental power for those critical, historical, and theological studies which are the indispensable conditions of serviceable preaching to modern congregations. A worthier obstacle to the Pulpit has been the immense increase of parochial duties. Whether this increase is wholly satisfactory may be doubted: whether the time and energy bestowed on the raising of money for a thousand objects, in the organizing of amusements, not always of the highest kind, could not be better employed, may well be questioned: yet, at least, it must be conceded that the motives which have led to that distracting multiplicity of parochial engagements, which threatens to make pastoral charge wholly incompatible with intellectual self-respect, are high and unselfish motives. Here I refer to the subject merely in its bearings on the lamentable Decline of the Pulpit, to which I have adverted. Of late years there has been a considerable increase of "Home Missions." Almost every parish of any size is subjected every few years to the Ordeal of a "Mission." The enormous demand for preachers has induced many of the more earnest and eloquent clergy to cultivate an emotional and declamatory type of preaching, which, though immediately effective and generally popular, is not free from very obvious and considerable perils. I think there are signs that the standard of Pulpit performance has been appreciably lowered by the development of "Mission preaching." Finally, the Sermon may have suffered by the competition of the religious newspaper and the religious book, though it may be doubted whether the readers of such are not generally the most assiduous auditors of Sermons.

Personally I think the influence of the press has been indirect. The best work is now rarely put into Sermons: it is reserved for publication. This is a natural, but a highly undesirable practice.

It has often occurred to me that there is a connection between the facts just stated and the grave difficulty which is now felt in obtaining suitable candidates for the Christian Ministry. No doubt the serious decline in clerical incomes has influenced parents in choosing careers for their sons; but there is compensation in the thought that poverty, though it may hinder some from entering Holy Orders, will purify the motives of many who, with the full knowledge of the distresses that await them, yet put their hand to the plough of the Divine Service. A more serious loss is inflicted on the Church when young men of intellectual gifts and high character turn away from Ordination because, under existing circumstances, they cannot hope for an adequate sphere for the exercise of their best powers. As matters stand now a musical voice is a better recommendation than academic distinction, a knowledge of athletics and theatricals outweighs habits of intellectual industry, and a solemn sense of the awfulness of religion. If indeed it be the case that the Church has no use for the higher gifts of mind and character, then it is nothing astonishing that her Ministry has little attraction for the gifted and devout. The higher the standard of Ministerial Duty the more attractive will the Ministerial Life be found; but no thoughtful and earnest man can readily accept a career, of which the principal tasks will be purely mechanical.

However this may be, the broad fact now stares the clergyman in the face that his principal instrument of teaching is breaking in his hands; the Pulpit seems to be discredited in the general mind, it is certainly ignored in the general practice. Therefore since teaching has always been and must remain the chiefest function of the Christian Ministry, the clergyman is driven to adopt various expedients by which to recover some opportunities for fulfilling his duty. Informal lectures, books written in a sufficiently popular style to secure the interest of average men, private conferences of one sort or another — these and similar methods are resorted to as substitutes for the Sermon.

These pages represent one modest attempt to bring before laymen in their homes subjects which had been better treated in Sermons, but which, since they will neither listen to Sermons nor read them, must be treated otherwise or not at all.

Urban life not only stimulates a passion for amusement, it also directly ministers to the cynical, sceptical disposition, which, not less than frivolity, obstructs the way of Religion. English people of the middle and lower classes, so far as I have observed, are not as a general rule well disposed towards definite infidelity; but they seem to be falling into a vague unbelief, which does not care enough about spiritual things to positively contradict, but which tacitly rejects the teachings of the Gospel. There is a widely-extended distrust of the good faith of the clergy in matters of Religion. It is thought that language is used in the pulpit which does not correspond with any actual convictions. The destructive aspects of Biblical criticism are becoming generally known, and something like contempt is not rarely expressed at the unrelaxed hold on the least defensible views which the clergy, in too many cases, display. With this contempt it is difficult not to feel a measure of sympathy. The timidity of the clergy scarcely respects the boundaries of Christian principle when it insists on ignoring the conclusions of Biblical Science. The manly attitude of S. Paul condemns such nervous dishonesty:—"Therefore seeing we have this Ministry, even as we obtained mercy, we faint not; but we have renounced the hidden things of shame, not walking in craftiness, nor handling the Word of God deceitfully; but by the manifestation of the truth commending ourselves to every man's conscience in the sight of God."*

The most urgent necessity of the present juncture seems to be the recovery of public confidence in the clergy. As one step, and a considerable one towards that end, I have urged, as well by example as by precept, the general adoption of the Revised Version in the public services of the Church. Without denying or minimizing the faults of that Version, I submit as an absolutely incontrovertible proposition, that for all the purposes which a Version of the Bible exists to serve, it is the best Version in existence. To go on using an inferior Version, when a superior is accessible, is not in my deliberate judgment to be reconciled with pastoral integrity. I need say no

---

* 2 Cor. iv. 1, 2.

more to explain my use of the Revised Version in this volume.

Urban life, it must be added, tends always towards sensuality. In the first century this was certainly the case; by many melancholy and scandalous tokens we know that in this respect the nineteenth century can claim no exemption from the same burden. Personally I am convinced that the most formidable obstacle to Christianity at this moment is the wasting and furtive viciousness which, in many forms, corrupts our city population. Drunkenness is a lesser evil than sensuality; it is neither so degrading to the character, nor so deadening to the soul. Weizäcker speaks of "the gigantic war which Christendom in general, and Paul in particular, had to wage with immorality." The same formula might be employed to express the duty of the modern Church. Unhappily it does not express the actual procedure of the Church as a whole.

Frivolity, cynical scepticism, sensuality — these notes of urban life are always recognizable. Two millenniums of Christianity have not altered the inveterate characteristics of great cities. Apostolic Christianity—as Professor Ramsay has reminded us—was almost exclusively urban. Hence the study at every point suggests parallels to contemporary experience, and it is literally true to say that the least archaic period of ecclesiastical history is the most remote.

The Apostolic Age has been of late years made known to us by the labours of many brilliant and indefatigable students. The effect of their work is a new revelation. The first beginnings of Christianity are now understood, as they have never been understood before. The conflict of the critics over the documents has incidentally brought together a mass of information about the first century, which enables the English student at the end of the nineteenth century to appreciate the standpoints and sympathize with the difficulties of the Christians of Jerusalem and Corinth, to whom the Apostles preached. Unhappily the rank and file of English Churchmen are still suspicious and fearful of the new knowledge. They read their New Testament, or neglect to read it, with the paramount conviction that it is all a solemn and blessed miracle, which has no real connection with actual, normal human experience. To such I respectfully address this volume. The history of its origin is briefly this. I read the Corinthian Epistles with classes of men both in Barking and in Ilford, and found it serviceable to put together into separate addresses the leading subjects dealt with by the Apostle. These were found helpful, and I was urged by many, both laymen and clergy (to whom my notes were submitted), to bring the whole into connected form and publish it. This account of the origin of this book will, perhaps, go some way towards explaining some sufficiently obvious faults of arrangement and style.

This volume, it is hardly necessary to explain, is not addressed to scholars, nor does it attempt an exact or continuous interpretation of the Corinthian Epistles, on which, nevertheless, it may be called in some sense a commentary. I have throughout endeavoured to be honest and clear, not greatly regarding a certain looseness of arrangement if only the broad outlines of the subject could be plainly marked. I have not scrupled to draw practical inferences; and though I have tried not to read into the first century the ideas of the nineteenth, yet I have everywhere assumed the continuity of ecclesiastical life.

I fear that repetition has not been as successfully avoided as I could wish. Partly this arises from the circumstance that the first four chapters were originally composed as a thesis independently of the rest of the book, which, as I have said, was in the first instance designed for public delivery. This also may explain a certain difference of style.

References have only been given when it seemed to me desirable to indicate to the reader either the authority for an opinion which might seem novel, or the direction in which fuller information might be obtained. I have given the Greek text of quotations from the New Testament wherever it seemed to me that anything turned upon an exact rendering of the original. Histories of the Apostolic Age abound, and there are numerous commentaries on the Epistles to the Corinthians. Many of these I have used.

It will be manifest on every page how much I owe to the works of Rénan, Weizäcker, Godet, Ramsay, Hort, and Bishop Lightfoot. Perhaps I may be permitted to make special mention of two authors—the one a great preacher of the fourth century, the other a great preacher of the nineteenth—S. Chrysostom and F. W. Robertson. Both have taught me much; both considered the Corinthian Epistles of S. Paul from the standpoint of men set to teach civilized people under urban conditions; and both, therefore, enter into the Apostle's mind more deeply than more learned exegetes.

If this little book shall induce in anyone a desire to know something more about the great subject of which it treats, my labour will not have been thrown away. To me it has been a labour of love, from which I rise with the conviction that in the Apostolic Age the latest Christian century must find its guidance. In reverting to first principles the Church must recover that Christian allegiance which she has now so largely forfeited. We are haunted and burdened by the idiosyncrasies of the later history. We are slaves to the fourth century, or to the Ages of Faith, or to the Reformation, or to the Zeitgeist of our own generation. Hence our impossible demands, our obdurate divisions, our desperate rivalries. Behind all that long apostasy we call Church History is the Age of the Apostles, when the mind of the Spirit was reflected in the life of the Society with a fidelity which has never since been witnessed. There we may discover the original principles of Christianity, return to which is the supreme spiritual necessity of our time.

CONTENTS

Part I.

THE APOSTOLIC ECCLESIA, OR LOCAL CHURCH

	PAGE
I. Influence of the Synagogue on the Organization of the Ecclesia	3
II. Limits to Autonomy of the Local Ecclesia	7
III. Discipline of the Religious Assemblies	16
IV. Moral Discipline of the Local Ecclesia	34

Part II.

PRELIMINARY DATA

CHAP.
I. The Epistles of S. Paul	41
II. The Founding of the Church in Corinth	54
III. The Letter from Corinth	66

Part III.

DOCTRINE AND THE SACRAMENTS

I. The Historic Christ	81
II. The Resurrection	94
III. The Corinthian Heretics	107
IV. The Apostolic Creed	120
V. Baptism	134
VI. The Holy Communion	150

Part IV.
Organization and Practice

CHAP.		PAGE
I. The Church		173
II. The Ministry		187
III. Public Worship		201
IV. The Gift of Tongues		214
V. Miracles		227
VI. The Christian Prophets		239
VII. Women in the Church		252
VIII. Apostolic Finance		266
IX. Conclusions		282

APPENDICES

I. S. Paul's Teaching in Corinth	297
II. Apostolic Succession	300
III. Confession	306
IV. Celibacy	312

TWO DISCOURSES

I. The Administration of Holy Baptism in Large Urban Parishes	319
II. The Social Influence of Christianity	336

Part I.

THE APOSTOLIC ECCLESIA OR LOCAL CHURCH

I. INFLUENCE OF THE SYNAGOGUE ON THE ORGANIZATION OF THE ECCLESIA

II. LIMITS TO THE AUTONOMY OF THE LOCAL ECCLESIA

III. DISCIPLINE OF THE RELIGIOUS ASSEMBLIES

IV. INTERNAL DISCIPLINE OF THE LOCAL ECCLESIA

THE APOSTOLIC ECCLESIA OR LOCAL CHURCH

I. INFLUENCE OF THE SYNAGOGUE ON THE ECCLESIA.

THE Church of Christ received from the Divine Founder no rigid and detailed constitution. Neither the faith, nor the government, nor the discipline of the Christian society were defined in advance. The Apostles, to whom the task of founding the Church was given, were assured the presence of the guiding "*Spirit of Truth*," and sent out into the world to learn by experiment and failure the right methods of organization. The conditions under which they went about their work were difficult and various. In Palestine they acted under the overmastering influence of ancestral Judaism: when the Gospel had spread beyond the limits of Palestine it advanced still on Jewish lines. The synagogues of the Hellenistic Diaspora became the first preaching centres of the Christian Faith in Gentile lands, and the earliest models of Church organization. Moreover, the fact that without exception the Apostles were Jews, and particularly that the most active missionary of them all, Paul of Tarsus, was a Rabbinist of distinction, tended to strengthen the influence of the old system upon the development of the new. The Christian Church was literally the off-spring of the synagogue. In Jerusalem we learn from the Epistle of S. James* that the name "*synagogue*" was actually applied to the Christian assembly. Probably this was customary throughout the Jewish congregations. The record of the Acts suggests that the Apostles hoped and even expected to win over to Christianity entire synagogues. They were frankly admitted as co-religionists by the synagogue authorities, and allowed in the ordinary course of the worship to advocate the Messianic claims of Jesus Christ. Thus S. Luke records of *Paul and his company* that at Antioch, in Pisidia, "*they went into the synagogue on the Sabbath, and sat down. And after the reading of the law and the prophets the rulers of the synagogue sent unto them, saying, Brethren, if ye have any word of exhortation for the people, say on.*"† The synagogue was, indeed, the common starting-point of evangelistic work. At Iconium, at Thessalonica, at Berœa, at Corinth, at Ephesus we read that S. Paul began his preaching of the Gospel in the local synagogue. The authorities were extremely long-suffering; in no case does it appear that the Apostle was refused permission to preach, or promptly ejected after the nature of his preaching had become evident. Even at Thessalonica,‡ where the Jews showed themselves very hostile, we read that the Christian preaching was tolerated for three successive

* S. James ii. 2. † Acts xiii. 14, 15.
‡ Acts xvii. 2.

Sabbaths. At Corinth* the narrative suggests that a considerable time elapsed before the violent breach with the synagogue, and at Ephesus† it is on record that S. Paul continued his preaching in the synagogue for no less than three months. It would be no extravagant assumption that in many instances the Apostles succeeded in carrying with them the entire synagogue, which passed without difficulty from Judaism to Christianity.‡ But where this was not so, and the Christian synagogue came into existence as a Schismatic congregation, it is certain that the general system of the parent synagogue would be maintained in the separated body.§ At Corinth and at Ephesus the transition was abrupt and violent. S. Paul made his final departure from the Corinthian synagogue with every demonstration of anger. The violence of the Jews was met by an outburst of righteous resentment. "*When they opposed themselves and blasphemed he shook out his raiment, and said unto them, Your blood be on your own heads: I am clean: from henceforth I will go unto the Gentiles.*" This indignant language was immediately followed by decisive action. The Apostle organized a Christian synagogue in the house of a Corinthian proselyte who dwelt hard by the synagogue of the Jews. The real meaning of his conduct was evident when Crispus, the ruler of the synagogue (ὁ ἀρχισυνάγωγος), professed himself a believer, and joined the new society. Much the same course was followed at Ephesus: there the

* Acts xviii. 4. † Acts xix. 8.
‡ *v*. B. L. HATCH, p. 60. § B. L. HATCH, p. 60-62.

schoolroom of Tyrannus served to shelter the new Christian community which organized itself as a rival synagogue outside the limits of Israel. These conspicuous examples were undoubtedly typical of the common procedure. Everywhere outside the Jewish synagogue was formed a rival, organized on the same lines and preserving unaltered the same aspect. The influx of Gentile converts must have quickly affected the organization of these Christian synagogues. New conditions of existence involved new problems, and the solution of those problems necessitated extensive modification of the original Jewish model. The history of the Church in Corinth enables us to follow the course of development. The conditions under which that Church took shape were thoroughly representative. Originating in a secession from the Jewish synagogue, it rapidly attracted the Gentiles, until it became predominantly non-Jewish. The society to which the Pauline Epistles are addressed is clearly composed mostly of converts from heathenism. Apostolic discipline represents a compromise between the tradition of the Jewish synagogue and the needs of the Gentile disciples. The compromise was gradually reached, for the needs to which it was adapted only revealed themselves gradually, but throughout this was its character —an adaptation of the original Hebrew system to the changed circumstances and wider functions of a Christian Ecclesia.

II. LIMITS TO AUTONOMY OF THE ECCLESIA.

The original Christian Ecclesia, as it is pictured in the Corinthian Epistles, was by no means destitute of the machinery of government. Whether there existed a ministry in the traditional Christian sense may be fairly questioned. The idea of a free republic rather than that of a society governed by an ordained ministry is suggested by the Apostle's language: yet this freedom was neither absolute nor unrestricted. Large, indeed, were the powers of the Corinthian Ecclesia, but they were subjected to four important authorities. These must be carefully considered.

1. *Laws of Christ.*

The supreme and ultimate authority was the commandment of Christ. It is certain that at the time when the Corinthian Epistles were written (probably in A.D. 57) the Evangelic tradition had not been committed to writing. The oral Gospel, agreeing, we may believe, in the main with the canonical narratives, varied considerably in detail. Yet wherever it could be adduced, the Authority of the Divine Founder was final. Thus in the discussion on the right of the Christian ministry to maintenance by the Church. S. Paul, after advancing arguments drawn from the practice of the older Apostles, from the analogy of common life, from the practice of contemporary Judaism, reaches the climax of his reasoning in the words, "*Even so did the Lord ordain that they which proclaim the Gospel should live of the Gospel."* *

Whether we understand these words as a free rendering of Christ's language addressed to the Twelve, according to the first Synoptic,† to the Seventy according to the third,‡ or as a separate "logion" which has no place in the Canonical Gospels, it makes no matter. The Apostle evidently adduces the authority of our Lord as closing the question. Similarly, when dealing with the difficult subject of domestic ties, which had been submitted to his judgment by the Corinthians, S. Paul sharply distinguishes his own authority from that of Christ. "*Unto the married I give charge, yea not I, but the Lord, . . . but to the rest say I, not the Lord.*"§ At that early stage, when the memory of the Life of the Founder was yet fresh in Christian minds, the authority of Christ, the Lord, as He was emphatically styled, was conceived as immediate as well as final. Discipleship resolved itself into the frank and affectionate recognition of that supreme and operative Lordship. While the tradition of the Founder was recent and powerful, the lesser authority of the Christian society played but little part in the history; but manifestly, as the years passed, that tradition tended to grow weaker, and as it waned the ecclesiastical power, properly so called, continuously waxed.

* 1 Cor. ix. 14. † S. Matt. x. 10.
‡ S. Luke x. 7, 8. § 1 Cor. vii. 10–12.

2. *Mosaic Law and Old Testament.*

S. Paul certainly regarded the Christian Ecclesia to be subject to the Jewish law so far as it dealt with morals. He assumes among his converts a complete acceptance of the Jewish Scriptures. His quotations from the Old Testament presuppose in his readers a familiarity with the sacred writings. Undoubtedly the Greek Version of the Canon was generally known throughout the sphere of the synagogue, and its acceptance was naturally transferred from the synagogue to the society, which found in the synagogue its origin and its model. Examples of an appeal to the Scripture are numerous in the Corinthian Epistles. Fornication is condemned by a reference to the Book of Genesis. "*The twain, saith he, shall become one flesh.*"* The Mosaic rule, "*Thou shalt not muzzle the ox when he treadeth out the corn,*" is applied to the case of the Christian minister claiming maintenance from the Ecclesia which he serves.† The history of Israel supplies precedents of warning or encouragement. Indeed, the Apostle ascribes to the Corinthian Church the character of sacred distinction which belonged to the chosen people. To his thinking the Ecclesia succeeded to the position which the synagogue had forfeited.‡ The experiences of ancient Israel are the heritage of the spiritual Israel of Christian believers. "*For I would not, brethren, have you ignorant, how that our fathers*

---

* 1 Cor. vi. 16 = Genesis ii. 24. † 1 Cor. ix. 9.
‡ *cf.* Gal. vi. 16, where S. Paul calls the Church "the Israel of God."

were all under the cloud, and passed through the sea. ... Now these things were our examples ... now these things happened unto them by way of example: and they were written for our admonition, upon whom the ends of the ages are come."* The silence of women in the religious assemblies is based on the Mosaic law, by which we must understand the Rabbinic tradition in which S. Paul had been trained. *"Let the women keep silence in the churches: for it is not permitted unto them to speak; but let them be in subjection, as also saith the law."* †

These direct references to the Jewish law by no means adequately express the extent of the restriction on Christian liberty involved in the Apostle's assumption that the Church was the true successor of the synagogue, and as such subject to the moral rules, not only of Scripture but also of the established Rabbinic tradition.

3. *Apostolic Authority.*

Moreover, the Church was subject to the Apostolic Authority, and in S. Paul's hands that authority was neither narrow in range nor feeble in exercise. It is evident that the Apostle claimed for himself over the Churches which he founded an authority supreme within the limits of his apostolic commission, divine in essence, independent, therefore, of external control, and unaffected by human judgment, which could be exercised either in person, or by letter, or by a duly accredited envoy. S. Paul

---

* 1 Cor. x. 1, 6, 11.   † 1 Cor. xiv. 34.

dwells much on his own authority, and resents, almost passionately, the attacks upon it, which were both frequent and vigorous.

He planted the Church [ἐγὼ ἐφύτευσα, iii. 6]; in so doing he was indeed a fellow-worker with God. [Θεοῦ γαρ ἐσμεν συνεργοί, iii. 9.] He is the wise master-builder [σοφὸς ἀρχιτέκτων, iii. 10], who has laid the one foundation [θεμέλιον] on which all the rest must build, either well or ill. He repudiates human judgment as indifferent, and indeed irrelevant, in the case of one who holds a Divine Commission to be the servant of Christ and steward of the mysteries of God. [οὕτως ἡμᾶς λογιζέσθω ἄνθρωπος, ὡς ὑπηρέτας Χριστοῦ καὶ οἰκονόμους μυστηρίων Θεοῦ, iv. 1.] This, indeed, might be said of all Christian ministers, but he was the spiritual father of the Corinthians, and as such could claim over them an unique authority. He addressed them not merely as a tutor [παιδαγωγός], but as the father who "*in Christ Jesus had begotten them through the Gospel.*" (iv. 14, 15.) This authority he would exert in gentleness, but if necessary with severity. [τί θέλετε; ἐν ῥάβδῳ ἔλθω πρὸς ὑμᾶς; ἢ ἐν ἀγάπῃ πνεύματί τε πραότητος; iv. 21.] His relation of Founder authorized him to claim from the Corinthians a provision for his maintenance [μὴ οὐκ ἔχομεν ἐξουσίαν φαγεῖν καὶ πιεῖν, ix. 4], but this right he had not exercised, preferring not to associate his preaching with any personal claims, however legitimate. (ix. 15–17.) The "traditions" [παραδόσεις] which he had delivered to the Corinthians were binding upon them. (xi. 2.) In case of doubt as to their application the reference lay to him, and from his decision there was no appeal. He was the channel through which the Evangelic History had reached them, and he necessarily determined its practical bearings. He speaks by way of command rather than of exhortation or advice, and though he is careful to separate his personal opinion from his inspired decision, it does not appear that he would tolerate any disregard of the less authoritative utterance. In the second epistle, which has much the appearance of a personal "Apologia," S. Paul dwells at length* on his position towards the Churches of his own foundation. He evidently considers himself exclusively charged with their spiritual oversight, and pathetically declares that besides his normal sufferings at the hands of persecutors and opponents, "*there is that which presseth upon me daily, anxiety for all the Churches.*"†

As the Churches grew more numerous, and were scattered over a wider area, the Apostle found himself compelled to exercise his episcopal functions by means of messengers and of letters. To this necessity the Church owes those incomparable compositions, the Epistles of S. Paul, which, originally called forth by special emergencies, were made the vehicles of eternal truth, and rapidly secured among Christians the supreme position which they merited, and which in the next century caused them to take rank as inspired Scripture. M. Rénan has pointed out that the idea of utilizing epistles‡ as instruments of government was not

---

* Especially 2 Cor. x. 7-16.   † 2 Cor. xi. 28.
‡ RÉNAN, *S. Paul*, p. 228.

original, but borrowed, in common with so much else, from the practice of the synagogue. In S. Paul's hands, however, the Epistle became, as we have said, not merely a means of ruling congregations, but also of teaching religion. Finally, in the administration of discipline within the local Churches S. Paul held himself to be supreme. He issued his sentence from a distance, and determined both the character and the duration of punishment. But to this point we shall recur at a later stage of our inquiry.

4. *General Custom of Ecclesia.*

The local Churches were self-governing, but not independent. The general custom of the Christian society was held to be binding on particular congregations. This recognition of the unity of the Church was seriously threatened at Corinth, where tendencies to ecclesiastical individualism were unusually strong. The behaviour of women in the religious assemblies was a case in point. It appears that some of the Corinthian women ventured to appear unveiled in the congregation, and actually usurped a share in the conduct of service. S. Paul's Rabbinic training rendered such licence particularly abhorrent to him; his good sense warned him that the gravest offence, possibly leading to a rupture of Communion, would be given to the Churches of Judæa. Moreover, he had but too good reason for suspecting the moral effect of such perilous liberty upon the Corinthian community. He condemns the conduct of the women as an unwarrantable departure from the general practice of the Christian society. He concludes the discussion about veiling with this brusque observation: "*But if any man seemeth to be contentious* [φιλόνεικος], *we have no such custom* [συνήθειαν], *neither the Churches of God*"* and he closes his prohibition of the public prophesying of the women still more peremptorily. "*What? was it from you that the Word of God went forth? or came it unto you alone?*"† The Apostolic Church was assuredly not "congregational" in the modern sense, any more than it was "presbyterian" or "episcopal": the notion of an external unity, superior to local particularism and restraining it, did certainly exist; and in the autocracy of the Apostles over the Churches which they planted was the principle of the later episcopal *régime*. In face of the evidence of the Acts and the Pastoral Epistles it seems difficult to deny that the notion of transmitting ministerial authority by a formal act of ordination was established in the earliest Church. From these premisses the conclusion of episcopacy would seem to be as logically irresistible as it has been historically evident.

Official Ministry. Thus the local Churches in the Apostolic period were held together in a loose, but not ineffective union. The task of maintaining order within those little communities must have devolved upon officials. The synagogue, upon which the Christian Ecclesia was modelled, had its duly ordained officials; it is barely conceivable that these could have been dispensed with in the new societies.

* 1 Cor. xi. 16.   † 1 Cor. xiv. 36.

THE APOSTOLIC ECCLESIA

It is not, indeed, necessary to assume that in those early days there existed the sharply defined "orders" of a later age, but that some ministry existed, howsoever designated or regarded, seems to be proved by the Pauline Epistles. Possibly, as Weizäcker suggests, the earliest converts became the first ministers.* In their houses would the little congregation of converts ordinarily come together, and their claim to the submission of their brethren would be largely based on the substantial services which they rendered to the common cause.

It must, however, be conceded that the regular ordained ministry was, in Apostolic times, dwarfed by the exceptional ministries which then principally engaged the attention of the Church. The diffusion of extraordinary gifts rendered the maintenance of order extremely difficult. At Corinth it is probable that the circumstances were exceptional, but everywhere in the Apostolic age the "deacon," the "presbyter," and the "episcopos" count for little beside the "apostle," the "prophet," the "speaker in a tongue." It is remarkable that neither when rebuking the disorders which disgraced the Agape, and even the Eucharist, nor when regulating the procedure of the normal religious assemblies at Corinth, does S. Paul address himself to those who, on the hypothesis that an ordained ministry existed in that Church, must have been primarily responsible for the disorders and the natural agents of reformation.

* *Vide Apostolic Age,* vol. ii. p. 320; *cf.* also HORT, *Christian Ecclesia,* p. 117.

III. DISCIPLINE OF THE RELIGIOUS ASSEMBLIES.

1. *Domestic.*

The religious assemblies were either domestic or public. To the former none but the baptized had access; the latter appear to have been open to the entrance of the heathen [ἄπιστοι, 1 Cor. xiv. 22], and perhaps were designed with a view to their conversion. The domestic assemblies were the Agapæ or Love-feasts, and the Lord's Supper.* At this early time these were united, the Agape forming a preliminary to the more solemn rite.† Later, probably as a consequence of the persecutions, the Agape was wholly discontinued, and the Holy Communion transferred to the early morning. This arrangement, originating under the pressure of calamity, speedily commended itself as convenient, and from the second century until the nineteenth the practice of celebrating the Holy Eucharist in the evening has been abandoned.

That grave disorders had made their appearance in the Corinthian Church is evident from S. Paul's letter. The Corinthians carried over into their Agapæ the licentious and ostentatious habits of their præ-Christian life. The Apostle's indignant language conveys a melancholy picture of excess and anti-social arrogance. The Corinthians, when they came together for the Agape, drew apart in cliques, severed from one another by doctrinal differences or by variant customs. The mutual dislike and suspicion of these

* S. Jude 12. † S. Peter xi. 13.

factions destroyed the harmony and threatened the unity of the Ecclesia. More scandalous, however, was the ostentatious gluttony of the wealthier members, and the evident hunger of the poorer. It would seem that at Corinth everyone brought with him not—as was the later and more creditable practice—a contribution to the common provision, but his own supper. The rich ate to excess, the poor had little or nothing; and when in due course the Agape was succeeded by the Mysteries of the Eucharist the awful profanity of drunken communicants might be observed. "*When therefore ye assemble yourselves together, it is not possible to eat the Lord's Supper:* [Κυριακὸν δεῖπνον φαγεῖν] *for in your eating each one taketh before other his own supper: and one is hungry and another is drunken. What? have ye not houses to eat and to drink in? or despise ye the Church of God* [ἢ τῆς ἐκλλησίας τοῦ θεοῦ καταφρονεῖτε], *and put them to shame that have not?*" After rehearsing the history of the Institution of the Eucharist, and pointing out in terms of the greatest solemnity the guiltiness of the Corinthians, the Apostle concludes, "*Wherefore, my brethren, when ye come together to eat, wait one for another. If any man is hungry let him eat at home: that your coming together be not unto judgment.*" [ἵνα μὴ εἰς κρίμα συνέρχησθε, 1 Cor. xi. 20, 21; 33, 34.]

2. *Public.*

Quite distinct from the Agape and the Lord's Supper, which followed it, was the public service of the Church. The former were domestic and social, the latter was public and didactic. It may safely be asserted that the ordinary service of the synagogue provided the model upon which the public service of the Ecclesia was formed. The reading of the Old Testament, probably in the Septuagint Version, and in fixed portions or lessons, the recitation and singing of the Psalms, the offering of prayer, and preaching were common to both. Very early the practice was introduced of reading the Apostolic Epistles, and, when the Evangelic tradition had been committed to writing, the Gospel narratives,* S. Paul instructs the Colossians not only to read in the public assembly of the Church the Epistle which he had addressed to them, but to forward it to the Church of the Laodiceans for similar public reading, and to receive in exchange the Epistle from Laodicea.† The arrangement of the congregation customary in the Jewish was reproduced in the Christian synagogue. In both women were present, and joined in the singing and the "Amen"; but in neither were they permitted to appear unveiled, or to take any prominent share in the service. It appears that the men prayed uncovered, according to the general custom of the Greeks. The practice of veiling the head in token of reverence and penitence, which certainly prevailed among the later Jews, did not perhaps obtain in the Apostolic age.‡ Possibly there was a formal allocation of seats to the "unbelievers" who attended these assemblies, such as was customary in the next century.

These arrangements, borrowed from the syna-

* S. Mark xiii. 14.   † Col. iv. 16.   ‡ 1 Cor. xiv. 16.

gogue, were necessarily modified by the conditions under which the Christian Ecclesia existed. On the one hand, the extraordinary diffusion of χαρισματα, on the other hand, the rapid expansion of the society by the admission of converts from heathenism, necessarily affected the constitution and order of the Ecclesia. The fourteenth chapter of the first Corinthian Epistles throws a strong light on the subject, and must, therefore, receive the close attention of the student of Apostolic Christianity.

S. Paul evidently combats an exaggerated estimate of the socially valueless χάρισμα, described by the ambiguous expression, speaking γλώσσῃ or γλώσσαις. He contrasts it very disadvantageously with the χάρισμα of προφητεία. The basis of his judgment is the assumption that the measure of worth is the power to edify. "*He that speaketh in a tongue edifieth himself, but he that prophesieth edifieth the Church. Now I would have you all speak with tongues, but rather that ye should prophesy: and greater is he that prophesieth than he that speaketh with tongues, except he interpret, that the Church may receive edifying*" (*vv.*4,5). Here it may be noticed that the Apostle evidently contemplates the very widest diffusion of χαρισματα. There is no suggestion of an official ministry, charged with the conduct of "Divine Service." S. Paul assumes the possibility, and even the desirableness of an arrangement by which, without confusion, every member (no doubt, every adult male member) of the Ecclesia should lead the public devotions. He rebukes the disorderly exercise of the χαρίσματα: he does not deprecate all exercise. "*What is it,* *then, brethren? When ye come together, each one hath a psalm, hath a teaching, hath a revelation, hath a tongue, hath an interpretation.*" There was no agreement beforehand as to the nature and order of the religious exercises, nor yet any settled principle by which the exercise of the χαρίσματα might be directed and restrained. The Ecclesia tended to present to view a scandalous spectacle of disorder and competitive display. The Apostle lays down the broad principle, "*Let all things be done to edifying,*" and proceeds to apply the rules of the synagogue to remedy the confusions of the Church. The Rabbins required that the reading and interpreting of the Scripture should be orderly, the ministers succeeding one another in due rotation.* So in the Ecclesia. "*If any man speaketh in a tongue, let it be by two, or at the most three, and that in turn: and let one interpret: but if there be no interpreter, let him keep silence in the Church: and let him speak to himself and to God. And let the prophets speak by two or three, and let the others discern.* [διακρινέτωσαν.] *But if a revelation be made to another sitting by, let the first keep silence.*" It would seem that the prophets formed a distinct class, and sate together in the assembly. But they were not officials. The prophetic inspiration might come upon any member of the Ecclesia, and its character was "discerned" or recognized by infallible tokens. Once admitted into the category of the prophets, the position seems to have been permanently retained. S. Paul refused to allow the strength of the prophetic impulse to be

* LIGHTFOOT, *Works*, xii. 542.

pleaded as an excuse for breaking up the order of the worship. Disorder could not be justified: it involved an insult to the Author of all order. "*For ye all can prophesy one by one, that all may learn, and all may be comforted: and the spirits of the prophets are subject to the prophets, for God is not a God of confusion, but of peace: as in all the Churches of the Saints.*"* The Apostle takes for granted that his counsels, conceived in the interests of order, will be affirmed by the genuine prophets. He boldly proposes such affirmation as a test of genuineness. "*If any man thinketh himself to be a prophet, or spiritual, let him take knowledge of the things which I write unto you, that they are the commandment of the Lord.*" (*v.* 37.) The ideal which he offers to the Corinthians unites the highest appreciation of the χαρίσματα with the keenest jealousy of disorder· "*Wherefore, my brethren, desire earnestly to prophesy, and forbid not to speak with tongues. But let all things be done decently and in order.*" [πάντα δε εὐσχημόνως καὶ κατὰ τάξιν γινέσθω.]

The necessity of thus laying stress on the importance of order was evident from another point of view. The heathen were wont to attend the meetings of the Ecclesia, and the impressions they received determined their permanent attitude towards Christianity. There was much suspicion of the new religion among them, and the malignant jealousy of the Jews was at all times eager to minister to that suspicion the stimulus and direction of malicious suggestion. It was clearly important to vigilantly

* xiv. 31–33.

guard against discreditable appearances, which, in the existing state of opinion, could hardly fail to receive the worst possible construction. S. Paul is fully awake to this danger, and warns the Corinthians against it. He describes the case of a simple heathen, drawn by curiosity to visit the Christian Assembly. He is startled by the confused and meaningless clamour of the "unknown tongue," which in the extravagance of unrestrained enthusiasm is poured forth at once from many persons. His astonishment is quickly replaced by disgust, and he leaves the meeting convinced that Christians are the victims of insanity. Against this melancholy picture the Apostle sets the case of a man who has found himself encountered by the solemn, spirit-searching utterances of the prophets, as in due order they succeeded one another in speaking to men "*edification, and comfort, and consolation.*" He feels irresistibly that he is in a divine presence; his conscience is stirred, his fears are waked, and he lends a willing and respectful audience to the Gospel. "*If therefore the whole Church be gathered together, and all speak with tongues, and there come in men unlearned or unbelieving* [ἰδιῶται η ἄπιστοι], *will they not say that ye are mad? But if all prophesy, and there come in one unbelieving or unlearned, he is reproved* [ἐλέγχεται] *by all, he is judged* [ἀνακρίνεται] *by all: the secrets of his heart are made manifest: and so he will fall down on his face and worship God, declaring that God is among you indeed.*"*

* xiv. 23-25.

3. *Moral Discipline.*

The close contact with the heathen in the necessary intercourse of urban life forced into prominence the organization of an effective moral discipline. The paramount character of Apostolic Christianity in a great heathen city was that of revolt against the established morality. The ancients were sufficiently familiar with novelties in doctrine to regard with equanimity the addition of one more religious theory to the many already in existence.* The variety of rites and ceremonies was so great that if the Christian observances had been far more novel than they actually were, they would hardly, of themselves, have occasioned much alarm, or provoked much opposition, but the case was different in the region of practical morality. The Christians there stood out in sharp contrast to the rest of society, they were committed to a position of arrogant isolation, they seemed plainly guilty of anti-social conspiracy. The very violence of the rupture with society necessitated by discipleship rendered the maintenance of moral discipline at once the most arduous and the most important function of the Christian Ecclesia. The Corinthian Epistles reveal the gravity of the perils which threatened the morality of the infant Church, and the means by which the Church endeavoured to guard her purity.

* *Cf.* the scene at Athens. Acts xvii. 16 fol.

CASE OF THE INCESTUOUS CORINTHIAN.

A gross scandal at Corinth had been brought to the Apostle's knowledge, and his directions for dealing with it enable us to learn the nature of the discipline then established.* The case is thus described by S. Paul. "*It is actually reported that there is fornication* [πορνεία] *among you, and such fornication as is not even among the Gentiles, that one of you hath his father's wife. And ye are puffed up, and did not rather mourn, that he that hath done this deed might be taken away from among you. For I verily, being absent in body but present in spirit, have already, as though I were present, judged him that hath so wrought this thing in the name of our Lord Jesus, ye being gathered together, and my spirit, with the power of our Lord Jesus to deliver such a one unto Satan for the destruction of the flesh, that the spirit may be saved in the day of the Lord Jesus.*" Here we may separately consider: (1) the offence; (2) the procedure; (3) the sentence.

1. *Offence.*

The offence of the incestuous Corinthian was not directly an ecclesiastical offence. It was a breach of the moral law involving scandal, and, therefore, came within the jurisdiction of the Ecclesia. The predominant character of Apostolic Christianity being moral, gross breaches of morality involved a negation of discipleship. S. Paul enumerates the offences which

* 1 Cor. v. 1–5.

THE APOSTOLIC ECCLESIA

were of this fatal character. How far it is possible to extract from his language anything of the nature of a formal classification of sins may well be doubted. It appears that objection had been taken to his ruling in a letter, which is no longer extant, as impracticable. In justifying his decision, which had been misunderstood, the Apostle seizes the opportunity for developing his moral teaching. "*I wrote unto you in my epistle to have no company with fornicators; not altogether with the fornicators of this world, or with the covetous and extortioners, or with idolaters: for then must ye needs go out of the world: But now I write unto you not to keep company, if any man that is named a brother* [ἐάν τις ἀδελφὸς ὀνομαζόμενος] *be a fornicator* [πόρνος], *or covetous* [πλεονέκτης], *or an idolater* [εἰδωλολάτρης], *or a reviler* [λοίδορος], *or a drunkard* [μέθυσος], *or an extortioner* [ἅρπαξ], *with such a one no, not to eat. For what have I to do with judging them that are without* [τοὺς ἔξω]? *Do not ye judge them that are within* [τοὺς ἔσω], *whereas them that are without God judgeth? Put away* [ἐξάρατε] *the wicked man from among yourselves.*"* This language is explicit. S. Paul, distinctly repudiating the notion of passing judgment on non-Christians, enumerates six offences as involving loss of communion, and, as a consequence of loss of communion, cessation of social intercourse. These offences are: 1, fornication; 2, covetousness; 3, idolatry; 4, reviling; 5, drunkenness; 6, extortion.

A little further on in the Epistle he repeats in a more rhetorical shape his enumeration of offences

* 1 Cor. v. 9-13.

fatal to Christian fellowship.* To the six sins already mentioned he adds four: adultery, effeminacy, sodomy, theft. These, however, would seem to be really included in the shorter enumeration. Thus the more general πόρνοι would seem to include the particular variety μοιχοί, and less obviously the darker types of sensuality. "Thieves" might be included in "extortioners." The Apostle names the varieties of sensuality in an ascending scale of gravity. Fornication was in the actual experience of the Corinthians aggravated by religious connections, and became idolatry. It might involve also a grave social offence as adultery; nay, lust had yet darker developments —it passed into those offences which the usage of Christendom abhors as "unnatural." Clearly the immediate needs of the Corinthian Ecclesia are the governing influences in these Corinthian catalogues. Crimes of violence are altogether omitted; crimes of sensuality are elaborately enumerated.

In the Epistle to the Galatians S. Paul† sets down a long list of fifteen "works of the flesh," but the passage is obviously rhetorical, and need not be further considered.

2. *Procedure.*

The disciplinary procedure is sufficiently indicated in the passage quoted above. The whole Ecclesia was specially convened, and the guilty member set forward in the midst. A solemn invocation of Christ, conceived as actually present, for the Apostolic

---

* 1 Cor. vi. 9, 10.   † v. 19.

THE APOSTOLIC ECCLESIA

Church literally believed the promise in the Gospel,[*] introduced the formal treatment of the case. Probably the commandment of the absent Apostle was read aloud in order that the greatest possible authority might attach to the action of the Church, and the sentence was pronounced in his name. The formula of excommunication may be recognized in S. Paul's Epistle. The offender was delivered unto Satan for the destruction of the flesh, that the spirit might be saved in the day of the Lord Jesus.[†]

Assuming with most authorities that the sequel to the case of the incestuous Corinthian is to be found in the second Epistle,[‡] we can learn that unanimity was not necessary in order to pass sentence of excommunication. A majority sufficed.[§] This, indeed, was the case in this instance. S. Paul's severity did not commend itself to all the members of the Corinthian Ecclesia. His decision was resisted by a minority, but the sentence of the majority was accepted as final. The offender, declared excommunicate, manifested every token of genuine repentance. Indeed, his sorrow was so extreme as to threaten despair. So the Apostle intervened in the

---

[*] S. Matt. xviii. 20.

[†] 2 Cor. ii. 5-11.

[‡] Weizäcker (*Apostolic Christianity*, vol. i. pp. 349-353) argues that the connection between the excommunication in the first Epistle and the absolution in the second is untenable. But his reasoning is weakened by an obvious desire to magnify the opposition to S. Paul's Apostolic authority in Corinth. The matter is not of importance so far as the argument in the text is concerned.

[§] Godet repudiates the notion of a formal sentence by vote of the Ecclesia as absurd; but his reasons are not convincing. (*Cor.* i. 228-9.)

interest of mercy. In the second Epistle he urges the penitent's restoration, and undertakes to ratify the action of the Corinthians in rescinding the excommunication. We may conclude that the restoration of the offender* was not less public, solemn, and formal than his expulsion.

3. *Sentence.*

What ought to be understood by the apostolic formula of excommunication? M. Rénan understands the language of S. Paul in the Corinthian Epistle quite literally. "Il ne faut pas en douter: c'est une condamnation a mort que Paul prononce."† There is much to be said for this view. The case of Ananias and Sapphira, recorded in the Acts, may be adduced in support of it, nevertheless it cannot be accepted without modification.

Under the circumstances of the Apostolic Church mere exclusion from the Christian society was a very serious matter. The sentence extended not only to the religious assemblies from which the excommunicate was banished, but also to the friendly and almost indispensable intercourse of society. Christianity drew the line very sharply between the Church and Pagan society: to be excluded from the Church was to be an outcast from all men.

---

* Probably the penitent was restored to communion by the laying on of hands. The exhortation in 1 Tim. v. 22, "Lay hands hastily on no one," may be, with large probability, referred to "the act of blessing by which penitents were received back into the communion of the faithful." It is so understood by Dr. Hort (*Christian Ecclesia*, p. 214) and by Bishop Ellicott (*Pastoral Epistles*, p. 83, 5th ed.).

† *S. Paul*, p. 392.

The excommunicate Christian was the object of general abhorrence. The terrors of superstition were added to his actual misery. He had been publicly "*delivered to Satan for the destruction of the flesh.*" The terrible formula was no merely conventional phrase, of which the meaning had been quietly worn away by familiarity.* It was a new formula, expressing at once the Christian belief in the power of evil, and the apostolic authority in the spiritual sphere. Thrust outside the protected area of the Church, the excommunicate lay exposed to every spiritual adversary. Even S. Paul held the prevailing doctrine that the heathen deities were demons. (1 Cor. x. 20.) We may be sure that the Corinthian converts held it far more strongly. What must have been the mental and spiritual anguish of the wretch thus abandoned to the vengeance of the idol-demons, whom he had deserted in order to join that Church which now disowns him? It is not difficult to believe that, as a matter of fact, excommunication was often followed by disease and death. The consequences which followed the desecration of the Eucharist at Corinth would follow expulsion from the Church. "*For this cause many among you are weak and sickly, and not a few sleep.*"† The "destruction of the flesh" would bear a terribly literal meaning; and the connection between excommunication and physical disaster, once established in the general mind by some striking examples, would tend to justify itself by means of the fears it provoked.

* Lightfoot, vol. xii. p. 475.
† 1 Cor. xi. 30.

It has been hitherto assumed without hesitation that the delivery unto Satan and excommunication were identical, but this identity has by no means been generally maintained, and we must therefore not pass away from the subject without giving some reasons for our position.

M. Godet insists, with great positiveness, on distinguishing between excommunication, which was an act of the local Ecclesia, and this sentence of delivery to Satan, which was exclusively an Apostolic act. The latter might or might not be added to the former, and it alone carried with it a physical penalty. The Corinthians, indeed, by prayer might have obtained at God's hand the destruction of the excommunicate,* and they were blameworthy in not doing so; but what their prayers might have effected the authority of the Apostle could inflict. "La seule différence entre ce châtiment qu'a décrété l'apôtre et celui que les Corinthiens auraient dû réclamer d'en haut, c'est que l'église s'en serait rémise à Dieu pour le mode d'éxécution, tandis que Paul, en vertu de sa position spirituelle supérieure à celle de l'église, se permet de déterminer le moyen dont le Seigneur se servira, car il connait la pensée du Seigneur."† (ii. 16.)

Weizäcker, on the other hand, takes for granted that excommunication involved (according to the belief of the Apostle) the dreadful physical consequences implied by "delivery unto Satan." "Exclusion from the Church was not, however, all that was involved. Paul associated with that the idea derived

---
* 1 Cor. v. 2, αἴρειν, equal to destroy, according to M. Godet.
† GODET, *Corinthiens*, vol. i. p. 232.

THE APOSTOLIC ECCLESIA

from the old institution of the ban, that the excommunicated person would necessarily die. He would be given over bodily to Satan for destruction, and the sentence of the Church thereby only effected what he himself effected who took part unworthily in the Lord's Supper, and who was in consequence punished with sickness and death."*

It is not disputed that the Church borrowed from the synagogue the procedure of excommunication. That procedure involved a graduation of penalties. Lightfoot has described the disciplinary system of the Jews in his "exercitations" on the Corinthian Epistle.† We learn that excommunication was in three stages of advancing severity. (1) Simple excommunication, which was called Niddui, in which there was not absolute cursing, and which lasted thirty days. During that time the excommunicate might make his submission and receive absolution. (2) Excommunication with a curse, Shammatha, which involved the publication of the offence in the synagogue, and also lasted thirty days. (3) Anathema, which was the final sentence. "And this is much more heavy than either Niddui or Shammatha. For in this is both excommunication, and cursing, and the forbidding the use of any men, unless in those things only which belong to the sustaining of life. And they anathematize not, but when a man hath hardened himself against the bench once and again." Lightfoot himself concludes that "delivery unto Satan" was not excommunication, but "a miracu-

* WEIZÄCKER, *Apostolic Age*, vol. ii. p. 379, Eng. Trans.
† LIGHTFOOT, *Works*, vol. xii. p. 466, fol. London, 1823.

lous action, namely, of the real delivery of this (incestuous) person into the hands and power of Satan, to be scourged by him, and tormented by him with diseases, tortures, and affrightments." We should rather conclude that the more dreadful consequences of Christian excommunication did but reflect the superiority of the Church over the synagogue; the graduated system of Jewish discipline was adopted by the Church, and in the Church necessarily received a more mysterious and dreadful character. In the case of the incestuous Corinthian, the Ecclesia had not even taken the first step in the disciplinary process. S. Paul, to mark at once his horror of the crime and his indignation at the laxity which condoned it, insists upon the final sentence of Anathema, *i.e.*, delivery unto Satan for the destruction of the flesh. His language appears to convey this. The exceptional circumstance of his absence from Corinth is not to interfere with the formality of the proceedings. The Ecclesia is to meet, and his sentence, conveyed beforehand in the Epistle, is to be considered precisely equivalent to a declaration from him actually present.

That there was a graduated system of discipline in the Apostolic Church is evident from several passages in the Epistles. The passages in the Epistle to the Thessalonians and the Galatians are of especial value in illustrating the language of the Corinthian Epistles. Excommunication of the milder, preliminary type is suggested by 2 Thessalonians iii. 14: "*And if any man obeyeth not our word by this epistle, note that man, that ye have no company with him to the end that he may be ashamed. And yet count him not as an enemy, but admonish him as a brother.*" The extremest possible condemnation is suggested by the language in Galatians i. 8, 9: "*But though we, or an angel from heaven, should preach unto you any gospel other than that which we preached unto you, let him be anathema. As we have said before, so say I now again, if any man preacheth unto you any gospel other than that which ye received, let him be anathema.*" In the Epistle to Titus* we find the following very specific injunction: "*A man that is heretical after a first and second admonition refuse: knowing that such a one is perverted, and sinneth, being self-condemned.*" This injunction seems to be directly suggested by the words of our Saviour, which must be regarded as the charter of the Church's discipline, and which may possibly have been committed to writing at the time when the Pastoral Epistles were written. It is, indeed, true that our Lord contemplated "offences against the brethren," while S. Paul treats of heresy (which his excommunication of Hymenæus and Alexander compels us to understand in the technical sense), but the transference of the discipline from the sphere of conduct to that of opinion would present no difficulty to one who held S. Paul's view as to the nature and claims of the doctrine he preached. The Dominical injunctions in S. Matthew xviii. 15–17 run as follows: "*And if thy brother sin against thee, go, show him his fault between thee and him alone: if he hear thee thou hast gained thy brother. But if he*

---

* iii. 10, 11.

hear thee not, take with thee one or two more, that at the mouth of two witnesses or three every word may be established. And if he refuse to hear them, tell it unto the Church, and if he refuse to hear the Church also, let him be unto thee as the Gentile and the publican." The elaborated discipline of the later Church followed the lines here laid down.

Finally, the Apostolic conception on the one hand of the organized powers of evil, and on the other of the Church, appears to require the association of spiritual abandonment with the fact of exclusion from the Christian Society. A passage from the Colossian Epistle will sufficiently illustrate this. The Apostle exhorts to thankfulness for the inestimable gift of the Gospel. "*Giving thanks unto the Father, who made us meet to be partakers of the inheritance of the saints in light: who delivered us out of the power of darkness and translated us into the kingdom of the Son of His love.*" The Church was a protected sphere, an asylum of safety in a demon-ridden world, over which Satan wielded empire. To be thrust out from the Church was to be exposed without defence to the assaults of Satan.

ARBITRATION IN THE ECCLESIA TO REPLACE LAWSUITS.

Interposed between the discussion of the Corinthian scandal and a fervid denunciation of impurity is a paragraph dealing with the subject of lawsuits. The disgraceful inactivity of the Ecclesia in the matter of the incestuous communicant indicated a singular inability to grasp the full greatness of its own position. The same fact lay at the root of the practice, which had reached discreditable proportions, of carrying disputes between Christians before heathen tribunals. The members of the Church in Corinth were mostly drawn from the humbler ranks of a Greek commercial community. They belonged to the race and to the class in which petty disputes about property have the greatest importance and evoke the keenest interest. This litigiousness was bad in itself as tending to strengthen a hard, grasping disposition, directly opposed to the spirit of Christian fraternity. It was scandalous in effect, as leading to a public exhibition before the heathen of the domestic bickerings of the disciples of Christ. It was distinctly perilous as bringing Christians into close contact with the heathen life, out of which Christianity had drawn them, and as establishing in their minds a mean estimate of the authority of the Ecclesia. The language of S. Paul reveals a very keen perception of all these mischiefs. He lays particular stress on the implied insult to the Ecclesia, and the evident breach of fraternity. The analogy of the synagogue is plainly paramount in his mind. The Jews, under the tolerant sway of the Roman Empire, were permitted to retain their own judicial institutions, and among these were reckoned the synagogues. It is not uninteresting that at Corinth the judicial independence of the Jewish community in reference to certain classes of questions had been publicly asserted by a Roman proconsul.*

* Acts xviii. 15.

The Christian Ecclesia in Corinth owed its origin to a rupture within the Jewish synagogue,* and bore the aspect, and, probably, advanced the claims of a rival synagogue. The Roman Government at this early period drew no distinction between Jew and Christian. The privileges of the synagogue might be appropriated by the Church. This, in effect, is what the Apostle aimed at. From his standpoint the Jewish synagogue in rejecting the Gospel had fallen into apostasy and forfeited its claim to be regarded as a synagogue. To that claim the Christian synagogue was rightful heir. Lightfoot thinks that S. Paul's language directly contemplates the judicial arrangements of the synagogue, and the antecedent probabilities point in that direction. In every synagogue there were three tribunals, known respectively as the Bench of Three, composed of duly ordained elders, the "Authorized" or "Mumchin," whose members commonly held this office by some special patent from the Sanhedrim, and "the Bench not Authorized," of which the members were elected by the litigants. The first of these courts dealt with ordinary suits, the second confined itself to ritual matters, and the third had the range and the limitations of a board of arbitrators. It is to this last, according to Lightfoot, that S. Paul refers in the Epistle. "To this very ordinary bench among the Jews the apostle seems to have respect in this place, and to prescribe it to the Corinthians for a means of ending their differences, which was easy, common, and void of

* *Ibid.* 5-8.

cost and charges. The Bench of Mumchin one may not unfitly call τοὺς αὐθεντημένους, such as were deputed by authority: this Bench consisting of . . . those that were not Mumchin, he calls ἐξουθενημένους, not 'vile' or 'contemptible,' but such as were 'not authorized.' He exhorteth, therefore, that if at any time suits arise among them, concerning pecuniary or other matters, they by no means run to heathen courts, but rather choose some private men among themselves, as judges and arbitrators in such matters."* This may well have been in the Apostle's mind, but it is obscured by the indignation which shapes his actual language. "*Dare* [τολμᾷ] *any of you, having a matter against his neighbour, go to law before the unrighteous, and not before the saints? or know ye not that the saints shall judge the world? and if the world is judged by you, are ye unworthy to judge the smallest matters* [κριτηρίων ἐλαχίστων]? *Know ye not that we shall judge angels? how much more things that pertain to this life* [βιωτικά]? *if then ye have to judge things pertaining to this life* [βιωτικὰ κριτήρια], *set them to judge who are of no account in the Church.* [τοὺς ἐξουθενημένους ἐν τῇ ἐκκλησίᾳ τούτους καθίζετε.] *I say this to move you to shame. Is it so that there cannot be found among you one wise man, who shall be able to decide between his brethren, but brother goeth to law with brother, and that before unbelievers? Nay, already it is altogether a defect in you* [ὅλως ἥττημα ὑμῖν] *that ye have lawsuits* [κρίματα] *one with another. Why not rather take wrong? why not rather be*

* *Works*, xii. pp. 484, 485.

defrauded? Nay, but ye yourselves do wrong, and defraud, and that your brethren."

Whether or not this language is to be understood as actually instituting a tribunal in the Ecclesia for the adjudication of suits between Christians, certain it is that it became the authority upon which such institution justified itself in the next century. The change of attitude towards Christianity which speedily took place on the part of the Empire, and led to the settled policy of persecution, destroyed the protection which had resulted from identification with Judaism, and rendered all Church organization hazardous and difficult. Less and less must discipline have been a matter of fixed rules and courts, more and more must it have taken the character of moral influence. As the theory of the Church developed, the practical effect of Church censures increased. Tertullian's well-known description of Christian worship may be adduced. The discipline was not the less effective for being purely moral: its sanctions were found in the convictions of the community. "Nam et judicatur magno cum pondere, ut apud certos de dei conspectu, summumque futuri judicii praejudicium est, si quis ita deliquerit, ut a communicatione orationis et conventus et omnis sancti commercii relegetur."*

* *Apol.* 39.

Part II.
PRELIMINARY DATA

CHAPTER I.

THE EPISTLES OF S. PAUL

THE Epistles of S. Paul form the principal authority upon which the student of Apostolic Christianity must build his theory; and we must, therefore, begin our present inquiry by briefly describing the nature and importance of those primary documents, with two of which we shall be in this volume mainly concerned. The exceptional character of the Apostle's writings was recognized from the first. An example is found in the second Corinthian Epistle. "His letters, they say, are weighty and strong; but his bodily presence is weak, and his speech of no account."

These words are the judgment of hostile contemporaries upon S. Paul. How far they may express a real contrast between the personal insignificance and the literary ability of the Apostle we can hardly now appreciate. Probably they have the measure of truthfulness which belongs to malicious but successful caricature. S. Paul was not physically imposing,*

---

* The Acts of Paul and Thekla (a second century document) contains a description of the Apostle which, in Prof. Ramsay's opinion, "seems to embody a very early tradition." It is not flattering. Onesiphorus goes out to meet S. Paul. "And he saw Paul coming, a man small in size, with meeting eyebrows, with a rather large nose,

nor did his speech possess the characteristics of the most generally approved eloquence. So far his adversaries may be allowed to have the advantage of him. But even they were compelled to admit that "*his letters were weighty and strong.*" [βαρεῖαι κ. ἰσχυραί.] Their reluctant admission inadequately represents the high estimate of these writings, which has from the earliest times obtained among Christians.

The importance of these Epistles is by no means sufficiently indicated by the fact that they form not less than one-fourth of the New Testament. They include the earliest of existing Christian documents: the whole series were written between the years 52 and 67 of our era. They have been subjected to the rigorous examination of keen and learned, and not always friendly criticism for many years, and we may certainly say that the general result has been to confirm the traditional theory of their authorship. " I must needs believe that all the Epistles of S. Paul which have come down to us as his are genuine." This is the deliberate conclusion of a very learned and acute scholar, Professor Sanday, and if any object that he is a Christian, I will content myself with replying, first, that his Christianity never, as far as I know, interferes with the honest exercise of his critical faculty ; and next, that his favourable opinion of the Pauline Epistles is shared by all competent

---

bald-headed, bow-legged, strongly built, full of grace, for at times he looked like a man, and at times he had the face of an angel." Conybeare and Howson have put together the traditional conception of S. Paul's appearance.—*Vide Life and Epistles*, chap. vii., end.

critics with regard to four, by most with regard to seven, and by many with regard to ten out of the thirteen ascribed to the Apostle in the Canon. The Pastoral Epistles* are admittedly the most disputed and the most disputable members of the series, but Professor Ramsay's† recent and most interesting discoveries of the actual relations which existed between the Roman State and the Apostolic Church have gone far to strengthen their position. It may be useful to have before us the list of undisputed and practically undisputed Epistles. Undisputed are the Epistle to the Romans, the two to the Corinthians, and that to the Galatians; practically undisputed are the First Epistle to the Thessalonians, the Epistle to the Philippians, and that to Philemon. The rest are disputed, but not very successfully. We may be content with the position of most English critical scholars that no real case has been made out against any of them.‡ In the present state of opinion the

---

* "There are features of the Pastoral Epistles which legitimately provoke suspicion. *To the best of my belief, however, they are genuine*, and that not merely in parts: the theory of large early interpolations does not work out at all well in detail."—HORT, *Judaistic Christianity*, p. 130.

† *Vide Church in the Roman Empire*, pp. 245-251. "Incidentally we may here note that the tone of the Pastoral Epistles in this respect (persecution) is consistent only with an early date. It is difficult for the historian of the Empire to admit that they were composed after that development of the Imperial policy towards the Christians which occurred . . . under the Flavian Emperors."

‡ *Weizäcker* admits Romans, 1, 2 Corinthians, Galatians, 1 Thess., Philippians, *i.e.*, six epistles, is doubtful about Colossians and Philemon, and rejects the three Pastoral Ep., 2 Thess., and Ephesians.—*Vide Ap. Age*, p. 218.

Harnack admits all the Epistles except Ephesians, which he marks

private Christian appears to have good reason for accepting with confidence the traditional theory of the Church.

These thirteen letters (for the Epistle to the Hebrews, which is sometimes reckoned as a fourteenth Pauline letter, is agreed on all hands to be the work of an unknown writer of the Apostolic age), including the oldest Christian documents, have formed and must always form the starting point, and the foundation of whatever knowledge we can obtain as to the beginnings of Christianity. They are the principal, because the primary witnesses to the truth of those facts of the life of Christ, and of that presentment of the character of Christ, which together form the basis of the Christian Religion. The four Gospels are alike anonymous and undated; the letters of S. Paul, of which the date is well known, and the authority cannot be denied, form a most valuable test by which to appraise the historical worth of those sacred narratives. We shall see, in the course of our inquiry, how far the Epistles to the Corinthians confirm the statements of the evangelists. Again, all Christians are agreed in deferring to the authority of the Apostles. The most ignorant member of the smallest and youngest sect appeals to that tribunal not less than the most cultivated member of the most venerable Church. The Creed of Christendom

---

as doubtful, and the Pastorals. He thinks that the latter were based on genuine Epistles of S. Paul. His chronology is remarkable. He places S. Paul's conversion in the same year as the Crucifixion, A.D. 30, and his death in A.D. 64.—*Vide die Chronologie der alt lit.*, p. 233, fol. Leipzig, 1897.

lays emphasis upon the "Apostolic" character of the Catholic Church. It cannot then be a matter of indifference to us what the Apostles actually taught and ordered in the Churches which they founded. And we shall not well learn this from the lips of controversialists, or the assertions of partisans. We must not pile together texts, and so wring from the New Testament some kind of assent to the doctrines we already have decided to maintain. We must rather let the Epistles tell their own tale, and bear their own witness in their own way.

The practice of writing doctrinal Epistles may have been suggested to S. Paul by "the so-called Epistles of Jeremiah and Baruch and the Epistles at the beginning of 2 Maccabees.* The Old Testament contains at least one specimen of such compositions in the letter sent by the prophet Jeremiah to the exiles in Babylon.† Probably the practice grew out of the necessities of experience. The rapid success which followed the missionary labours of the great Apostle had scattered little Christian communities over a great part of the Roman Empire. How were the new converts to be spiritually governed except by means of letters? S. Paul himself says that he was burdened with "*anxiety for all the churches.*"‡ That anxiety found

---

* SANDAY, *Bampton Lectures*, p. 335, note.

† *Vide* RÉNAN, *S. Paul*, p. 228. "La correspondance entre synagogues existait déjà dans le judaïsme ; l'envoyé chargé de porter les lettres était même un dignitaire attitré des synagogues." This whole chapter gives a most interesting view of the circumstances under which the Apostle wrote, and the actual conditions of the Churches to which he wrote. ‡ 2 Cor. xi. 28.

expression in the Epistles. From the circumstances of their origin these documents derive both loss and gain. On the one hand, they often deal with questions which were at the time of urgent importance, but which have long ceased to be so. Thus in the Corinthian letters great space is taken up with two discussions, on the eating meat sacrificed to idols, and on the due exercise of miraculous gifts, neither of which have any direct reference to modern needs, although it must be allowed by all that the Apostle so handles these subjects as to provide principles of Christian conduct, which can never be wholly without relevance to Christian needs. *Directly*, however, these questions do not any longer concern us, and it is difficult to induce the careless reader to interest himself in them. Doubtless we have in this circumstance the explanation of the fact that some of S. Paul's letters—how many we do not know, but certainly several—have perished. One such letter is referred to in the first Corinthian Epistle. "*I wrote unto you in my epistle*" (*v.* 9), says S. Paul, but we cannot refer to the passage for the Epistle no longer survives. In the closing verses of the Epistle to the Colossians we perhaps have another lost letter mentioned. "*When this epistle hath been read among you, cause that it be also read in the church of the Laodiceans; and that ye also read the epistle from Laodicea.*"* The Epistle to Laodicea, however, has perished, unless the supposition be correct that it is to be identified with the Epistle to the Ephesians. There is an expression in the second Epistle to the

* Col. iv. 16.

Thessalonians which seems to indicate that several letters had preceded that Epistle, which is probably the earliest in date of all the existing letters save its predecessor to the same Church. "*The salutation of me, Paul, with mine own hand, which is the token in every epistle: so I write.*"*

"*Every epistle*" seems to indicate certainly more than one. The emphasis laid on the Apostle's autograph† appears also to show that the practice of forging letters was included among the weapons of his adversaries. Earlier in the same Epistle S. Paul exhorts the Thessalonians not to "*be troubled either by spirit, or by word, or by epistle as from us.*" We may take for granted that the lost letters dealt with matters of temporary though urgent importance, and so speedily fell out of use among Christians, and then, in the troublous days of persecution, perished altogether. We may admit that the study of the surviving Epistles is hindered by the aspect of obsoleteness, which in some places they present.

The gain, however, predominates over the loss. We owe to the practical exigencies out of which they came that practical tone, that sound insight into the actual conditions of temporal existence, that faithful portraiture of primitive Christianity which charac-

---

* 2 Thess. iii. 17.
† Rénan, *S. Paul*, p. 233. "Pour éviter les fraudes nombreuses auxquelles donnaient lieu les passions du temps, l'autorité de l'apôtre et les conditions matérielles de l'epistolographie antique, Paul avait coutume d'envoyer aux Églises un spécimen de son écriture, qui était facilement reconnaissable ; après quoi, il lui suffisait, selon un usage alors général, de mettre à la fin de ses lettres quelques mots de sa main pour en garantir l'authenticité."

terize these writings, and add so greatly to their interest and value. We may say with confidence that S. Paul was not unconscious of the importance of his Epistles. That he intended them for public use is evident from such passages as that which I have already quoted from the Colossian letter, and from the solemn adjuration which is added at the end of the First Epistle to the Thessalonians. "*I adjure you by the Lord that this epistle be read unto all the brethren.*" (*v.* 27.) He clearly believed himself to be writing with the assistance of the Holy Spirit. He knew himself to be inspired. This is evident from the careful distinction he draws between his own unassisted judgment, and the judgment to which he was led by the Spirit. The seventh chapter of the first Corinthian Epistle provides some very suggestive examples of such distinction. The different expressions employed by the Apostle deserve careful notice. "*This I say by way of permission, not of commandment.*" (*v.* 6.) "*Unto the married I give charge, yea not I, but the Lord.*" (*v.* 10.) "*And so ordain I in all the churches.*" (*v.* 17.) "*Now concerning virgins I have no commandment of the Lord: but I give my judgment, as one that hath obtained mercy of the Lord to be faithful. I think therefore that this is good by reason of the present distress.*" (*vv.* 25, 26.) "*She is happier if she abide as she is, after my judgment: and I think that I also have the Spirit of God.*" (*v.* 40.)

Such careful language does manifestly annihilate theories of verbal inspiration; but it does not less manifestly claim for the Apostle's language when not thus guarded a special authority.

"Paul declares that he does not teach of himself, and that he is but the organ of Him who has confided his mission to him. This is what he means to say when at the head of some of his letters he calls himself '*Apostle of Jesus Christ by the will of God.*' He puts his writing under the guarantee of Him who intrusted him with it."*

Largely, indeed, these Epistles are polemical, concerned with the calumnies of bitter personal antagonists, and the false teachings of dangerous heretics. The language faithfully reflects the vehemence of the writer's fear, or indignation, or joy, or affection. We know that S. Paul was wont to dictate his letters. Where, contrary to custom, he writes with his own hand he calls attention to the fact. "*See with how large letters I have written unto you with mine own hand*" he writes to the Galatians. Similarly, in the little epistle to Philemon, we find: "*I Paul write it with mine own hand, I will repay it.*" But, in this instance, there was an obvious motive for emphasizing the personal liability for the debt of Onesimus which the Apostle undertook. In one instance the amanuensis interpolates his own name. "*I Tertius, who write the epistle, salute you in the Lord*"† is almost abruptly introduced into the salutations with which the Apostle concludes the Epistle to the Romans.

Two results may be attributed to this practice of dictation. On the one hand, much would depend on the ability of the amanuensis to take down fully and accurately the utterances of S. Paul. "One might

* GODET, *Intro. to N. T.*, p. 123.   † Rom. xvi. 22.

take down the Apostle's words verbatim; then we should get a vivid, broken, natural style like that of Romans and First and Second Corinthians. Another might not succeed in getting down the exact words; and then when he came to work up his notes into a fair copy the structure of the sentences would be his own, and it might naturally seem more laboured." It has been plausibly suggested that the habit of the amanuensis may explain those differences in the "cast and structure of the sentences" which are apparent in the later Epistles, and have done yeoman's service to the cause of destructive criticism in the hands of the Germans. On the other hand, as has been already hinted, speech is a much more facile instrument of expression than writing. The astonishing irregularity which marks the glowing eloquence of the Apostle is easily explicable if the language be regarded as the unrestrained outpouring of his thoughts as they rushed to his lips clothed in the words which first presented themselves to his mind. There is precisely the aspect which we might expect to find in a speech, but which surprises us in an essay.

The Epistles were carried to their destination by disciples in whom S. Paul had confidence. Sometimes the messenger is mentioned and specially commended to the Church. "*I commend unto you Phœbe our sister*" occurs in the Epistle to the Romans.* Probably she was intrusted with that letter. "*All my affairs shall Tychicus make known unto you, the beloved brother and faithful minister*

* xvi. 1.

in the Lord: whom I have sent unto you for this very purpose, that ye may know our estate, and that he may comfort your hearts: together with Onesimus the faithful and beloved brother that is one of you." *
We may conclude that Tychicus was the bearer of the Epistle to Colossæ; we know that Onesimus carried a private letter to Philemon, the master from whom he had in former days run away under discreditable circumstances.

We must remember that communications were easy within the Roman Empire. Railways and telegraphs were indeed unknown; but roads were excellent, and there was a regular and efficient system of posts. It is probable that in the matter of material civilization the Roman Empire of S. Paul's day has not found its equal until the present century.†

Finally, we must remember the necessary limitations of the witness which Epistles, prompted by practical emergencies, and often directed to conditions of life and thought which were transitory, and have in fact long since passed away, can yield to the great subject of Christianity. If we expect to find in S. Paul's Letters a methodical and detailed exposition of the Christian Creed, we shall certainly be disappointed. The Epistle to the Romans most nearly corresponds to our idea of a theological treatise, and even in that instance the correspondence is not very close. Still less shall we find in these letters a complete system of Church polity. If we look to discover in them the model

---

* Col. iv. 7–9.   † GIBBON, *Decline and Fall*, chap. ii.

of any existing ecclesiastical system, we shall certainly find them contradict our expectations. S. Paul was writing to Christian people, and he takes for granted their acquaintance with and belief of the Christian Faith. What the Christian Faith involves in the matter of articles of belief it is not hard to discover by legitimate inference from the Letters; but it is nowhere expressly stated, except, indeed, with reference to certain fundamental truths, upon which the Apostle is led to insist by the necessities of polemical argument. So with regard to Church government. We may infer with more or less probability what the system was, but it is nowhere formally declared. The Church at that early period was taking shape, and the agents which influenced the final result were neither few nor simple. Certain elements existed which were derived from the ultimate authority of our Lord; certain principles were accepted which derived their origin from no inferior source; there was an intense conviction of the presence and guiding action within the Christian Society of the Holy Ghost; there existed in S. Paul a singularly rich, strong, original character: in his converts a wealth of material, almost infinitely diverse in quality, and subjected to the formative influence of the most various forces. The Epistles reveal the process of settlement, of definition, of development which created the Catholic Church of Christian History. The source and character of the process are thus described by the great Apostle in a passage from the Epistle, which will form the principal authority in our present inquiry:—

"*Now there are diversities of gifts, but the same Spirit. And there are diversities of ministrations, and the same Lord. And there are diversities of workings, but the same God who worketh all things in all. But to each one is given the manifestation of the Spirit to profit withal. For to one is given through the Spirit the word of wisdom; and to another the word of knowledge according to the same Spirit; to another faith in the same Spirit; and to another gifts of healings in the one Spirit; and to another workings of miracles; and to another prophecy; and to another discernings of spirits; to another divers kinds of tongues; and to another the interpretation of tongues: but all these worketh the one and the same Spirit, dividing to each one severally even as He will.*"* We may add that among the numerous results of that Divine Energy working in the Christian Society none bear their origin more plainly impressed on them, none have exercised a wider and more beneficent influence in succeeding ages, none have more fully secured the ratifying acceptance of the general Christian conscience than these letters of S. Paul, which even the enemies of Christianity must acknowledge to be "*weighty and strong*," and which Christian students in every age, and never more confidently than in this, have believed to be inspired.

* 1 Cor. xii. 4-11.

CHAPTER II.

THE FOUNDING OF THE CHURCH IN CORINTH

IT needs but to glance at the map to see at once that the city of Corinth must have been one of the most important of the ancient world.* It "stood on the high road between Rome and the east, and was therefore one of the greatest centres of influence in the Roman world." With its two ports—Lechæum on the west, and Cenchreæ on the east—Corinth was a meeting place of merchants, wealthy with the exchange and commerce of nations, luxurious with the lavish luxury of wealth, profligate with the shamelessness of luxury. Its importance, both political and commercial, was long standing. It provoked the envy of monarchs and the more malignant jealousy of mercantile rivals. The greatest disaster of Corinthian history had its origin in "mer-

---

* GROTE, *History of Greece*, vol. ii. p. 224. "Corinth in ancient times served as an entrepôt for the trade between Italy and Asia Minor, goods being unshipped at Lechæum, the port on the Corinthian Gulf, and carried by land across to Kenchreæ, the port on the Saronic; indeed, even the merchant vessels themselves when not very large were conveyed across by the same route." For a description of the remains of the ancient city see *Dict. of the Bible*, art. "Corinth." Stanley has a picturesque account of the outward aspect of the city in S. Paul's age: *v. Corinthians*, p. 5.

cantile selfishness," which was strong enough to overcome in the Roman mind that admiration for all things Greek, which generally influenced the attitude of the Republic towards the communities of Hellas.* In the year 146 B.C. the Consul Mummius had besieged and taken Corinth. The sack of the city was memorable both for its ruthless character, and for the considerable effect produced by the transference to Rome of the numerous art-treasures of the greatest centre of Greek life. "The town was stripped of everything of value, and the works of art, pictures, statues, and ornaments of every description were collected for transport to Italy. Much, however, was spoilt by the greedy and ignorant soldiers, and Polybius—who had lately returned from a similar spectacle at Carthage—saw some of the finest pictures thrown on the ground and used as dice-boards. . . . Corinth was then dismantled and burnt, and remained a mere village until its restoration in 46 by Cæsar."† The sack of Corinth had taken place about two centuries before the arrival of S. Paul, but the memory of disasters lingers long, and we know that there existed in the restored city some relics—temples or other public buildings—which had escaped both the fierceness of the flames and the violence of the plunderers, surviving to perpetuate the tradition of the great overthrow from which they had emerged. We have

---

* MOMMSEN, *Provinces of the Roman Empire*, vol. i. p. 257. "In the treatment of Corinth mercantile selfishness had, after an ill-omened fashion, shown itself more powerful than all Philhellenism."
† SHUCKBURGH, *Hist. of Rome*, p. 525.

a parallel in our own history. Rather more than two centuries have elapsed since the Great Fire of London in Charles II.'s reign; but the memory of that immense conflagration is still green among us. We may detect a reference to the sack of Corinth in S. Paul's description of that fire of the Divine Judgment, which will consume everything that is not precious and solid. "*But if any man buildeth on the foundation gold, silver, costly stones, wood, hay, stubble; each man's work shall be made manifest: for the day shall declare it, because it is revealed in fire; and the fire itself shall prove each man's work of what sort it is.*"*

For a century Corinth remained in desolation, and then a new era in its history began, when "the greatest of all Romans and of all Philhellenes, the dictator Cæsar," made "the atonement for the sack of Corinth" by re-founding the city as a Roman colony. This was in the year 46 B.C. S. Paul came to the new city in the year 52 A.D. In this comparatively short period of 98 years the growth of Corinth had been extremely rapid. "The Greek merchants, who had fled on the Roman conquest to Delos and the neighbouring coasts, returned to their former home. The Jews settled themselves in a place most convenient both for the business of commerce and for communication with Jerusalem. Thus, when S. Paul arrived at Corinth after his sojourn at Athens, he found himself in the midst of a numerous population of Greeks and Jews. They were probably far more numerous than the Romans, though the city

* 1 Cor. iii. 12, 13.

had the constitution of a colony, and was the metropolis of a province."* Corinth, moreover, was associated with the famous Isthmian games, which every second year attracted a vast concourse of Greeks. It seems probable that, during his residence in the city, the Apostle actually was present during the games:† it is certain that he was both interested in them and familiar with the rules under which they were carried on. Many allusions to athletics may be found in his Epistles. It will suffice to quote one from the First Epistle to the Corinthians. He compares the Christian to an athlete contending in the foot-races which were the favourite contests of the ancient Greeks. "*Know ye not that they which run in a race run all, but one receiveth the prize? Even so run that ye may attain. And every man that striveth in the games is temperate in all things. Now they do it to receive a corruptible crown; but we an incorruptible. I therefore so run, as not uncertainly; so fight I, as not beating the air; but I buffet my body, and bring it into bondage: lest by any means, after that I have preached to others, I myself should be rejected.*"‡ The visitor to the site of ancient Corinth will be able to trace the remains of the Posidonium or sanctuary of Neptune, the scene of the Isthmian games. "The exact site of the temple is doubtful, and the objects of interest, which Pausanias describes as seen by him within the enclosure, have vanished;

---

* CONYBEARE and HOWSON, xii.

† "It may be confidently concluded that he was there at one of the festivals. (*Ibid.* c. xx.)

‡ 1 Cor. ix. 24-27.

but to the south are the remains of the stadium, where the foot-races were run; to the east are those of the theatre, which was probably the scene of the pugilistic contests; and abundant on the shore are the small green pine trees, which gave the fading wreath to the victors in the games."* Religiously Corinth enjoyed an evil prominence as the centre of "the abandoned and unclean worship of Aphrodite, to whose temple more than a thousand priestesses of loose character were attached." This circumstance may explain the anxious and reiterated emphasis on the duty of purity which marks the Epistles to Corinth, and the constant association in S. Paul's thought of idolatry with sensuality.

The record of the founding of the Christian Church in Corinth is contained in the 18th chapter of the Book of the Acts. "*After these things* (*i.e.*, the visit to Athens and disputation there with the philosophers) *he departed from Athens and came to Corinth. And he found a certain Jew named Aquila, a man of Pontus by race, lately come from Italy, with his wife Priscilla, because Claudius had commanded all the Jews to depart from Rome.*" We may notice the reference to Imperial history. The Roman historian Suetonius, who, though writing at a later date, probably reproduces the words of a contemporary document, states that this edict of Claudius was occasioned by disturbances at Rome led by one Chrestus, by whom we must understand the leader of the Chrestians or Christians, whom the ill-informed Romans supposed to be still living. The narrative proceeds:—"*And he came unto them; and*

* *Dict. of the Bible*, art. "Corinth."

because he was of the same trade, he abode with them, and they wrought; for by their trade they were tent-makers." We have here an interesting indication of the strict Rabbinic influences under which S. Paul had been brought up. The Rabbis strongly insisted that every boy ought to be taught a trade. " He that teacheth not his son a trade, doth the same as if he taught him to be a thief" is a saying of Rabbi Judah.

We may learn from the Epistles how great store the Apostle set by the independence which his ability to earn his own living secured to him. He made the Gospel without charge to his converts. He took advantage of no man. "*Ye yourselves know,*" he said to the Ephesian presbyters, "*that these hands ministered unto my necessities, and to them that were with me.*"* Following his custom in every city where the Jews were numerous, S. Paul first addressed himself to the authorities of the synagogue. Doubtless the scene in Pisidian Antioch was repeated in Corinth. "*After the reading of the law and the prophets the rulers of the synagogue sent unto them, saying, Brethren, if ye have any word of exhortation for the people, say on.*"† The Apostle at first met with considerable success. The earlier stages of his preaching contained little that would offend the prejudices of his hearers, while his fervent loyalty to the spiritual destiny of Israel, his profound knowledge of the Scriptures, and his earnest eloquence would go far to conciliate the most suspicious. A change, however, happened when he passed on to the central element of his message. "*But when Silas and Timothy came*

* Acts xx. 34.   † *Ibid.* xiii. 15.

down from Macedonia, Paul was constrained by the Word (συνείχετο τῷ λόγῳ), *testifying to the Jews that Jesus was the Christ.*" It is not easy to connect the arrival of S. Paul's companions with his increased energy in preaching. It has been suggested that they brought a supply of money, and so enabled the Apostle to leave tent-making and give himself up wholly to his preaching. It is certainly true that the Philippians did minister to S. Paul's necessities, for he gratefully acknowledges their bounty in his Epistle to them (iv. 15); but it seems difficult to reconcile this sense with the structure of the passage in the Acts. We may learn from S. Paul's own account of his preaching at Corinth that it presented marked features. "*And I, brethren,*" so he writes to the Corinthians, "*when I came unto you, came not with excellency of speech or of wisdom, proclaiming to you the mystery of God. For I determined not to know anything among you, save Jesus Christ, and Him crucified. And I was with you in weakness, and in fear, and in much trembling. And my speech and my preaching were not in persuasive words of wisdom, but in demonstration of the Spirit and of power: that your faith should not stand in the wisdom of men, but in the power of God.*" (ii. 1–5.)

Perhaps the Apostle looked back with half-regretful feelings on his disputation at Athens, when he had laid aside the manner of an apostle in order to contend in the character of a sophist with the sophists of the Athenian schools. "It would appear," observes Professor Ramsay, "that Paul was disappointed and perhaps disillusioned by his experience in Athens."* Certainly his insistence on the crucifixion of the Messiah would be as offensive to the Jews as it was ridiculous to the philosophers. We are not surprised to learn that opposition manifested itself, and soon took a violent form. The Apostle was little disposed to conciliate or compromise with the Jews. "*And when they opposed themselves, and blasphemed, he shook out his raiment, and said unto them, Your blood be upon your own heads; I am clean: from henceforth I will go unto the Gentiles. And he departed thence, and went into the house of a certain man named Titus Justus, one that worshipped God, whose house joined hard to the synagogue. And Crispus, the ruler of the synagogue, believed in the Lord with all his house; and many of the Corinthians hearing believed, and were baptized.*" The open breach with the synagogue must have taken place sooner or later, wherever the Gospel was preached in the synagogue; here in Corinth the process was carried through by the Apostle himself. The house of the converted proselyte became the first independent Christian Church; for the first time the connection with the venerable system of Judaism was repudiated; Christianity stood out in its true character as a new religion. This important event took place amid circumstances of great disturbance and difficulty, which, however, eventually turned out to the furtherance of the Christian cause. S. Paul had clearly gauged the critical character of his action, and braced himself for conflict. He was inwardly strengthened by renewed assurance of the

* S. *Paul, the Traveller and the Roman Citizen*, p. 252.

Divine Protection. "*And the Lord said unto Paul in the night by a vision, Be not afraid, but speak, and hold not thy peace: for I am with thee, and no man shall set on thee to harm thee: for I have much people in this city. And he dwelt there a year and six months, teaching the Word of God among them.*" We can imagine how bitter were the feelings with which the Jews regarded the seceders from the synagogue. Corinth had easy communication by sea with Palestine. We may be sure that the malignant enemies of S. Paul at Jerusalem exerted their influence to stimulate and organize the opposition against him in Corinth. An opportunity for action was provided by the arrival in the city of a new proconsul of Achaia. "*But when Gallio was proconsul of Achaia, the Jews with one accord rose up against Paul, and brought him before the judgment seat, saying, This man persuadeth men to worship God contrary to the law. But when Paul was about to open his mouth, Gallio said unto the Jews, If indeed it were a matter of wrong or of wicked villany, O ye Jews, reason would that I should bear with you: but if they are questions about words and names and your own law, look to it yourselves; I am not minded to be a judge of these matters.*"

"It is clear," observes Professor Ramsay, "that Gallio's short speech represents the conclusion of a series of inquiries, for the accusation, as it is quoted, does not refer to words or names, but only to the law. But it is reasonable to suppose that the Jews put their accusation at first in a serious light, with a view to some serious penalty being inflicted; and Gallio, on probing their allegations, reduced the matter to its true dimensions as a question that concerned only the self-administering community of 'the Nation of the Jews in Corinth.'"* The governor's action gave great satisfaction to the Greeks of Corinth, with whom the Jews were probably extremely unpopular. A demonstration of public feeling was made in the very presence of the proconsul. "*They all*" (*i.e.*, the Greeks) "*laid hold on Sosthenes, the ruler of the synagogue, and beat him before the judgment seat.*" Even this violence did not disturb the placid mind of Gallio. He "*cared for none of these things.*" Shortly afterwards Paul himself left Corinth, and sailed for Syria. It is curious that precisely at this time, when his relations with the Jews were so strained, and when he had himself conducted an open secession from their synagogue, we should read of his performing a ritual act required by Jewish law. He shaved his head in Cenchreæ; for he had a vow. Perhaps he was already preparing for his encounter with the intensely Judaistic Church of Jerusalem, in which he knew himself to be the object of general suspicion, and not a little positive hostility. He was acting on that conciliatory principle which he had laid aside in the conflict with the Corinthian Jews, but which marked his conduct at Jerusalem. "*I am become all things to all men, that I may by all means save some,*" is his own account of himself. The episode before the proconsul's judgment seat illustrates the neutral attitude which, in the earliest period of Church History, was maintained by the Roman Government

* *S. Paul*, pp. 258-9.

towards Christianity. At the same moment the sharpest contrast was presented between the fanatical hatred of the Jews and the impartial justice of the Empire. The impression made by the contrast on S. Paul's mind is reflected in the Epistles to the Thessalonians, which were written during his residence in Corinth. In no other of his letters does the Apostle write with such bitterness of his own nation. "*Ye also suffered the same things of your own countrymen even as they*" (*i.e.*, the Christians of Judæa) "*did of the Jews; who both killed the Lord Jesus and the prophets, and drave out us, and please not God, and are contrary to all men; forbidding us to speak to the Gentiles that they may be saved; to fill up their sins alway: but the wrath is come upon them to the uttermost.*"* This is the language of deep indignation. S. Paul has clearly come to the decision that there is no hope of working through the Jews or with them. His separation of the disciples, and organization of an independent congregation in the house of Titus Justus, was but the expression in act of the sentiments he expressed in the Epistles to Thessalonians. On the other hand, he gained a new estimate of the spiritual value of the mighty organization of the Empire which had rescued him from his adversaries and authorized the existence of the Church. We may truly say that "the residence at Corinth was an epoch in Paul's life." His view of the Roman Government as the providential agent for enabling the preaching of the Gospel is ambiguously expressed in the second

* 1 Thess. ii. 14 16.

Thessalonian letter, in which he speaks of the restraining force which at present checks the "*mystery of lawlessness*," and the removal of which will be the signal for the great catastrophe of the second Advent.* In the Epistles to the Galatians and Romans his language is definite and clear :—"*The powers that be are ordained of God.*"†

We gather from the Epistles to the Corinthians that the Church in Corinth was mainly composed of Gentiles. The name of "*Sosthenes our brother*" is associated with the Apostle's in the opening verse of the first Epistle; and it is natural to conjecture that he may be identical with the ruler of the synagogue, whom the rabble beat before Gallio's judgment seat; but there is nothing beyond the identity of names to show that so conspicuous a success had been vouchsafed to the Church. The general drift of the Epistles prohibits the notion that any large proportion of the Corinthian Christians were Jews; yet the numerous references to Scripture and to the system of Judaism make it certain that knowledge of both was general in the Church. Probably Titus Justus, whose name sufficiently indicates that he belonged to the Italian colony, and who is expressly described as a proselyte, was representative of many. The core of the Church in Corinth, as in most of the great cities of the Empire, was found in the Greek proselytes, who possessed the Scriptures, and attended the worship of the synagogues of the Dispersion.

* 2 Thess. ii. 7. † Rom. xiii. 1.

CHAPTER III.

THE LETTER FROM CORINTH

AFTER his acquittal before the tribunal of Gallio, or to speak more exactly, his escape from trial through the imperturbable neutrality of the proconsul, S. Paul yet *tarried many days* in Corinth;* then, solemnly bidding farewell to the Church, he started on a leisurely journey to Syria by way of Ephesus. While he was visiting Cæsarea, and making a general visitation of the Churches which he had founded, there came to Ephesus a learned and eloquent Alexandrian Jew, named Apollos. Ignorant of the Gospel history, "*knowing only the baptism of John*," Apollos "*was mighty in the Scriptures*," and his reasonings were entirely favourable, so far as they went, to Christianity.

Happily Priscilla and Aquila (who had left Corinth in S. Paul's company) had remained at Ephesus when the Apostle went forward to Cæsarea, and from them Apollos learned "*the way of God more carefully.*" He professed himself a Christian, and in that character was formally commended by the Ephesian brethren to the kindly reception of the Corinthian Church. His influence at Corinth rapidly

* Acts xviii. 18.

extended; especially in controversy with the parent synagogue his labours were rewarded by great success, "*for he powerfully confuted the Jews, and that publicly, showing by the Scriptures that Jesus was the Christ.*" While he was thus active at Corinth S. Paul had returned to Ephesus and entered on a lengthened ministry there, which, though marked by many crises of danger, resulted not only in the firm foundation of the Church in Ephesus itself, but also in the wide extension of Christian influence in the province of Asia. Shortly after S. Paul's settlement in the city ominous reports reached him from Corinth. The servants of Chloe brought tidings of divisions among the Christians, divisions which were only the more offensive since they sheltered themselves under the authority of justly venerated names. Apollos arrived from Corinth, and his tidings were in the main confirmatory of these reports. Especially, he had to tell of grave departures from the law of Christian purity. The heathen laxity in which the Corinthians had grown up, and by which they were surrounded, was asserting itself most manifestly among the baptized. S. Paul wrote a short Epistle on the subject of purity; this Epistle is referred to in the first of the canonical writings, but has not survived.

Hearing further reports he determined to visit Macedonia and Achaia on his journey to Jerusalem, where his presence was required in the matter of the general collection for the poverty-stricken Christians of Judæa, which he had agreed to make among the Gentile converts, and which he designed to serve as an assertion of unity. With this plan in view he sent on in advance two of his most trusted disciples—Timothy and Erastus—with instructions to organize the collection against his own arrival, and to rectify the disorders at Corinth.* In the interval, however, there arrived in Ephesus a deputation from the Corinthians, composed of three members—Stephanas and Fortunatus and Achaicus† —and charged with a letter from the Church. To this Corinthian letter S. Paul made answer in the First Epistle to the Corinthians, and we are able to discover from the latter the outline of the contents of the former.

The Corinthians appealed to S. Paul for direction on five matters of practical importance. The answers of the Apostle are marked by a tone of authority, which makes it evident that he regarded himself as the supreme ruler of his converts in spiritual matters.

I. The first and, from some points of view, the most important question in the letter had reference to the subject of marriage. It is discussed and answered in the seventh chapter of our Epistle. The actual inquiry had reference to celibacy. Was it a legitimate state? Under what limitations and for what reasons was it to be commended? It is not very obvious to the modern reader why such an inquiry should have been made; but a little reflection, and a study of S. Paul's reply, make it evident that the subject was

---

* Acts xix. 21, 22.
† 1 Cor. xvi. 17, "And I rejoice at the coming of Stephanas and Fortunatus and Achaicus." It will be observed that the names are obviously Gentile.

both urgent and difficult. The relations of husband and wife within the married state were rendered extremely complicated by the advent of Christianity. How far did the heathen husband's authority extend over the Christian wife? How far was the heathen wife to be considered subject to the Christian husband? Did the marriage hold good when one of the parties became Christian? What was the position of the children? Might new marriages between Christians and heathen be rightfully contracted? How was the Christian doctrine of the spiritual equality of the sexes to be reconciled with the subordination of wife to husband in the married state? What about divorce? The question of the Corinthians was neither simple nor unimportant: it dealt with real difficulties: and it is not too much to say that the highest interests of society were at stake in S. Paul's treatment of it. Moreover, in ancient as in modern times, though far more powerfully, there has worked in devout minds that ascetic principle, which assuredly true in itself, does easily lend itself, and has constantly lent itself to the most disastrous errors. Was the single state religiously preferable to the married? *That*, S. Paul answers, must be determined by considerations of expediency.* His own opinion was that in view of the approaching Advent of Christ, an event which would be preceded by great catastrophes, and in view of the claims of the religious life, it was better to remain single: but

* *Cf.* Eph. v. 22-33. This passage cuts up by the roots the idea that S. Paul believed in the superiority of the single life in itself. His own example sufficiently proves that he regarded it as superior in some circumstances and for some work.

he refused to advance beyond that position. That there was any inherent spiritual superiority in the unmarried state he would not allow. The false asceticism which degraded marriage found in S. Paul the most uncompromising antagonist. Unmarried himself, it is yet to him that we owe that sublime doctrine of marriage which makes it the symbol of the highest and holiest fellowship, which consecrates it as inherently spiritual, and associates it for ever with the very centre of Christian discipleship.

II. The second question dealt with a practical matter of great urgency. S. Paul answers it in the eighth and tenth chapters of the Epistle. Apparently there were three inquiries:—

1. Was it permissible to buy and eat the meat publicly offered for sale in the market-place, although it was known that according to custom the sellers had offered it to idols?

S. Paul replies in the affirmative. "*Whatsoever is sold in the shambles, eat, asking no question for conscience sake: for the earth is the Lord's, and the fulness thereof.*" *

2. Was it permissible for a Christian to join with his neighbours in the feasts, which were held in the heathen temples, and formed, perhaps, the principal social gatherings?

It seems probable that S. Paul has preserved the actual language of the Corinthian letter. "*Now concerning things sacrificed to idols: we know that we all have knowledge: we know that no idol is anything in the world, that 'all things are lawful.'*" These

* x. 25, 26.

THE LETTER FROM CORINTH

phrases were perhaps much on the lips of the Corinthians, especially of those who called themselves the *"strong"* members, and regarded with ample disdain their more scrupulous brethren. S. Paul returns to the Corinthian question a twofold negative. Under existing circumstances their liberty to feast in heathen temples would hurt the consciences of many, and so break the supreme law of charity. "It may be true, as you say, that '*meat will not commend us to God*': that '*neither if we eat not are we the worse: nor, if we eat, are we the better*': but your point of view is wrong: you treat the subject purely in its selfish aspects." "*Take heed lest this liberty of yours become a stumbling-block to the weak. For if a man see thee which hast knowledge sitting at meat in an idol's temple, will not his conscience, if he is weak, be emboldened to eat things sacrificed to idols? For through thy knowledge he that is weak perisheth, the brother for whose sake Christ died. And thus, sinning against the brethren, and wounding their conscience when it is weak, ye sin against Christ.*" How the petty ritual point grows in S. Paul's hands into a nobler thing, is transformed until the whole issue is lifted out of the controversial atmosphere of Corinth and judged at the foot of the Cross! On the other hand, the Apostle condemns the practice of attending idolatrous feasts as involving positive disloyalty to our Lord. *He apparently

---

* *Cf.* 1 Cor. x. 19-21, with 1 Cor. viii. 4. Godet reconciles these apparently contradictory statements thus:—"Jupiter, Apollon, Vénus assurément ne sont pas des êtres réels: mais Satan est quelque chose. D'arrière toute cette fantasmagorie mythologique se cachent des puis-

believed the heathen gods to be demons—a belief which was general in the early Church, and therefore any participation in the heathen worships was a homage of Satan, and apostasy from Christ. "*What say I then? that a thing sacrificed to idols is anything, or that an idol is anything? But I say, that the things which the Gentiles sacrifice, they sacrifice to devils, and not to God: and I would not that ye should have communion with devils.*"

3. Finally, might a Christian accept a private invitation to dinner in the house of a heathen friend, although the meat set on the table would probably have been "*offered to idols*"?

Yes, replies S. Paul, he may go, but if his attention is directly called to the idolatrous character of the meat, so as to raise the question of religious principle, he must decline to partake of the meat. "*If one of them that believe not biddeth you to a feast, and ye are disposed to go: whatsoever is set before you, eat, asking no question for conscience sake. But if any man say unto you, This hath been offered in sacrifice, eat not, for his sake that showed it, and for conscience sake.*" (x. 27-28.) Such is S. Paul's treatment of this question, which for so many ages has ceased to be urgent in the Christian Church, save where the Corinthian conditions are reproduced among the newly-founded Churches in heathen lands. For missionaries the subject has a direct and living

---

sances malfaisantes, qui, sans être des divinités, n'en sont pas moins très-réelles, très-actives, et qui sont parvenues à fasciner l'imagination humaine et à détourner sur des êtres de fantaisie le sentiment religieux des nations païennes : de là les cultes idolâtres, cultes addressés à ces puissances diaboliques et non pas à Dieu."—*Corinthiens*, ii. p. 106.

interest, and even for other Christians, the members of an ancient Christian Church, the Apostle's teaching has a real value. I have sometimes reflected that under changed forms the inquiries of the Corinthians in the matter of idolatry still need answer. Many devout disciples are distressed in conscience by the apparent necessity under which they are placed to accept and in a measure support an order of social life which they are convinced is poisoned with injustice. They are fearful of incurring guilt by maintaining a system which involves the practice known as sweating, and in their anxiety they are sometimes prepared to attempt very perilous economic and moral experiments. I suggest that the Pauline principles might apply. "Whatsoever is sold in the shops, buy, asking no question for conscience sake. . . . But if any man say unto you, These goods are manufactured under disgraceful conditions, the work-people are oppressed and the materials are adulterated or inferior, buy not, for his sake that showed it, and for conscience sake."

III. The Corinthian letter raised another question, which again, at first, strikes us as rather trivial, but which, on investigation, is found to be of real importance. How ought women to behave in the religious assemblies? Were they to be veiled? Might they take part in the conduct of worship? We must remember that Christianity effected a great change in the position of women. It was by no means easy to determine the practical application of that equality in Christ on which all Christians were agreed. Moreover, there were considerable perils involved in any sudden extension of liberty to persons who were quite unaccustomed to its possession. In the profligate atmosphere of ancient Corinth these perils were obvious and grave. We shall have to return in a later chapter to the question of the conduct of public worship in the Corinthian Church, and I do not propose to anticipate here the discussion which will more properly be undertaken there. It will suffice to state that the Apostle insisted with some show of indignation that in the public assemblies the Christian women should be veiled, and that they should take no part in the actual conduct of the devotions. "*Let the women keep silence in the churches: for it is not permitted unto them to speak; but let them be in subjection, as also saith the law.*"*

IV. The Corinthian Church was richly endowed with spiritual gifts, but the sense of order was frail, and the temper of responsibility inadequate. The public assemblies became scenes of confusion, almost of conflict. The need of some regulations wherewith to check anarchic tendencies and to ensure a more edifying conduct of the common devotions was apparent. It is sufficiently evident that the Corinthian letter included a request that the Apostle would deal with the subject. The discussion of spiritual gifts forms the climax of the Epistle. The beautiful description of the Church under the metaphor of the natural body has passed into the very texture of Christian thought; the appended hymn on the glories of charity or love has taken its place in Christian literature as the unequalled unity of

* 1 Cor. xiv. 34.

THE LETTER FROM CORINTH

inspired thought and graceful though glowing language.* We owe both to the anarchy of the Corinthian assemblies. The fourteenth chapter contains the Apostle's actual rulings; incidentally it enables us to gain view of the Apostolic Church in real life. We refrain from commenting on it here, because we shall have to deal with the whole subject in a later chapter. In putting forward the principles which ought to control the exercise of spiritual gifts, S. Paul makes a significant appeal to those members of the Corinthian Church who claimed to be most richly endowed with these graces. "*If any man thinketh himself to be a prophet, or spiritual, let him take knowledge of the things which I write unto you, that they are the commandment of the Lord.*" (*v.* 37.)

V. The Corinthian letter appears to have made reference to "*the collection for the saints*" which S. Paul had pledged himself to organize throughout the Churches which he founded. In the Epistle to the Galatians the Apostle for polemical reasons is led to give an account of the circumstances under which he had done this. He is defending the cause of Christian liberty against the Judaizing fanatics who sought to impose on the Gentile Churches the yoke of the Mosaic law, and he narrates the history of his relations with the "*chiefest apostles*," "*James and Cephas and John, they who were reputed to be*

---

* RÉNAN's enthusiastic description of this thirteenth chapter is worth quoting:—"Emporté par un souffle vraiment prophétique au delà des idées mêlées des aberrations qu'il vient d'exposer, Paul écrit alors *cette page admirable, la seule de toute la litterature Chrétienne qui puisse être comparée aux discours de Jésus.*"—*S. Paul*, p. 408.

pillars." These unquestioned leaders of the Church had not insisted on the imposition of the Jewish law. On the contrary, "*when they perceived the grace that was given unto*" S. Paul they had readily consented to an arrangement by which, while they themselves undertook the conversion of the Jews, he should "*go unto the Gentiles*," one condition only they had insisted upon, and that S. Paul was more than willing to fulfil, "*only they would that we should remember the poor; which very thing I was also zealous to do.*" It is very evident that the success of this collection was earnestly desired by S. Paul.* It would cut the ground from under the feet of those who persistently accused him of disloyalty to the Mother Church of Jerusalem, and it would bring home to his Gentile converts the reality of their communion with their Jewish brethren. Yet he was clearly anxious as to the reception which his efforts would obtain at Jerusalem. He requests the prayers of the Roman Christians on his behalf, and his words convey the impression that he had misgivings as to the future. "*Now I beseech you, brethren, by our Lord Jesus Christ, and by the love of the Spirit, that ye strive together with me in your prayers to God for me; that I may be delivered from them that are disobedient in Judæa, and that my ministration which I have for Jerusalem may be acceptable to the saints; that I may come unto you in joy through the will of God, and together with you find rest.*"† That S. Paul's misgivings were justified by the event is manifest from the narrative in the Acts of his visit to

* *Vide* HORT, *Romans and Ephesians*, pp. 40-44.   † Rom. xv. 30-31.

THE LETTER FROM CORINTH

Jerusalem, a visit which led to his arrival in Rome as a state prisoner.

We conclude, then, that the collection was regarded both by S. Paul and by the Corinthians as a matter of considerable importance. They inquire by what methods the money is to be collected and forwarded, and this is the Apostle's answer: "*Now concerning the collection for the saints, as I gave order to the churches of Galatia, so also do ye. Upon the first day of the week let each one of you lay by him in store, as he may prosper, that no collections be made when I come. And when I arrive, whomsoever ye shall approve by letters, them will I send to carry your bounty unto Jerusalem: and if it be meet for me to go also, they shall go with me.*"* We learn from the second Epistle that the Corinthians were not so zealous in this matter as S. Paul had expected them to be. No less than two chapters—the eighth and the ninth—are devoted to the subject, and the embarrassed tone of the Apostle is very apparent. He courteously dwells on the liberality of the Corinthians, but he reminds them that "*he that soweth sparingly shall reap also sparingly,*" and that "*God loveth a cheerful giver.*"

S. Paul's answer to the Corinthian inquiry contains the earliest reference to the observance of the "*first day of the week.*" We learn from the record of the Acts that the Christians of the Apostolic age were accustomed to receive the Holy Communion on that day. At Troas it is related that "*upon the first day of the week, when we were gathered together to break bread, Paul discoursed with them,*

* xvi. 1-4.

intending to depart on the morrow: and prolonged his speech until midnight."* It does not indeed appear that S. Paul intended the Corinthians to make their weekly contributions at the religious service, his language seems rather to suggest that each one should set aside his alms at home, and bring the total to the common fund on the Apostle's arrival; but this in no way detracts from the significance of the reference. The *"first day of the week"* is mentioned as a matter of course; that was the obvious day which would suggest itself to every Christian mind when any matter connected with religion was in question. The explanation of this prominence, at once unquestioned and complete, points to the supreme event which was associated in Christian thought with the first day of the week. That event—the resurrection of Christ—stamped a character of greatness and joy upon the day, and endowed it with the name which has continued in use throughout the history of the Church, and remains the favourite name in the usage of disciples among themselves,—" the Lord's Day." Incidentally it is worth noticing that the Apostle provides a very remarkable piece of collateral evidence for the historic truth of that Article of the Creed, which perhaps may be described as the foundation of all the rest, "*On the third day He rose again.*"

* Acts xx. 7.

Part III.
DOCTRINE AND THE SACRAMENTS

CHAPTER I.

THE HISTORIC CHRIST

THE Corinthian Epistles were written before the canonical Gospels; they may represent, therefore, an earlier stage of the tradition about our Lord. By carefully studying them we shall be able to discover what was the *original* account of Jesus Christ, which was circulated in the Church. If they confirm the history as it is presented in the four Gospels, we certainly have added, and that in no slight measure, to the strength of the reasons which justify our acceptance of that history. Manifestly the inquiry which we have in hand touches the very centre of our religion. Everything depends on the validity of our belief that the Founder of our religion was, what the Creed asserts that He was, the Son of God; that being thus of divine origin and essence, He yet was very man; that His death on the cross was no mere martyrdom glorious with the barren majesty of unequalled fortitude, but an event, powerful for our salvation; that His resurrection was no fair dream of ardent friendship, unable to reconcile itself to the extinction of the hopes which had grown round His person, but a fact able to bear the weight of Christian faith. The truth of Christianity stands or falls with the truth of Christ's history. In the four Gospels we have a record of our Lord's life on earth, which for eighteen centuries has been accepted as a true record. This century, however, has brought that record under the scrutiny of a vigilant and rigorous criticism. Attention has been directed to the discrepancies in detail between the synoptic evangelists, to the remarkable difference between the history as presented by those writers and the history as presented by the author of the fourth Gospel. The discrepancies, even when the harmonists have tried their hardest, are real; the difference between the first three Gospels and the fourth is manifest to every student. Yet, in spite of these, I do not think any impartial person will deny that there is left upon the student's mind an impression at once distinct and absolutely unique. <u>The personality of Jesus looks out upon us from the Gospels, commanding, inscrutable, severe, yet beyond all parallel winning, tender, and pathetic. That personality constitutes the abiding charm of those writings. It is the secret of the power of Christianity.</u> It is the magnet of souls, drawing out to itself the involuntary homage of the good, the pure, the just in every age and in every land. The question proposes itself and presses for answer. Is the impression left on us by the Gospels a just one? Is the personality of Christ, presented in those writings, a creation of pious fancy, or is it a transcript from actual experience? In a word, are the Gospels in the main true? The inquiry which we have now in hand will help us towards the answer. If we can show that the Gospels do certainly present the earliest form of

Christ's history, that, whatever else may be said about the picture of our Lord which they contain, this at least must be conceded, that it is the original picture, the first, the oldest; that in the Gospels we have no later growth, no developed tradition, but in its essential features the same version of the life of Jesus as that which on the morrow of His death was accepted by the converts to Christianity—then, I submit, that we shall have advanced a long way towards the affirmative answer to the momentous questions we have proposed. Supposing, then, for the sake of our argument, that we had no other documents from which to form our conception of the history of Christ than these Epistles to the Corinthians, what should we know about that history? Or, to state the same thing in other words, what account of Christ did S. Paul give to the Corinthians?

Let me remind you that both the Corinthian letters were written in the year 57, that S. Paul had been at least for twenty years a professed disciple of Christ, that his knowledge of Christ's history must have been acquired at the time of his conversion, and that, therefore, the version of that history which these Epistles assume must have been current within the first eight or ten years after our Lord's crucifixion.* It cannot, I think, be reasonably disputed that whether we learn much, or whether we learn little from these writings about our Lord's life on earth, what we learn is certainly the original version of the history. We turn now to the Epistles themselves.

* This is probably an under-statement of the facts.

The most casual reader must be impressed by the prominence of Christ in these Corinthian letters. Unless my counting is at fault our Lord is mentioned by name sixty-nine times in the first Epistle, fifty-six times in the second. There are, besides, numerous references to Him more or less direct. He is referred to under two names, "*Jesus*" and "*Christ*"; often both names are combined, "*Jesus Christ*," or "*Christ Jesus.*" The title which is most commonly assigned to Him is "*Lord*"; except in quotations from the Old Testament, it would seem that wherever "*the Lord*" is mentioned, Christ is referred to. In one place he is emphatically described as the "*one Lord*" of Christians; and in another the recognition of His Lordship is referred to as the test of discipleship. The contrasted formulas in the following passage would seem to have been actually current in Corinth. The one, perhaps, was the battle-cry of the synagogue; the other, the rejoinder of the Church. "*I give you to understand, that no man speaking in the Spirit of God saith, Jesus is anathema; and no man can say, Jesus is Lord, but in the Holy Spirit.*"*

Two events in Christ's History are specifically dwelt upon—His Crucifixion and His Resurrection. "*We preach Christ crucified, unto Jews a stumbling-block, and unto Greeks foolishness.*"† S. Paul is fully conscious of the unpopularity of the fact upon which he constantly insists. "*I determined not to know anything among you, save Jesus Christ, and Him crucified.*"‡ This fact emerges again and again in the

* 1 Cor. xii. 3. † *Ibid.* i. 23. ‡ *Ibid.* ii. 2.

THE HISTORIC CHRIST

Apostle's thought. Does he urge the necessity of purity, and the jealous exclusion from Christian society of all that endangers purity? It is the death of Christ which supplies the basis of his appeal. "*Purge out the old leaven, that ye may be a new lamp, even as ye are unleavened. For our passover also hath been sacrificed, even Christ.*" "*Ye are not your own ; for ye were bought with a price : glorify God therefore in your body.*" *

Does he seek an argument which shall bring home to the "*strong*" members of the Corinthian Church the real meaning of that proud insistence on their liberty to which they clung? He finds it in the Death of Christ. "*Through thy knowledge he that is weak perisheth, the brother for whose sake Christ died.*"† Does he seek an explanation of that affliction which shadows his apostolate? It is here that he finds it. The Apostles are "*always bearing about in the body the dying of Jesus, that the life also of Jesus may be manifested in our body.*"‡ Will he confess the motive of his passion for souls? It is still the Cross. "*For the love of Christ constraineth us; because we thus judge, that One died for all, therefore all died; and He died for all, that they which live should no longer live unto themselves, but unto Him who for their sakes died and rose again.*"§ Do the Corinthians require an explanation of the contrast between his lofty insistence on obedience, and his harassed, feeble personality? He will yet point them to the paradox of Christ's Passion. "*Seeing*

---

* *Ibid.* v. 7, 8 ; vi. 19, 20. † *Ibid.* viii. 11.
‡ 2 Cor. iv. 10. § *Ibid.* v. 14–15.

that ye seek a proof of Christ that speaketh in me: who to youward is not weak, but is powerful in you: for He was crucified through weakness, yet He liveth through the power of God."*

Now this insistence on the fact of the Crucifixion would be inexplicable if it stood alone; but is not so much explicable as obvious when it is combined with the fact of the Resurrection. Regarded in the light of the triumph of Easter, the tragedy of Good Friday receives an interpretation which invests it with resistless attractiveness. "*Wherefore we henceforth know no man after the flesh; even though we have known Christ after the flesh, yet now we know Him so no more.*"† The Crucifixion is no longer merely or mainly the central Infamy of human history; it is a Pageant of Divine Love; it is the stepping forth into the vexed life of the Race of the Divine Helpfulness. "*God was in Christ reconciling the world unto Himself, not reckoning unto them their trespasses, and having committed unto us the word of reconciliation.*"‡ The Resurrection is affirmed with a solemnity and caution not inadequate to its crucial importance. The Apostle does not hesitate to stake on it the truth of Christianity. "*If Christ hath not been raised, your faith is vain; ye are yet in your sins.*"§ The testimonies collected together in the fifteenth chapter of the First Epistle are too important to be cursorily noticed here; we must consider them separately in the next chapter.

The Institution of the Eucharist is related in the

* 2 Cor. xiii. 3. † *Ibid.* v. 16.
‡ *Ibid.* v. 19. § 1 Cor. xv. 14.

eleventh chapter, and so close is the parallel with S. Luke's Gospel that it leaves us in little doubt as to the source from which the Evangelist drew some of his materials. The form of the account as it stands in the Epistle suggests that in liturgical use it had already established itself. Reserving to a later stage in our inquiry the discussion of this subject, we may here pause to notice that the Apostle follows exactly on the lines of the Gospels in giving so great prominence to the closing scenes of our Lord's life.

We learn that Christ was a Teacher, whose authority, indeed, is final in the Church. Twice, at least, S. Paul quotes the very words of Christ, and it is interesting to note that while in both instances the words are fairly representative of His teaching, in neither do the canonical Gospels contain the actual words attributed to our Lord. In treating of marriage the Apostle lays down this rule on the authority of Christ :—"*That the wife depart not from her husband, and that the husband leave not his wife.*" Again, in arguing the right of the clergy to the support of their flocks, he adduces as the final consideration this precept of Christ that "*they which proclaim the gospel should live of the gospel.*" It is worth noticing that in the farewell speech to the Ephesian presbyters attributed to S. Paul in the Acts, there is another saying of Christ quoted which also is not found in our Gospels. He bade the presbyters "*remember the words of the Lord Jesus, how He Himself said, It is more blessed to give than to receive.*" (xx. 35.)

We learn incidentally that Christ had "*brethren*" and "*apostles*," of whom *twelve* occupied a position of exceptional importance. One of these is mentioned by name, apparently as holding a certain recognized pre-eminence amongst them—*Cephas*. We also learn that one of Christ's brethren bore the name "*James.*" "*Have we no right to lead about a wife that is a believer, even as the rest of the apostles, and the brethren of the Lord, and Cephas?*"* It is evident that all these were well-known persons, whose authority no Christian would dream of disputing. In the testimonies of the Resurrection we find the following:—"*He appeared to Cephas; then to the twelve . . . then He appeared to James; then to all the apostles.*"† In the second Epistle we are able to discover that within the apostolic college there was recognized a certain gradation of authority. Some were regarded as superior to the rest, if not in position yet certainly in influence. "*I reckon that I am not a whit behind the very chiefest apostles.*"‡ We learn from the Epistle to the Galatians, which, you will remember, was written about the same time as the Corinthian Epistles, and is, like them, of undisputed authority, that these "*chiefest apostles*" were "*James and Cephas and John.*"

Moreover we have in these Epistles no obscure indications as to the character of the Historic Christ. It is assumed that the Corinthians are familiar with His self-abnegation. "*Ye know the grace of our Lord Jesus Christ, that, though He was rich, yet for your sakes He became poor, that ye through His poverty*

* 1 Cor. ix. 5.   † *Ibid.* xv. 5, 7.   ‡ 2 Cor. xi. 5.

might become rich." It is evident that the Christ of history was, in worldly circumstances, a poor man. His character was as notorious as his poverty. "*I Paul myself intreat you by the meekness and gentleness of Christ*,"† says the Apostle.

So far we have been concerned mainly with statements of fact, and I do not think anyone will deny that the agreement between the Gospels and these Epistles is, so far as it goes, complete. The Gospels confirm and explain the allusions in the letters, and are in the process themselves confirmed and explained. Now we may turn to the position assigned to Christ in these Epistles, and inquire how far it matches with the declarations about Himself which in the Gospels are attributed to our Lord. Here we should expect a large measure of variation; for here the idiosyncrasy of the Apostle would be free to assert itself. We shall find, however, that even here the witness of the Epistles to the Gospels is decisively favourable. We notice that great emphasis is laid by S. Paul on the Divine Sonship of Christ. God is described as the Father of Jesus Christ; the description seems to carry with it a version of the Divine character. "*The God and Father of the Lord Jesus, He who is blessed for evermore, knoweth that I lie not.*"‡ So Christ is called "*the image of God*," in whose "*face*" men may perceive "*the light of the knowledge of the glory of God.*"§ Would it be possible to find a better comment on these expressions than these words from the fourth Gospel:—"*No man hath seen God at any

---

* *Ibid.* viii. 9. † *Ibid.* x. 1.
‡ 2 Cor. xi. 31. § 2 Cor iv. 4–6.

time; *the only begotten Son, which is in the bosom of the Father, He hath declared Him."** Christ is presented in the Corinthian Epistles as a Divine Being, the object of Christian worship. The first Epistle is addressed not only to the "*saints*" at Corinth, but also to "*all that call upon the name of our Lord Jesus Christ in every place.*" To have the "mind of Christ" is to "*know the mind of*" God.† His name is united with that of God the Father in the Benedictions with which the second Epistle opens and concludes. S. Paul prayed to Him in tribulation and was strengthened. He is the Judge of the world before Whose Tribunal all men must be *made manifest*.‡ In His "*day*" the spirit of the sinner who has done penance for his sin shall be saved.§ He is the "*one foundation*" of discipleship.‖ He is the model which Christians must imitate.¶ He governs the Church with sovereign authority, allotting to every man his place, determining for every office its functions. He is the Head of the mystical Body into which Baptism admits, and in which the Holy Eucharist sustains men.** His grace is ineffably great; His dignity is supreme. Unworthily to receive the Holy Communion is to be "*guilty of the body and the blood of the Lord.*" Yet while so awful He is ever near at hand in watchful mercy. He will arrange the journeyings of S. Paul as well as afflict with fearful penalties the unrepenting sinners. No quotations can adequately express the intense conviction

---

* S. John i. 18.   † 1 Cor. ii. 16.   ‡ 2 Cor. v. 10.
§ 1 Cor. v. 5.   ‖ *Ibid*. iii. 11.   ¶ *Ibid*. xi 1.
** *Ibid*. xii.

of Christ's nearness which penetrates these Epistles. S. Paul naturally turns to Him for guidance, comfort, and strength. Nay, the astounding mystery is declared as a matter so surely established in the Christian consciousness as to be the very commonplace of discipleship that Christ inhabits the Christian. "*Know ye not as to your own selves, that Jesus Christ is in you? unless indeed ye be reprobate.*"*

The numerous references to the Holy Spirit are not less impressive, and they also tend in the same direction. The doctrine of the Blessed Trinity, nowhere formally defined, everywhere underlies S. Paul's language, and the Epistles conclude with a formula which is definitely Trinitarian. "*The grace of the Lord Jesus Christ, and the love of God, and the Communion of the Holy Ghost, be with you all.*"

Now compare this version of Christ (if I may be permitted the expression) with the version presented in the four Gospels. Can it be truthfully said that there is any substantial discrepancy between them? Is it not rather manifest that the agreement is remarkably close? Christ, as He is described in the Gospels, did claim to be the Son of the Father, the Light and Life of men, the Judge of the World, the King of the Kingdom, the Founder of the Church, the Model of Disciples. And you will not fail to notice that the parallel is particularly close with the Fourth Gospel. Whatever may be said—and I admit that much may be said—as to the form and language of that Gospel, I cannot question, with the Epistles of S. Paul before me, that the substance

* 2 Cor. xiii. 5.

is genuinely evangelic. We are led to the conclusion that the original version of Christ's life, the version that within eight years of His Death was set before the converted Pharisee, from whose extant writings we may still learn it, was essentially the same as that which for so many centuries has been the Baptismal Confession of Christendom, which has long been known in the Church as the Apostles' Creed. If the evidence cannot prove the truth of the Creed, it certainly can prove its original character, and in an historical question to get the original version of the facts is to get all the assurance of truth you are able to get from historical inquiry.

At the very beginning of Christian History the inquirer encounters the Problem of Jesus. The paradox which amazes, perhaps also offends him, is there already, before tradition has been swelled by myth and fable. He must find some other explanation of the Divine element in Christ's history than the obvious one of legendary expansion. Legend takes time to grow; myth does not spring up in a night; fable echoes faith, but cannot create it. The war of the critics over the documents cannot touch the facts of the Life of Christ. They are certified, so far as they can be certified, by the independent authority of the Pauline Epistles. Profoundly diverse in so many things, in this the nineteenth century finds itself at agreement with the first. <u>The one changeless element in Christian History is the Person of Jesus.</u> From It all grace proceeds; to It all problems come for solution. It reconciles the contradictions of experience, and creates unity of faith out of the chaos of opinions. For the Person of Jesus is both Divine and Human, since in Its indissoluble Oneness meet the perfect Nature of God, and the perfect nature of man. Yes, amid the shifting sands of speculation, here is the Rock. The Historic Christ, Who loved the society of little children, and felt no shame to be the Comrade of the strayed and exiled ones of the earth, Whose fierce anger rushed forth in anathema upon hypocrisy, and pride of place, and selfishness of class, Whose stainless purity shamed into silence His embittered foes, Who wrestled in strong prayer beneath the olives of Gethsemane and prayed for His murderers in the Hour of His Agony, the Cross of Whose Passion is clothed with Eternal Glory—the Historic Christ remains when the last word of criticism has been spoken, the Alpha and Omega of Christian Faith, the only sure Foundation of Human Hope.

CHAPTER II.

THE RESURRECTION

M. RÉNAN has observed that the Resurrection was of all the Christian dogmas the most repugnant to the Greek mind. We owe to the fact this memorable fifteenth chapter of the first Corinthian Epistle, perhaps the most important chapter in the Bible. It is evident that there were persons in Corinth who stumbled at this doctrine. "*How say some among you that there is no resurrection of the dead?*" asks S. Paul. The objectors do not seem to have questioned Christ's Resurrection; to do that would have been to stultify their position as Christians, but they denied the general Resurrection which—as the Apostle urged with unanswerable force—was really involved in the fact of Christ's rising. They may be compared with those heretics—*Hymenæus and Philetus*—whose "*profane babblings*" are censured in the second Pastoral Epistle, and who are described as "*men who concerning the truth have erred, saying that the resurrection is past already.*"* Among the Jews the Christian doctrine created no difficulties. The belief in resurrection and immortality was no new thing. "Within the Old Testament period, and even within Old Testament literature the gloom of Sheol begins to lighten, while between the Maccabean age and

* 2 Tim. ii. 17, 18.

THE RESURRECTION

the birth of Christ the 'larger hope' had become a permanent dogma of Judaism."* The doctrines of the immortality of the soul and the resurrection of the body were firmly held by the Pharisees, and their influence was generally supreme within the sphere of Judaism. Gibbon does not overstate the fact when he says that "the immortality of the soul became the prevailing sentiment of the synagogue under the reign of the Asmonean princes and pontiffs." The narrative of the Acts illustrates the different attitude of Jews and Greeks towards the message of the Resurrection. S. Paul could count on the sympathy of the Pharisees when he urged this doctrine. On one occasion he availed himself of that sympathy in order to avert a judicial condemnation. "*When Paul perceived that the one part* (of the Sanhedrim) *were Sadducees, and the other Pharisees, he cried out in the council, Brethren, I am a Pharisee, a son of Pharisees; touching the hope and resurrection of the dead I am called in question.*"† The result of this appeal abundantly justified the Apostle's expectation. The assembly was divided, and the "*scribes of the Pharisees part*" openly espoused his cause. On the other hand, the Greeks received the announcement of Christ's Resurrection with contemptuous incredulity. Of the Athenians we read that "*when they heard of the resurrection of the dead, some mocked.*"‡ The prominence given to the Resurrection in the preaching of S. Paul is apparent on the face of the history of the Acts. The Athenian philosophers, indeed, supposed that the "*Resur-*

* MONTEFIORE, *H. L.*, p. 455.   † Acts xxiii. 6.   ‡ *Ibid.* xvii. 32.

rection" was the name of a separate Deity. "*Certain of the Epicurean and Stoic philosophers encountered him. And some said, What would this babbler say? other some, He seemeth to be a setter-forth of strange gods: because* (adds the historian) *he preached Jesus and the resurrection.*"* Festus, also, was impressed with the Resurrection as the principal subject of S. Paul's teaching. He described his apostolic prisoner to King Agrippa as one who was not accused of any evil things, but whose enemies "*had certain questions against him of their own religion, and of one Jesus, who was dead, whom Paul affirmed to be alive.*"†

The case was not different with the older Apostles. They, indeed, were the original eye-witnesses, and their incommunicable function was to declare the fact of Christ's Resurrection. "*We are witnesses*," said S. Peter to Cornelius and his friends, "*of all things which He did both in the country of the Jews and in Jerusalem; whom also they slew, hanging Him on a tree. Him God raised up the third day, and gave Him to be made manifest, not to all the people, but unto witnesses that were chosen before of God, even to us, who did eat and drink with Him after He rose from the dead.*"‡ It is important to notice the emphasis laid on the testimony of the Apostles. The record of the Gospels represents the followers of Christ as entirely destitute of any expectation that He would rise from the dead. Some of them were actually bearing in their hands the spices with which they designed to bury His Body, when they were encountered by tidings of the empty sepulchre and

* Acts xvii. 18.   † *Ibid.* xxv. 18, 19.   ‡ *Ibid.* x. 39-41.

THE RESURRECTION

the vision of angels. The obstinate incredulity of S. Thomas refused belief to all testimony save that of his own senses. We may be sure that the Apostles were not more sceptical than the other disciples, nor disciples than the unbelieving Jews. From the first the belief in Christ's Resurrection was advanced on evidence which was considered to be irresistible, and was, in fact, generally accepted as such. S. Paul sets down in his Epistle to the Corinthians a list of testimonies which had been delivered to him soon after his conversion, and which he strengthens by the addition of his own personal testimony. He is careful to disclaim any originality for this summary of the Gospel. "*I delivered unto you first of all that which also I received.*" The expressions are identical with those adopted by the Apostle when treating of the Eucharist. "*I received ($\pi\alpha\rho\acute{\epsilon}\lambda\alpha\beta o\nu$) of the Lord that which also I delivered ($\pi\alpha\rho\acute{\epsilon}\delta\omega\kappa\alpha$) unto you.*" (xi. 23.) The kindred substantive to the verb here rendered to "deliver to" anyone is used by S. Paul in the second Thessalonian Epistle, where it is represented in English by the famous word "tradition," *i.e.*, something delivered to somebody. "*So then, brethren, stand fast, and hold the traditions ($\pi\alpha\rho\alpha\delta\acute{o}\sigma\epsilon\iota\varsigma$) which ye were taught, whether by word or by epistle of ours.*"*
Now S. Paul expressly says in the Galatian Epistle that he did not make the acquaintance of the older Apostles until some time had elapsed after his conversion. "*After three years I went up to Jerusalem to visit Cephas, and tarried with him fifteen days. But other of the Apostles saw I none, save James, the Lord's*

---

* 2 Thess. ii. 15.

brother." (i. 19.) It is significant that in the list of testimonies the only names mentioned are those of Cephas and James. This coincidence corresponds with the probabilities of the case in assigning the origin of this "tradition" which S. Paul delivered to the Corinthians to his visit to Jerusalem three years after his conversion. This visit may be reasonably ascribed to the year 38 of our era, that is, precisely eight years after the Crucifixion of our Lord. In Jerusalem, then, the scene of the alleged fact, where, if the statement were false, overwhelming evidence must have been at hand to demonstrate its falseness by the very men who had companied with Christ during His life, and had been panic-stricken by His Death—within eight years of the supposed occurrence, S. Paul received the following statement:—"*That Christ died for our sins according to the Scriptures; and that He was buried; and that He hath been raised on the third day according to the Scriptures; and that He appeared to Cephas; then to the twelve; then He appeared to above 500 brethren at once; then He appeared to James; then to all the Apostles.*" S. Paul, in rehearsing this "tradition," inserts a comment and makes an addition. Of the 500 brethren, he says, "*the greater part remain until now, but some are fallen asleep.*" Is it extravagant to infer from these words that S. Paul had known many of these brethren, and learned from their own lips the glorious Fact of which they had been spectators? He adds to the list his own testimony. "*And last of all, as unto one born out of due time, He appeared to me also,*" That vision of the Risen Lord was supremely important to S. Paul. Not only had it been the cause of his conversion, but it was the basis of his Apostolic authority. He could meet the insulting questions of his judaistic opponents with confidence. "*Am I not free? am I not an Apostle? have I not seen Jesus our Lord?*" It does not fall within the purpose of this inquiry to examine the evidences of the Resurrection; it is sufficient to show that in the Apostolic Church the fact of the Resurrection was presented to men as claiming their belief reasonably. It was matter of legitimate questioning; it challenged inquiry; it required proof; it possessed—so the Apostles maintained and so the Church believed—overwhelming proof. It may be permitted to remark that—apart from the refusal to allow any evidence as adequate to prove the Resurrection—the evidences which satisfied S. Paul remain to-day unshaken by centuries of questioning and criticism.

But what were the Corinthians taught about Christ's Resurrection? What was the understanding of the Fact which obtained in the Apostolic Church? The fifteenth chapter, which opens with the traditional testimonies to the fact, proceeds to expound the doctrine of the Resurrection. "*But now hath Christ been raised from the dead, the first-fruits of them that are asleep. For since by man came death, by man came also the resurrection of the dead. For as in Adam all die, so also in Christ shall all be made alive. But each in his own order; Christ the first-fruits; then they that are Christ's at His coming.*" Our Lord is the true representative of the race in its spiritual, as

Adam in its natural capacity. In His case the law is first operative, which shall in due course be operative in all His brethren. The Resurrection is not so much miraculous as natural; the working of the law, which is ultimately to work universally. S. Paul proceeds to argue the moral necessity of the Resurrection. The practice of baptizing for the dead assumed the life beyond the grave, in which the sacrament, thus vicariously received, could prove its efficacious virtue. "*Else what shall they do which are baptized for the dead? If the dead are not raised at all, why are they then baptized for the dead?*" Considerable doubt has been expressed as to the meaning of this "baptism for the dead." The difficulty hardly so much arises from any obscurity in S. Paul's language as from an unwillingness on the part of students to admit the existence in Apostolic times, and, apparently, under Apostolic auspices, of a practice which seems plainly superstitious. We do not share that unwillingness, and, therefore, do not perceive the difficulty. M. Rénan, perhaps, goes too far in his explanation of the Corinthian usage. "The faithful," he says, "called to mind their excellent ancestors, who had died without having known the truth which saves. A touching practice—baptism for the dead—was the consequence of this feeling. They believed that in being baptized for those of their ancestors, who had not received the sacred water, they conferred on them the merits of the sacrament; thus they allowed themselves to hope that they would not be parted from those whom they had loved." We cannot think that the practice had so wide an application. Rather we should suppose that it was limited to the case of those who being desirous of baptism were cut off by death before they could receive the Sacrament. This view is confirmed by the testimony of S. Chrysostom, who relates, not without expressions of contempt, the custom of certain Christians. "After a catechumen was dead they hid a living man under the bed of the deceased, then coming to the dead man they spoke to him and asked him whether he would receive baptism, and he making no answer the other replied in his stead, and so they baptized the living for the dead." The reason of their action is stated by Epiphanius. They feared "lest in the resurrection the dead should be punished for want of baptism." While we may agree with Dean Stanley in regarding this "baptism for the dead" as a "curious relic of primitive superstition," we shall maintain that the idea underlying the practice was a true one. S. Paul only appeals to the custom as an indication of the necessary assumption of the Resurrection which the Corinthians were making. He goes on to urge the kindred witness of all hardship borne for the sake of righteousness, nay, of all effort after righteousness. "*Why do we also stand in jeopardy every hour? I protest by that glorying in you, brethren, which I have in Christ Jesus our Lord, I die daily. If, after the manner of men, I fought with beasts at Ephesus, what doth it profit me? If the dead are not raised, let us eat and drink, for to-morrow we die.*" Loyalty to righteousness is an act of faith in that life beyond the grave, in which righteousness shall be seen to be victorious. Here in this strange world, where the wicked flourish as the bay tree and the heroes of self-sacrifice sink unregarded into their graves, the servant of Righteousness must "*endure as seeing Him, Who is invisible.*"

But a host of objections were urged, are still urged, in the name of reason, of physical science. "*But someone will say, How are the dead raised? And with what manner of body do they come?*" There are many in these days who object to the doctrine of the Resurrection its incompatibility with what are conveniently called the "laws of nature." S. Paul, as Christ had done before him,[*] points to the significant analogy of nature. "*Thou foolish one, that which thou thyself sowest is not quickened, except it die; and that which thou sowest, thou sowest not the body that shall be, but a bare grain, it may chance of wheat, or of some other kind; but God giveth it a body even as it pleased Him, and to each seed a body of its own. . . . So also is the resurrection of the dead. It is sown in corruption; it is raised in incorruption; it is sown in dishonour; it is raised in glory; it is sown in weakness; it is raised in power; it is sown a natural body; it is raised a spiritual body.*"

[*] *Cf.* ARCHBISHOP TEMPLE'S *Bampton Lectures*, pp. 196-7 (London, 1884). "It is quite possible that our Lord's Resurrection may be found hereafter to be no miracle at all in the scientific sense. It foreshadows and begins the general Resurrection; when that general Resurrection comes we may find that it is, after all, the natural issue of physical laws always at work. . . . We may find that even in the language of strict science ''He was the first-fruits of them that slept,'' and that His Resurrection was not a miracle, but the first instance of the working of a law till the last day quite unknown, but on that last day operative on all that ever lived."

The idea of "a spiritual body" takes the doctrine of the Resurrection out of the category of the physical, and relieves it from all objections which proceed on the materialist supposition. The best comment on the phrase is provided by the Evangelic accounts of Christ's Resurrection. Evidently the Body of the Risen Saviour was an enfranchized, glorious Body; no longer was It subject to the limiting conditions of terrestrial existence. It overpassed all physical impediments, coming and going in perfect obedience to the Will of Christ, recognizable as Christ's and yet different, so that only by an effort of awakened attention could the likeness be perceived. Read the last chapter of S. Luke's Gospel in connection with this fifteenth chapter of the Corinthian Epistle: remember that S. Luke probably drew from his great master, S. Paul, much of his knowledge of the Evangelic History, that the account of Christ's Risen Body may be regarded as correspondent with S. Paul's conception of the facts, and, therefore, as providing the basis of his doctrine of the spiritual body. You recall the experience of the two disciples with whom our Lord conversed on the way to Emmaus. "*It came to pass, when He had sat down with them to meat, He took the bread and blessed it, and brake, and gave to them. And their eyes were opened, and they knew Him, and He vanished out of their sight.*"* Our Lord Himself was the Author of the Pauline doctrine, when—as S. Matthew relates —He rebuked the coarse carnal notions of the Sadducees. "*Jesus answered and said unto them, Ye*

* S. Luke xxiv. 30.

do err, not knowing the Scriptures, nor the power of God. For in the resurrection they neither marry, nor are given in marriage, but are as angels in heaven." Such is the argument of the Apostle. "*Now this I say, brethren, that flesh and blood cannot inherit the kingdom of God; neither doth corruption inherit incorruption.*" In the silence of death the subtle alchemy of God shall work the great transformation; the carnal, perishable element shall be purged away, and the emancipated spiritual element alone survive. So death shall not be the final disappointment of Christian Hope, as the Corinthians, misled by their expectation of an immediate Advent of Christ, had been disposed to think, but a stage of preparation for the ultimate state of blessedness. "*Behold, I tell you a mystery,*" cries the Apostle, kindling with his sublime theme: "*We shall not all sleep, but we shall all be changed, in a moment, in the twinkling of an eye, at the last trump; for the trumpet shall sound, and the dead shall be raised incorruptible, and we shall be changed.*" Yes; the great transformation out of the material into the spiritual is the essential thing; whether by death or by some unknown process apart from death. "*We shall be changed. For this corruptible must put on incorruption, and this mortal must put on immortality. But when this corruptible shall have put on incorruption, and this mortal shall have put on immortality, then shall come to pass the saying that is written, Death is swallowed up in victory. O death, where is thy victory? O death, where is thy sting? The sting of death is sin;*

---

* S. Matt. xxii. 29, 30.

THE RESURRECTION

and the power of sin is the law; but thanks be to God, which giveth us the victory through our Lord Jesus Christ." S. Paul catches up into his impassioned speech the famous utterances of the prophets. Isaiah* had described the bliss of that great deliverance when the Lord God should have "*swallowed up death for ever*"; and Hosea† at a still remoter period had spoken even more wonderfully. "*I will ransom them from the power of the grave; I will redeem them from death; O death, where are thy plagues? O grave, where is thy destruction?*" The prophets were stirred by the thought of great national deliverances; the Apostle borrows their language to express a nobler victory.

The faith in the Resurrection, firmly built on the conviction that Christ had actually risen from the dead, was the source of that high courage which marked the primitive Christians, and was so splendidly conspicuous in the life of S. Paul. A new grandeur attached to life in the world when it was set free from servitude to physical conditions. "*We know that if the earthly house of our tabernacle be dissolved, we have a building from God, a house not made with hands, eternal in the heavens.*"‡ The humblest duties acquired a certain sanctity in view of the assurance of immortality. Among the Gentile converts there was, at first, a tendency to turn aside from the common tasks of life in order to reflect without distraction on the approaching glories of the Day of Christ. This tendency was, indeed, contrary to the mind of the Apostle, by

---

* Isaiah xxv. 8.   † Hosea xiii. 14.   ‡ 2 Cor. v. 1.

whom—in the Epistle to the Thessalonians—it was severely rebuked. Few things are more impressive than the calm, practical counsel with which S. Paul concludes the famous chapter we have been considering. He passes from his ecstasy of praise to the plain duties of the hour. "*Wherefore, my beloved brethren, be ye stedfast, unmoveable, always abounding in the work of the Lord, forasmuch as ye know that your labour is not vain in the Lord.*" Have not those strong, simple words sounded to many, standing beside the open grave into which has just been lowered the mortal remains of their best beloved, as a true message of God, restraining the bitterness of grief, hallowing the stroke of calamity, proclaiming the everlasting greatness of duty in the very face of Death? Otherwise considered, human labour—all the vain strivings of men, their splendid ambition, their sublime aspirations, are perishing and worthless; but from the empty tomb in the counsellor's garden streams on all honest work a new and nobler light. Henceforth all honest work is transacted "*in the Lord,*" and believers *know* (even as the tears fall for dear ones gone) "*that their labour is not in vain in the Lord.*"

CHAPTER III.

THE CORINTHIAN HERETICS

THE Revisers have made use of two words to render into English the Greek αἵρεσις. It is a "heresy" or a "faction." Thus in 1 Cor. xi. 19 the first is placed in the text, the last in the margin as an alternative rendering. "For there must be also heresies [margin, factions] among you, that they which are approved may be made manifest among you."

Perhaps "faction" does best render the sense of the Greek word, although in this passage the distinction is so clearly drawn between "*divisions*" or "*schisms*" and "*heresies*" or "*factions*," as to compel us to understand something more than the mere breach of unity. S. Paul seems to argue back from the external divisions to graver differences which they expressed. "*For, first of all, when ye come together in the church, I hear that divisions exist among you; and I partly believe it. For there must also be heresies among you.*" It will be worth while to notice the New Testament usage of this word which here is rendered "*heresy*" or "*faction*." Literally the word simply means "*choosing*"; then it is applied to the thing chosen, and so is used to describe opinions which men adopt with no better authority than their

own preference. Thus in the so-called second Epistle of S. Peter we read of "*false teachers, who shall privily bring in destructive heresies,*" or (as the margin reads) "sects of perdition," by which we understand private opinions of their own tending towards perdition. This is nearly the later ecclesiastical sense of *heresy;* more commonly in the New Testament the word is used to signify any body of men holding a particular opinion. Thus we read in the Acts of "*the αἵρεσις, or sect of the Sadducees,*" *
and of "*the αἵρεσις, or sect of the Pharisees.*" † S. Paul, in his defence before King Agrippa, said that "*after the straitest sect (αἵρεσις) of the Jews' religion he had, before his conversion, lived a Pharisee.*" ‡ Tertullus, the orator, when opening his case against S. Paul before the governor Felix, described him "*a ringleader of the sect (αἵρεσις) of the Nazarenes,*" § and the Apostle, when answering for himself, took up the expression. "*But this I confess unto thee, that after the Way which they call a sect (αἵρεσις) so serve I the God of our fathers.*" ‖ Finally, the Roman Jews when, in response to S. Paul's invitation, they visited him in prison, applied the word to the Christian community, "*as concerning this sect (αἵρεσις), it is known to us that everywhere it is spoken against.*" ¶ It is, I think, evident that the notion of doctrinal peculiarity is always present in this usage. The external separation which marked off Sadducees, Pharisees, or Christians, had its root in a divergence of belief. In short, *heresy* stands for private opinion

* Acts v. 17.   † *Ibid.* xv. 5.   ‡ *Ibid.* xxvi. 5.
§ *Ibid.* xxiv. 5.   ‖ *Ibid.* xxiv. 14.   ¶ *Ibid.* xxviii. 22.

in the sphere of religious doctrine. M. Godet's comment on 1 Cor. xi. 19 seems to bring out clearly the drift of the Apostle's thought:—

"To the simple divisions which arise from personal preferences or antipathies Paul foresees that there will succeed deep severances of another kind, based on various conceptions of Christian truth. He believes what he has been told about the first, because he expects the last. There will arise among them false doctrines, heresies, in the sense which the Greek word has taken in later ecclesiastical language, and there will result from thence divergences far more serious than actual divisions. Divisions (σχίσματα) are like mere rents in a piece of cloth; but heresies (αἱρέσεις) are rents which tear off a fragment and destroy the unity of the piece." In the Epistle to the Galatians S. Paul includes "*heresies*" in the long list of "*the works of the flesh*," and, perhaps, we may infer from its place in the catalogue, the special gravity which attached to it in the Apostle's mind— "*enmities, strife, jealousies, wraths, factions, divisions, heresies.*"

That "*heresy*" in the doctrinal sense was present in the Corinthian Church is evident from the Epistles. S. Paul exhorts to agreement in the opening chapter of his first Epistle to the Corinthians in terms which point to disunion in matters of faith, as well as in sentiment and conduct. "*Now I beseech you, brethren, through the name of our Lord Jesus Christ, that ye all speak the same thing, and that there be no divisions* (σχίσματα) *among you: but that ye be perfected together in the same mind and in the* *same judgment.*" Later in the Epistle S. Paul sets himself to oppose one particular heresy, which had reference to the fundamental doctrine of the Resurrection. "*Now if Christ is preached that He hath been raised from the dead, how say some among you that there is no resurrection of the dead?*"* What the precise teaching of the Corinthian heretics was it is not quite easy to gather. That they admitted the fact of Christ's Resurrection is the impression most naturally conveyed by the Apostle's language. He appears to make that universally accepted fact the basis of his argument. However, the evident anxiety with which S. Paul presses the reality of Christ's Resurrection, and the care with which he enumerates the historic evidences for the fact, may show that unbelief had extended itself even to this central doctrine. In the second Pastoral Epistle there is reference made to the heretics, "*Hymenæus and Philetus, men who concerning the truth have erred, saying that the resurrection is past already, and overthrow the faith of some.*" The essence of this heresy was probably that false view of the body as the enemy of the soul, which marked the early Ascetics. The Resurrection of the body was a prospect entirely irreconcilable with their philosophy. The destruction of the body from their point of view was the enfranchisement of the soul, and death, as involving such destruction, not so much to be abhorred as desired. "Death and resurrection were terms which had with these false teachers only a *spiritual* meaning and application; 'they allegorized

* 1 Cor. xv. 12.

away the doctrine, and turned all into figure and metaphor.'"* They understood by "resurrection" only that spiritual quickening which belonged to discipleship; in this sense they taught that "*the resurrection was past already.*"

In the second Epistle S. Paul speaks with almost passionate earnestness about the false teachers, who were assaulting the faith of the Corinthians. "*But I fear, lest by any means, as the serpent beguiled Eve in his craftiness, your minds should be corrupted from the simplicity and the purity that is toward Christ. For if he that cometh preacheth another Jesus, whom we did not preach, or if ye receive a different spirit, which ye did not receive, or a different gospel, which ye did not accept, ye do well to bear with him.*"† The Apostle speaks ironically. The ready welcome extended by the Corinthians to these heretics moved his scorn, even while it alarmed his affection. It was a painful revelation of religious levity in his converts that they should find so little difficulty in abandoning the truth which they had received from the Apostle, and that, moreover, at the instigation of persons who had no title whatever to their audience.

That in the very lifetime of the Apostles heretics should have made their appearance may well astonish those who have been accustomed to think of the Apostolic age as a golden time, when faith was inviolate and unity unbroken. The manner in which heresy was rebuked in the first age is eminently worthy our notice. S. Paul applies a two-fold test

* BISHOP ELLICOTT, *Epistles to Timothy and Titus*, p. 134.
† 2 Cor. xi. 3.

to the doctrines which came before him for judgment. The one, we may call, the historical test; the other, the moral test. He appealed to the facts of the Evangelic Tradition, which formed the basis of Christianity. Opinions which could not be reconciled with those facts must necessarily be rejected as incompatible with discipleship. You will observe that the Apostle regards himself as the faithful steward, charged loyally to transmit the treasure of Divine truth. He does not claim an original authority; it is his function to carry to others the message he has himself received. "*I received of the Lord that which also I delivered unto you*" is the formula with which he introduces his account of the Institution of the Eucharist. "*I delivered unto you, first of all, that which also I received*" is the phrase with which he prefaces what may almost be called a solemn creed or profession of belief. S. Paul disclaims that speculative "*wisdom*" which the Corinthians admired. Christ had sent him not to play the philosopher, but the Apostle, and it was not for him to mitigate the harshness or explain away the difficulties of the Divine Gospel. "*Christ sent me not to baptize, but to preach the Gospel; not in wisdom of words, lest the cross of Christ should be made void.*"* Experience made clear at once the disadvantages and the power of that unyielding Message. Jews and Greeks alike were disappointed and repelled, yet from both it drew to itself those who found it "*life from the dead.*" "*Seeing that Jews ask for signs, and Greeks seek after wisdom:*

* 1 Cor. i. 17.

but we preach Christ crucified, unto Jews a stumbling-block, and unto Gentiles foolishness; but unto them that are called, both Jews and Greeks, Christ the power of God, and the wisdom of God."* Eloquence and philosophy were almost impertinent when a Divine Message was in question. The Gospel could not need such auxiliaries. They might easily obstruct its grace. So, for himself, S. Paul renounced them, and set before his mind as an ideal the absolute honesty which should distinguish a loyal ambassador. "*I determined not to know anything among you, save Jesus Christ, and Him crucified. And I was with you in weakness, and in fear, and in much trembling. And my speech and my preaching were not in persuasive words of wisdom, but in demonstration of the Spirit and of power: that your faith should not stand in the wisdom of men, but in the power of God.*"† Sincerity, straight-dealing are the qualities which he emphasizes as properly characteristic of a Christian Minister's work. "*We have renounced the hidden things of shame, not walking in craftiness, nor handling the Word of God deceitfully, but by the manifestation of the truth commending ourselves to every man's conscience in the sight of God.*" ‡

Necessarily, as time passed, fidelity in the Christian took the shape of orthodoxy. For the guidance and help of the new converts the foundation facts of the Evangelic Tradition were expressed in a formula of belief, a creed in fact. We have already had

---

* 1 Cor. i. 22-23.   † *Ibid.* ii. 2-4   ‡ 2 Cor. iv. 2.

occasion to notice that in the Pastoral Epistles, written at the close of S. Paul's career, there are frequent references to "*the faith*," by which evidently is understood a concrete body of doctrine. Heretics are described as those that "*fall away from the faith*";* it is the mark of the "*good minister of Jesus Christ*" that he is "*nourished in the words of the faith.*" † The very mark of the presumptuous wrangler is departure from the Christian tradition. "*If any man teacheth a different doctrine, and consenteth not to sound words, even the words of our Lord Jesus Christ, and to the doctrine which is according to godliness, he is puffed up, knowing nothing,* etc." ‡ It is the duty of the Christian Minister to "*fight the good fight of the faith.*" § In the second Pastoral Epistle we find mention of a "*pattern of sound words*" which S. Timothy is exhorted to *hold fast.* ‖ It would be true to say that S. Paul tested religious opinions by the fundamental beliefs of Christians, the articles of the Creed.

His second test was moral. Did the new opinions make for righteousness, or was their tendency in the opposite direction? It goes a long way to justify the extreme indignation which S. Paul manifests against the heretical teachers, that for the most part their heresies had a very evil effect on conduct. Thus that false asceticism which despised the body and denied the Resurrection easily passed into a profligacy, which better matched the habits of paganism than the precepts of the Gospel. The ardent champions of "Christian liberty" were but

---

* 1 Tim. iv. 1.   † *Ibid.* v. 6.   ‡ *Ibid.* vi. 3.   § *Ibid.* v. 12.
‖ 2 Tim. i. 13.

THE CORINTHIAN HERETICS

too often found to be as contemptuous of moral restraints as of ritual distinctions. The zealots for Mosaic ceremonial were commonly found to be strangely indifferent to evangelic righteousness. S. Paul — it is manifest from every line of the Epistles—was a zealot for righteousness. Discipleship in his mind was synonymous with the conflict against sin. He ever speaks of baptism, the decisive act which introduced men into the Church and declared them disciples of Christ, as involving a crisis of moral change, which the subsequent Christian life attested and revealed. "*Are ye ignorant that all we who were baptized into Christ Jesus were baptized into His death? We were buried therefore with Him through baptism into death: that like as Christ was raised from the dead through the glory of the Father, so we also might walk in newness of life.*"* The association of right faith and righteous conduct was as natural in S. Paul's mind as that of heresy and vicious living, and commonly experience justified it. This must be remembered when we read the stern counsel given to S. Titus: "*A man that is heretical after a first and second admonition refuse; knowing that such a one is perverted, and sinneth, being self-condemned.*"† For, if we direct our gaze upon Christian history, we cannot avoid the impression that, while the Apostle's severity has been vastly increased towards "*heretics*," the Apostle's tests of heresy have been almost wholly neglected. Again and again the Church of Christ has oppressed and even caused to be slain as heretics men who had been driven into revolt by her own portentous

* Romans vi. 3.   † Titus iii. 10.

departures both from primitive faith and from essential righteousness. One of the most awful scenes in history is that presented by the condemnation, betrayal, and execution of John Huss by authority of the most numerous council of ecclesiastics ever assembled in Christendom. Huss —I borrow the words of the present Bishop of London—was "stirred only by his desire for greater holiness in the Church." His own life was pure;* his teachings were mostly based on the Scriptures; his personal influence was always good; yet he was murdered by the assembled chiefs of Christendom, the very men who—such is the irony of history— had been engaged in deposing a Pope for monstrous crimes.† The action of the Council of Constance represents in an extreme and astounding form the general attitude of the Church towards "*heresy*" through the greater part of her history. Is it any wonder that there should have been provoked in men's minds so powerful a reaction, that now little if any sense of the peril and sinfulness of "*heresy*" survives among us? The grotesque extravagances

* "Of pure and austere life, his countenance bore the traces of constant self-denial, and his loftiness of purpose lent force to his words." (p. 314.) "His letters show us neither a fanatic nor a passionate party leader, but a man of childlike spirit, whose one desire was to discharge faithfully his pastoral duties, and do all things as in the sight of God, and not of man."—*History of Papacy*, vol. i. p. 330.

† To fully state the irony of history it is necessary to add that the cardinal doctrine enunciated at Constance, which was, indeed, the assumption of the Council's action, viz., the superiority of a General Council to a Pope, is now by the Vatican Council declared to be heresy. It is permissible to think that in due course the same fate will overtake the foolish and arrogant dogma of "Papal Infallibility." The instability of dogma is one of the plainest and most consolatory lessons of history.

which arise and flourish in the religious sphere, provoking the contemptuous ridicule of unbelievers and the grief of all thoughtful Christians, must be regarded as the direct outcome of the abuse of authority, which for so many ages was normal in Christendom. Discipleship to Jesus Christ does involve belief in a divinely-revealed doctrine, to disbelieve which is spiritually perilous, and may be spiritually sinful. But the essence of *heresy* is wilfulness, the deliberate choice of error in face of a clear perception of the truth; and there may be —we know there is—much formal heresy which has no wilfulness in it. Concerning such we cannot rightly speak of guilt, we can only speak of spiritual loss. Yet for ourselves we should be wise to adopt a severer standard than that which we apply to others. We are far more responsible for our opinions than we choose to remember. Unhappily it has become a common practice for men to speak about their opinions as matters which stand outside all laws. Yet there are laws of right thinking, to disregard which is to stand self-condemned of folly. The laws of language, of mathematics, of logic— these cannot be set at naught by a rational thinker under pain of exclusion from the intercourse of sane men. Analogous to this is the case in the sphere of religion. Christians are men who believe that Christ's revelation of truth constitutes a law of right thinking about religion, which cannot be set aside without grievous loss. Christians are men whose consciences have ratified and made response to Christ's claim; and departure from His teaching must in this case involve a certain infidelity to conscience. Nor does even this state the whole truth. It is no real excuse for a man who thinks unreasonably that he never cared to understand the laws which govern thought. We say, and rightly, that it is every man's duty to understand and obey those laws. Mere indolence or mere wilfulness are not accepted as an excuse for folly. So also in the religious sphere. Heresy may, and generally does, result as much from ignorance as from wilfulness; but ignorance itself has an origin, and that, for most of us, is our own lazy indifference to truth. Surely we are responsible for the religious errors into which we fall, because we are too idle to learn or too vain to obey. S. Paul's admonition to the Thessalonians is not superfluous for the modern Church: "*Prove all things; hold fast that which is good.*"* And this "*proving*" or "*testing*" to which the Apostle exhorts his converts — and which, we may add, was never more needed than in this age and land of unchecked liberty of thought and speech—can only lead to right results if it be pursued by right methods. Still the touchstone of heresy must be S. Paul's two-fold test. Does it correspond with the fundamental facts of the Christian faith? Does it make for righteousness? Nor do I think that for the mass of men there is any real force in the common excuse that the fundamental facts of Christianity are not apparent to all students of the Scripture, or equally conceived by all professed Christians. For most men the Creed, which has for more than fifteen centuries officially expressed the essential elements of Christian

* 1 Thess. v. 21.

belief, will be sufficiently authoritative. Few will be disposed to ask for a better statement of the faith than that to which they were solemnly pledged in baptism. The manifold and subtle heresy of the present time may serve to sift the Church, as formerly among the Corinthians the "*heresies* *made manifest those that were approved.*" Men show the metal of their character under trial. Christians show the quality of their discipleship in times of doubt and difficulty. "*Watch ye, stand fast in the faith, quit you like men, be strong. Let all that ye do be done in love.*"* That is the counsel with which S. Paul concludes the first Corinthian Epistle. Heresy in their midst is to make the Corinthians more vigilant, more loyal, more resolute. They are to guard the sacred deposit of revealed truth against the assault of error, but let them remember that even that high warfare is not exempt from the danger that belongs to all warfare. The combatant may be hurried by the ardour of conflict into breaches of that supreme and ultimate law of Christ — the law of Love — apart from obedience to which even loyalty to truth shrivels into fanaticism, and vigilance against error hardens into a rigid refusal to consider anything which is unfamiliar or unpalatable. But still "*let love be without hypocrisy.*" Let no man plead charity as an excuse for disloyalty to the truth. Be honest as well as charitable, faithful as well as courteous; true as well as liberal; and thus "*speaking truth in love*" be ready to "*contend earnestly for the faith which was once for all delivered to the saints.*"†

* 1 Cor. xvi. 13, 14.   † Jude iii.

CHAPTER IV.

THE APOSTOLIC CREED

THE famous Creeds of Christendom do not belong to the earliest ages of Christian History; this, indeed, is what we might expect, since, for the most part, those Creeds represent the self-defensive action of the Church rendered necessary by the assaults of error. Definition of belief must be subsequent to belief; and, perhaps, marks the decline of the fresh ardour of conviction. Definition belongs to the calmer, colder period of reflection, of examination, of deliberation. So it may not be doubted that the intensity of belief is greatest when creeds are shortest; and length of creeds is a safe index to the decay of faith. In our Prayer-book we have three Creeds, and the latest is the longest. The Athanasian Creed, as it is called, belongs obviously to a time of religious controversy, when the creed was more a subject of desperate disputing than of devout conviction. Long, however, as is the Athanasian Creed, it is a small thing beside the doctrinal confessions of the sixteenth century, the Creed of Pius IV., or the Confession of Augsburg, or our own Thirty-nine Articles. But these lengthy formulas faithfully reflect the aspect of an age which, beyond all ages, was distracted by religious questioning. In the earliest times of the Church, then, we shall not look to find long and elaborate Creeds, nor, indeed, any fixed and generally authoritative written Creeds at all; but we shall expect to find what may be called rudimentary Creeds, crystallisation of Christian conviction on certain subjects, real though undefined terms of Christian fellowship.

We must, on the threshold of our inquiry, try to realize the convictions which the Christian Missionaries found ready to hand in their converts. The Religion of Christ arose in the midst of Judaism; it was, and it professed to be, the true development of Judaism; and it built itself on the foundation of Jewish belief. Now Judaism was a national and exclusive system, and the very characteristic of Christianity is universality. So far the old religion and the new were directly opposed; but the opposition was more manifest in the region of theory than of fact. Judaism, at the time of the beginning of Christianity, had acquired by a variety of circumstances a cosmopolitan character. The Diaspora, or Dispersion, was spread abroad in all lands. The translation of the Hebrew Scriptures into Greek had introduced the history and theology of Israel to the multitudes of the Greek-speaking population; the synagogue system had easily lent itself to the purposes of a propaganda, and myriads of proselytes gathered round the Chosen People. While the Hebrews of Palestine laboured to draw ever more decisively the dividing-line between Israel and the world, the Hellenists, Greek-speaking Jews of the

Dispersion, whose principal centre was the renowned Greek colony, Alexandria, had admitted into their religion wider ideas, and established relations of a friendly character with their Greek neighbours. "That non-Palestinian Judaism," it has been remarked, "formed the bridge between the Jewish Church and the Roman Empire, together with its culture. The Gospel passed into the world chiefly by this bridge." We know that the Apostles found everywhere in the synagogues their first preaching centres, and in the heathen proselytes who frequented the synagogues their earliest converts. It has even been questioned whether S. Paul ever counted among his converts any who had not gained from the synagogue a knowledge of the Jewish Scriptures. Certainly his Epistles, with their frequent reference to the system and sacred writings of the Jews, make it evident that such knowledge was very widely possessed. The Apostolic Creed, then, included the beliefs of Judaism. The unity and holiness of God, the vocation of Israel, the authority of the Moral Law, the inspiration of the Old Testament—these were taken for granted by the first Christian preachers. They formed the foundation upon which to erect the fabric of distinctively Christian conviction. We advance to inquire what was the distinctively Christian message? If we study the New Testament we shall be at no loss for the answer. The expressions employed in the Acts to describe the Apostolic preaching convey a clear notion of its character. "*They taught the people, and proclaimed in Jesus the resurrection from the dead.*"* "*Every day,*

* iv. 2.

in the temple and at home, they ceased not to teach and to preach Jesus as the Christ."* "*Philip went down to the city of Samaria, and proclaimed unto them the Christ."* † "*Straightway in the synagogues he proclaimed Jesus that He is the Son of God."* ‡ S. Paul, addressing the Ephesian presbyters on the sea-shore of Miletus, summed up his own preaching in these terms. "*I shrank not from declaring unto you anything that was profitable, and teaching you publicly, and from house to house, testifying both to Jews and to Greeks repentance toward God and faith toward our Lord Jesus Christ."* § And with this we may compare the same Apostle's declaration before King Agrippa. "*Having therefore obtained the help that is from God, I stand unto this day testifying both to small and great, saying nothing but what the prophets and Moses did say should come; how that the Christ must suffer, and how that He first by the resurrection of the dead should proclaim light both to the people and to the Gentiles."* ‖ From these and many similar passages we conclude that the central Christian message was that Christ, the promised Messiah, had come, died on the Cross for the sins of men, had risen gloriously, and would speedily return to judge the world. The crucial question of discipleship was whether this view of Christ would be accepted or not.

There are two narratives of conversion in the Book of the Acts, which set out very clearly the actual manner in which the great issue was presented to men. The first is in the eighth chapter, and records the conversion of the Ethiopian

* v. 42.   † viii. 5.   ‡ ix. 20.   § xx. 20, 21.   ‖ xxvi. 22, 23.

eunuch. It is worth while to recall the episode. As the evangelist approached the pious traveller he heard him reading aloud to himself the 53rd chapter of Isaiah, and immediately volunteered his help as an expositor of the sacred and mysterious text. "*Philip opened his mouth, and beginning from this scripture, preached unto him Jesus. And as they went on the way, they came unto a certain water; and the eunuch saith, Behold here is water; what doth hinder me to be baptized?*" You will observe in passing that S. Philip had evidently represented Baptism as the necessary act of professing discipleship. Here there has been interpolated into the text a passage of considerable importance, of which the antiquity is certainly great, and which may be fairly considered to represent the practice of the Apostolic age. It forms part of the text in the Authorised Version, but has been relegated to the margin in the more accurate Revised Version.* "*And Philip said, If thou believest with all thy heart, thou mayest. And he answered and said, I believe that Jesus Christ is the Son of God.*" The eunuch's profession fairly represents the Apostolic Creed.

* Dean Alford's note on the interpolation is the following:—"The insertion appears to have been made to suit the formularies of the baptismal liturgies, it being considered strange that the eunuch should have been baptized without some such confession. It appears to have been one of those remarkable additions to the text of the Acts common in D. (Codex Bezæ), which is here deficient, and its cognates: few of which, however, have found their way into the received text. This was made very early, as Irenæus has it. The manuscripts which contain it vary exceedingly: another strong mark of spuriousness in a disputed passage." Professor Ramsay has an interesting discussion of the problem presented by Codex Bezæ in *The Church in the Roman Empire*, pp. 151-168. He concludes that "the revision can hardly be dated later than A.D. 150-160."

The other history is in the sixteenth chapter, and relates the conversion of the Philippian jailor. The circumstances of that conversion were unusual; amid the excitement and terror doubtless words were not very carefully weighed; it is, however, precisely in such spontaneous utterances that men discover their real convictions. "*Sirs, what must I do to be saved?*" cried the jailor, kneeling before his prisoners. "*And they said, Believe on the Lord Jesus, and thou shalt be saved, thou and thy house. And they spake the word of the Lord unto him, with all that were in his house. And he took them the same hour of the night, and washed their stripes; and was baptized, he and all his, immediately.*" Here we get again the same Apostolic Creed. "I believe on the Lord Jesus." We may compare with these narratives from the Acts the testimony of the Corinthian Epistles. S. Paul seems to be appealing to the notorious belief of Christians when he writes: "*For though there are that are called gods, whether in heaven or on earth; as there are gods many, and lords many: yet to us there is one God, the Father, of Whom are all things, and we unto Him; and one Lord, Jesus Christ, through Whom are all things, and we through Him.*"* Here the Apostolic Creed is gathered into two Articles. "I believe in one God the Father, and in one Lord, Jesus Christ." We have in another passage a still shorter formula. "*Wherefore I give you to understand that . . . . no man can say, Jesus is Lord, but in the Holy Spirit.*"† "This solemn protestation," observes

* viii. 5-7.   † xii. 3.

Harnack, "shows that he who acknowledged Jesus as the Lord, and accordingly believed in the resurrection of Jesus, was regarded as a full-born Christian." We may compare a passage from the second Epistle. "*For we preach not ourselves, but Christ Jesus as Lord, and ourselves as your servants for Jesus' sake.*"* The great argument about the Resurrection in 1 Cor. xv. is prefaced by a careful and detailed statement of Christian belief. It is at once the longest and most significant declaration of faith which the Epistles contain. The solemnity with which it is introduced may, perhaps, indicate a settled and recognized form. "*Now I make known unto you, brethren, the gospel which I preached unto you, which also ye received, wherein also ye stand, by which also ye are saved; I make known, I say, in what words I preached it unto you, if ye hold it fast, except ye believed in vain. For I delivered unto you first of all that which also I received, how that Christ died for our sins according to the Scriptures; and that He was buried; and that He hath been raised on the third day according to the Scriptures.*" We conclude, then, that the Apostolic Creed, the specifically Christian doctrine, which was added to the belief about God, inherited from the Jews, was the confession of Jesus Christ as Lord, including in that title the fact of His Resurrection from the dead.

The rapid extension of Christianity would speedily compel the Apostles to make some provision for the teaching of their numerous converts. The simple acknowledgment of the Lordship of Jesus might,

* iv. 5.

indeed, suffice for admission into the Christian society, but some completer statement of the truth would be required to provide, in the absence of the Apostles, a groundwork for Christian teaching and a barrier against error. We may infer from the language of S. Paul's Epistles that such a statement had even at that early stage been put forward. There are three passages in the Epistle to the Romans (which is nearly coincident in date with the Corinthian Letters) to which I will call your attention. In the sixth chapter the Apostle blesses God for the conversion of the Romans. "*But thanks be to God*," he writes, "*that, whereas ye were servants of sin, ye became obedient from the heart to that form of teaching whereunto ye were delivered.*" The "*form*" or "*pattern*" ($\tau\acute{u}\pi o\varsigma$) of teaching seems to mean an authoritative statement of Christian doctrine. We may conjecture that since no Apostle had yet visited Rome, such a statement would be almost indispensable for the Church in that city. In the tenth chapter we find a passage, which certainly seems to indicate a formal profession of belief as inseparable from Christian discipleship. "*The word is nigh thee,*" says S. Paul, "*in thy mouth, and in thy heart; that is the word of faith, which we preach; because if thou shalt confess with thy mouth Jesus as Lord, and shalt believe in thy heart that God raised Him from the dead, thou shalt be saved; for with the heart man believeth unto righteousness; and with the mouth confession is made unto salvation.*" Among the closing exhortations of the Epistle the Apostle includes an urgent warning against certain disorderly brethren, who disturbed the peace of the Church. "*Now I beseech you, brethren, mark them which are causing the divisions and occasions of stumbling, contrary to the doctrine which ye learned; and turn away from them.*" A common profession of faith in the terms of an authorized statement would powerfully assert and protect the unity of the Church, and nothing could more plainly reveal the spirit of division than the refusal to accept the established formula. So we find S. Paul, in rebuking the incipient schisms of Corinth, lays emphasis on this matter. "*Now I beseech you, brethren, through the name of our Lord Jesus Christ, that ye all speak the same thing, and that there be no divisions among you; but that ye be perfected together in the same mind and in the same judgment.*" S. Paul, indeed, directly claims Divine authority for the language by which he had expressed the verities of revelation. "*Which things also we speak, not in words which man's wisdom teacheth, but which the Spirit teacheth: comparing spiritual things with spiritual,*" or as perhaps the original may better be rendered, "*interpreting spiritual things in spiritual terms.*"* "Christianity," observes M. Rénan, "not finding in the ancient languages

* "ἃ καὶ λαλοῦμεν, οὐκ ἐν διδακτοῖς ἀνθρωπίνης σοφίας λόγοις, ἀλλ' ἐν διδακτοῖς Πνεύματος, πνευματικοῖς πνευματικὰ συγκρίνοντες, '*combining the spiritual with the spiritual*,' *i.e.*, applying spiritual methods to explain spiritual truths. . . . This is the proper meaning of συγκρίνειν, 'to combine,' as διακρίνειν is 'to separate.' Συγκρίνειν, it is true, sometimes gets the sense of 'compare,' as in 2 Cor. x. 12; but it does not suit context here, whether explained, as by Chrysostom and others, of comparing the types of the Old Testament with the tidings of the New, or more generally."—BP. LIGHTFOOT, *Notes on Epp. of S. Paul*, p. 180.

an instrument adapted to its needs, has broken them up."* It is certainly true that Christianity has created for itself a new vocabulary, of which, indeed, the words are old, but the rich spiritual sense is wholly new.

The necessity for Creeds, in the modern sense of the term, would become apparent when Apostles were withdrawn from the Church. We possess in the Pastoral Epistles what may be called counsels for governing the Church when the Apostles have disappeared. S. Paul, in those Epistles, appears to contemplate the future, and, as far as he can, to arrange for its requirements. It is, then, natural that he should directly refer to a fixed form of belief. He calls it "*the faith,*" or "*the mystery of the faith,*" or "*the sound doctrine,*" or "*the deposit,*" or "*the pattern of sound words,*" or "*the faithful word which is according to the teaching,*" or "*the mystery of godliness.*" He seems to quote it when he bids S. Timothy "*Remember Jesus Christ, risen from the dead, of the seed of David, according to my gospel.*"† "*Without controversy,*" he cries, "*great is the mystery of godliness; He Who was manifested in the flesh, justified in the spirit, seen of angels, preached among the nations, believed on in the world, received up in glory.*"‡ And again, "*There is one God, one Mediator also between God and man, Himself man, Christ Jesus, Who gave Himself a ransom for all.*"§ This Creed is the touchstone of heresy and the test of orthodoxy; it is to

---

* "Le christianisme, ne trouvant pas dans les langues anciennes un instrument approprié á ses besoins, les a brisées."
† 2 Tim. ii. 8.   ‡ 1 Tim. iii. 16.   § *Ibid.* ii. 5.

be held fast, and fought for by the faithful Christian. Timothy is to carefully transmit it to the succeeding age. "*The things which thou hast heard from me among many witnesses, the same commit thou to faithful men, who shall be able to teach others also.*"* This Apostolic Creed seems to have substantially coincided with the formula which for sixteen centuries has been the Baptismal Confession of Christendom, which we rehearse in our public worship, and know by the not unsuitable name of "the Apostles' Creed." It is the oldest and the simplest of the Creeds.

It would surely be a mistake to limit the belief of the Apostolic Church to the few articles which (as we have shown) formed its creed. We have but to read these Corinthian Epistles to perceive how rich was the faith of the first believers. "*Of Him are ye in Christ Jesus, Who was made unto us wisdom from God, and righteousness and sanctification and redemption.*"† All theology is grandly summarized in that one verse. But the aim of the Apostolic Creed was not to state the whole faith, but its essence. That essence is still, as at the first, discipleship to a living Teacher. "Jesus is Lord." "The essence of the matter," observes Harnock, "is a personal life which awakens life around it as the fire of one torch kindles another."‡

It may be that in these later ages of the Church, when the faith of the Christian is set forth in many and lengthy doctrinal formulas, and has been "de-

---

* 2 Tim. ii. 2.   † 1 Cor. i. 30.
‡ *History of Dogma*, vol. i. p. 71. (Theol. Trans. Lib.; Williams and Norgate.)

veloped" into an elaborate and coherent theology, that its original essence has, in a measure, been buried and forgotten. Christianity has been regarded as pre-eminently a matter of orthodox profession; it has ceased to be primarily what it is essentially, discipleship to a living Lord. Perhaps we may find here that most significant combination, which surely is not the least remarkable sign of the times,—on the one hand, ardent admiration of Jesus Christ, on the other, avowed hostility to current Christianity. There is an intuitive perception in many minds that for modern Christians the faith of Jesus has undergone a transformation not for the better, but for the worse. The living Lord has retired into the background of Christian thought, and His place in the affections of those who own His Lordship has been filled by theology, or the Church, or even the Church policy. If this be so, and in so far as it is so, we have, indeed, grave and urgent cause for self-examination and searching of heart. We have need to return to the Apostolic Creed, to bring ourselves, it may be for the first time, into the presence of Jesus, to submit ourselves frankly to the influence of His Personality, to own Him from our hearts to be what we have so often asserted with our lips, our Lord, in a word, to be disciples.

This shall be our orthodoxy, our standard of fellowship, even S. Paul's. "*If any man loveth not the Lord, let him be anathema.*"* In the light of this discipleship the Creeds, the Church, the Sacraments, the Preaching, the Discipline of Christianity will take their

* 1 Cor. xvi. 22.

right place; real, precious, even necessary to discipleship, but empty, valueless, even harmful apart from discipleship. The old order will be re-asserted in our experience. First we shall be disciples, then brethren and members. The positive laws of ordered religion will be obeyed in the loving spirit of true discipleship. Self-suppression will no longer be the arduous achievement of discipline, but the eager sacrifice of love. The Blessed Sacrament will take <u>its supreme place in our spiritual life when we realize that therein we are brought into the closest fellowship with Jesus.</u> The grace of that Adorable Eucharist will flow forth into our lives, enriching them with tender consolations and sublime hopes. Failure and disappointment, inexorable hardships of undeserved obloquy, the silent gnawing of unappeasable desire, the unuttered sorrows of defeated purpose—all the mysterious shadows which lie darkly on life, defrauding it of sunshine, and driving the chill of despair into the hearts of men—all these passing into His Presence, seen in relation to His Person, borne for His sake, shall underpass a strange and blessed transfigurement. Instead of their former repulsive aspect they shall acquire a new character, a new use, becoming so many mystic links binding our experiences into His, and us to Him. So the Enigma of Christian Heroism shall be renewed in the humblest disciple's life, and the great language of the Apostle express a normal and common conviction. "*We are pressed on every side, yet not straitened: perplexed yet not unto despair: pursued, yet not forsaken; smitten down, yet not destroyed;*

THE APOSTOLIC CREED

always bearing about in the body the dying of Jesus, that the life also of Jesus may be manifested in our body." *

Nor is it only in the activities of life that the power of this discipleship shall be proved. When the last crisis comes upon us, and by manifold tokens we know ourselves to be passing into the "valley of the shadow of death," when we are alone in the drear naked solitude of the last hour,—in that time of rigorous testing, when all that is earthly, all that is merely human, all that is not real, shall fall from our side,—not even then shall the Apostolic Creed have lost its virtue. Jesus shall fill our failing vision. Jesus shall meet us on the eternal shore. It is the same Sun which shrouds in splendour the dying day, and lightens in the East the waxing glory of the dawn.

* 2 Cor. iv. 8-10.

CHAPTER V.

BAPTISM.

THE subject of this chapter bears a character which must be described as contentious ; among English-speaking Christians it has been made the occasion of extensive and obdurate separation. It does not, however, correspond with the character of this volume to discuss it from a contentious standpoint, or in a contentious spirit. Our primary object is not to justify or to condemn any modern doctrines or usages, but to discover what was the real aspect of Apostolic Christianity. When by honest and fearless examination of the evidences we have obtained a definite conception of the original belief and order of the Church of Christ, we shall be in a better position to decide upon the validity of modern versions of that belief and order. Our discussion may conveniently fall into three parts. In the first, we shall discuss the practice and method of Holy Baptism; in the second, the prerequisites of the Sacrament ; in the third, its grace. Our chief authority throughout must be the New Testament, and, according to our general plan, we shall particularly consider the witness of the Corinthian Epistles.

I. We found occasion to observe with reference to the Apostolic Creed that it included the fundamental beliefs of Judaism; much the same might be said with respect to the usages of the Apostolic Church. Our Blessed Lord adopted ceremonies which were familiar and generally significant not only among the Jews, though undoubtedly among them in special measure, but even among the heathen. The idea of religious purification as symbolized, and in some sense realized by the "*washing of water*," was rooted in Jewish and Gentile religion. Christ took up the well-known usage of Baptism, and filled it with deeper significance. He created the Sacrament out of existing religious material. If it be allowed—and certainly the position seems extremely probable—that as early as the beginning of the first century of our era the Jews were wont to baptize proselytes, then we have an extremely close parallel to the Christian rite actually established in contemporary Judaism. How close is the parallel will be manifest from the following account of the Jewish Baptism:—

"It was indeed a great thing when, in the words of Maimonides, a stranger sought shelter under the wings of the Shekinah, and the change of condition which he underwent was regarded as complete. The waters of Baptism were to him in very truth, though in a far different from the Christian sense, the 'bath of regeneration.' As he stepped out of these waters he was considered as 'born anew,' in the language of the Rabbis, as if he were 'a little child just born,' as 'a child of one day.' But this new birth was not 'a birth from above' in the sense of moral or spiritual renovation, but only as implying a new relationship to God, to Israel, and to his own past, present, and future. It was expressly enjoined that all the difficulties of his new citizenship should first be set before him, and if, after that, he took upon himself the yoke of the law, he should be told how all those sorrows and persecutions were intended to convey a greater blessing, and all those commandments to redound to greater merit. More especially was he to regard himself as a new man in reference to his past. Country, home, habits, friends, and relations were all changed. The past, with all that had belonged to it, was past, and he was a new man—the old, with its defilements, was buried in the waters of Baptism."*

On the assumption that Baptism with this significance was familiarly known to the numerous Gentiles who as "proselytes of the gate," or as "proselytes of righteousness," or "proselytes of the covenant," had been drawn into a relationship, more or less intimate, with the Jewish system, and reminding ourselves that the converts to Christianity were in Apostolic times mainly drawn from these proselytes, we can understand how easily and naturally the new Christian Sacrament would commend itself to the hearers of the Gospel. The Ethiopian eunuch's question to S. Philip—"*What doth hinder me to be baptized?*"—would occur to most of those who were impressed with the truth of the Christian message. Moreover, in direct relation to the mission of our Lord stood the mission of S. John the Baptist, whose familiar appellation points to the most conspicuous feature of his ministry. The Evangelists relate that S. John described his Baptism as the

* EDERSHEIM, *Jesus, the Messiah*, App. xii. vol. ii. p. 746.

prophetic type of a Baptism shortly to be inaugurated of more mysterious character and diviner virtue. "*I indeed baptize you with water unto repentance: but He that cometh after me is mightier than I, whose shoes I am not worthy to bear: He shall baptize you with the Holy Ghost and with fire.*"* Several of Christ's apostles, many of His personal disciples, were drawn from the number of the Baptist's followers, and this fact also leads us to conclude that the Christian Sacrament at its first introduction did not wear a novel appearance, but harmonized with the customs and expectations of the disciples.

We learn from the history of the Acts that from the very beginning the practice of baptizing converts was followed; and indeed we cannot doubt, in face of the evidence, that it was invariably followed. Moreover, it seems evident that almost, if not quite universally, the method of Baptism was that which is known as total immersion. That was the Jewish method; that also was the method of S. John; that is the method suggested by every reference to Christian Baptism which the New Testament contains. The impressive imagery of the Sacrament, on which S. Paul dwells in several of his epistles, appears to require it. Nor do I attribute very much weight to the common and, at first sight, weighty arguments based on the practical impossibility of immersing 3000 persons in Jerusalem, a city by no means well supplied with water, or on the similar difficulty in the case of the Philippian jailor. It is hardly clear how the narrative in the

* S. Matt. iii. 11.

Acts ought to be understood; and the difficulties of a literal understanding appear to me more formidable the more I consider the narrative; moreover it is by no means true that the water supply of Jerusalem was so meagre as to negative a numerous baptism by immersion. In the jailor's case the assumed difficulty in the way of immersion does not appear to exist. There was a river at Philippi, on the bank of which, apparently, the Jewish residents were wont to meet for prayer. The Apostle had already baptized Lydia and her household, doubtless in the river; it is by no means improbable that the jailor, who seems from his appeal to his Christian prisoners to have had some notion of the new religion, was acquainted with the circumstance of the purple-seller's conversion. S. Paul would naturally suggest to the convert a visit to the river-bank for the purpose of his Baptism; and since the jailor is expressly said to have given liberty to the Apostle and his companion, there seems no reason why the Baptism should not have been easily performed. But while I thus insist that there is no evidence in the New Testament of any other method of Baptism than that of total immersion, I do not for one moment believe that the Apostles would have condemned another method under special circumstances. I believe the Apostolic administration of the Sacrament is very fairly represented by the rules in the *Teaching of the Twelve Apostles*, as it is called, a little manual discovered a few years ago, and apparently with good reason supposed to have been written about the close of the Apostolic age,* and at one time read in the public assemblies of the faithful as an Apostolic document. We conclude this part of our discussion by reading the rules there laid down :—

"But concerning Baptism baptize thus: Having said beforehand all these things (*i.e.*, the moral teachings which fill the preceding part of the treatise), baptize ye in the name of the Father, and of the Son, and of the Holy Ghost, in living water."†

Probably at first Baptism was "*into the name of the Lord Jesus*," as is stated in the account of the Baptism of the twelve disciples of S. John the Baptist, whom S. Paul baptized at Ephesus. "Living water" is, of course, running water; all the earliest representations in art of Holy Baptism represent the baptized as standing in a stream up to the knees or even the middle, and the baptizer standing on the bank, apparently intending to

---

* "Eusebius puts the Didache last among the ecclesiastical but uncanonical and spurious books (ἐν τοῖς νόθοις), and in the same category with 'The Acts of Paul,' 'The Shepherd of Hermas,' 'The Apocalypse of Peter,' 'The Epistle of Barnabas,' *i.e.*, with writings which were publicly used in some churches, but which he himself as an historian with good reason did not find sufficiently authenticated and intrinsically important enough to entitle them to a place among the 'Homologumena,' or even among the seven 'Antilegomena,' which are now parts of the New Testament canon." (SCHAFF, *The Oldest Church Manual*, p. 116.) This writer "assigns the Didache with some confidence to the closing years of the first century, say, between A.D. 90 and 100." This seems to be Bishop Lightfoot's opinion also. See *Apostolic Fathers*, vol. i. p. 390, note 1. [Harnack, however, places the Didache later, 131–c. 160. *Die Chronologie der Altch. Litt.*, p. 438.]

† vii. 1.

plunge or dip him in the water. The manual proceeds:—

"But if thou hast not living (or running) water, baptize in other water; and if thou canst not in cold, then in warm. But if thou have not either, pour water thrice upon the head in the name of the Father, and the Son, and the Holy Ghost."*

This is the earliest recognition of the sufficiency of the method, now generally prevailing in the Church, of "affusion" or "pouring." As far as I know the method of "sprinkling" has no authority, either ancient or modern. The rules conclude with the following:—"But before the Baptism let him that baptizeth and him that is baptized fast, and any others who can; but thou shalt bid him that is baptized fast one or two days before."†

II. We proceed to inquire what were the pre-requisites of Baptism in the Apostolic age? They are summed up in the two words, repentance and faith. The record of the earliest Baptism no doubt reflects the normal process of the Sacrament. The spoken message struck home to the consciences of the hearers; they appealed for guidance to the Christian Preacher; in every case the same demand was made upon them. Repent and be baptized. "*Let all the house of Israel know assuredly, that God hath made Him both Lord and Christ, this Jesus, Whom ye crucified.*"‡ There was the Gospel in a sentence: the very core and pith of the message. "*Now when they heard this, they were pricked in their heart, and said unto Peter and the rest of the Apostles,*

* *Ibid.* 2, 3.   † *Ibid.* 4.   ‡ Acts ii. 36.

BAPTISM

Brethren, what shall we do? And Peter said unto them, Repent ye, and be baptized, every one of you, in the Name of Jesus Christ unto the remission of sins; and ye shall receive the gift of the Holy Ghost. . . . They then that received his word were baptized."

The question will probably arise, Were infants baptized in the Apostles' times? The question is not wholly easy to answer. That the children of Christians were believed to inherit a measure of religious advantage cannot be questioned. Even one Christian parent sufficed to convey a sacred character to the children. So S. Paul writes to the Corinthians, "*For the unbelieving husband is sanctified in the wife, and the unbelieving wife sanctified in the brother: else were your children unclean; but now are they holy.*"* Accordingly we find that S. Paul accounts children to be members of the Church; they are included in the exhortations which he addresses to the Christians of Ephesus and Colossæ. "*Children,*

---

* 1 Cor. vii. 14. ἡγίασται γαρ ὁ ἀνὴρ ὁ ἄπιστος ἐν τῇ γυναικί, καὶ ἡγίασται ἡ γυνὴ ἡ ἄπιστος ἐν τῷ ἀδελφῷ· ἐπεὶ ἄρα τὰ τέκνα ὑμῶν ἀκάθαρτά ἐστι, νῦν δὲ ἅγιά ἐστιν. Godet discusses this passage at some length, and insists that the reference is to Infant Baptism. (*Corinthiens*, i. p. 312-318.) Bp. Lightfoot is neutral, though clearly in sympathy with a baptismal reference. "The passage is not to be pressed on either side; no inference can be drawn here against the practice of Infant Baptism. On the contrary, the expression tells rather in its favour. Certainly it enunciates the principle which leads to Infant Baptism, viz., that the child of Christian parents shall be treated as a Christian." (*Notes on Epp. of S. Paul*, p. 226.) It is worth noting that S. Chrysostom does not seem to understand any reference to Baptism. Robertson, of Brighton, writes characteristically: *v*. Lecture XV. on the Epp. to the Corinthians. The bearing of the passage on the modern practice of indiscriminate baptizing of infants is important. See the Discourse on this subject appended to this volume.

obey your parents in the Lord." "Children, obey your parents in all things, for this is well-pleasing in the Lord." Fathers are exhorted to "*nurture them in the chastening and admonition of the Lord.*" In the Pastoral Epistles the emphasis laid on the right conduct of the bishop's or deacon's family points in the same direction. Thus the bishop or presbyter must be "*one that ruleth well his own house, having his children in subjection with all gravity; (but if a man knoweth not how to rule his own house, how shall he take care of the church of God?*")* S. Paul almost suggests that the family should be organized as a little model of the larger family of the Church.† S. Titus is admonished to "*appoint elders in every city,*"‡ men whose qualifications include the possession of a Christian family. "*If any man is blameless, the husband of one wife having children that believe, who are not accused of riot or unruly.*" It seems impossible to avoid the conclusion that the children of Christian parents were regarded as naturally entitled to receive Baptism, and did, as a matter of fact, ordinarily receive the Sacrament. This conclusion is strengthened by the undoubted fact that Baptism was regarded as the parallel in the new Covenant of circumcision in the Old; that, accordingly, it served all the purposes of circumcision, while it completely superseded it, being transcendently superior in grace and dignity. "*In whom*" (*i.e.*, in Christ), writes S. Paul to the Colossians, "*ye were*

---

* 1 Tim. iii. 4-5.
† *Cf.* S. Chrysostom's expression, "a house is a little church," ἡ οἰκία γὰρ Ἐκκλησία ἐστὶ μικρά. Hom. XX. in Eph. (Gaume vol. xi. p. 173.)
‡ Titus i. 5.

also circumcised with a circumcision not made with hands, in the putting off of the body of the flesh, in the circumcision of Christ; having been buried with Him in Baptism." *

The beautiful passage in which Irenæus describes the method and virtue of Christ's Incarnation seems to assume the Baptism of children.† "For He came to save all through Himself; all, I mean, who through Him are born anew unto God, infants, and little children, and boys, and youths, and elders. Accordingly He came through every age, with infants becoming an infant, hallowing infants; among little children a little child, hallowing those of that very age, at the same time making Himself to them an example of dutifulness and righteousness, and subjection; among young men a young man, becoming an example to young men, and hallowing them to the Lord. So also an elder among elders, that He might be a perfect Teacher in all things, not only as regards the setting forth of the Truth, but also as regards age, at the same time hallowing also the elders, becoming likewise an example to them. Lastly, He came also even unto death, that He might be the first begotten from the dead, Himself holding the primacy in all things, the Author of life, before all things, and having precedence of all things."

I think, therefore, that the evidence justifies the consistent belief and practice of the Church in the matter of baptizing infants. For the most part, however, the Church, in Apostolic times, was com-

---
* ii. 11, 12.
† Dr. Hort's translation in *Ante-Nicene Fathers*, p. 72.

posed of men and women who had been converted in adult life, and who were baptized as adults. We have already considered what was the nature of the profession of belief which they were required to make; what their repentance was, I need not say, every penitent will understand it; yet it is requisite to point out that it seems to have been expressed in Apostolic times by a public confession of sin. The scene at Ephesus was typical. "*Many that had believed came, confessing and declaring their deeds.*"* But, indeed, in the New Testament repentance and audible, detailed confession seem inseparable.

III. Finally, we turn to consider the Apostolic doctrine of Holy Baptism. What did the first Christians believe to be the effect of the simple and familiar ceremony by which they were publicly and formally constituted disciples of Jesus Christ? In the very brief time at my disposal I can do no more than indicate the merest outlines of their belief. Holy Baptism was believed to change the spiritual status of the baptized. He henceforward stood towards Almighty God in a new relationship. It was no excessive use of language to describe the change as a passing out of death into life. "*And you did He quicken,*" is S. Paul's phrase to the Ephesians, "*when ye were dead through your trespasses and sins.*"† The baptized person was by his Baptism wonderfully and most really associated with the Death and Resurrection of Jesus. This, indeed, was the manifest teaching of the external ceremony: the disappearance under the water

* Acts xix. 18. † Eph. ii. 1.

pictured burial; the reappearance pictured the life from the grave. "*Are ye ignorant,*" writes S. Paul to the Romans, "*that all we who were baptized into Christ Jesus were baptized into His Death? We were buried therefore with Him through Baptism into death: that like as Christ was raised from the dead through the glory of the Father, so we also might walk in newness of life.*" * From this union of the baptized with Christ two consequences flowed. On the one hand, it cancelled the sins of the past; on the other hand, it imparted a principle of Divine Life to the baptized. The water of Baptism was the means by which the Blood of Jesus was applied to the penitent and believing sinner. So S. Paul, warning the Corinthians against sin, reminds them in these impressive words of their Baptism. "*Ye were washed, ye were sanctified, ye were justified in the Name of the Lord Jesus Christ, and in the Spirit of our God.*" † This grace of Baptism was, indeed,

* vi. 3-4.
† 1 Cor. vi. 11. ἀλλὰ ἀπελούσασθε, ἀλλὰ ἡγιάσθητε, ἀλλ' ἐδικαιώθητε ἐν τῷ ὀνόματι τοῦ Κυρίου Ἰησοῦ Χριστοῦ καὶ ἐν τῷ Πνεύματι τοῦ Θεοῦ ἡμῶν. Godet understands here a reference to the full baptismal formula. (S. Matthew xxviii. 19.) In confirmation of this view he adduces Acts xix. 1-6, where S. Paul's question, "Into what then were ye baptized?" seems to involve an accustomed mention of the Holy Ghost in Baptism. The common expression, "to baptize into the name of Jesus," "est une forme abrégée pour designer le baptême chrétien en général." He further adduces the fact that the Trinitarian formula is found in the Didache. [*vide Corinthiens*, i. pp. 275-6.] On the other hand, the evidence of early Church history is not favourable to this view: "After the third century the formula of Baptism was the name of the Trinity, and Baptism otherwise performed was declared invalid. But in the early Church, as also in the Apostolic age, there is evidence that the baptismal formula of the name of Jesus only was not unusual."—ALLEN, *Christian Institutions*, p. 403.

L

the most prominent of all. To sin-burdened men the remission of sins was of all spiritual boons the most precious. The exhortation of Ananias to the penitent Saul at Damascus was the most welcome message conceivable. "*And now why tarriest thou? arise and be baptized, and wash away thy sins, calling on His Name.*"* But vast as is this boon of remission, it were but a transitory, nay, an illusory possession, if it added no securities for future forgiveness. No doubt the theory of discipleship supposed a life of holiness following upon the death to sin in Baptism; and very awful language was employed to describe the guilt and peril of sin in the baptized. The probable interpretation of the terrible passage in the Epistle to the Hebrews understands the "enlightenment" which may not be renewed of Baptism. "*For as touching those who were once enlightened and tasted of the heavenly gift, and were made partakers of the Holy Ghost, and tasted the good word of God, and the powers of the age to come, and then fell away, it is impossible to renew them again unto repentance; seeing they crucify to themselves the Son of God afresh, and put Him to an open shame.*"† The exact sense of this fatal "falling away" is hard to determine; but the whole tone of the Epistles precludes the notion that it is identical with sin as such. The Corinthian Epistles are conspicuously full of warnings against sin, even gross sin, yet they are addressed to "*saints*," that is, baptized Christians. The "one Baptism for the remission of sins" carried its blessed virtue not alone to the past, but also to all the life

* Acts xxii. 16. † Heb. vi. 4-5.

of the baptized. For it placed him within the sphere of forgiveness; it made him member of the Divine Society which has received from Jesus Christ the "power of the Keys." So to repentance the promise of renewed forgiveness is ever sure. "*Godly sorrow worketh repentance unto salvation,*" writes S. Paul, "*a repentance which bringeth no regret*";* and S. John speaks very plainly: "*If we say that we have no sin, we deceive ourselves, and the truth is not in us. If we confess our sins, He is faithful and righteous to forgive us our sins, and to cleanse us from all unrighteousness.*"† And with these teachings of Apostles accords the word spoken by Jesus Christ in the Upper Room, and always understood by the Church of Baptism. "*He that is bathed needeth not save to wash his feet, but is clean every whit.*"‡ Within the Church men are ever within reach of forgiveness. No sins are too gross, no rebellion is too obdurate and protracted to defeat the virtue of Christ's Atonement, so only the sinner truly repent, and make honest confession, and renounce his sin. "*The Blood of Jesus His Son cleanseth us from all sin.*"

Baptism introduces into the sphere of the Holy Ghost—it is the "*laver of regeneration*";§—in it men are "*born of water and the Spirit.*"‖ Hence it is the basis of Christian equality. All secular distinctions lose their meaning in the new Life therein conferred. Within the family of God all by title of their common origin are equal. "*For ye are all*

---

* 2 Cor. vii. 10.   † 1 John i. 8 9.   ‡ S. John xiii. 10.
§ Titus iii. 5.   ‖ S. John iii. 5.

Sons of God, through faith in Christ Jesus," writes S. Paul to the Galatians, and he immediately adds an explanation. "*For as many of you as were baptized into Christ did put on Christ. There can be neither Jew nor Greek, there can be neither bond nor free, there can be no male or female, for ye are all one man in Christ Jesus.*"* Baptism being thus the basis of Christian equality is also the basis of Christian fellowship, the principle of Church unity. "*For in one Spirit were we all baptized into one body, whether Jews or Greeks, whether bond or free; and were all made to drink of one Spirit.*" † Christians are one because they live by virtue of the same life-giving inspiration; they are all inhabited by the same Spirit. "*Know ye not*"—is the earnest phrase of the Apostle—"*Know ye not that your body is a temple of the Holy Ghost which is in you, which ye have from God?*" ‡

We may read in the wonderful eighth chapter of the Roman Epistle what an Apostle considered the meaning of the Baptismal Gift of the Holy Ghost. "*If any man hath not the Spirit of Christ, he is none of His. . . . But if the Spirit of Him which raised up Jesus from the dead dwelleth in you, He that raised up Christ Jesus from the dead shall quicken also your mortal bodies through His Spirit that dwelleth in you.*"

S. Peter's famous parallel between the water of Baptism and the water which floated the Ark of Salvation expresses the general doctrine of the New Testament. Then, in the traditional Deluge,

* Gal. iii. 26-28.   † I Cor. xii. 13.   ‡ *Ibid.* vi. 19.

the saving agent was water; so it is still: "*After a true likeness (water) doth now save you, even Baptism, not the putting away of the filth of the flesh, but the interrogation of a good conscience toward God, through the resurrection of Jesus Christ.*"* The humble and familiar agent carries to the penitent and believing soul the saving power of Christ's Risen Life. The simple Sacrament at once tries faith and helps it; by its simplicity confounding natural wisdom, and altogether disappointing human pride; by its Divine Authority consoling the misgivings of the lowly, and firing the heart of the disciple with the passion of conviction. In Baptism man is nothing; God is everything. "*When the kindness of God our Saviour and His love toward man appeared, not by works done in righteousness, which we did ourselves, but according to His mercy He saved us, through the washing of regeneration and renewing of the Holy Ghost which He poured out upon us richly, through Jesus Christ.*"†

* 1 Peter iii. 21.   † Titus iii. 4-5.

CHAPTER VI.

THE HOLY COMMUNION

WE may repudiate at once all intention of embarking on the large and important subject of Eucharistic controversy. Not one chapter, but a bulky volume would be necessary, I do not say, to do justice to that subject, but even to present it in any tolerable shape. Moreover, such a discussion hardly belongs to our present inquiry. We are seeking to gain a true conception of Apostolic Christianity, and our principal authority is S. Paul, who, in the Epistles to Corinth, has given us a picture, drawn by a master's hand, of an Apostolic Church. We shall divide our discussion into two parts: in the first, we shall discuss the administration of the Holy Communion; in the second, the doctrine held by the Corinthians as to the Sacrament.

But first let me repeat a warning. We must not look for detailed and thorough teaching about the Holy Eucharist in the Epistles before us. We showed above that the conditions under which these writings took shape preclude the notion of systematic instruction. S. Paul deals with practical matters, which were urgent, which were causing scandal, which threatened worse scandal. In so far as the Holy Sacrament was concerned in the disorders the Apostle deals with it, but no farther. As a matter of fact the Corinthian disorders did affect, and that very closely, their treatment of the Eucharist, and, therefore, the Epistle designed to correct them is rich beyond all other New Testament writings, save the fourth Gospel, in sacramental teaching. But we must be careful to appreciate justly the language used: and, in order to do so, we must endeavour to place ourselves in the position of the Corinthians, and to understand the Apostle's words from their standpoint. We shall return to this point presently.

We observe that the Sacrament was evidently the central act of Christian worship. It superseded the sacrifices and sacrificial meals of the heathen; it was to the Jewish Christian all and more than all that his Passover had been. It had been instituted by the Lord Himself in direct connexion with His own Redemptive Death. We cannot fail to recognize the close agreement which all this presents between the Epistles and the Evangelic narratives. We have already alluded to the evidential importance of this agreement; here we content ourselves with merely pointing to it.

The fullest account of the administration of the Holy Communion is contained in the eleventh chapter. The Apostle, having ordered that in the religious assemblies the women should be veiled, continues: "*But in giving you this charge, I praise you not, that ye come together not for the better but for the worse. For, first of all, when ye come together in the church* [*i.e.*, in religious assembly], *I hear that divisions exist among you; and I partly believe it. For there must be also heresies* [or factions] *among you, that they which are approved may be made manifest among you.*" S. Paul has had occasion earlier in the Epistle to denounce the factions of Corinth; he is now about to deal with their most scandalous exhibition. "*When therefore ye assemble yourselves together, it is not possible to eat the Lord's Supper: for in your eating each one taketh before other his own supper; and one is hungry and another is drunken. What? have ye not houses to eat and to drink in? or despise ye the Church of God, and put them to shame that have not? What shall I say to you? shall I praise you in this? I praise you not.*" We may remark that in this passage S. Paul goes some way towards using the word "Church," ἐκκλησία, in the familiar modern sense of a consecrated building. We know that in Apostolic times there were no churches; but the faithful assembled in one another's houses.

There can be no doubt that the Lord's Supper was preceded by the common meal, or Agape, and that the shocking abuses denounced by S. Paul belonged primarily to the latter. The association seems to have continued far into the sub-Apostolic age. The name "Eucharist" seems to have extended both to the Agape and to the Lord's Supper. At the very beginning of the second century we have the authority of Pliny's letter to the Emperor Trajan for saying that the two rites were separated. The language of the letter is not free from ambiguity; but on the whole it may be

THE HOLY COMMUNION 153

most reasonably understood as a description of the Holy Communion in the early morning. Pliny is reporting what he had discovered about the Christians in Bithynia, and this is what he says:—

"They maintained that the amount of their fault or error was this, that it was their habit on a fixed day to assemble before daylight and sing by turns a hymn to Christ as a god; and that they bound themselves with an oath (*sacramento*) not for any crime, but not to commit theft or robbery or adultery, not to break their word, and not to deny a deposit when demanded. After this was done their custom was to depart and meet together again to take food; and even this (they said) they had given up doing after the issue of my edict, by which in accordance with your commands I had forbidden the existence of clubs."*

It is possible that Trajan's edict suppressing the clubs, which for the time destroyed the Agapæ, may have actually brought about the separation of the Lord's Supper from the common meal. This may be doubted. One thing, however, is certain:

* Professor Ramsay (*The Church in the Roman Empire*) discusses Pliny's Report and Trajan's Rescript. "Among the strict regulations about societies, the Roman Government expressly allowed to all people the right of meeting for purely religious purposes. The morning meeting of the Christians was religious; but the evening meeting was social, including a common meal, and therefore constituted the Christian community a *sodalitas*. The Christians abandoned the illegal meeting, but continued the legal one. The fact is one of the utmost consequence. It shows that the Christian communities were quite alive to the necessity of acting according to the law, and of using the forms of the law to screen themselves as far as was consistent with their principles." (p. 219.) Bishop Lightfoot, however, thinks that the Agape was still united with the Eucharist when Ignatius wrote

the language of S. Paul in censure of the Corinthian excesses necessitated the formal severance, after a longer or shorter interval, of the social feast from the religious Communion. The character of those excesses more than justified the Apostle's severity. They not only destroyed the character of the Agape, but they defamed the more awful mystery which followed the Agape.

"The abuses which he (S. Paul) reproved and sought to abolish were of two kinds," observes Weizäcker. "First, the congregation divided into groups, the rich having their meals prepared without reference to the others, and the poor requiring to wait. Thus the difference in means and style of living could not but wound, while the meal of the wealthier degenerated into sensuality. In consequence of this, again, the Lord's Supper itself, the commemoration, was neglected, if not altogether given up. The feeling for it was lost, the order thrown into confusion, the very formula had to be insisted upon by Paul." The Apostle introduces that formula with great solemnity; as it stands in

nis Epistles, *i.e.*, A.D. 100-118. "In the Apostolic age the Eucharist formed part of the Agape. The original form of the Lord's Supper, as it was first instituted by Christ, was thus in a manner kept up. This appears from 1 Corinthians xi. 17 *sq.* (compare Acts xx. 7), from which passage we infer that the Celebration of the Eucharist came, as it naturally would, at a late stage in the entertainment. In the Doctr. Apost., 10, this early practice is still observed. In after times, however, the Agape was held at a separate time from the Eucharist. Had this change taken place before Ignatius wrote? I think not." The Bishop describes as "*precarious*" the inference drawn from Pliny's letter by Professor Ramsay and others. (*Vide Apostolic Fathers*, Part II. vol. ii. p. 313-4.) For the subsequent history of the Agape see note at end of chapter.

THE HOLY COMMUNION

the text of the Epistle it forms the oldest account we possess of the Institution of the Eucharist.

"*For I received* [παρέλαβον] *of the Lord that which also I delivered* [παρέδωκα] *unto you, how that the Lord Jesus in the night in which He was betrayed took bread; and when He had given thanks, He brake it, and said, This is My Body, which is for you; this do in remembrance of Me* [εἰς τὴν ἐμὴν ἀνάμνησαν]. *In like manner also the Cup, after Supper, saying, This Cup is the new Covenant in My Blood; this do as oft as ye drink it, in remembrance of Me.*" That was the Formula of Consecration used at Corinth, and doubtless everywhere in Apostolic times; it was not written down; the New Testament as yet did not exist, and the Liturgies were yet unknown; but it had become customary; it had taken a definite shape; it was an incipient "Canon of the Mass." The slight differences which are noticeable between the four accounts of the Institution, extremely interesting and suggestive in themselves, do but serve to bring into prominence the practical identity of formula used by the Apostolic Church in the Holy Communion. S. Paul adds a comment, which might well arrest the most reckless of the offending Corinthians. "*For as often as ye eat this bread, and drink the Cup, ye proclaim the Lord's Death till He come. Wherefore whosoever shall eat the bread and drink the cup of the Lord unworthily, shall be guilty of the Body and the Blood of the Lord. But let a man prove himself, and so let him eat of the bread, and drink of the Cup. For he that eateth and drinketh, eateth and drinketh judgment* [κρίμα] *unto himself, if he discern not the body."* S. Paul does not scruple to ascribe the sickness and mortality then prevalent among the Corinthians to their sins against the Sacrament. *"For this cause many among you are weak and sickly, and not a few sleep."*

It seems sufficiently evident that all the members of the Church received the Eucharist. We may be sure that others were not only not permitted to receive, but were not even permitted to be present. In course of time the dismissal of the non-communicants became a recognized feature of the Liturgy; and, curiously enough, it has provided the name by which in the Latin Church the Sacrament has been for many centuries commonly called. As is well known, the word "Mass" is only a corruption of missa, or missio, the dismissal, which formerly took place at a fixed point in the service. Some such procedure must have existed even in the Apostolic Church, for it is evident from the fourteenth chapter of the Epistle before us that the Christian assemblies were accessible even to unbelievers, who certainly could not have witnessed the "breaking of bread." S. Justin Martyr, in his account of the Celebration, says :—

"And this Food is called by us Eucharist, and it is not lawful for any man to partake of it, but he who believes our teaching to be true, and has been washed with the washing which is for the forgiveness of sins and unto a new birth, and is so living as Christ commanded. For not as common bread and common drink do we receive these; but like as Jesus Christ our Saviour being made flesh through the Word of God had both flesh and blood for our salvation, so also were we taught that the food for which thanks are given by the prayer of His word, and from which our blood and flesh by conversion are nourished, is both flesh and blood of that Jesus who was made flesh."*

We may be sure that the Holy Communion was commonly administered on the Lord's day, that is, among the Jewish Christians on the Sabbath evening, which would be considered the beginning of the Lord's day. Such, probably, was the case at Troas, where we read that "*upon the first day of the week, when we (i.e.,* S. Luke and the Apostle's company) *were gathered together to break bread, Paul discoursed*" at such length, as to prolong the assembly until daybreak.† Thus the celebration was originally a night-service; and, after the Agape had been definitely separated from it, the service took place in the early morning. It has been well observed‡ that this arrangement was almost a necessity of the case in a society numbering many slaves among its members, who would, of course, have to work on Sunday as well as on other days. "The Sacrament of the Eucharist," observes Tertullian, "though it was commanded by the Lord at meal-time and to all, we take in assemblies before daybreak, and from the hand of no others except our Presidents." The older practice of evening communion lingered in

* *Apologia*, i. 66. S. Justin proceeds to describe the method of Christian worship.

† Acts xx. 7, 8, 11.

‡ By Bishop WORDSWORTH, *The Holy Communion*, p. 59. I have drawn much from this valuable book, where the references are collected.

the remoter districts, as for instance in Egypt, as late as the fifth century; but generally from the close of the first century the custom of the Church has been to celebrate the Holy Eucharist in the morning, and to insist upon fasting as a condition of reception. It is greatly to be deplored that in recent years a certain number of English clergymen—not, I think, a large number, and, I believe, a diminishing number —have permitted themselves to violate the settled custom of the Church through eighteen centuries, by celebrating the Holy Communion in the evening, and encouraging the practice of non-fasting Communion. It is not in my opinion a subject for discussion. It comes within the class of those matters which must be and ought to be settled by the general conduct of the Church. I answer the objector in S. Paul's words. "*If any man seemeth to be contentious, we have no such custom, neither the Churches of God.*"* We may conclude this part of our discussion by reading the rules of the little treatise known as *The Teaching of the Twelve Apostles*, which does probably present a very faithful picture of Apostolic Christianity. It is deserving of notice that here, as in S. Justin's description and in Pliny's Letter, there is an inseparable connection between conduct and Holy Communion.

"And on the Lord's own day gather yourselves together and break bread and give thanks, first confessing your transgressions, that your sacrifice may be pure. And let no man, having his dispute with his fellow, join your assembly until they have been reconciled, that your sacrifice may not be

* 1 Cor. xi. 16.

defiled; for this sacrifice it is that was spoken of by the Lord. *In every place and at every time offer Me a pure sacrifice; for I am a great King, saith the Lord, and My Name is wonderful among the nations."*

We pass on now to gather in very brief outline the Sacramental Teaching of these Corinthian Epistles. What did S. Paul teach his converts as to the grace and dignity of the Holy Eucharist? "If we compare 1 Cor. x. 17 and xi. 27," says Weizäcker, "then it is clear that by *the body* Paul alternately understands the Church and Jesus Himself, applying it to the former, doubtless, by means of the interpretation of the simile of the bread, as a unity composed of many grains of corn. xii. 27 furnishes the connecting link between the two applications: the Church is *one body*, but *the body of Christ* Himself." It is necessary to consider these three passages more carefully.

In the tenth chapter S. Paul is warning the Corinthians against idolatry. They were disposed to minimize the significance of their presence at the idolatrous feasts, and partaking of sacrificial meats. "What difference can the idols make?" they said, "we know idols are really mere shams. Why should we hold aloof from the society of our neighbours, because they are so stupid as to think the feasts and the meats in some sense sacred to the idols?" S. Paul's method of arguing is this. He points the Corinthians to the Sacrament. What that Sacrament means to you Christians, he says, that the Idol-feasts mean to your neighbours, and will be

* Chap. xiv.

understood to mean to you also. The heathen expressed their religious unity with one another, and with their gods by those sacrificial feasts. To partake at the idol table was to publicly unite oneself to the body of devotees, and to make oneself by solemn symbolic act partaker of the idol's life. Therefore, such partaking involved nothing less than the negation of discipleship. It stultified the Christian position. "*I speak as to wise men; judge ye what I say. The cup of blessing which we bless, is it not a communion* [κοινωνία] *of* (*i.e.*, participation in) *the Blood of Christ? The bread which we break, is it not a communion* [κοινωνία] *of the body of Christ? seeing that we, who are many, are one bread, one body; for we all partake of the one bread. . . . Ye cannot drink the cup of the Lord, and the cup of devils; ye cannot partake of the table of the Lord, and of the table of devils.*" We may compare the expressions in the Eucharistic petition contained in *The Teaching*.

"As this broken bread was scattered upon the mountains and gathered together became one, so let Thy Church be gathered together from the ends of the earth into Thy kingdom, for Thine is the glory and the power through Jesus Christ for ever."

The Holy Communion was not only the external sign by which the disciples of Christ might be recognized, but it conveyed the Divine Life by which the individual disciples were united by a living bond with Jesus Christ. It sustained the mystic union with the Lord which Holy Baptism had created. So necessarily the idea of the mystical Body, the Church, passed into the idea of Christ

Himself as, through the Sacrament, bestowing His own life-giving Presence. Christians became one Body because they received one Divine Life.

The consecrated Elements were seen to possess a more awful character. They conveyed the very Life of the Lord; they were spiritually His Body and His Blood. Therefore the gross irreverence of the Corinthians had a more heinous guilt; it involved the ignoring, perhaps the scorning of the Lord Himself. *"For as often as ye eat this bread, and drink the cup, ye proclaim the Lord's Death till He come. Wherefore whosoever shall eat the bread or drink the cup of the Lord unworthily* [ἀναξίως] *shall be guilty* [ἔνοχος] *of the body and the blood of the Lord."** We

* S. Chrysostom interprets "unworthy receiving" in two ways. 1. Generally, of that hard, shameless temper which permits in the communicant open breaches of the Christian law, and especially (cf. v. 22) contempt of the poor. "These things let us also listen to, all of us, as many as in this place approach with the poor to this Holy Table, but when we go out, do not seem even to have seen them, but are both drunken, and pass heedlessly by the hungry; the very things whereof the Corinthians were then accused. And when is this done? say you. At all times, indeed, but especially at the festivals, where, above all times, it ought not so to be. Is it not so, that at such times, immediately after the Communion, drunkenness succeeds, and contempt of the poor?" (Hom. XXVII. c. 5 in 1 Cor.) 2. More exactly, of a gross forgetfulness of the inherent dignity of the Sacrament. "Not discerning the Lord's Body, *i.e.*, not examining well, not bearing in mind as he ought, the greatness of the things set before him; not estimating the dignity [ὄγκον] of the gift. For if thou shouldest accurately learn who it is that lies before thee [τίς ποτέ ἐστιν ὁ προκείμενος] and who He is that gives Himself, and to whom, thou wouldest need no other argument, but this is enough for thee to use all diligence, unless thou art wholly abandoned." (Hom. XXVIII. 1, in 1 Cor.) I have appended to this chapter S. Chrysostom's excellent observations on the custom of communicating at festivals. His words are as necessary for English Churchmen in the nineteenth century as for Antiochenes in the fourth.

M

learn from the context the nature of such unworthy eating and drinking, and S. Paul states it plainly in the next verse. It is the undiscerning, undiscriminating reception of the Sacrament, the reception which makes no difference between those hallowed Elements and common food, which sees nothing more in them than the lowly creatures of bread and wine they are, and continue to be, which has no reverence because it has no faith. *"For he that eateth and drinketh eateth and drinketh judgment unto himself, if he discern not the Body."** This blindness to the spiritual dignity attaching to the Sacrament was, in essence, the very fault of the Jews, who murdered the Prince of Life. They were so gross of understanding, so carnal-minded, that when the Spiritual King stood before them they could—in the phrase of the prophet—*see no comeliness in him* to move their *desire*. So we can recognize the real identity of disposition between those who despise Christ present in the Sacrament, and those who despised Him before the tribunal of Pilate. Both were in the awful language of S. Paul, *"guilty of the Body and the Blood of the Lord."*†

* ὁ γὰρ ἐσθίων καὶ πίνων κρίμα ἑαυτῷ ἐσθίει καὶ πίνει μὴ διακρίνων τὸ σῶμα.

† It is indeed far from my intention to suggest that a devout and edifying reception of the Holy Communion must involve the acceptance of a specific theory of the Mode of Christ's Presence in the Sacrament. I hold firmly that the precise contrary is true. But, apart from such specific theories, the disciple cannot escape from (1) Christ's clear commandment; (2) His emphatic teaching in S. John vi., xiii., xvi., which, whatever other reference it may possess, cannot be supposed to have no reference to the Sacrament; (3) The positive law and unbroken tradition of the Christian Society. Under all the circumstances—

The Apostle's language in this Epistle compels us to give a directly Sacramental application to S. John's record of our Lord's great discourse at Capernaum; and we are thus permitted to borrow from the Evangelist the "catalogue of those spiritual privileges" belonging to Holy Communion, to which S. Paul but indirectly refers. "It contains," says Waterland, "1. A title to a happy resurrection; for such as spiritually feed on Christ, Christ will '*raise up at the last day.*' 2. A title to eternal life; for our Lord expressly says, '*Whoso eateth My Flesh, and drinketh My Blood, hath eternal life.*' 3. A mystical union with Christ in His Whole Person; or, more particularly, a presential union with Him in His Divine Nature. '*He that eateth My flesh, etc., dwelleth in Me, and I in him.*' 4. In these are implied (though not directly expressed by our Lord in that discourse) remission of sins, and sanctification of the Holy Spirit."*

But no summary can do justice to Christ's teaching on that memorable occasion. Let any thoughtful and unprejudiced man read the sixth chapter of S. John's Gospel from the first verse to the last, let him remember that the primary, though not exclusive reference of Christ's words was to the Holy Communion, let him read the language of S. Paul to the Corinthians,

---

always supposing a knowledge of the facts—it seems impossible to reconcile a contemptuous attitude towards Holy Communion with any real conviction of Christ's Lordship. But when all is said the human heart is inscrutable, and while we may, and, I think, ought to grasp for ourselves the solemn significance of neglecting or despising the Sacrament, we had best refrain from sentence on others.

*. p. 192.

and on the authority of these distinct yet complementary testimonies let him determine the Sacramental belief of the Apostolic Church. He will hardly fail to conclude that the first disciples held a doctrine of the Eucharist which in point of loftiness and solemnity has never since been surpassed in the Church.* "*Now ye are the Body of Christ,*" writes S. Paul, "*and severally members thereof.*"† The statement at once explains, and is explained by, the words already quoted. "*The Bread which we break, is it not a communion of the Body of Christ? seeing that we, who are many, are one bread, one body: for we all partake of the one bread.*" Plainly, then, the Apostolic Church considered the regular receiving of Holy Communion necessary for the maintenance of Church membership, necessary for the maintenance of living connection with the Source of all Grace, our Lord Himself. We cannot doubt that S. Paul would have regarded neglect of Holy Communion as involving the cutting off from the soul of the Divine Life, which Christ gives in the Sacrament. Christ's own words are thus explained, words spoken at the very time when He instituted the Holy Eucharist. "*As the branch cannot bear fruit of itself, except it abide in the Vine; so neither can ye, except ye abide in Me. I am the Vine; ye are the branches; he that abideth in Me, and I in him, the same beareth much fruit; for apart from Me ye can do nothing. If a man abide not in Me, he is cast forth as a branch, and is withered; and they gather them, and cast them into the fire, and*

---

* ὑμεῖς δέ ἐστε σῶμα Χριστοῦ καὶ μέλη ἐκ μέρους.
† 1 Cor. xii. 27.

they are burned." * Far be it from me to limit the application of Christ's words. They bear profounder sense than attaches to any one application, however true; but I cannot see my way to doubt that they describe, and were designed to describe, the relation into which Christ enters with the faithful disciple in the Blessed Sacrament, and the most solemn and terrible results involved in the interruption, through deliberate neglect of the Blessed Sacrament, of that relation. I cannot see my way to doubt that the regular and devout receiving of Holy Communion is the natural, and, so far as we know, the only ordinary mode by which the Christian can remain within the unity of Christ's Mystical Body.

NOTE.—S. Chrysostom, Hom. XXVIII. 1 in 1 Cor.

After some preliminary remarks about S. Paul's habit of turning aside from his main argument in order to follow up some side issue, he continues:—" Now the same thing he hath also done here; in that having once found occasion to remind them of the Mysteries, he judged it necessary to proceed with that subject. For indeed it was no ordinary one. Wherefore also he discoursed very awfully concerning it, providing for that which is the sum of all good things, viz., their approaching those Mysteries with a pure conscience. Whence neither was he content with the things said before alone, but adds these also, saying, But let a man examine himself, which also he saith in the second Epistle: prove yourselves, examine yourselves; *not as we do now, approaching because of the season rather than from any earnestness of mind.* For we do not consider how we may

---

* S. John xv. 4-6.

approach prepared, with the ills that were within us purged out, and full of compunction, *but how we may come at festivals, and whenever all do so.* But not thus did Paul bid us come; he knoweth only one season of access and communion, the purity of a man's conscience. Since if even that kind of banquet which the senses take cognizance of cannot be partaken of by us, when feverish and full of bad humours, without risk of perishing; much more is it unlawful for us to touch this Table with profane lusts, which are more grievous than fevers. Now when I say profane lusts I mean both the desires of the body, and of money, and of anger, and of malice, and, in a word, all that are profane. And it becomes him that approacheth, first, to empty himself of all these things, and so to touch that pure sacrifice [Θυσίας]. *And neither, if indolently disposed and reluctantly, ought he to be compelled to approach by reason of the festival; nor, on the other hand, if penitent and prepared, should any one prevent him because it is not a festival.* For a festival is the shewing forth of good works, and reverence of soul, and exactness of conversation. And if thou hast these things thou mayest at all times keep festival, and at all times approach. Wherefore he saith, But let each man examine himself, and then let him approach. *And he bids not one examine another, but a man himself, making the tribunal not a public one, and the conviction without a witness.*"

The last sentence is of special interest as showing how far the Church of the fourth century stood from the modern rule, which makes confession to the priest the necessary preliminary to reception of the Sacrament. It is very unfortunate that the great Church Festivals synchronize with the popular holidays. The special temptations of a "Bank Holiday" prove too much for the fragile virtue of many communicants. The most miserable days in the year for the priest of a large parish are Boxing Day, Easter Monday, and Whit-Monday. The zeal for religious statistics operates as a strong pressure on careless Christians to communicate on the Festivals, and thus directly ministers to deplorable profanation.

THE AGAPE

It may fairly be doubted whether, in the Apostolic age, the term "Agape" was employed to describe the common meal of the Ecclesia. The term is certainly absent from the Pauline Epistles, and from the Acts. It would seem barely possible for S. Paul to write the famous chapter, 1 Cor. xiii., on ἀγάπη without reference to the technical meaning of the word, if at that time such existed. In Jude 12 and 2 Peter ii. 13, the Agape is mentioned, but in neither case is the reading undisputed. In both cases—assuming that R.V. has the right text—abuses of the gravest kind are denounced. "*These are they that are hidden rocks in your love-feasts when they feast with you, shepherds that without fear feed themselves.*"[*] "*Men that count it pleasure to revel in the daytime, spots and blemishes, revelling in their love-feasts while they feast with you.*"[†]

Evidently the Agape was used as an instrument for self-indulgence by persons in authority, "*shepherds.*" This marks a later stage of Church life than that described in the Corinthian Epistles, and is naturally connected with the curious regulation in the Didache, which requires that the Prophet shall not partake of the feast which he orders. "And no Prophet that orders a table in the spirit eats of it [himself] unless he is a false prophet."[‡]

The history of the Agape may be conveniently summarized as follows :—

1. In Apostolic and in sub-Apostolic times it was

---

[*] Jude 12.   [†] 2 Peter ii. 13.   [‡] xi. 9.

united with the Eucharist proper, to which it formed the normal preliminary.

2. Under pressure of persecution it was generally abandoned as provocative to the authorities of the Empire.

3. In the third century it was generally separated from the Eucharistic Celebration, and tended to become either a mere entertainment, or a distribution of provisions to the poor.

4. In the fourth century its secular character was indicated and emphasized by exclusion from the Churches. It generally connected itself with the rapidly developing cult of the martyrs.

5. It quickly became disreputable, was discountenanced by the Church, and fell into desuetude.

"The name, indeed, still lingered as given to the annual dedication feasts of Churches at Rome in the sixth century, and the practice left traces of itself, in the bread, blest as distinct from consecrated, which under the title of Eulogia was distributed in Churches, or taken from them to absent members of the congregation, (2) in the practice, prohibited by the Apostolic canons, and by the Council in Trullo, of bringing to the Altar honey, milk, grapes, poultry, joints of meat, that the priest might bless them there before they were eaten at a common table. The grapes appear, indeed, to have been actually distributed with the ἅγια, or consecrated elements, while the joints of meat are mentioned as a special enormity of the Armenian Church. (3) Traces of the Agape are to be found, lastly, in the practice which prevailed in Egypt, from the neighbourhood of Alexandria to the Thebaid in the fifth century, of meeting on the *evening* of Saturday for a common meal, generally full and varied in its materials, *after* which those who were present partook of the 'mysteries.' (*Dict. of Christian Antiquities*, Art. 'Agapæ,' where the facts are put together and references given.) Among the attempts to restore the system of primitive Christianity which marked the Methodist movement so distinctly and honourably must be counted the revival of 'Love-feasts.' For this John Wesley himself was responsible. 'In order,' he says, 'to increase in them a grateful sense of all God's mercies, I desire that, one evening in a quarter, all the men in band; on a second, all the women would meet; and on a third, both men and women together, that we might together "eat bread," as the ancient Christians did, "with gladness and singleness of heart." At these Love-feasts (so we termed them, retaining the name, as well as the thing, which was in use from the beginning) our food is only a little plain cake and water. But we seldom return from them without being fed, not only with "the meat which perisheth," but with "that which endureth to everlasting life." Subsequently the Love-feasts were not confined to the bands, but open to the whole Society.'"

OVERTON, *J. Wesley*, p. 129.

Part IV.

ORGANIZATION AND PRACTICE

CHAPTER I.

THE CHURCH

THE original character of the Corinthian Church was that of a secession from the Corinthian synagogue. It is, indeed, certain that as a general rule the Christian religion followed the Jewish Dispersion, and the synagogue was the forerunner of the Church. This fact had important effect on the organization of the new community, as we shall have occasion to show when we come to treat of the Christian Ministry, Discipline, and Worship. Here we must attempt a double task. On the one hand, we have to form some idea of the Apostolic Church as it actually was, not as it has been represented by the grateful fancy or the more deliberate purpose of later generations. On the other hand, we must learn the doctrine about the Church which was taught by the Apostles.

That Christianity should be organized in a society was almost inevitable. Apart altogether from theological considerations, this result might have arisen from the circumstances amid which the religion of Christ began its course in the world. It has been often remarked that the first century of our era was marked by a general and powerful tendency towards association.

"There were then, as now," writes Dr. Hatch, "associations for almost innumerable purposes in almost all parts of the empire. There were trade guilds and dramatic guilds; there were athletic clubs and burial clubs, and dining clubs; there were friendly societies, and literary societies, and financial societies; if we omit those special products of our own time, natural science and social science, there was scarcely an object for which men combine now for which they did not combine then."* Thus it was the most natural thing in the world for the converts to Christianity to form an association. They had the models of such association ready to hand in the familiar institutions of society, and those models were closely followed. To the outside observer the Christian communities appeared to belong to the general type of associations, and, as a matter of fact, they were so regarded by the Roman Government when they first attracted its notice.

The basis of association was discipleship to Jesus Christ, crucified and risen. S. Paul has made it very clear that in his preaching the central element was the personal Lord. This was the gospel, that Christ the Messiah had come in fulfilment of the Old Testament prophecy, that His Death on the Cross had reconciled man to God, by making Atonement for the World's sin, that He was reigning at the Right Hand of God in the Power of the Resurrection, that He would shortly return to judge the world. The

* HATCH, *B. L.* p. 26.

THE CHURCH

Jews were arrested by the proclamation of Christ as the Messiah. The Apostolic preaching consisted primarily in the proof, out of the Old Testament Scriptures, of that fundamental position. The account in the Acts of the proceedings at Thessalonica is doubtless representative. "*Paul, as his custom was, went in unto them* [the Jews], *and for three sabbath days reasoned with them from the scriptures, opening and alleging, that it behoved the Christ to suffer, and to rise again from the dead; and that this Jesus, Whom, said he, I proclaim unto you, is the Christ.*"* The Gentiles rather fastened on the doctrines of Atonement and Judgment certain and near at hand. We gather from the Acts that S. Paul was wont to dwell most on these parts of his message when he found himself face to face with Gentiles. He called to repentance; he announced the Judge. He attacked idolatry and the foul immorality which idolatry fostered, and even necessitated. His appeal was direct to the conscience of his hearers. Take, for example, the conclusion of his sermon at Athens. "*The times of ignorance, therefore, God overlooked; but now He commandeth men that they should all everywhere repent: inasmuch as He hath appointed a day in the which He will judge the world in righteousness by the Man Whom He hath ordained; whereof He hath given assurance unto all men, in that He hath raised Him from the dead.*" † The well-known description of the Apostle's preaching before the governor Felix is probably true of his general method. "*He reasoned of righteousness and temper-*

* Acts xvii. 2. † *Ibid.* xvii. 30, 31.

ance, and the judgment to come." Where, then, the Jews formed the majority of the Church the prevailing temper remained intensely Jewish. Righteousness was the noble heritage of Israel; discipleship did not involve a moral transformation. The religious and moral system in which the Jews had grown up received the doctrine of Christ's Messiahship, and the Evangelic tradition of His Life and Teaching, but the addition did not seem to necessitate any breach with the past. But where, as in Corinth, the Church was predominantly Gentile the case was otherwise. Christ the Saviour, Christ the Pattern, Christ the Grace-giver, Christ the Judge—in every character He faced the guilty conscience. He demanded the violent, immediate, and complete renunciation of the sinful habits of life. He upheld the winning Model of the New Life; He threatened with inexorable punishment the old sins. Discipleship among the Gentiles was emphatically an affair of the conscience. It involved a sharp conversion, which cleft life asunder, repudiating the past, transforming the present. The converts from heathenism were literally "an elect race," a "holy nation,"[*] called out from a world, perishing in its rottenness, into the new life of purity and love. This was the immense significance of their Baptism, which formally and publicly marked the great transition. So S. Paul addresses the Corinthians in anxious warning, setting in contrast

---

[*] Dr. Hort reminds us that the common explanation of the famous word Ecclesia, as meaning the "called-out" people, cannot be maintained. The idea itself, however, is thoroughly true and apostolic. —*Vide* HORT, *Christian Ecclesia*, p. 5.

their past iniquities and their present profession. "*Be not deceived: neither fornicators, nor idolaters, nor adulterers, nor effeminate, nor abusers of themselves with men, nor thieves, nor covetous, nor drunkards, nor revilers, nor extortioners, shall inherit the kingdom of God. And such were some of you: but ye were washed, but ye were sanctified, but ye were justified in the name of the Lord Jesus Christ, and in the spirit of our God."* *
Thus the Church was a society organized on the basis of the belief in Christ as Saviour, Model, Lord, Judge, in opposition to the prevailing wickedness of society. Its missionary method was a frank, straight appeal to the Conscience. Now the prevailing wickedness of the Imperial Society of that age may be grouped under the two heads of uncleanness and cruelty. The Church, then, was an association for the maintenance of purity and charity. This twofold character is indicated by the two names commonly used to describe the members of the Church. They are "*saints*" and "*brethren*." This twofold character expressed itself in the necessarily Catholic basis of membership. Discipleship being an affair of the conscience appealed to men as such, apart altogether from all conventional distinctions. S. Paul, writing to the Romans, dwells much on the universal relevancy of the Gospel of Redemption. The Church did, indeed, like the net in the parable, gather of every kind; yet mostly, as perhaps was natural, she draw her members from the humbler ranks of society. This was notably the case at Corinth, as S. Paul reminded the Corinthians.

* 1 Cor. vi. 9.

"*For behold your calling, brethren, how that not many wise after the flesh, not many mighty, not many noble, are called.*" * Doubtless many were slaves. The Apostle directly addresses himself to such, deprecating the not unnatural idea that discipleship was incompatible with their servile condition. "*Wast thou called being a bondservant? care not for it: but if thou canst become free, use it rather. For he that was called in the Lord, being a bondservant, is the Lord's freedman: likewise he that was called, being free, is Christ's bondservant. Ye were bought with a price; become not bondservants of men. Brethren, let each man, wherein he was called, therein abide with God.*" † M. Rénan reminds us that the servile class of the Roman Empire included many of the more intelligent and educated people. "The servile condition," he says, "included persons who were cultivated, contented, virtuous, well-informed, well brought-up. The highest teachings of morality came from slaves: Epictetus passed in servitude a great part of his life. The Stoics, the sages said, as S. Paul to the slave—'Remain where you are: do not think of enfranchisement.' We must not judge the popular classes in the Greek towns by our populations—sullen, brutal, coarse, incapable of understanding. That element of fineness, delicacy, polish, which we perceive in the relations of the first Christians is the tradition of Greek refinement. The humble artisans of Ephesus, whom S. Paul salutes with so much cordiality, were certainly sweet persons, of touching probity, set off by excellent manners and by that

* 1 Cor. i. 26.   † *Ibid.* vii. 21-24.

peculiar charm which there is in the courtesy of simple folks. Their serenity of mind, their content, were a perpetual sermon. 'See how they love one another,' was the remark of the heathen, astonished by this innocent and tranquil aspect, by this profound and attractive cheerfulness. Next to the preaching of Jesus this is the Divine Achievement of Christianity: this is its second miracle—a miracle, verily drawn from the living forces of humanity, and all that is best and holiest in humanity."* We may allow something for the characteristic style of the eloquent Frenchman, and something for his standpoint, but surely he does not overstate the fact. Perhaps our first impression as we read these Corinthian Epistles is one of disappointment. Those bitter partisan rivalries, that terrible profligacy, that discreditable anarchy, that frightful misconduct at the holiest time, at once amaze and repel us. We expected better things of the Church which listened to the living voices of the Apostles, in which the memory of the Son of God was yet recent. In our disappointment we may readily be unjust to these first believers, unjust to Christianity. We have before us the picture of the Church's scandals; but we forget the state of society amid which the Church existed. Think what it meant for Corinth, for the world, that in an age which delighted in the brutal butcheries of the Amphitheatre, in a place where the central shrine of the popular Religion was nothing better than a vast brothel,† there should yet exist and

---

* RENAN, S. Paul, pp. 436, 437. Paris, 1869.
† "L'affluence des marins attirés par les deux ports avait fait de

spread a society of which the purpose was the making possible for men the life of brotherly love and personal purity. Read the thirteenth chapter of the first Corinthian Letter, that sweet Hymn of Charity which stirs within us infinite yearnings and tender hopes, and think what it meant for Corinth and the world, that in the foul, cruel, pagan city companies of men and women had been drawn together into a fellowship so real, so divine, that there was nothing exaggerated or unreal in addressing to them those glowing words. When the "hard, pagan world" of imperial Rome was at the height of its blood-stained magnificence, is it not a portent indeed that in "upper rooms," in the cavernous catacombs of the dead, in the waste places, on the mountains, human ears should receive, and human lips rehearse such words as these? "*Love suffereth long and is kind; love envieth not; love vaunteth not itself, is not puffed up, doth not behave itself unseemly, seeketh not its own, is not provoked, taketh not account of evil, rejoiceth not in unrighteousness, but rejoiceth with the truth, beareth all things, believeth all things, hopeth all things, endureth all things.*" This at least may be said for the Church of the first days, that its practice was not wholly unworthy of such words. Can as much be said for the Church of any later age?

We said that the Church wore the aspect of those

Corinthe le dernier sanctuaire du culte de la Vénus Pandémos, reste des anciens établissements phéniciens. Le grand temple de Vénus avait plus de mille courtisanes sacrées : la ville entière était comme un vaste mauvais lieu, où de nombreux étrangers, des marins surtout, vénaient follement dépenser leurs richesses."—*Ibid.*, p. 214.

THE CHURCH

associations, which were the most conspicuous feature of the social life of the Roman Empire. Its purpose was, indeed, vastly superior, its spirit fraternal, but its general organization was remarkably similar. It might be an easy matter for the more unspiritual Christians to think of the Church much as their heathen neighbours thought about it—it was just one more religious association in Corinth. S. Paul intervenes with his doctrine of the Body of Christ. He compels the Corinthians to regard their association as not only superior to all other associations, but as a thing wholly apart, belonging to an order of its own, with claims and graces unparalleled elsewhere. His teachings about the Church are scattered over the Epistles, but they are summed up in the twelfth chapter. The Apostle begins by tracing every genuine profession of discipleship to the Holy Spirit. "*Wherefore I give you to understand, that no man speaking in the Spirit of God saith, Jesus is anathema; and no man can say, Jesus is Lord, but in the Holy Spirit.*" And so with those "*spiritual gifts*" which the Corinthians so greatly admired, and so extensively abused, their Author was the Holy Spirit. From this fact it followed that the distribution of those gifts was not capricious, nor yet determined by individual merit, but expressed the purpose of the Holy Spirit, and was designed to serve the general edification. The Corinthians were treating their several gifts as private possessions; S. Paul teaches them to rather regard them as Divine trusts. "*To each one is given the manifestation of the Spirit to profit withal.*" The gifts are various, indicating by their variety that none are sufficient standing alone, but all are designed to assist and complement one another: their value lies in their due correlation, their virtue depends on their co-exercise. "*All these worketh the one and the same Spirit, dividing to each one severally even as He will.*" In fact, Christians are not so many separate individuals, but severally members of an inspired society. S. Paul describes the Church under the metaphor of the human body.* "*For as the body is one, and hath many members, and all the members of the body, being many, are one body; so also is Christ. For in one Spirit were we all baptized into one body, whether Jews or Greeks, whether bond or free; and were all made to drink of one Spirit.*" "Think," he says, "what is involved in that common gift of the Spirit in Holy Baptism. You stand on a basis of equality; and yet this equality co-exists with an almost infinite diversity of function. You are severally placed by the Divine Architect as 'living stones' in His Spiritual temple. You depend on one another; you cannot dispense with one another; you cannot transfer to any other your own function. You may not despise one another." "*For the body is not one member, but many. If the foot shall say, Because I am not the hand, I am not of the body; it is not therefore not of the body. And if the ear shall say, Because I am not the eye, I am not of the body: it is not therefore not of the body. If the*

---

* This metaphor was not original. The Stoics especially were wont to employ it; but nowhere is it used with such range and power as in this Epistle.

THE CHURCH

whole body were an eye, where were the hearing? if the whole were hearing, where were the smelling? But now hath God set the members each of them in the body, even as it pleased Him." After his fashion the Apostle is led away by his metaphor; he draws out fresh lessons for the rebuke of the loveless anarchy of Corinth, for the eternal guidance of disciples. "It is, you see, absurd to draw distinctions between the members, calling this one honourable and that one uncomely. All are necessary: and all are so closely bound together that their fortunes are the same." "*And whether one member suffereth, all the members suffer with it; or one member is honoured, all the members rejoice with it.*" Then comes the direct application of the metaphor. "*Now ye are the body of Christ, and severally members thereof. And God hath set some in the church, first apostles, secondly prophets, thirdly teachers, then miracles, then gifts of healings, helps, governments, divers kinds of tongues. Are all apostles? are all prophets? are all teachers? are all workers of miracles? have all gifts of healings? do all speak with tongues? do all interpret? But desire earnestly the greater gifts. And a still more excellent way shew I unto you.*" That "*more excellent way*" is the way of love, which forms the subject of the thirteenth chapter.

It is evident that S. Paul's notion of the Church was very exalted. Breach of unity was to his thinking grievous sin: it contradicted the very fundamental conditions of discipleship. So he treated the divisions among the Corinthians as very serious matters. '*Now I beseech you, brethren, through the name of our*

Lord Jesus Christ, that ye all speak the same thing, and that there be no divisions among you; but that ye be perfected together in the same mind and in the same judgment." The Apostle would have had small patience with the popular modern notion that every disciple is free to follow his own private choice in the matter of public worship. Such individualism was, in the judgment of S. Paul, "*sin against the brethren.*" In like manner the conduct of every member was of direct interest to the whole Church. The Corinthians forgot this when they treated with indulgence that incestuous Christian, whose crime shocked even the heathen. "*Know ye not that a little leaven leaveneth the whole lump? Purge out the old leaven, that ye may be a new lump, even as ye are leavened. . . . Put away the wicked man from among yourselves.*" The litigiousness of the Corinthians was so particularly blameworthy because it argued contempt for the "*Body of Christ.*" "*Is it so*"— demands the indignant Apostle—"*that there cannot be found among you one wise man, who shall be able to decide between his brethren, but brother goeth to law with brother, and that before unbelievers?*" It is the sacred character of the Christian society that makes so guilty that reckless exercise of liberty which hurts the consciences of the weaker brethren. Liberty must be conditioned by expediency, regulated by charity, if it is not to degenerate into guilty license. "*All things are lawful; but all things are not expedient. All things are lawful; but all things edify not. Let no man seek his own, but each his neighbour's good.*" The same considerations must determine the

THE CHURCH

relations between Corinthian Christians and the rest of the Church. Large as is the liberty of the local church, it may not be so extended as to break the unity of the whole Christian fellowship. "*If any man seemeth to be contentious, we have no such custom, neither the churches of God.*" "*God is not a God of confusion, but of peace; as in all the churches of the saints.*" "*What? was it from you that the word of God went forth? or came it unto you alone?*" Clearly S. Paul's authority cannot be pleaded in justification of the congregational theory of the Church.* He represses the notion of such independence with a peremptory decisiveness that admits of no misunderstanding. The "*Body of Christ*" can never be narrowed down to the limits of a congregation, or even, we may add, in deference to later Christian experience, of a denomination. It must never be thought of as anything less than "the whole company of faithful people dispersed through-

---

* It seems impossible to reconcile the Church theory of the Pauline Epistles with such a theory as the following, which was propounded in 1658 by a representative body of independents in "a declaration of the faith and order owned and practised in the congregational churches in England":—"That every particular society of visible professors agreeing to walk together in the faith and order of the gospel is a complete church, and has full power within itself to elect and ordain all church officers, to exclude all offenders, and to do all other acts relating to the edification and well-being of the Church."

"They disallow the power of all stated synods, presbyteries, convocations, and assemblies of divines, over particular churches; but admit that in cases of difficulty, or difference relating to doctrine or order, churches may meet together by their messengers in synods or councils, to consider and give advice, but without exercising any jurisdiction." (NEAL's *History of Puritans*, vol. ii. p. 692. London, 1837.) These declarations reflect very plainly the influence of contemporary politics.

out the whole world." Nor did S. Paul consider this wide fellowship to be merely matter of phrase or sentiment. He insisted that the fraternity of believers must express itself in action. During the Famine in Palestine, when the Jewish Christians were reduced to great want, he exerted himself with much energy to obtain liberal contributions from the members of the Gentile churches.

CHAPTER II.

THE MINISTRY

S. PAUL was in exceptional degree the victim of calumny and misrepresentation. His character was defamed; his teaching contradicted; his Apostolic authority questioned; his success belittled; even his physical appearance ridiculed. It is astonishing what bitter malignity he provoked. The personal fortunes of the Apostle are reflected in his Epistles. We can detect the note of ceaseless conflict throughout them. They constantly tend to become apologies for the writer. One result of this circumstance is to secure for the Christian ministry a very large place in the Pauline Epistles. The Apostle, driven by his opponents to justify his actions and the large authority he claimed over the churches he had planted, is led to write at length of the Apostolic Office in particular and of the ministerial office in general. In the last years of his life he was forced, by the rude pressure of persecution, to consider the contingency of his own withdrawal from the government of the churches. He was thus led to write the three Pastoral Epistles, in which he directly and formally treats of the pastoral office. Indeed, those Epistles might not inaptly be called the Apostle's Manual for Bishops.

It is noteworthy that in the Apostolic age the Christian ministry was still largely undeveloped. It was latent in the Apostolate. Ecclesiastical terms were not definitely fixed; they reflected, in the looseness of their application, the bewilderment of the time. The Church was taking shape. In the process many factors were operative; but the supreme principle which governed their operation was that which was enshrined in the name "Apostle," and which the Apostolic ministry most conspicuously asserted—the principle of Divine Mission.* For the rest, the actual form which the Christian ministry ultimately assumed was very obviously determined by secular conditions. The names, presbyter, episkopos or bishop, deacon, were familiar in current experience. The infant Church naturally modelled itself on the organization out of which, in a sense, it grew—the synagogue, or the Greek Club. It adopted for its own purposes the institutions and the very names of Judaism or paganism; but it brought everything under the control of the supreme Apostolic idea. Here, as it seems to me, is the mistake of those industrious and learned students

* S. Paul assumes that the Christian preacher stands in the position of the prophet of Hebrew History; mission is essential to the prophetic character. So in Romans x. 14, 15 the Apostle writes, "How shall they hear without a preacher? and *how shall they preach except they be sent?*" A generation after S. Paul the Church believed that the "sending" of the Apostolic ministry was solemnly effected by the Risen Christ on Easter Evening. (See S. John xx. 21-23.) Most Christians will need no better assurance of this fact of Divine Mission than the record of the fourth Gospel.

who endeavour to provide a merely Jewish or merely heathen origin for the Christian ministry. They are very successful in showing the reproduction within the Christian Church of the established institutions and officials of the older systems, but they forget the dominant doctrine which determined the character of the ministry—the doctrine of a Divine Mission.

In the Corinthian Epistles we observe S. Paul directly dealing with a disposition on the one hand to magnify the power of religious teachers; on the other hand, to degrade their character. The Corinthians were inclined to constitute the Apostles their masters in the sense of the sophist schools. They would transform the Church into the Academy, discipleship into philosophy, Apostles into the leaders of philosophy: but so doing they would give Apostolic authority no better basis than the Apostle's ability, no longer existence than the Apostle's popularity. Their view of the ministry was frankly carnal, "*of the earth, earthy*": it left no place anywhere for a Divine Commission. You remember how S. Paul deals with it :—

"*When one saith, I am of Paul; and another I am of Apollos: are ye not men? What then is Apollos? and what is Paul? Ministers* [διάκονοι] *through whom ye believed: and each as the Lord gave to him. I planted, Apollos watered: but God gave the increase. So then neither is he that planteth anything, neither is he that watereth; but God that giveth the increase. Now he that planteth and he that watereth are one* [ἓν εἰσιν]: *but each shall receive his own reward according to his* *own labour. For we are God's fellow-workers, ye are God's husbandry, God's building.*"* It would be difficult to repudiate more absolutely the Corinthian partisan conception of the Christian ministry; but the Apostle proceeds to develop the true doctrine. If the essential element of the ministerial character be indeed a Divine Commission, then obviously serious consequences must follow; the Christian minister is at once weighed with an awful responsibility, and strengthened by a sublime independence. "*Let a man so account of us, as of ministers* [ὑπηρέτας] *of Christ, and stewards* [οἰκονόμους] *of the mysteries of God. Here, moreover, it is required in stewards, that a man be found faithful. But with me it is a very small thing that I should be judged of you, or of man's judgment* [ἢ ὑπὸ ἀνθρωπίκης ἡμέρας]: *yea, I judge not mine own self. For I know nothing against myself: yet am I not hereby justified; but he that judgeth me is the Lord. Wherefore judge nothing before the time until the Lord come, who will both bring to light the hidden things of darkness and make manifest the counsels of the hearts; and then shall each man have his praise from God.*"† This language is strong, almost aggressive in its egotism: but it is the egotism of a man defending himself against unrighteous attack. S. Paul is careful to show the necessity of the ministry to the Church, and he separates his argument from his own person. He describes the Church as a living, complex organism, "*the Body of Christ*": inspired by the Holy Spirit, almost infinitely rich in variety of

* 1 Cor. iii. 4-9. † *Ibid.* iv. 1-5.

structure and function, depending for its health upon the harmonious interaction of all its organs, every one fulfilling its own separate task, and thereby ministering to the common welfare. Many disputations are raised about the Church; there are many theories in the air; and those theories do not agree together. I know no clearer, no more beautiful, and no more authoritative teaching on the subject than that of S. Paul in the twelfth chapter of the first Corinthian Epistle, and the fourth chapter of the Epistle to the Ephesians. That teaching represents the Christian ministry as essential to the Church: the clergy are organs of the Body, and as such indispensable. "*Now ye are the body of Christ, and severally members thereof. And God hath set* [ἔθετο] *some in the church, first apostles, secondly prophets, thirdly teachers, then miracles, then gifts of healings, helps, governments, divers kinds of tongues. Are all apostles? are all prophets? are all teachers? are all workers of miracles? have all gifts of healings? do all speak with tongues? do all interpret?*"

Here we find not only the assertion of the Divine institution of the Christian ministry, and of its necessity to the Church, but also the statement that the ministry as constituted by God is various in order and function. The parallel passage in the Ephesian Epistle gives a slightly different list. "*And He* (i.e. Christ) *gave* [ἔδωκεν] *some to be apostles; and some, prophets; and some, evangelists; and some, pastors and teachers; for the perfecting of the saints, unto the work of ministering, unto the building up of the body of Christ.*" You will observe that in neither list do we find the famous names which have been permanent in the Church, "bishops, presbyters, and deacons." We know that all these terms were current in the Apostolic Church. The Epistle to the Philippians is addressed "*to all the saints in Christ Jesus which are at Philippi, with the bishops and deacons*" [σὺν ἐπισκόποις και διακόνοις]. The Pastoral Epistles make frequent mention of bishops and deacons. Nowhere, however, in the Pauline writings are the presbyters or elders mentioned, a circumstance the more perplexing since we are assured in the Book of the Acts that the Apostle was accustomed to "*ordain presbyters in every city*"; and in the Epistles of S. Peter and S. James the "*presbyters*" are mentioned. The true explanation probably is the old one, that in the earliest times "presbyters" or elders and "episkopoi" or bishops were alternative names for the same officer, the former title being in common use among the Jewish Christians, the latter among the Gentile.

I have already observed that the nomenclature of the Apostolic Church was in a fluid state; meanings had not been finally fixed to names. We must here note that there was a broad distinction between the ministry of evangelisation and the ministry of pastoral charge. The Apostolic Church was mainly a missionary church; its organization was determined by the necessities of that warfare against paganism to which it owed its existence. The Apostles and prophets represent the missionary stage of the history; but so soon as the Church had been planted in any place the need for a pastoral ministry made itself felt. The bishops, or presbyters, and the deacons represent the settled stage of the history. It is remarkable that the *Teaching of the Twelve Apostles* describes both types of the ministry; but it is not difficult to see that in the Church, as described by that little treatise, there was a certain suspicion attaching to the "Apostles" and "prophets." The Evangelistic ministry was receding into the background, and the settled ministry of edification replacing it. There are rules laid down for the due testing of the wandering Apostles and prophets, and the contingency of impostors is plainly contemplated. "Not every one that speaketh in the spirit is a prophet, but only if he have the behaviour of the Lord. By their behaviour then shall the false prophet and the prophet be known." The regular, fixed ministry is still reckoned to belong to an inferior type, but it is evidently growing in importance. "Elect, therefore, for yourselves bishops and deacons worthy of the Lord, men meek, and not lovers of money, and truthful, and approved, for they too minister to you the ministry of the prophets and teachers. Therefore despise them not, for they are those that are honoured of you with the prophets and teachers."

It has been suggested, and the suggestion is very probable in itself, that commonly the first local ministers were the first converts. They would be the chief organizers of the Church life; they would have a claim on the gratitude of their fellow-disciples.

"*We beseech you, brethren,*" writes S. Paul to the Thessalonians, "*to know them that labour among you,* and are over you in the Lord [τοὺς κοπιῶντας ἐν ὑμῖν κ. προϊσταμένους ὑμῶν ἐν κυρίῳ], *and admonish you ; and to esteem them exceeding highly in love for their work's sake."* In the Corinthian Epistle we have a still clearer indication of this personal ministry based on service. *"Now I beseech you, brethren,"* writes S. Paul to the Corinthians, *"(ye know the house of Stephanas, that it is the firstfruits of Achaia, and that they have set themselves to minister unto the saints), that ye also be in subjection unto such, and to every one that helpeth in the work and laboureth."* †

"According to this there were a number of people who were to be regarded as superintendents in the Church. The claim was based on their having been the first to believe and on their maintaining the Church by their ministry. The Apostle's exhortation shows accordingly that here again it was not a question of an office that had been instituted, but

---

* 1 Thess. v. 12, 13.
† xvi. 15, 16. παρακαλῶ δὲ ὑμᾶς, ἀδελφοί (οἴδατε τὴν οἰκίαν Στεφανᾶ, ὅτι ἐστὶν ἀπαρχὴ τῆς Ἀχαΐας, καὶ εἰς διακονίαν τοῖς ἁγίοις ἔταξαν ἑαυτούς), ἵνα καὶ ὑμεῖς ὑποτάσσησθε τοῖς τοιούτοις, καὶ παντὶ τῷ συνεργοῦντι καὶ κοπιῶντι.

"These words suggest that Stephanas was a wealthy or otherwise influential Corinthian, who with his household made it his aim to use his position for the benefit of Christians travelling to Corinth from a distance, all of whom in Apostolic language were saints or holy, as all alike members of a holy community, and consecrated to a holy life. Services like these rendered by a man of social eminence made it good for the members of the Corinthian Ecclesia to look up to him as a leader. He was, in fact, affording an example of what S. Paul meant by ὁ προϊστάμενος, in Rom. xii. 8." (HORT, *Christian Ecclesia*, p. 207.) So Godet, "Rien n'indique qu'il s'agisse ici d'une charge ecclésiastique proprement dite."

of a relationship that had grown out of facts, a relationship founded constantly on voluntary work, and dependent on the goodwill of the community." This is very true, but, with the Pauline Epistles before us, it seems to me impossible to doubt that the local ministers, however chosen and however called, were all solemnly ordained to their ministry. Apart from such Ordination I cannot see what intelligible meaning can be attached to the solemn language continually used by S. Paul when speaking of the ministry. The most natural interpretation of the Apostle's message to Archippus understands it as referring to his ordination. "*Say to Archippus, Take heed to the ministry* [διακονίαν] *which thou hast received of the Lord, that thou fulfil it.*"* The well-known words to S. Timothy may be compared, in which S. Paul bids him "*stir up the gift of God, which is in thee through the laying on of my* [S. Paul's] *hands*"; and the very solemn charge to the presbyters of Ephesus. "*Take heed unto yourselves, and to all the flock, in the which the Holy Ghost hath made you bishops, to feed the Church of God, which He purchased with His own blood.*"† There is a passage in the Epistle of S. Clement of Rome which may well be quoted here. S. Clement was the presiding presbyter of Rome at the end of the first century: he wrote his Epistle

---

* Col. iv. 17.

† Acts xx. 28. προσέχετε ἐαυτοῖς καὶ παντὶ τῷ ποιμνίῳ, ἐν ᾧ ὑμᾶς τὸ πνεῦμα τὸ ἅγιον ἔθετο ἐπισκόπους, ποιμαίνειν τὴν ἐκκλησίαν τοῦ θεοῦ, ἣν περιποιήσατο διὰ τοῦ αἵματος τοῦ ἰδίου. S. Paul himself had "ordained" these presbyters: it is evident that he believed intensely in the sacramental efficacy of such ordination.

in the name of the Roman Church to the Church of the Corinthians about the year 95 : the Epistle is therefore well within the Apostolic period : S. John was yet living when it was written. S. Clement wrote on account of disorders which had broken out at Corinth : there was a kind of revolt against the local presbyters. In order to restore peace the writer dwells on the dignity and authority of the presbyter's office, and he gives the following account of the origin of the Christian ministry :—

"The Apostles received the Gospel for us from the Lord Jesus Christ : Jesus Christ was sent forth from God. So then Christ is from God, and the Apostles are from Jesus Christ. Both therefore came of the will of God in the appointed order. Having, therefore, received a charge, and having been fully assured through the resurrection of our Lord Jesus Christ and confirmed in the Word of God with full assurance of the Holy Ghost, they went forth with the glad tidings that the kingdom of God should come. So preaching everywhere in country and town, they appointed their first-fruits when they had proved them by the Spirit to be bishops and deacons unto them that should believe." (c. 42.) . . . "And our Apostles knew through our Lord Jesus Christ that there would be strife over the bishop's office. For this cause, therefore, having received complete foreknowledge, they appointed the aforesaid persons, and afterwards they provided a continuance, that if these should fall asleep other approved men should succeed to their ministration. Those, therefore, who were appointed by them, or afterward by other men of repute with the consent of the whole Church, and have ministered unblameably to the flock of Christ in lowliness of mind, peacefully and with all modesty, and for a long time have borne a good report with all—these men we consider to be unjustly thrust out from their ministration." (c. 44.) S. Clement bases his exhortation to the disorderly Corinthians on the Divine Authority, which the presbyters possessed by virtue of their Ordination by the Apostles, or in succession from them. In the same way S. Paul bases the right of the ministry to receive maintenance from the Church on the commandment of Christ Himself. "*Even so did the Lord ordain that they which proclaim the gospel should live of the gospel.*"*

The ideal which S. Paul set before himself, which in his writings he has set before his successors in the Christian ministry, is indeed a noble one. "*We are ambassadors therefore on behalf of Christ as though God were intreating by us: we beseech you on behalf of Christ, be ye reconciled to God.*" † He felt himself endowed with Divine Authority, strengthened with Divine grace. This faith in their Commission is to be to the Christian ministers of every age their

---

* 1 Cor. ix. 14. It is not clear whether S. Paul is quoting an actual "logion" of our Lord, or summarising shortly His teaching on the subject. Probably the former. The Apostle certainly quoted a saying of Christ, not in the Gospels, in Acts xx. 35, "It is more blessed to give than to receive"; and, probably, he does the same in 1 Cor. vii. 10, 11. There must certainly have been many of Christ's sayings current in the Apostolic Church, which have now perished. Possibly the graves of Egypt may yet yield some genuine "words of Jesus."

† 2 Cor. v. 20.

stay in troublous times, the spring of their courage, the unfailing sustenance of their fortitude: it is to react upon their characters, purging, humbling, ennobling them: it is to win a way for their message in the hearts of men, bringing God near to them, and opening the locked Treasure-house of Eternity. "*Therefore seeing we have this ministry, even as we obtained mercy, we faint not: but we have renounced the hidden things of shame, not walking in craftiness, nor handling the word of God deceitfully: but by the manifestation of the truth commending ourselves to every man's conscience in the sight of God.*"*

Even so the message will often fail to win acceptance: men will harden their hearts, and avert their eyes. What shall the messenger do? It is the bitterest of all experiences. He is rent by a thousand anxieties. Why that failure? "*His blood will I require at thy hand.*" Was it his own blunder, or dishonesty, or stumbling-block of sin? Did not the Lord pronounce His woe on him who caused the least of His simple ones to stumble? Let him take courage: rejection is the lot of the holiest, even of the Master. "*But and if our gospel is veiled, it is veiled in them that are perishing: in whom the god of this world hath blinded the minds of the unbelieving, that the light of the gospel of the glory of Christ, Who is the image of God, should not dawn upon them. For we preach not ourselves, but Christ Jesus as Lord, and ourselves as your servants for Jesus' sake.*† Ah, S. Paul would say, it is not your sacred character that men will resent: it is your self-

* 2 Cor. iii. 1, 2.   † *Ibid.* iii. 3-5.

assertion: your Divine Commission will only wake resistance when you make it the occasion of vanity, and the servant of self-interest. Live humbly, speak truly, and you need not fear; "*in everything commending ourselves, as ministers of God, in much patience, in afflictions, in necessities, in distresses, in stripes, in imprisonments, in tumults, in labours, in watchings, in fastings; in pureness, in knowledge, in long-suffering, in kindness, in the Holy Ghost, in love unfeigned, in the word of truth, in the power of God; by the armour of righteousness on the right hand and on the left, by glory and dishonour, by evil report and good report; as deceivers, and yet true: as unknown, and yet well known: as dying, and behold, we live; as chastened, and not killed: as sorrowful, yet alway rejoicing: as poor, yet making many rich; as having nothing, and yet possessing all things.*"*

Such is the Ministerial Ideal: how it mocks selfish lives and feeble faith. Set it beside the ministry of Christian History, of contemporary experience, and how eloquent it is of censure and shame. "*Who is sufficient for these things?*" Who, indeed? Yet the Christian ministers of later ages may echo the words of the Apostle, "*Our sufficiency is of God*"; and, as we look back across the ages of Christian History, and around on the tumultuous life of our own time, surely we find abundant authentication of the words. Two facts about the Christian ministry stand out with luminous clearness. On the one hand, the incalculably great evils which flow from its corruption; on the other, the rare moral beauty with which it has enriched discipleship. The necessity of the

* *Ibid.* vi. 4-10.

ministry might be deduced from this circumstance, that apart from its healthy working the Church of Christ languishes, or perishes altogether. Despise it if you will: heap ridicule upon it: deny its claims: dispute its value: you cannot escape from the fact that upon it depends the well-being of Christianity. The clergy are, and always have been, the unfailing indicator of the Church's spiritual health. What the clergy are that the Church will become. Alas! that the failures should have been so many: the scandals so gross and so obdurate. They who bear the Lord's Commission may well bend their heads in shame and confusion of face as they recall the iniquities of the past, and the treasons of the present. Again and again, by their pride, their ambition, their rivalries, their corruptions, they have made the Lord's people to transgress. But there has been another side to the record of the Christian ministry. The Church counts among the saints and martyrs many, very many, of the Lord's ambassadors: saintly priests, learned Divines, missionaries burning with holy zeal, pastors who laid down their lives for their flocks, far-sighted prelates, guiding the Church in difficult times. Nor has the great succession ceased. Sometimes from scenes of holy toil, without recognition and without reward, as the world counts, the splendid devotion of the Christian Ministry startles the world; and sometimes the same high witness is yielded from seats of power, on which beats the fiercest light of public scrutiny.

CHAPTER III.

PUBLIC WORSHIP

IT is evident to the most superficial student of Christian antiquity that the earliest and most effectual influence, which shaped the organization of the Church, was that of the Jewish synagogue. In no direction is the effect of that influence more apparent than in the arrangements for public worship in the Christian assemblies. "It would hardly be an exaggeration to say," observes Dean Plumptre, "that the worship of the Church was identical with that of the synagogue, modified (1) by the new truths, (2) by the new institution of the supper of the Lord, (3) by the spiritual Charismata."* This close modelling of the Church upon the synagogue resulted from the actual circumstances under which the Church came into existence. The Christian Church was literally the offspring of the synagogue. In Jerusalem, and perhaps generally throughout the Jewish congregations, the name was adopted. S. James speaks in his Epistle of the Christian synagogue. We may suppose, without extravagance, that in many cases the entire Jewish community accepted the Apostolic message, and that the worship

* *Dictionary of the Bible*, art. "Synagogue."

of the Church succeeded without breach of continuity to the worship of the synagogue. The same building continued to serve the same purposes under the new, as formerly under the old *régime*.

It is evident, therefore, that in order to understand the conduct of public worship in the Apostolic Church, we ought in the first place to enquire into the arrangements actually in existence for the service of the synagogue.* Those arrangements are sufficiently well known. The service consisted of fixed forms of prayer, of psalms, hymns, doxologies, lessons from the Law and the Prophets, preaching. In the New Testament we find many references to the synagogue worship. Thus we read of Christ, that at Nazareth "*He entered, as His custom was, into the synagogue on the sabbath day, and stood up to read. And there was delivered unto Him the book (or roll) of the prophet Isaiah.*† After reading a passage, perhaps the lesson for the day,‡ "*He closed the book (roll) and gave it back to the attendant and sat down.*" We get a clear view of the proceedings. The prayers and psalms were ended. The first lesson from the Law had been read, and Christ had intervened to read the second lesson from the Prophets, and to give the customary

* A full and interesting account of the Synagogue, etc., and its arrangements may be found in EDERSHEIM, *Life and Times of Jesus the Messiah*, vol. i. p. 430 fol.

† S. Luke iv. 16.

‡ "No doubt there was even in ancient times a lectionary, though certainly not that presently in use, which occupies exactly a year." "Certain it is that the present lectionary from the prophets did not exist in early times; nor does it seem unlikely that the choice of the passage was left to the reader himself."—*Ibid.* p. 443, 444.

exhortation. In the Book of the Acts we find a similar episode in the history of S. Paul and S. Barnabas. At Antioch, in Pisidia, "*they went into the synagogue on the sabbath day, and sat down. And after the reading of the law and the prophets the rulers of the synagogue sent unto them, saying, Brethren, if ye have any word of exhortation for the people, say on.*"*

If we turn to the first Corinthian Epistle, and especially to the fourteenth chapter, we shall find evident correspondence with the organization of the synagogue. With the main subject of that chapter—the exercise of the *charismata*—we are not here concerned, but its incidental references to the public worship of the Corinthian Church must be carefully noted. We observe, in the first place, that the services were open to all. Undoubtedly the Agapæ and the Lord's Supper were rigidly guarded against the intrusion of strangers: but these more ordinary assemblies were intended not only to edify the faithful, but also to impress the heathen. S. Paul speaks of the "*men unlearned or unbelieving.*" Just as the Greeks and proselytes attended the service of the synagogue, so did the general multitude have free access to the public service of the Church. It is worthy our notice that the Apostle insists on taking thought for the impression likely to be made upon these non-Christian visitors by the proceedings they witnessed. The Corinthians were greatly disposed to regard with supercilious contempt those who were less instructed or more scrupulous than themselves.

* Acts xiii. 14, 15.

S. Paul's profounder insight perceived the mischiefs which would inevitably flow from that uncharitable contempt of appearances, which, veiling itself under the masque of liberty or devotion, scandalized the heathen and discredited the Church.

Some discussion has been raised as to the precise meaning to be attached to the word rendered in our Bibles "*unlearned*" (ἰδιώτης). Does it merely mean simple people, whose ignorance would lay them open to mistaken ideas of what they saw? or, does it bear a more technical meaning, and indicate the catechumens, who had not yet been admitted by baptism into the full membership of the Church? or, does it signify ungifted Christians as contrasted with those who possessed a *charisma*? or, private Christians as against those who held office in the Church? The word was applied by the Sanhedrists to the Apostles, whose courage amazed them. "*When they beheld the boldness of Peter and John, and had perceived that they were unlearned and ignorant men* [ἀγράμματοί κ. ἰδιῶται], *they marvelled.*"* Perhaps it is not necessary to suppose that S. Paul intended more than a general meaning. He is insisting on the unedifying character of that unintelligible devotion "*in a tongue,*" by which the Corinthians set great store. Intelligibility, he argues, is the first condition of edification. "*Else, if thou bless with the spirit, how shall he that filleth the place of the unlearned say the Amen at thy giving of thanks, seeing he knoweth not what thou sayest? For thou verily givest thanks well, but the other is not edified.*" The use of "the

* Acts iv. 13.

Amen" was directly borrowed from the synagogue. It assumes the adoption of fixed forms of prayer intelligibly read. *The Rabbis were wont to describe the meaningless Amen of the worshipper, who understood not the prayer to which he thus made response, by a quaint term. They styled it the "Orphan Amen," just as they styled a psalm to which neither the name of the author nor the occasion of its composing is inscribed, an "Orphan Psalm."

The expression "*he that filleth the place of the unlearned*"† has been thought by some to indicate an actual allotment of space. This seems improbable, yet we may hardly doubt that in the internal arrangement of the place of meeting the Christians followed the model of the synagogue. In both at the upper end would be the ark or chest containing the sacred rolls, from which the lessons were read, and later those new documents, Epistles and Gospels, which in time came to form the "New Testament." Around this ark would be placed the "*chief seats*" which the Rabbis coveted, and which, we may suppose, were, in the Corinthian Assembly, occupied by the "*prophets.*" To these "*good places*" in the Christian synagogue of Jerusalem the "*man with a gold ring, in fine clothing*," was respectfully escorted, while the "*poor man in vile clothing*" was left to stand, or given the worst seat in the *synagogue*. Perhaps the Jewish

* *Vide* LIGHTFOOT, *Works*, xii. p. 545. London, 1823.

† ὁ ἀναπληρῶν τὸν τόπον τοῦ ἰδιώτου πῶς ἐρεῖ τό 'Ἀμήν ἐπὶ τῇ σῇ εὐχαριστίᾳ.

[But WEIZÄCKER (ii. p. 250) seems to take the view that a special place is indicated.]

practice of placing an eight-branched lamp in front of the Ark may have been adopted. Lights were certainly the earliest Christian symbols. In the centre was the lectern or pulpit on a raised platform. Here the lessons were read, and teaching given. The sexes were divided, " men on one side, women on the other, a low partition, five or six feet high, running between them." We may doubt whether the partition existed in any but the assemblies of Jewish Christians. We are told that the synagogues had "alms-boxes at or near the door, after the pattern of those at the temple, one for the poor of Jerusalem, the other for local charities ; notice-boards, on which were written the names of offenders who had been 'put out of the synagogue'; a chest for trumpets and other musical instruments, used at the New Years, Sabbaths, and other festivals."* All these arrangements were probably reproduced with little alteration in the Church. Certainly the Christian Church would not be behind the Jewish synagogue in its care for the poor, in its zeal for discipline, in its use of musical instruments in the service of God. The pipe, the harp, and the trumpet are mentioned in 1 Corinthians xiv., and if it would be excessive to build anything on an admittedly vague and incidental reference, yet we may urge that S. Paul's description of Christian worship in the Ephesian Epistle—"*speaking one with another in psalms and hymns and spiritual songs, singing and making melody with your heart to the Lord*"—is most

* *Dictionary of Bible*, art. "Synagogue." See also EDERSHEIM, *l. c.*, p. 436.

naturally understood as assuming the use of musical instruments.

The Jewish practice of standing at prayer with uplifted or outstretched hands was adopted by the Church. "*I desire therefore that the men pray in every place, lifting up holy hands, without wrath and disputing.*"* In one respect, however, S. Paul distinctly departed from the model of the synagogue, which, as a rule, he so closely followed. The Jews were accustomed to veil themselves in token of penitence and humility when they stood to pray. This practice the Apostle condemned. The Greek custom of praying with uncovered head was established as the rule of the Church. "*Every man praying or prophesying, having his head covered, dishonoureth his head. But every woman praying or prophesying with her head unveiled dishonoureth her head.*"† The energy with which S. Paul presses the matter seems to indicate that there was a strong movement among the Corinthians to adopt the practice he condemns. "*Judge ye in yourselves: is it seemly that a woman pray unto God unveiled? Doth not even nature itself teach you, that, if a man have long hair, it is a dishonour to him? But if a woman have long hair it is a glory to her: for her hair is given her for a covering. But if any man seemeth to be contentious we have no such custom, neither the churches of God.*" We shall have to consider this language more carefully when we treat of the position of women in the Apostolic Church.

Undoubtedly a great place was filled in the public

* 1 Timothy ii. 8. † 1 Cor. xi. 4.

worship of the Christian assembly by the unpremeditated outpourings of gifted individuals; nevertheless, even in that early time the solid framework of the service was carefully prescribed by authority. The Psalms and lessons were no doubt selected on some definite plan, either that of the synagogue or some other. The prayers were not wholly unregulated. S. Paul in the first Pastoral Epistle insists on a certain order and range of subjects. "*I exhort, therefore, first of all, that supplications, prayers, intercessions, thanksgivings, be made for all men; for kings and all that are in high place: that we may lead a tranquil and quiet life in all godliness and gravity.*"*

This solid framework of the service was, perhaps, under the control of the ordained ministry. That throughout his discussion of the disorders connected with the public worship of the Corinthian Church S. Paul should not make a single reference to the resident officials is, indeed, very astonishing; it must, however, be remembered that he was directly concerned with regulating the exercise of the *charismata*, which admittedly lay outside the authority of the ordained ministry. That such a ministry existed, and was charged with the oversight of the worship, cannot be regarded as an extravagant assumption in view of the general character of the Epistles, the analogy of the synagogue, and the subsequent development of the Church. These Corinthian Epistles treat at great length of the status and responsibility of the ordained ministry. Moreover,

* 1 Timothy ii. 1, 2.

we have the direct testimony of the Acts that it was the normal Apostolic practice to provide for the government of the churches they founded by ordaining "*presbyters*." S. Paul emphasized the pastoral character of the episcopate to which the Ephesian presbyters had been admitted. "*To feed the Church of God*" would seem in the first place to carry the notion of teaching. Apart from rhapsodies and revelations there was the steady, continuous necessity of instruction, and that must have been the specific charge of the official ministry. In reference to this matter, also, the precedent of the synagogue was most influential. A fully organized synagogue had its college of elders or presbyters, and its official executive—the "ruler" or "rulers," the collectors of the alms, the minister, whose functions seem to have much resembled those of a modern verger.* Assuming that the Christian synagogue was similarly organized, the normal conduct of public worship would be in the hands of such officials, save in so far as the *charismata* superseded all ordinary system; and when, with the

* Edersheim enumerates the following synagogue officials:—

(1) "The *Chazzan*, or minister, who often acts also as a schoolmaster.

(2) "The elders (Zegenin), or rulers (ἄρχοντες), whose chief is the Archisynagogos, or Rosh-ha-Keneseth. These are the rulers (Paruasim), or shepherds (ποιμένες). These formed the local sanhedrim or tribunal. But their election depended on the choice of the congregation.

(3) "Officials who officiated during the service, the *Sheliach Tsibbur*, or delegate of the congregation—who, as its mouthpiece, conducted the devotions—the Interpreter or *Methurgeman*, and those who were called on to read in the Law and the Prophets, or else to preach."— *Vide Life and Times of Jesus*, i. pp. 438, 439.

Canon Gore (*The Church and the Ministry*, pp. 399-410) has a learned

wider extension of the Church, the extraordinary phenomena which marked its beginning became of rarer occurrence, and finally ceased altogether, these officials, *i.e.*, the ordained clergy, came to possess the exclusive control which has ever since belonged to them. The great principles which S. Paul lays down have determined the development of the liturgical worship, which everywhere has replaced the more spontaneous service of the early days. "*Let all things be done to edifying.*" "*Let all things be done decently and in order.*" The sphere of Divine Worship is the least suited of all spheres for the display of personal preferences, and the exaltation of personal importance. The less experiment, the less novelty, above all, the less excitement the better. Two paramount considerations, always present, should chasten individualism and prohibit irreverence—the permanent needs of the human worshipper, the revealed character of Almighty God. There *are* permanent spiritual needs, and these are not always as carefully provided for as their importance requires. Fashions in public worship make

and interesting note on "The Origin of the Titles 'Bishop,' 'Presbyter,' 'Deacon,'" in which he discusses the relation between the synagogue officials and the officials of the Church. He concludes "that the Christian Church borrowed none of the Jewish titles except that of 'presbyter'" . . . "that all our evidence goes to show that the Christian Church had only one organization, while the Jews with their temple, schools, synagogue, and sanhedrim, had four." He hardly seems to allow enough for the necessities of the situation; but with certain reservations I do not dispute his conclusion. "All the functions and powers of the Church were, in fact, summed up at first in the apostles, and were gradually imparted under their authority and leading to different officers, who shared the same ministry in distinct grades." The whole note should be read.

their appearance at intervals, and seem to carry all before them. Now it is extempore prayer, now it is hymn singing, now it is elaborate music, now it is ornate ritual, now it is sensational preaching. The fickle multitude easily deserts the familiar but comparatively uninteresting system of the Church, and flocks greedily after the latest thing in religion. Yet our needs do not vary with our preferences, nor can they be conformed to our fashions; and the Church, whose ancient system does in the main represent a continuous effort to match human need, secures in the long run the loyal acceptance of faithful disciples. Still more important is the argument which the Apostle builds on the known character of Him whom we worship. "*God is not a God of confusion, but of peace.*" The worship which is acceptable to Him must correspond to His character. Above all, it must be intelligent, and devout, and orderly. When public worship degenerates into mere lifeless formalism, or into mere empty convention, or into a wild chaos of unchecked excitement, how gross is the offence, how scandalous the spectacle! Yet who will deny that such degeneration is both facile and frequent? We should be ever vigilant against the irreverence of self-assertion. Our needs and God's majesty must be the restraints of our frivolity, and the rebukes of our pride. The counsels of the Preacher of Israel may well be in our minds as we cross the threshold of the Lord's House. "*Keep thy foot when thou goest to the house of God: for to draw nigh to hear is better than to give the sacrifice of fools: for they know not that they do evil. Be not rash with thy mouth, and let not thine heart be hasty before God: for God is in heaven and thou upon earth: therefore let thy words be few.*" The more we cultivate the true, sober, restrained temper of devotion, the more dear to us will become the ordered worship of the Church of England. There is a modern fashion of speaking contemptuously about Matins and Evensong, as if those services represented the very antithesis of the worship which devout souls would naturally seek. Of course these services cannot take the place, and were never intended to take the place, of the supreme action of Christian Worship—the Holy Eucharist, from which, according to the wholesome discipline of the Apostolic Church, all save communicants were excluded; but for the purpose of that public worship, which is the ordinary witness to the outside world of Christian truth, which is to secure regular teaching, and to provide a channel for the general praise, these services of Matins and Evensong, with their fixed elements of prayer, psalms, confession of faith, reading of the Scriptures, preaching, do seem to approve themselves to all who acknowledge the authority of Apostolic precedents, and have regard to the standing necessities of human souls.*

---

* Bp. Lightfoot's dissertation on the liturgical ending of S. Clement's Epistle is of extreme interest, and directly bears on the subject here discussed. It must suffice to quote the following :—

"The earliest services of the Christian Church, so far as they were grafted on the worship of the Jews, would be indebted to the synagogue rather than to the temple. Recent archæological discoveries, more especially in Galilee and in Eastern Palestine, have enlarged our ideas on this subject. The number, the capacity, and even (in some cases) the magnificence of the synagogues are attested by their ruins. What we find at such Jewish centres as Capernaum would certainly not be wanting in the mighty cities of the world, like Alexandria and Rome. The ritual would bear some proportion to the buildings; and thus the early Christian congregations would find in their Jewish surroundings ample precedent for any ritual development which for some generations they could desire or compass. Again, as regards the substance of public worship, they would naturally build upon the lines traced by their Jewish predecessors. The common prayer, the lessons from the law, the lessons from the prophets, the chanting of the psalms or of hymns, the exposition or homily, all were there ready for adoption. The eucharistic Celebration—the commemoration of and participation in the Lord's Passion—was the new and vivifying principle, the centre round which these adopted elements ranged themselves, being modified as the circumstances suggested. The earliest account of the Christian eucharist, as given by Justin Martyr, shows that this is no merely conjectural view of the genesis of the Christian Celebration."

Apostolic Fathers, part I, vol. i. pp. 392, 393.

CHAPTER IV.

THE GIFT OF TONGUES

IN the appendix to S. Mark's Gospel we read that before His ascension our Lord foretold to His disciples that among the "*signs*" which should follow upon acceptance of the Christian message should be the power of speaking "*with new tongues*" (γλώσσαις καιναῖς). On the Day of Pentecost His assurance was justified by a miraculous gift of utterance, which the author of the Book of Acts believed to be the faculty of speaking divers languages, of which the inspired speakers had previously possessed no knowledge.* That this is the sacred historian's meaning there can be no question. The festival crowd, including representatives of many nationalities, are said to have recognized with amazement the familiar sounds of their respective languages. "*When this sound was heard the multitude came together, and were confounded, because that every man heard them speaking in his own language*" (τῇ ἰδίᾳ διαλέκτῳ).† If these passages exhausted the witness of the New Testament on the subject there would be little room for discussion.

* Unfortunately this literal and—as I hold—untenable view is embedded in our Communion Service. The Whit-Sunday preface specifically asserts that the χαρισμα of Pentecost was "the gift of divers languages." † Acts ii. 6.

We should be encountered by a prodigy which has no parallel in human experience, and which, as far as we know, has had very little influence on human history. In the Epistle before us, however, we possess a detailed and strictly contemporary account of an extraordinary phenomenon in the Corinthian Church, which all are agreed to identify with the gift of Pentecost, and which certainly was not the power of speaking divers languages, whatever else it may have been. It is important to remember that S. Paul's Epistle to the Corinthians is earlier in point of time than either the appendix to S. Mark's Gospel or the Book of the Acts, and possesses, therefore, a superior historical value within its own sphere. The section of the Epistle, which includes the xii., xiii., and xiv. chapters, treats of the *spiritual gifts*, or *charismata*, the undisciplined exercise of which had led to serious confusion and even scandal. Among these *charismata* S. Paul mentions "*divers kinds of tongues*" (γένη γλωσσῶν), and a supplemental gift which seems connected with this mysterious utterance, "*the interpretation of tongues*" (ἑρμηνεία γλωσσῶν). Having set forth with singular force and beauty the conception of the Church which underlay his view of the *charismata*, and having exalted in a passage of imperishable charm the supreme virtue of love, the Apostle in the fourteenth chapter grapples with the practical question, and proposes certain regulations in restraint of the Corinthian abuses. From this chapter we are able to gather some information about the mysterious *charisma*, which we are here considering. Putting together the indications before us, we learn that the *charisma* of "*the tongue*" was always unintelligible to the hearers unless they possessed the power—itself a *charisma*—of *interpretation* (*v.* 2); that, therefore, its value as an element in the public worship of the Church was entirely contingent on the presence of an interpreter (*v.* 5); that, though generally useless for the purpose of general edification, it edified the speaker himself (*v.* 4): however, even this was not necessarily the case, for the speaker might himself be ignorant of the meaning of the words which rushed from his lips (*v.* 14); that this gift, both as unintelligible and, probably, as accompanied by violent physical excitement, was not calculated to make a favourable impression on casual observers, who might easily mistake it for insanity (*v.* 23); finally, that in spite of its mysterious and even violent character, it was not really outside the control of the individual (*vv.* 27, 28). S. Paul, though he thus takes a very unfavourable view of the practical worth of the *charisma* in question, did most certainly hold it to be a genuine and, for its own purposes, a precious gift of the Holy Spirit. He himself was richly endowed. "*I thank God, I speak with tongues more than you all: howbeit in the church* [ἐν ἐκκλησίᾳ = in an assembly] *I had rather speak five words with my understanding, that I might instruct others also, than ten thousand words in a tongue.*"* Perhaps we may recognize in S. Paul's description of his vision an analogous experience to that here referred to. The abrupt and involved language seems to suggest the awful nature of the

* 1 Cor. xiv. 18, 19.

ecstasy it attempts to describe. "*I know a man in Christ, fourteen years ago (whether in the body, I know not; or whether out of the body, I know not; God knoweth), such a one caught up even to the third heaven. And I know such a man (whether in the body, or apart from the body, I know not; God knoweth), how that he was caught up into Paradise, and heard unspeakable words, which it is not lawful for a man to utter.*"* This unutterableness of the Divine communication, arising from the sublime character of truths "too deep for words," which could be felt but could not be spoken, is mentioned also in the Roman Epistle, where the Apostle speaks of the influence of the Holy Ghost upon the Christian, "*the Spirit Himself maketh intercessions for us with groanings which cannot be uttered.*"† So in 1 Cor. xiv. 2, "*He that speaketh in a tongue speaketh not unto men, but unto God, for no man understandeth; but in the spirit he speaketh mysteries.*"

‡ It is, I think, quite evident that the notion of a

* 2 Cor. xii. 2-4.   † Rom. viii. 26.
‡ *Vide* E. DE PRESSENSÉ, *Le Siècle Apostolique*, 1ʳᵉ Periode, p. 153 fol. His decision seems the only reasonable one. "La tradition a pu subir quelques modifications." He points out that the languages-theory is really contradicted by the New Testament itself. "Le style des écrivains sacrés nous montre clairement qu'ils ont appris la langue grecque, cars ils l'écrivent sans correction et la surchargent de locutions hébraïques."
    The traditional view is very moderately stated by Dean PLUMPTRE in the *Dict. of the Bible*, art. "Tongues," where the whole subject is fully discussed. The whole question really turns on the authority assigned to Acts ii. If the actual language of that chapter must be maintained, then the traditional view with its immense difficulties follows obviously; but if ordinary rules of criticism are to be applied to New Testament documents, then certainly Acts ii. must be corrected by 1 Cor. xiv.

miraculous knowledge of languages must be rejected. The narrative of the Pentecostal Outpouring stands quite by itself, and is not compatible with the rest of the evidence. It represents a developed tradition of the history, rather than the history itself. The subsequent references to the gift of tongues in the Book of the Acts are in agreement with the Pauline Epistles. It is not seriously suggested that when Cornelius and his friends received the Holy Ghost and began to speak with tongues, they were suddenly breaking out in various and hitherto unknown languages. It is particularly worthy of notice that S. Peter, in relating this occurrence to the Church in Jerusalem, expressly identified the *charisma* of Cornelius with that of Pentecost. "*As I began to speak, the Holy Ghost fell on them, even as on us at the beginning.*" * Similarly in the case of the twelve disciples of S. John the Baptist, whom S. Paul found at Ephesus and whom he baptized. No one supposes that they spoke foreign languages when, after the laying on of the Apostle's hands, "*the Holy Ghost came on them, and they spake with tongues, and prophesied.*" † Moreover, it seems to me that the record in the second chapter of the Acts is hardly compatible with the assumption, which the author undoubtedly makes, that the "*tongues*" were divers languages. The observation of the scoffers, "*They are filled with new wine,*" does not seem very relevant to a preaching, of which the chief distinction was that it was expressed, contrary to their expectation, in their respective mother tongues. S. Peter's defence

* Acts xi. 15.   † *Ibid.* xix. 6.

is hardly what we should expect if the phenomena which he had to justify was a supernatural knowledge of foreign languages. The prophecy of Joel, which he quotes, has no reference to anything at once so amazing and so commonplace, while it is very relevant indeed to such manifestations of the Divine Influence as those which were common among the Corinthians. If a knowledge of languages was supernaturally conveyed, it must have been designed to facilitate the missionary labours of the Church. Such, indeed, has been the general belief. But it is impossible to produce a single instance that any such knowledge was either possessed or used. All the evidence points in the opposite direction. The narrative of the Apostolic preaching at Lystra clearly indicates that S. Paul and S. Barnabas were ignorant of "*the speech of Lycaonia*," and only learnt by degrees the idolatrous intentions of the people.*
It was a matter of astonishment to the chief captain that S. Paul could speak Greek, which would hardly have been the case if the knowledge of languages had been a characteristic of the Christians.†

The scoffers at Jerusalem derided the inspired disciples as "*filled with new wine*." It is not without significance that S. Paul himself should institute a comparison between such inspiration and drunkenness. "*And be not drunken with wine, wherein is riot*," he writes to the Ephesians, "*but be filled with*

---

* Acts xiv. 11, 13, 14. The exclamation of the Lycaonians was unintelligible to the Apostles, who only grasped the situation when "the priest of Jupiter, whose temple was before the city, brought oxen and garlands unto the gates, and would have done sacrifice with the multitudes." † *Ibid.* xxi. 37.

*the Spirit."** M. Godet thus describes the state of the Christian under the influence of this *charisma* :—

"While drawing him into a state of ecstasy the Divine Spirit separates him for the moment from his understanding, which is a faculty of the soul, or rather the soul herself in its thinking capacity. Thus his impressions take the character of pure sentiment, of ineffable emotion: it is a state of spiritual exhilaration, of which drunkenness is as it were the coarse counterpart. Such a state was revealed by extraordinary utterances, consisting of prayers, praises, or thanksgivings, and expressing the satisfaction and the aspirations of the saved soul. Only with such a state the understanding was not associated. It was, as the Apostle says, "*unfruitful.*"

It is particularly noteworthy that S. Paul does not draw the inference that the *charisma* is therefore valueless, and should be suppressed. Rather he insists on an intelligent and responsible exercise of it. "*What is it then? I will pray with the spirit, and I will pray with the understanding also: I will sing with the spirit, and I will sing with the understanding also.*" The Apostle seems to mention the two principal manifestations of the *charisma* in question — prayer and singing. We naturally compare the familiar language of the Epistle to the Ephesians, "*Speaking one to another in psalms and hymns and spiritual songs, singing and making melody with your heart to the Lord.*" Joy was, perhaps, the prevailing temper of Apostolic Christianity. The Gospel meant so much to men who

* Eph. v. 18.

had groaned under the rigid despotism of the Rabbinic system, or groped despairingly amid the gross errors of paganism. "*Tidings of great joy*" was the announcement of the herald angel, and every page of the New Testament reveals the fitness of the description. Everywhere the acceptance of Christianity expressed itself in a wonderful light-heartedness, as of men suddenly set free from some oppressive anxiety. So the converts of Pentecost "*took their food with gladness and singleness of heart, praising God*";[*] so, on the morrow of their conversion, "*there was much joy in the city*"[†] of the Samaritans; so at Iconium "*the disciples were filled with joy and with the Holy Ghost.*"[‡] Continually this joy of discipleship breaks through the language of the Epistles. Christians in those first days were like happy children, too happy to put into intelligible words their feelings, but singing and humming, and dancing for joy. Now the *charisma* of the tongue seems to me the organ through which most conspicuously this joy of discipleship expressed itself. That joy had two elements—the blessed sense of peace with God, reconciliation with the Father and the full heart of gratitude for the Redemption; and these elements were represented in the fellowship of fervent prayer, and in the ecstatic pouring forth of improvised hymns of thanksgiving. The violence of the phenomenon—inarticulate cries, loud voice, excitement which almost suggested insanity or intoxication—only reflected the greatness of the spiritual crisis through which men were passing. We may

[*] Acts ii. 46, 47.   [†] *Ibid.* viii. 8.   [‡] *Ibid.* xiii. 52.

find many illustrations in the history of later Christianity. The gift of tongues itself soon disappeared from the normal life of the Church. S. Irenæus, indeed, in the second century relates that in his day there were brethren "who had prophetic gifts, and spoke through the Spirit in all kinds of tongues"; but his evidence stands alone, for the prophetess mentioned by Tertullian was a heretic. S. Chrysostom begins his comments on the passage in the Corinthian Epistle, which treats of spiritual gifts, with these words: "This whole place is very obscure; but the obscurity is produced by our ignorance of the facts referred to, and by their cessation, being such as then used to occur, but now no longer take place." Neither in the Pastoral, nor in the General Epistles, nor in the Epistle to the Hebrews is there any clear reference to this *charisma*. The little treatise known as *The Teaching of the Twelve Apostles* is equally silent, a fact which is the more significant since the conditions under which the kindred *charisma* of prophecy should be exercised are carefully prescribed. At intervals, however, generally in sects or communities which are subjected to circumstances of extreme difficulty and pressure, there have appeared phenomena which have a close resemblance to the charisma as described by S. Paul. "The movement of the mendicant orders in the thirteenth century, the prophesyings of the sixteenth in England, the early history of the disciples of George Fox, that of the Jansenists in France, the Revivals under Wesley and Whitefield, those of a later date in Sweden, America, and

Ireland, have in like manner been fruitful in ecstatic phenomena more or less closely resembling those which we are now discussing." Still closer parallels were presented in France at the beginning of the last century, and in England about sixty years ago.* In every case, however, these exhibitions have been too definitely connected with extravagances of doctrine to permit of their being placed on a level with the manifestation which in the first Christian

---

* Dean Stanley has an interesting and elaborate discussion of the "Gift of Tongues" in his *Commentary on the Corinthian Epistles*, pp. 243--257. He endeavours with more ingenuity than success to reconcile the phenomena described in Acts ii. with those described in 1 Cor. xiv. His suggestion is that "as even in common life persons in a highly wrought state of feeling are enabled to understand each other, though not speaking the same language, so this gift, which above all others lifted the speaker out of himself, might have the same effect." He suggests that "Hellenistic Greek, compounded as it was of Greek, Latin, and Hebrew, and instinct with that peculiar life and energy which we see it assume in the various styles of the New Testament, especially in S. Paul and in the Apocalypse, was almost in itself a 'speaking' in divers kinds of tongues." "All the various elements of Aramaic and Hellenic speech, latent in the usual language of the time, would be quickened under the power of this gift into a new life, sometimes intelligible, sometimes unintelligible to those who heard it, but always expressive of the vitality and energy of the Spirit by which it was animated." He gives two descriptions of the so-called "gift of tongues" in the followers of Mr. Irving, about 1831-1833, by a sympathetic and an unsympathetic eye-witness. Dr. Arnold's opinion about those occurrences is expressed in a letter to Rev. F. C. Blackstone. (*Stanley's Life*, p. 241.) "If the thing be real I should take it merely as a sign of the coming of the day of the Lord—the only use, as far as I can make out, that ever was derived from the gift of tongues. I do not see that it was ever made a vehicle of instruction, or ever superseded the study of tongues, but that it was merely a sign of the power of God, a man being for the time transformed into a mere instrument to utter sounds which he himself understood not." Also *Ibid.*, p. 360, at greater length.

age testified to the presence of the Divine Spirit.*
"Prayer and singing"—the natural victims of undisciplined enthusiasm at all times! Do I mistake in thinking that the Apostle's rules for controlling the "*gift of tongues*" are not without relevance still in respect of those matters? Restraint of private feelings in public, reverence,—these, surely, are not superfluous counsels in these days, when men's feelings are proposed as the very bases of their faith, and a strange familiarity, not to say a disrespect, is indulged in by Christians when addressing the Almighty, and even exalted as the proper expression of the filial relationship, into which, by the adoption of grace, Christians have been admitted. Extempore prayers and popular hymns have renewed in our own times the extravagances, without the excuses, of Corinth. "There is a great danger in ungoverned feeling," observes one of the wisest spiritual teachers of this century.† "There are persons more highly gifted with fine delicate sensibilities than others; they are not moved to action like others, by convictions of the intellect or by a strong sense of duty; they can do nothing except through their affections. All this is very precious, no doubt, if well used; but just in proportion as

---

* "Michael Maurice went himself to London, and was simply shocked by what he saw and heard at Mr. Irving's church--the wild voices and artificial excitement." (*Life of F. D. Maurice*, vol. i. p. 116.) Dr. Arnold (*l. c.*) was offended by the religious arrogance of the Irvingites. "The intolerance of their presumption in calling themselves the only true Church would, to my mind, go very near to decide against them."

† F. W. ROBERTSON, *Lectures on Epistle to the Corinthians*, p. 236.

feelings are strong do they require discipline. The temptation is great to indulge from mere pleasure of indulgence, and from the admiration given to feeling. It is easier to gain credit for goodness by a glistening eye, while listening to some story of self-sacrifice, than by patient usefulness. It is easier to get credit for spirituality by thrilling at some impassioned speech on the platform, or sermon from the pulpit, than by living a life of justice, mercy, and truth. And hence religious life degenerates into mere indulgence of feeling, the excitement of religious meetings, or the *utterance* of strong emotion. In this sickly strife life wastes away, and the man or woman becomes weak, instead of strong; for invariably utterance weakens feeling."

"Feelings" may not be despised, but they must always be checked, and never wholly trusted. "*Quench not the spirit*,"—writes S. Paul, perhaps with the "*gift of tongues*" in his mind—"*despise not prophesyings; prove all things; hold fast that which is good; abstain from every form of evil.*" The same balanced sympathy and caution speak in the conclusion to the discussion of the *charismata* in 1 Cor. xiv., "*Wherefore, my brethren, desire earnestly to prophesy, and forbid not to speak with tongues. But let all things be done decently and in order.*" Be slow to condemn enthusiasm, for it may, indeed—in spite of external appearances, which suggest fanaticism—indicate a genuine working of God upon the human spirit. Be slower still to give enthusiasm free scope, for under the masque of its fervour strange elements may come into play

—pride, and self-centredness, and self-advertisement. Always keep before you the essential superiority of the serviceable over the merely devotional activities of discipleship. "There are gifts which draw admiration to a man's self, others which solace and soothe him personally, and a third class which benefit others. The world and the Bible are at issue as to the comparative worth of these. A gifted singer soon makes a fortune, and men give their guinea and their ten guineas ungrudgingly for a morning's enjoyment. A humble teacher in a school or a missionary can often but only just live. Gifts that are showy and gifts that please—before these the world yields her homage, while the lowly teachers of the poor and the ignorant are forgotten and unnoticed. Only remember that in the sight of the Everlasting Eye the one is creating sounds which perish with the hour that gave them birth, the other is doing a work that is for ever—building and forming for the eternal world an immortal human spirit."

CHAPTER V.

MIRACLES

IT does not fall within the scope of this volume to discuss miracles in themselves. I take for granted their possibility, and address myself to the task of discovering the place they held in the Apostolic Church. My method is sufficiently simple. In the first place, I shall briefly put together the evidence which we possess; in the next place, I shall endeavour to appreciate the facts.

The earliest and in all respects the weightiest testimony on the subject is that of the Corinthian Epistles. Miracles are included among the *charismata* of the Spirit. They fall into two classes. On the one hand, there are *"gifts of healings"* (χαρίσματα ἰαμάτων). These may be illustrated by the well-known passage in S. James' Epistle, where the association of physical illness with sin is evident. *"Is any among you sick? let him call for the elders of the church: and let them pray over him, anointing him with oil in the name of the Lord: and the prayer of faith shall save him that is sick, and the Lord shall raise him up: and if he have committed sins, it shall be forgiven him. Confess therefore your sins one to another, and pray for one another that ye may be healed.*

The supplication of a righteous man availeth much in its working.* Here, however, there is no mention of a special *charisma* of healing, but only of the efficacy of prayer. A better parallel is provided by the records in the Acts. Thus of the cripple at Lystra we read that S. Paul "*fastening his eyes upon him, and seeing that he had faith to be made whole, said to him with a loud voice, Stand upright on thy feet.*"† Similar action is attributed to S. Peter, who healed a paralyzed man at Lydda with the words, "*Æneas, Jesus Christ healeth thee: arise, and make thy bed.*"‡ The *charisma* evidently included the power to recognize a suitable subject for treatment. The exercise of the miraculous power—if such we ought to call an action which scarcely lies outside general experience—was limited in range. Only persons of a certain temperament, and, perhaps, only certain classes of physical infirmity, could yield to the influence of this *charisma*. Certainly the existence within the Church of inspired faith-healers§ did not exclude the necessity of physicians. S. Paul himself was afflicted with bad health: and neither his own prayers nor the miraculous powers which he possessed could remove his ailment. S. Luke, "*the beloved physician,*" ‖ had to bring his medical skill to the Apostle's aid. S. Timothy's "*often infirmities*" ¶ were to be corrected not by religious exercises, but by a change of diet. I see no reason to think that

---

* S. James v. 14-17. † Acts xiv. 9. ‡ *Ibid.* ix. 34.

§ I would refer the reader to Archbishop Temple's *Bampton Lectures,* "The Relations between Religion and Science," especially Lecture VII.

‖ Col. iv. 14. ¶ 1 Tim. v. 23.

the Christian of the first century as such ordinarily enjoyed any advantage from the "*gifts of healings.*" These may have served a useful purpose as occasional demonstrations of apparently superhuman power, arresting the notice of the heathen, and inducing their belief, but in the normal life of the Christian community they counted for little. We read in two passages of the Acts* of many amazing miracles wrought by S. Peter, and, later, by S. Paul; but the account in both cases has an unusual and, so to say, hyperbolical aspect, which perhaps permits us to regard it as less historical than the rest of the narrative, and on any showing these displays of wonder-working did not continue. Commonly the Christians were as the rest of men, save for the comforts and encouragements of their faith. They fell sick, and died like their neighbours; like them they associated sickness and death very closely with the hostile or penal action of spiritual powers, and had recourse, therefore, to acts of religion for their relief in time of illness. Often, no doubt, where will was strong and faith was ardent very astonishing recoveries took place, as, indeed, they do still; but for the most part the sick had to surrender them-

* (1) Acts v. 12-16. "They even carried out the sick into the streets and laid them on beds and couches, that, as Peter came by, at the least his shadow might overshadow some one of them."

(2) Acts xix. 11, 12. "And God wrought special miracles by the hands of Paul: insomuch that unto the sick were carried away from his body handkerchiefs or aprons, and the diseases departed from them, and the evil spirits went out." The curious story of the Exorcists, who imitated S. Paul's method with calamitous results to themselves, then follows, and, as a consequence from it, the sacrifice of "vanities" by the Ephesians. The whole narrative is extremely difficult.

selves to the risks of medical treatment in an age when medical science was in its infancy. The counsels of the son of Sirach were certainly familiar to S. Paul, and probably to his converts also. "*My son, in thy sickness be not negligent: but pray unto the Lord, and He shall heal thee. Put away wrong doing, and order thine hands aright, and cleanse thy heart from all manner of sin. . . . Then give place to the physician, for verily the Lord hath created him: and let him not go from thee, for thou hast need of him.*"*

On the other hand, are the "*workings of miracles*" (ἐνεργήματα δυνάμεων) a general expression, of which it is not easy to fix the meaning? "Paul would speak"—comments M. Godet—"of the faculty of working every kind of miraculous act, other than simple healings, and designed to match the needs of the different situations in which the servant of Christ may find himself; resurrections of the dead, castings-out of demons, chastisements inflicted on faithless Christians or on adversaries, such as Ananias or Elymas, deliverance such as Paul's at Melita."†

It is to be remembered that S. Paul claims for himself this wonder-working power, and advances the fact as an evidence of his own equality with "*the very chiefest apostles.*"‡ "*Truly the signs of an apostle were wrought among you*"—he writes to the Corinthians in his second Epistle—"*in all

---

* Eccles. xxxviii. 9, 10, 12.   † Vol. ii. p. 207.
‡ 2 Cor. xii. 2. οὐδὲν γὰρ ὑστέρησα τῶν ὑπερλίαν ἀποστόλων, εἰ καὶ οὐδέν εἰμι· τὰ μὲν σημεῖα τοῦ ἀποστόλου κατειργάσθη ἐν ὑμῖν ἐν πάσῃ ὑπομονῇ, σημείοις τε καὶ τέρασιν καὶ δυνάμεσιν.

patience, by signs and wonders and mighty works." Similarly in the first Epistle he declares that "*his speech and his preaching were not in persuasive words of wisdom, but in demonstration of the spirit and of power.*" * It is not a little astonishing in view of these statements that in the record of the Acts there is no hint of miracles at Corinth; perhaps it is not necessary to assume that in speaking of "*signs and wonders and mighty works*" the Apostle meant physical prodigies. The establishment of the Church in Corinth, effected in the teeth of bitter and powerful opposition, was itself an evident "*demonstration of the spirit.*" It must, however, be conceded that the words are more naturally interpreted of miracles in the technical sense.

If we examine the recorded miracles of S. Paul we find that, apart from acts of healing, they consisted either of punishments inflicted on opponents, or of exorcism. The raising to life of Eutychus I leave out of reckoning, because I think the narrative may be fairly read as the record of a natural event. The young man was at first assumed to be dead, but the Apostle discovered the falseness of the assumption. "*Make ye no ado*"—he said—"*for his life is in him.*" An accident of that kind would almost certainly acquire a miraculous aspect in so credulous an age, but there is really nothing miraculous about it.†

---

* 1 Cor. ii. 4. καὶ ὁ λόγος μου καὶ τὸ κήρυγμά μου οὐκ ἐν πιθοῖς σοφίας λόγοις ἀλλ' ἐν ἀποδείξει πνεύματος καὶ δυνάμεως, ἵνα ἡ πίστις ὑμῶν μὴ ᾖ ἐν σοφίᾳ ἀνθρώπων ἀλλ' ἐν δυνάμει θεοῦ.

† Acts xx. 7-12. It is to be noted that this is one of the "we" passages, which are universally recognized as of the highest historical authority. Yet v. 13 suggests that his companions had left the Apostle

We have already, in a previous chapter, considered the meaning of that "*delivery unto Satan for the destruction of the flesh,*" and we then saw how it assumed the Apostolic belief in the empire of Satan in the world, and how under the circumstances of the time there would be a large probability of its literal interpretation in fact. In the Acts we read of the punishment inflicted on Elymas the Sorcerer. The Apostle "*filled with the Holy Ghost, fastened his eyes on him, and said, O full of all guile and all villany, thou son of the devil, thou enemy of all righteousness, wilt thou not cease to pervert the right ways of the Lord? And now, behold, the hand of the Lord is upon thee, and thou shalt be blind, not seeing the sun for a season. And immediately there fell on him a mist and a darkness: and he went about seeking some to lead him by the hand.*"* This must be regarded as an extraordinary exercise of a power, which normally was used as the sanction of Church discipline. Commonly S. Paul declined to exercise authority over those who were not members of the Church. "*What have I to do with judging them that are without?*" he asks in the Epistle before us. We must assume that there were special circumstances of aggravation in the case of the sorcerer Elymas, which justified S. Paul in departing from his general rule.

---

still speaking, and were not, therefore, actually present at the episode in question. However this may be, I do not see any necessity for understanding more than is actually stated; S. Paul's expression literally precludes the notion of a resurrection.

* Acts xiii. 9-11.

Probably the commonest type of miracle was that known as "exorcism." The passage in the Acts, to which I have already alluded as scarcely historical, gives prominence to S. Paul's power as an exorcist, and describes the ignoble failure which followed upon the attempt made by the sons of Seeva to imitate his method. "*And God wrought special miracles by the hands of Paul: insomuch that unto the sick were carried away from his body handkerchiefs or aprons, and the diseases departed from them, and the evil spirits went out.*" The history of the Jewish exorcists, and as a result the burning of the magical books of the Ephesians, then follow. We are not here concerned with this remarkable narrative save in so far as it supports the contention that the "*miracles*" of the early Church, apart from healings and judgments, were mostly acts of exorcism. The casting out of devils has a very prominent place in the Gospels. It is recorded that our Saviour gave to His Apostles and to the Seventy "*power and authority over all devils.*"* We learn that there was a disposition to exult in the possession of this mysterious power, and that Christ rebuked this disposition. "*Behold, I have given you authority to tread upon serpents and scorpions, and over all the power of the enemy: and nothing shall in any wise hurt you. Howbeit in this rejoice not, that the spirits are subject unto you: but rejoice that your names are written in heaven.*"† The authority, however, was not limited to the disciples, nor would Christ permit it to be limited. On one occasion we read that the question was raised by the

---

* S. Luke ix. 1. † *Ibid.* x. 19, 20.

Apostles, and decisively answered by our Lord. "*John answered and said, Master, we saw one casting out devils in Thy name; and we forbade him, because he followeth not with us. But Jesus saith unto him, Forbid him not: for he that is not against you is for you.*"* In the appendix to S. Mark's Gospel the power to cast out devils is included among the "*signs*" which "*shall follow them that believe.*"† It cannot be questioned that in that age the practice of exorcism was the normal characteristic of religious prominence. It attracted general notice, and provoked little, if any, criticism. Exorcism perpetuated itself in the Church, while every other type of miracle quickly ceased. The Roman Church to this day includes among the "minor orders" of clergy that of the exorcist. In early times this mysterious power was not limited to an Order, but supposed to belong to every Christian as such. Now exorcism was precisely the form of miracle which least affected the normal course of human life. It is to this conclusion that I would bring my discussion. Miracles played a very small part in the actual experience of the Church. The crises of need, through which then, as in later times, Christians had to pass, were met by the commonplace resources of prudence and charity. No miracle provided relief for the poor Christians of Judæa during the famine which Agabus foretold. Such relief as came to them was obtained from the collection in the Gentile Churches, which S. Paul promoted with such ardour. The Apostle himself never drew upon his miraculous

* *Ibid*. ix. 49, 50. † S. Mark xvi. 17.

powers for that sustenance which he earned by his labour as a tentmaker, or, where that was impossible, accepted as a gift from the most devoted of his converts. Always miracles were "*signs*," not exemptions for the Church from normal terrestrial conditions, still less the decoration of individuals; but "*signs*," convincing indications of superhuman power mercifully offered to the heathen, to whom in the first instance, without traditions and without commendations, the gospel was presented. "Miracles," it has been truly said, "are the swaddling clothes of the infant Churches." It is deeply significant that in the miraculous age the inspired Authors of the New Testament should have subordinated them to the more prosaic and enduring virtues of the Christian character. A few sentences, a few more vague references, are all that the Epistles contain about those miraculous powers which have loomed so large in the misty retrospect of history; but the sacred writers never tire of urging upon Christians the practical duties of that righteous life to which their discipleship committed them The "fruits of the Spirit" will remain the authentic marks of discipleship when miracles are but a faint memory. "*Love never faileth; but whether there be prophecies, they shall be done away; whether there be tongues, they shall cease: whether there be knowledge, it shall be done away.*" Miracles—it must never be forgotten—have been the familiar tokens of falsehood; and, historically, the claim to work miracles is inseparably connected with religious imposture. Our Lord prophesied that this should be so. "*There shall arise false Christs, and false prophets, and shall show great signs and wonders: so as to lead astray, if possible, even the elect."** S. Paul, in like manner, associates great displays of miraculous power with "*the lawless one,*" of whom he writes mysteriously to the Thessalonians, "*even he, whose coming is according to the working of Satan with all power and signs and lying wonders.*"† In the Sermon on the Mount our Saviour warns us that the power to work miracles may co-exist with a cold heart, and a dead faith, and an evil life. "*Many will say to Me in that day, Lord, Lord, did we not prophesy by Thy Name, and by Thy Name cast out devils, and by thy Name do many mighty works? And then will I profess unto them, I never knew you: depart from Me, ye that work iniquity.*"‡ It is this constant depreciation of miracles as compared with moral qualities which distinguishes the New Testament from most religious literature of succeeding ages. The closest to His Master's Heart of all the Apostles was S. John; and as S. Chrysostom long ago observed, no miracle is directly ascribed to him. It was no sign of grace in Simon Magus to offer money for the miraculous power which he observed in the Apostles, and which degraded those holy men in his mind to his own category of imposture. It would seem, however, that Simon Magus, rather than S. Peter, has determined the later estimate of prodigies in the Christian Church. So far from the apostolic standpoint have Christians travelled that now the rule of the Roman

---

* S. Matt. xxiv. 24.   † 2 Thess. ii. 9.
‡ S. Matt. vii. 22.

MIRACLES

Church has made the working of miracles the very test of sanctity.

The craving for the miraculous appears to be an unfailing evidence of religious decline. The history of all the great religions of the world will provide examples of this law. Christianity is no exception. The individual disciple, not less than the society of disciples, reveals its working. What is superstition but the craving for the miraculous? and when did superstition fail to disturb the moral perspective, and minister to weakening of character? It is said that in the heart of our sceptical modern civilization, notably in France and in the great cities of America, to a less extent but in growing measure in this country, quasi-miraculous movements are attracting no little attention, and drawing after them no small number of adherents. Spiritualism, theosophy, esoteric Buddhism, or by whatever other name these new Gospels of the Mysterious may be known —all at least have this in common with debased religion in every age, that they appeal to that lust for miracle which our Lord and His Apostles so constantly rebuked. Perhaps that circumstance would suffice to assure a reflective man that in those movements there is scanty promise for society. They will not minister strength to the will, or impose the restraints of principle upon the wayward appetites of our nature. In seeking after the miraculous men miss the obvious. Star-gazers are apt to find themselves in ditches. The one perpetual miracle, which is accessible to all, and which alone can sustain the searching criticism of the human conscience, is the miracle of a holy life. For there can be no mistake about the source or the witness of a holy life. Miracles in the common sense can be imitated and misunderstood; a holy life never. It is quite manifest to the simplest understanding, a message fresh from God, which commands the audience of every conscience. "*A good tree cannot bring forth evil fruit: neither can a corrupt tree bring forth good fruit.*" * Men know *that* in their inmost hearts, and therefore, in the long run, they do homage to righteousness. This is the normal witness of Christ's disciples; it is the only test of truth the world is authorised to demand, or the Church is able to offer. It is a real test; for a holy life is manifestly supernatural. "*No man can say, Jesus is Lord but in the Holy Spirit.*" † To own the Lordship of the Crucified in any worthy and effectual measure means much, too much for mere human virtue, howsoever buttressed by high traditions and helped forward by large approbation, *so* much that only the grace of God, earnestly sought in prayer and discipline, can enable anyone to achieve it. It means the miraculous life inspired by the miraculous presence. "*Know ye not as to your own selves,*" reproachfully asks S. Paul of the Corinthians, "*that Jesus Christ is in you? unless indeed ye be reprobate.*" ‡ Beside *that* miracle all else is petty.

---

* S. Matt. vii. 18.   † 1 Cor. xii. 3.   ‡ 2 Cor. xiii. 5.

CHAPTER VI.

THE CHRISTIAN PROPHETS

NO one can read the New Testament, and especially the Pauline Epistles, with any care and not perceive the great place which in the Apostolic Church was filled by the prophets. The Church is said to be "*built upon the foundation of the apostles and prophets, Christ Jesus Himself being the chief corner stone.*"* In the Apocalypse we read that "*the testimony of Jesus is the spirit of prophecy.*" † It would be easy to multiply quotations; but there is no need. Their importance is sufficiently manifest, but their precise functions are not so clear. The language of S. Paul seems contradictory. On the one hand, he speaks of the "*prophets*" as constituting a distinct class; both in the Corinthian and in the Ephesian lists of Christian ministers they are placed next in order to the "*apostles.*" "*And God hath set some in the church, first apostles, secondly prophets, thirdly teachers,*" is the language of the one; "*And He gave some to be apostles; and some prophets; and some evangelists; and some pastors and teachers*"— is that of the other. In 1 Cor. xiv. the "*prophets*" appear as a very well-defined group, accustomed to

---
* Eph. ii. 20.   † Rev. xix. 10.

take an important share in the conduct of public worship, and perhaps occupying official seats in the Christian assembly. On the other hand, the Apostle contemplates the prophesying of the entire Church as a desirable and not improbable contingency. "*For ye all can prophesy one by one,*" he writes, "*that all may learn, and all may be comforted.*" * He bids the Corinthians "*desire earnestly to prophesy.*" † Not even women were excluded from the prophetic gift. Nay, S. Paul contemplates their publicly exercising it. "*But every woman praying or prophesying with her head unveiled dishonoureth her head.*" ‡ In the Acts we read of S. Philip the Evangelist that he "*had four daughters which did prophesy.*" § The contradiction, however, is only on the surface, and arises rather from our preconceived notions of Church order than from any obscurity in the language of S. Paul. Three things are quite evident. The prophets were not an order of the ministry in the traditional sense of the phrase. I see no reason for thinking that they received any formal Ordination, though I observe that the contrary is very commonly assumed. Moreover, the prophetic inspiration might come, and often did come, to private Christians of both sexes. Finally, that inspiration, though occasional and, so to say, intermittent, was considered to permanently attach to whomsoever it had once been given. The prophets, both men and women, were not an ordained official ministry, but they were a definite, recognized class, recruited

* 1 Cor. xiv. 31. † *Ibid.* 39.
‡ 1 Cor. xi. 5. § Acts xxi. 2.

supernaturally from the body of the faithful. The prominence of the prophets in the Church was very brief; in the Pastoral Epistles prophecy is just alluded to. S. Timothy is reminded of "*the prophecies which went before on him*,"* and which apparently marked him out for the work of the ministry, as on a memorable occasion S. Paul himself had been marked out for a missionary venture by the prophets of Antioch. In the same epistle prophecy is spoken of as associated with S. Timothy's ordination. "*Neglect not the gift that is in thee, which was given thee by prophecy, with the laying on of the hands of the presbytery.*"† How far prophecy continued in the Church after the Apostolic age had ended it is by no means easy to determine. The evidence is conflicting. Canon Gore makes the most of it in this passage:—

"The gift of prophecy continued as a recognized endowment of the Church into the second or third centuries. Certain people were recognized as prophets, *e.g.*, Ignatius, Polycarp, and Quadratus.... As in the Apostolic Church there had been prophetesses, so too they had their late representative in Ammia at Philadelphia. S. Irenæus, besides denouncing false prophets, protests against those who would banish prophecy from the Church under pretence of exposing such pretenders, and witnesses, like Justin Martyr, to the continuance of prophetic

* κατὰ τὰς προαγούσας ἐπὶ σὲ προφητείας. (1 Tim. i. 18.) See Dr. HORT's very interesting explanation of this passage in *Christian Ecclesia*, p. 181 foll. He translates "which led the way to thee."

† 1 Tim. iv. 14. μὴ ἀμέλει τοῦ ἐν σοὶ χαρίσματος, ὃ ἐδόθη σοι διὰ προφητείας μετὰ ἐπιθέσεως τῶν χειρῶν τοῦ πρεσβυτερίου.

gifts in his day. . . . As a matter of fact, however, the genuine gift seems to have become exceedingly rare; Origen speaks of slight traces of it remaining to his time."*

The functions of the prophets and the range of their prophecy may be gathered from the New Testament. They succeeded to the character of the Jewish prophets of the former dispensation, and modelled their behaviour on the precedents of the Old Testament. Thus they were considered to stand in such immediate relationship with the Almighty that their inspired directions could not be resisted without impiety. As a matter of fact the conduct of the Church and of individuals was determined at crises by the revelations of the prophets. The history of S. Paul provides many instances of such prophetic guidance. His long residence at Corinth was thus determined by a vision in which Christ exhorted him to constancy and assured him of success. Perhaps the most remarkable account of this government by revelation is the following: "*And they went through the region of Phrygia and Galatia,* HAVING BEEN FORBIDDEN OF THE HOLY GHOST *to speak the Word in Asia; and when they were come over against Mysia they assayed to go into Bithynia;* AND THE SPIRIT OF JESUS SUFFERED THEM NOT; *and passing by Mysia, they came down to Troas. And* A VISION APPEARED TO PAUL *in the night. There was a man of Macedonia standing, beseeching him, and saying, Come over into Macedonia and help us. And when he had seen the vision, straightway we sought to go forth into*

* GORE, *The Christian Ministry,* pp. 396, 397.

Macedonia, concluding that GOD HAD CALLED US *for to preach the Gospel unto them.*"* The supernatural guidance is assumed as a matter of course. God was very near to Christians in the Apostolic age: and His normal instruments of communication with the Church were the prophets. In 1 Cor. xiv. S. Paul contemplates Divine revelations as quite naturally to be looked for in the Christian assembly. "*Let the prophets speak by two or three, and let the others discern. But if a revelation be made to another sitting by, let the first keep silence. For ye all can prophesy one by one, that all may learn, and all may be comforted: and the spirits of the prophets are subject to the prophets.*" Here the Apostle indicates that the Church was the critic as well as the recipient of prophetic communications, and that apart from special revelations the prophets had messages to deliver in the assembly. By some unmistakable tokens the advent of a new revelation in the prophet's mind made itself known: the more normal prophesying was suspended in order that the most recent "*Word of the Lord*" might be delivered.

What was the nature of what I have called, for lack of a better phrase, normal prophesying? Perhaps we have the answer in the text, "*He that prophesieth speaketh unto men edification, and comfort, and consolation.*"† S. Ambrose, three centuries later, regarded interpreters of the Scriptures as the representatives of the prophets. Perhaps

---

* Acts xvi. 6-10.

† 1 Cor. xiv. 3. ὁ δὲ προφητεύων ἀνθρώποις λαλεῖ οἰκοδομὴν καὶ παράκλησιν καὶ παραμυθίαν.

preaching, especially that which is either addressed directly to the conscience of the sinner with a view to his conversion, or is directed to the devout understanding of the believer in order to edify him by deeper knowledge of Divine truth, presents the nearest modern parallel to the ordinary prophesying of the Apostolic Church. The New Testament contains a specimen of Apostolic prophecy in the Apocalypse. That book, in the words of Weizäcker, "has preserved for us a complete picture of the prophetic work of the Church."* The central subject of all prophecy was "the expected appearing of Christ, and everything that had the most remote connexion with it in the shape of preparation, associations, and consequences." The Apostolic Church lived in the light of that eager hope, guided itself by the rule of that masterful motive, purified itself by the terror of that tremendous thought, "*Maran-atha, the Lord is at hand.*" Of this belief the prophets were the exponents: prophecy may be said to have waned and passed with the conviction of Christ's speedy return. Only when that distracting delusion had disappeared could the Church attain that permanence of constitution which protracted residence in the world demanded.

The Church is the critic of prophecy. We are reminded at once that in Apostolic times, as ever since, over against every genuine element of Church life has arisen some base counterfeit. Prophecy was no exception to the general rule. "*Let the prophets speak by two or three, and let the others discern,*" or

* *Apostolic Age*, vol. ii. p. 269, E.T.

THE CHRISTIAN PROPHETS 245

discriminate.* We learn that among the *charismata* of the Holy Ghost there was one which specifically had reference to the critical function of the Church— "*discernings of spirits*" (διακρίσεις πνευμάτων). Those members of the Church who possessed this special gift were charged to exercise it in the assembly. The inspired critics of prophecy were not left without any guidance.

"Assuredly," observes M. Godet, "it is not for nothing that the Apostle has begun this whole discussion on the spiritual gifts by indicating the precise character which distinguishes true and false inspirations, by recalling that the one have as their common character and essence this cry of adoration —*Jesus, Lord!* whilst the others tend to the humiliation and rejection of Jesus. It was sufficient then to place every prophecy in relation with this centre of the entire Christian revelation, the Person of Christ, and to see to what result the prophecy which had been heard tended to make little of Him or to glorify Him." †

We may here consider the passage in the Epistle to the Romans. ‡ "*Having gifts differing according*

---

* 1 Cor. xiv. 29.

† ii. p. 206. *Cf.* M. RÉNAN (*S. Paul*, p. 412), who gives a different application to the "discerning of spirits."

"Quelques sons bizarres que prononçaient les glossolales, et où se mélaient le grec, le syriaque, les mots anathema, maranatha, les noms de Jésus, de 'Seigneur,' embarrassaient fort les simples gens. Paul, consulté à ce sujet, pratique ce qu'on appelait 'le discernement des esprits,' et cherche à démêler dans ce jargon confus ce qui pouvait venir de l'Esprit et ce qui n'en venait pas."

‡ ἔχοντες δὲ χαρίσματα κατὰ τὴν χάριν τὴν δοθεῖσαν ἡμῖν διάφορα, εἴτε προφητείαν κατὰ τὴν ἀναλογίαν τῆς πίστεως.

to the grace that was given unto us, whether prophecy, let us prophesy according to the proportion of our faith" [or perhaps "*of the faith.*"] The general drift of the passage seems to prohibit the common and attractive interpretation, which would understand the Apostle to refer to the body of revealed truth, and to warn against any distortion of its balanced harmony. Rather S. Paul is urging the duty of modesty. The prophet is to gauge accurately his own spiritual possibilities. He must not "strain after effects for which his faith is insufficient."*

So understood the passage may best be compared with the Apostle's insistence in the Corinthian Epistle upon the responsibility of the prophet for the orderly exercise of his *charisma*. "*The spirits of the prophets are subject to the prophets.*"† In marked contrast to the frenzied rhapsodies of the pagan priests of Oracular shrines the Christian prophet never lost his self-control in the access of inspiration. S. Paul himself lays emphasis on this fundamental distinction. "*Ye know that when ye were Gentiles ye were led away unto those dumb idols, howsoever ye might be led. Wherefore I give you to understand, that no man speaking in the Spirit of God saith, Jesus is anathema: and no man can say, Jesus is Lord, but in the Holy Spirit.*"‡ The test of prophecy, then, was its bearing upon the Person of Jesus Christ. S. John speaks to the same effect in his first Epistle, "*Beloved, believe not every spirit,*

---

* *Vide* SANDAY and HEADLAM, *Romans*, p. 354. A very learned, interesting, and serviceable commentary.

† xiv. 32.   ‡ 1 Cor. xii. 2, 3.

but prove the spirits whether they are of God: because many false prophets are gone out into the world. Hereby know ye the Spirit of God: every spirit which confesseth that Jesus Christ is come in the flesh is of God: and every spirit which confesseth not Jesus is not of God: and this is the Spirit of antichrist, whereof ye have heard that it cometh: and now it is in the world already."* The author of the so-called second Epistle of S. Peter, in like manner, makes disloyalty to our Saviour the mark of the false prophet. "*But there arose false prophets also among the people, as among you also there shall be false teachers, who shall privily bring in destructive heresies, denying even the Master that bought them, bringing upon themselves swift destruction.*"† Thus the test of prophecy was doctrinal; under the actual circumstances of the time, however, it was not less truly a moral test, for the heresies to which the sacred writers refer had direct connexion with the practical question, Does discipleship necessitate righteousness? In the strong phrase of S. Jude the false prophets were "*ungodly men, turning the grace of our God into lasciviousness, and denying our only Master and Lord, Jesus Christ.*"

The moral test of the Gospels thus inevitably became the doctrinal test of the Epistles. The Lordship of Jesus involves the reign of righteousness; repudiation of righteousness is the practical expression of apostacy from Christ. "*Beware of false prophets,*" so ran the warning in the Sermon on the Mount, "*which come to you in sheep's clothing, but*

* 1 John iv. 1-3.   † 2 Peter ii. 1.

inwardly are ravening wolves. By their fruits ye shall know them." As if His eyes were resting on the history of His Church, marking the baleful tendency to drive the moral into the background and set up arbitrary tests of doctrinal orthodoxy and ecclesiastical allegiance, He went on to warn us in words of merciless lucidity to be under no delusions. Discipleship did not consist in public acknowledgment of His Lordship, nor were its evidences to be sought in ardour of profession, in zeal of active work, in large apparent success, but always and everywhere in the moral obedience which induces righteousness. "*Not every one that saith unto Me, Lord, Lord, shall enter into the kingdom of heaven: but he that doeth the will of My Father which is in heaven.*" It was then a thoroughly sound instinct which led the early Church in laying down definite rules for the regulation of the prophets to make everything turn on the practical and obvious matter of conduct. The rules laid down in *The Teaching of the Twelve Apostles* insist upon a righteous life as the unfailing test of the genuine prophet. "Not every one that speaketh in the spirit is a prophet, but only if he have the behaviour of the Lord. By their behaviour then shall the false prophet and the prophet be known. . . .

"And every prophet that teacheth the truth if he doeth not what he teacheth is a false prophet.

"But whosoever saith in the spirit, Give me money or any other things, ye shall not hearken to him, but if he bid to give for others that lack, let no one judge him."*

* Chap. xi.

Prophecy, we have said, finds its modern form in preaching. We may agree with S. Chrysostom that* "now we retain only the symbols of those gifts" which cast so bright a lustre on the Apostolic Church. In his day it would appear that the Pauline rule was still followed. "For now also," he says, "we speak two or three, and by course, and when one is silent another begins. But these are only signs and memorials of those things. Wherefore when we begin to speak, the people respond '*with Thy Spirit*,' indicating that of old they thus used to speak, not of their own wisdom, but moved by the Spirit. But not so now (I speak of mine own case so far). But the present Church is like a woman who hath fallen from her former prosperous days, and in many respects retains the symbols only of that ancient prosperity, displaying, indeed, the re-

---

* Hom. XXXVI. 4 in 1 Cor. (*Opera*, x. p. 395. Paris, 1837.) The Saint gives a lively picture of the Church in Antioch :—

"There the very houses were churches; but now the church itself is a house, or rather worse than any house. For in a house one may see much good order, since both the mistress of the house is seated on her chair with all seemliness, and the maidens weave in silence, and each of the domestics hath his appointed task in hand. But here great is the tumult, great the confusion, and our assemblies differ in nothing from a vintner's shop, so loud is the laughter, so great the disturbance; as in baths, as in markets, the cry and tumult is universal. And these things are here only; since elsewhere it is not permitted even to address one's neighbour in the Church, not even if one have received back a long absent friend; but these things are done without, and very properly." He says that the church had become a trysting place for profligates, for business men making bargains, for scandal-bearers, and the purveyors of political gossip. The whole description is a suggestive comment on Church life in the "golden age" of that "undivided Church," which some people would make the norm of our doctrine and discipline.

positories and caskets of her golden ornaments, but bereft of her wealth; such an one doth the present Church resemble." So S. Chrysostom, whom all Christendom for fifteen centuries has venerated as the prince of Christian preachers. What words of humility shall be lowly enough to bewail our present degradation! The glorious rhapsody of inspiration, the vision which opened heaven, the unutterable ecstasy, the intuition of truth so powerful and so clear as to constitute a revelation of God, the Divine insight into the hearts of men—these are no longer ours, or are ours so faintly and so rarely that in the common course of our Church life they escape notice, yet something remains. Still the Christian preacher's function is prophetic. He is set to proclaim, to justify, and (alas! for the weakness of mortal man) to illustrate the Lordship of Jesus; still, in the Church "*he that prophesieth speaketh unto men edification, and comfort, and consolation.*" And still the old test of prophecy holds true of preaching, "*No man speaking in the Spirit of God saith, Jesus is anathema: and no man can say, Jesus is Lord, but in the Holy Spirit.*" What is the general drift and tendency of the preaching? Does it bring home to men's consciences as the very central fact of existence the presence in their midst of Jesus Christ— living, loving, ruling? Men clamour for much from the preacher. They seek for eloquence, for originality, for sensation, for pathos, sometimes (though this is not often) for honesty and learning, and they criticise freely the preacher's performances; but do they remember his real function? do they compassionate his awful lot? do they in any measure help him to preserve single and inviolate his loyalty to Him, whose representative and mouthpiece he is? In those first days prophecy, as we have seen, was no mere function of an official ministry, it was poured out on every receptive spirit. Should it not still be so? Public Order, of course, will preclude the preaching of private Christians; the conditions of this late age — the complexity of its problems, the mass and variety of its knowledge—would deter untrained men from the task, even if no law prohibited. But public preaching does not exhaust the prophetic mission of the Church. Still the Pauline counsel may be offered, "*desire earnestly to prophesy*," for the intercourse of common life is rich in opportunities of that service which prophecy can render, and prophecy alone. It is not only in Church that the words are true, "*he* (or, for the matter of that, she) *that prophesieth speaketh unto men edification, and comfort, and consolation*," though the scene of that prophecy be the lowliest home, or the commonest intercourse of business, or the comradeship of recreation. And still the essence of prophecy changes not. Then and now, by preacher or by private Christian, in public or in private, the old definition holds true: "*the testimony of Jesus is the Spirit of prophecy*."

CHAPTER VII.

WOMEN IN THE CHURCH

THE first Corinthian epistle deals at some length with the relation of the sexes in the union of marriage and in the intercourse of discipleship. The Apostle was led to devote so much attention to the subject by the direct request of the Corinthian Christians. Evidently in Corinth the position assigned to women by the Gospel was much discussed and largely misunderstood. The normal relations of the sexes seemed to be irreconcilable with the new conditions introduced by Christianity. If, as S. Paul was wont to insist, "*there can be no male and female* *in Christ Jesus*,*" that is, if the basal inequality of sex had been destroyed, then by what right could the ancient badges and limitations of inequality continue in the Christian community? Nay, how could the subordination of the female in the relationship of marriage be any longer insisted on? In Corinth we infer from the Epistles there was a strong party devoted to the advocacy of the extreme consequences of Christian equality. They would cancel the subjection based on the natural distinction of sex, and destroy at once and for ever the limitations

* Galatians iii. 28.

imposed by law and custom upon the activity of women. Against this party S. Paul ranged himself as an uncompromising opponent. He refused to recognize the claim of the Christian wife in the interest of devotion to repudiate the marriage bond;* he insisted on maintaining in the Church that public subordination of women which was established in the general custom of society;† he declined to allow the possession of high spiritual gifts to be made the plea for setting aside the decent reticence which ought always to mark the public behaviour of women.‡ S. Paul prevailed: his doctrine has determined the position of the female sex in Christian society; and it will undoubtedly be approved or condemned in proportion as that position is considered favourable or the reverse. It is notorious that a large and perhaps an increasing body of opinion inclines to regard the Apostle in no friendly spirit. He is a narrow Rabbinist, binding upon the infant Church the chains of his own præ-Christian prejudices; he is a hard celibate, infecting Christianity with his own personal contempt for the gentler side of human life; he is at bottom under the Apostle and the Christian always the Oriental, with the Oriental's conviction of the intrinsic inferiority of the weaker sex. In all this—it would be dishonest to deny—there is an element of truth. S. Paul's Rabbinic training undoubtedly affected his doctrine, as it certainly determined his arguments. His reasoning is obviously Rabbinic. It has been maintained with large justification that the intrinsic superiority of the single over

* vii. 3-5.   † xi. 3-16.   ‡ xiv. 34-36.

the married state is the underlying assumption of the seventh chapter. The Apostle would have been more than human if he had succeeded in wholly divesting himself of the prevailing Oriental notions about the female sex. We may allow that Weizäcker says truly :* " Paul did not in any way go beyond the conception of woman's position, which at bottom belonged to the whole ancient world," provided always that we have fairly grasped the new conditions under which in Christian circles that conception would have to find practical expression. In that process the conception itself would be necessarily modified and even transformed.

The Christian view of woman shaped itself under four powerful influences. In the first place stands the Evangelic Tradition. No one can read the Gospels and observe the place filled by women in the history of Jesus Christ and fail to perceive that a low view of woman, that any view short of the highest, is plainly incompatible with the Christian religion. We may remark in passing that the influence of the Gospels has tended to increase with the progress of time. As the truth about Jesus Christ became apparent to the understanding of believers, so the mystery of His Incarnation drew forth more and more their interest, and stimulated their devout reflexion. The central figure in the history of the Incarnation, our Lord Himself apart, is a woman—the Blessed Virgin Mary. It seems too evident to require proof that belief in the Incarnation involves the highest possible view of

* But see Appendix IV., " Celibacy."

woman. At the first preaching of the Gospel attention was mainly centred on the Crucifixion and Resurrection of our Lord; the facts connected with His miraculous Birth were little known, and, in any case, were not well adapted for the immediate purposes of the missionaries; but when the Evangelic Tradition had been committed to writing, and the Gospels, substantially in their present form, had been generally circulated, then the full meaning of the Incarnation began to reveal itself to the general body of Christians. There are in human life normal forces which ever tend to the degradation of women; assuredly those forces have been at work within the sphere of Christianity; but always behind them has stood this influence of the Gospel, appealing, and not in vain, to the conscience of discipleship, and restraining, where it cannot destroy, the power of evil. The Christian practice of publicly reading the Gospels in the regular worship of the Church has certainly secured from all danger of oblivion the evangelic prominence of women. The Virgin Mother of Bethlehem, the sisters of Bethany, the heroic mourners on Calvary, the holy women at the Tomb have been stamped ineffaceably on the memory of Christendom. Nay, as if to cut the roots of that cynicism which prompts low views of woman, the Gospel sets in prominence the pathetic figures of the adulteress and the harlot. The woman taken in adultery, that other woman whose sins He forgave *because she loved much*, the weeping Magdalen, from whom He drave the seven demons—who more precious than these to the thought of discipleship?

Who more potent to chasten the sensual, and quicken the despairing, and cleanse the polluted?

And next, there was the Christian doctrine of marriage. That doctrine, which was certainly insisted on from the first as an express commandment of Christ, must have revolutionized the position of women wherever it obtained acceptance. We may allow—what, indeed, seems to have been the fact—that the Jews, in spite of the technical lawfulness of polygamy, were practically in that age monogamists; we may recognize to the full whatever provisions for securing the rights of women the Jewish law contained; and even so it is impossible to overstate the importance of the change which our Lord effected by His Law of Marriage. Consider what is involved by the question of the Pharisees addressed to Christ, "*Is it lawful for a man to put away his wife for every cause?*" We are reminded at once on how low a level the marriage bond was then discussed. There was a standing dispute between the two great theological schools of the period on the question not whether divorce was permissible, but for what causes. "The Shammaites restricted them to the commission of an iniquitous action by the wife (probably adultery); the Hillelites, going to an opposite extreme, . . . inferred that a divorce was warranted even when the wife had only spoiled her husband's dinner. Rabbi Akiba endeavoured, in the same manner, to prove that a man might lawfully dismiss his wife if he found another more attractive."* How wide a

---

* EDERSHEIM, *History of the Jewish Nation*, p. 274.

chasm separates such licentious frivolity from the majestically simple Law of Christ. Yet that law at its first promulgation seemed intolerable, impossible, even to the disciples. "*If the case of the man is so with his wife, it is not expedient to marry,*"* they cried in consternation. A few years passed, and S. Paul, steeped in Rabbinic prejudices by his training, but liberated by the love of Christ, can write about marriage in those dignified and moving words, which have ever since been treasured by the Church as setting forth the true ideal of Christian marriage.

"*Wives, be in subjection unto your own husbands, as unto the Lord. For the husband is the head of the wife, as Christ also is the head of the Church, being Himself the saviour of the body. But as the Church is subject to Christ, so let the wives also be to their husbands in everything. Husbands, love your wives, even as Christ also loved the Church, and gave Himself up for it: that He might sanctify it, having cleansed it by the washing of water with the word, that He might present the Church to Himself a glorious Church, not having spot or wrinkle or any such thing; but that it should be holy and without blemish. Even so ought husbands also to love their own wives as their own bodies. He that loveth his own wife loveth himself: for no man ever hated his own flesh; but nourished and cherished it, even as Christ also the Church: because we are members of His body. For this cause shall a man leave his father and mother, and shall cleave to his wife: and the twain shall become one flesh. This mystery is*

---

* S. Matt. xix. 10.

great: but I speak in regard of Christ and of the Church. Nevertheless do ye also severally love each one his own wife even as himself: and let the wife see that she fear her husband." *

Now it is easy to perceive in this passage the traces of the Rabbinic influence under which the Apostle had been trained, but it is evident that the dominating principle is no longer Rabbinic. Marriage has been lifted out of the merely physical category in which the Rabbis placed it, and has been brought into direct relation with the very central belief of discipleship. It is no mean symbol of that mystic union which binds together Christ and the Church. Wifely love may take the character of that self-surrender in obedience which marks the Church's love for Christ. The husband's love may represent, and not unfaithfully, that self-surrender in sacrifice

---

* Eph. v. 22-33.

Dr. R. W. Dale has a lecture on this passage filled full of sound thought, tersely and eloquently expressed, *vide Ephesians*, pp. 349-377.

Canon Gore, in a recent volume, *The Epistle to the Ephesians*, pp. 212-228, discusses S. Paul's teaching on the subject of marriage with characteristic lucidity and force. He boldly maintains the inferiority of woman "in the moral qualities which are concerned with government—in justice, love of truth and judgment, stability and reasonableness." "To maintain that men and women are only physiologically different is to run one's head against the brick wall of fact and science, no less than against S. Paul's and S. Peter's principles."

For an extremely curious and characteristic exhortation to husbands and wives see S. Chrysostom's comment on this passage, Hom. XX. in Eph. (*Opera*, xi. p. 163). It indicates the profound difference between Eastern and Western standpoints, and gives an interesting view of domestic life in Constantinople in the fourth century. The preacher's preference for celibacy is not concealed, yet he draws an attractive picture of Christian marriage.

which marks Christ's love for the Church. The union in both cases is eternal, mysterious, spiritual.

In the third place there was the evident fact that the marvellous gifts of the Spirit were given to women as well as to men. It was impossible to maintain the inequality of the sexes when God Himself was plainly treating them as equal.

Finally, there was the logic of experience. In the history of S. Paul women played no insignificant part. Sometimes as opponents, sometimes as allies, he had to reckon with their influence. "*The devout women of honourable estate*" took the lead in driving him from Antioch in Pisidia; at Thessalonica, though the fury of the Jews was extreme, not a few of the "*chief women*" accepted the Gospel; among the noble-hearted Berœans, who heard without prejudice and searched the Scriptures for themselves, were many "*Greek women of honourable estate.*" Among the few converts at Athens, we are expressly told, was "*a woman named Damaris.*" The leading members of the Philippian Church were the two women, *Euodia and Syntyche*, whose rivalries caused some anxiety to the Apostle. He was on terms of close friendship with *Priscilla or Prisca*, whose importance may perhaps be inferred from the fact that she is generally named in front of her husband, Aquila. *Phœbe the deaconess of the Church in Cenchreœ*, is the subject of a separate and very eulogistic commendation in the Epistle to the Romans, and among the salutations which conclude that Epistle we find mention of the names of several Christian women, generally with a kind little comment added, "*Salute Mary, who bestowed much labour on you.*" "*Salute Tryphæna and Tryphosa, who labour in the Lord.*" "*Salute Persis, the beloved, which laboured much in the Lord,*" and so forth. All of these, if we may judge by their names, were slaves or freedwomen, but their importance in the Church had a better basis than that of social consequence. They were great in service and in suffering.

The expansion of the Church discovered new problems, in the solution of which women were indispensable. It is certain that in the Apostolic age the office, perhaps even the order of deaconesses, already existed.

"It is difficult," says M. de Pressensé, "to describe exactly the deaconesses of the primitive Church. They had their part in distributing alms and visiting the sick; undoubtedly also they were occupied with the Agapæ, and lent their aid to the deacons for whatever required their care in the conduct of public worship. We know that in the second century the deaconesses used to assist women at their Baptism. That custom, so convenient and so natural, must have been introduced into the Church from the first century. The widows above the age of sixty years registered on the roll of the Church, of whom S. Paul speaks in his first letter to Timothy, were probably deaconesses. In fact, we should not understand the duties which were imposed on them if we should think only of a regular assistance. On the contrary, nothing is more accordant with the spirit of the Apostolic Church than to give employment to the spirit of all its members, and to establish a holy reciprocity between the generous gifts made to poverty and the precious services which poverty can render. The widow was indeed better fitted than the virgin for the office of deaconess, for she had experience of human life, she knew its great sufferings, and found thus in her position a quite special aptitude for exercising a ministry of consolation."*

While, then, women secured their position within the Church on these firm foundations of principle and utility, the danger made its appearance that they should miss the lesson of their own success, and by intruding into spheres where, for fundamental reasons of physique and function, they had no place, should endanger their newly-acquired liberty. Among the Jewish Christians, perhaps, the Rabbinic Tradition was strong enough to counteract this peril; but among the freer and more licentious Gentiles the case was otherwise, and S. Paul found it necessary to exert his authority to maintain as consistent with Christian equality the subordination of the female sex. He insists on the use of the veil in the public assemblies. The point strikes us at first as scarcely adequate, and the argument has a somewhat fantastic appearance; but we should greatly err if we misconceived the real importance of the one or the permanent truth of the other. Veiling is but a fashion of dress, and has no abiding authority; but in that age veiling was the general custom of society, and represented, in the general mind, the vital and eternal interest of modesty. The question at stake

* DE PRESSENSÉ, *Le Siècle Apostolique*, ii. p. 243.

was really this: ought the Church of Christ to despise and disregard the established conventions of men in matters where the truth was not concerned? S. Paul's principle is stated in his exhortation to the Romans. "*Take thought for things honourable in the sight of all men.*" It is equally arrogant and uncharitable to offend against the legitimate custom of general society.

But there was more. The veil represented the fact of dependence, and its rejection argued revolt against the Divine government of the universe. "There exist three relations," comments M. Godet, "which form between them a kind of hierarchy: at the bottom, the purely human relation of man and woman; higher, the Divine-human relation of Christ and man; at the top, the wholly Divine relation between Christ and God. The common term by which Paul describes these three relations is that of *head*. This figurative expression includes two ideas: that of a community of life, and that of an inequality within that community. Thus between man and woman; by the tie of marriage there is formed between them the tie of a common life, but of such a kind that the one is the strong and directing element, the other the receptive and dependent element. It is the same in the relation between Christ and man. Formed by the tie of faith, it constitutes also a community of life in which are distinguished an active and directing principle, and a receptive and directed factor. An analogous relation presents itself higher still in the mystery of the Divine Essence. By the tie of sonship there is between Christ and God communion of Divine life, but of such kind that the communication (*l'impulsion*) proceeds from the Father, and that '*the Son can do nothing but what He seeth the Father doing.*'"*

In thus linking on the subordination of women, which he advocates, to the "vast system of subordination running through the universe" and ultimately arising from the very Being of God, the Apostle effectually guards against any distortion of his teaching into a denial of Christian equality. Subordination is one thing, inferiority is another. The one touches the order of life, the other the nature of men. Variety of function entails no inequality of dignity. Loss of dignity can only result from failure to perform specific function. This was S. Chrysostom's answer to the champion of those women's rights which consist in imitating the specific habits and activities of men, and it is the true answer. "But if any say, 'Nay, how can this be a shame to the women, if she mount up to the glory of the man?' we might make this answer, 'She doth not mount up, but rather falls from her own proper honour.' Since not to abide within our own limits, and the laws ordained of God, but to go beyond is not an addition, but a diminution . . . the woman acquireth not the man's dignity, but loseth even the woman's comeliness."†

S. Paul makes appeal to nature. He points to the broad physical distinction between the sexes,

---

* *Commentaire sur la* 1ʳᵉ *Épitre aux Corinthiens,* vol. ii. pp. 124-5.
† Hom. XXVI. in 1 Cor. (*Opera,* x. p. 272).

indicating distinctiveness of function, and necessitating a distinctive ordering of life, and he insists on respecting this natural dividing line between man and woman. Herein surely he asserts a principle of permanent importance. "Fanaticism defies nature" —I borrow the language of F. W. Robertson— "Christianity refines it and respects it. Christianity does not denaturalize, but only sanctifies and refines according to the laws of nature. Christianity does not destroy our natural instincts, but gives them a higher and a nobler direction. . . . And just as the white light of heaven does not make all things white, but the intenser it is so much more intense becomes the green, the blue, or the red; and just as the rain of heaven falling on tree and plant develops the vigour of each—every tree and herb *yielding seed after his kind*; and just as leaven does not change the mass into something new, but makes elastic and firm and springy that which was dull and heavy before; so the Spirit of Christ develops each nation, sex, and individual, according to their own nature, and not the nature of another —making man more manly and woman more womanly."*

There are many causes at work in modern society tending to what is called the "emancipation of woman": in so far as the movement follows on the lines of Christian principle it is indeed worthily styled a movement of emancipation. The functions of women more justly considered are seen to be more honourable and essential to the well-being of

* *Lectures on the Corinthians*, pp. 192, 193.

society; her fellowship with man in the holy marriage bond, rising above the merely physical union, is seen to extend into the intellectual and spiritual spheres. It becomes an equal comradeship. All this is thoroughly accordant with the Gospel. But the advocate of woman's emancipation does not always take that line. There is a note of contempt in the references to woman's sublimest function—motherhood; a note of rebellion against woman's true and normal relationship—wifehood; and that note is thoroughly anti-Christian. Whatsoever proceeds on the theory that woman is man's true, equal, honourable partner in bearing the strange burden of existence has its roots in the teaching of Jesus Christ. Whatsoever proceeds on the theory that woman is man's rival, meeting him on terms of competition in every sphere that is his, and repudiating as far as possible the inexorably marked limits of the sphere that is her own, ministers ultimately not to the enfranchisement, but to the degradation of woman.

CHAPTER VIII.

APOSTOLIC FINANCE

WE had occasion to observe in an earlier chapter that the Apostolic Church found ready to hand both in Jewish and in heathen society models of association upon which it might fashion its polity. It is, I think, sufficiently evident that in the organization of finance the Apostles adopted arrangements then existing in the world, and already familiar to their converts. Externally the Christian communities wore the aspect of those associations for almost every conceivable purpose, secular and religious, with which the Roman law was well acquainted.

"They had the same names for their meetings, and some of the same names for their officers. The basis of association, in the one case as in the other, was the profession of a common religion. The members, in the one case as in the other, contributed to or received from a common fund, and in many cases, if not universally, shared in a common meal. Admission was open in the one case as in the other, not only to free-born citizens, but to women and strangers, to freedmen and slaves."*

* HATCH, *Bampton Lectures*, p. 30.

APOSTOLIC FINANCE

The Church in those first days needed considerable funds in order to meet her normal expenditure. Putting together the scattered notices of the Epistles, we learn that this normal expenditure fell under five heads :—

(1) The maintenance of the ministry.
(2) Hospitality.
(3) Maintenance of widows.
(4) Relief of the poor.
(5) Assistance to the persecuted.

I. There can be no doubt whatever that from the first it has been held to be indispensable to the well-being of the Church that the task of ministry should be entrusted to a class of official teachers, who, laying aside other occupations, should make that task the business of their lives. The provision for the maintenance of these persons, thus excluded from the ordinary employments by which men are sustained, has necessarily been a first charge on the resources of the Church. S. Paul insists on "*the right*" of Christian ministers to their maintenance. "*Have we no right to eat and to drink?*"* he asks. They are workers, and, as such, entitled to their hire; they are ministers of religion, and, as such, entitled to "*have their portion with the altar.*" They confer great benefits on the congregations to whom they minister, and, as benefactors, they have a claim on the gratitude of the Church. "*What soldier ever serveth at his own charges? If we sowed unto you spiritual things, is it a great*

* μὴ οὐκ ἔχομεν ἐξουσίαν φαγεῖν καὶ πεῖν. 1 Cor. ix. 4.

matter if we shall reap your carnal things? Know ye not that they which minister about sacred things eat of the things of the temple, and they which wait upon the altar have their portion with the altar?"

These reasons and analogies might suffice, but in this case they are but the slighter part of the argument. The maintenance of the clergy is expressly commanded by Jesus Christ. "*Even so did the Lord ordain that they which proclaim the Gospel should live of the Gospel.*"†

But the justice of the claim could not exorcise its inherent peril. The devotion of the faithful facilitated the degradation of the clergy. There is a melancholy suggestiveness about the constant warnings against "*filthy lucre*" which are addressed to the clergy.‡ To many, even in that age, "*godliness*" had come to commend itself as "*a way of gain.*" That is not to say that the clergy were worse than other men, but that, being dedicated to the service of

---

* 1 Cor. ix. 13. This parallel between the Jewish priesthood and the Christian ministry is very suggestive of a clear and coherent doctrine of "Holy Orders." It is easy to make too much of this; but at present, in some quarters, there seems a disposition to make too little.

† 1 Cor. ix. 14. οὕτως καὶ ὁ κύριος διέταξεν τοῖς τὸ εὐαγγέλιον καταγγέλλουσιν ἐκ τοῦ εὐαγγελίου ζῆν.

‡ *Cf.* S. Paul's words to the Ephesian presbyters, Acts xx. 33, and the qualification for a "bishop" in 1 Tim. iii. 3, "no lover of money," ἀφιλάργυρον: for a "deacon," *ibid.* 8, "not greedy of filthy lucre," μὴ αἰσχροκερδεῖς. The Apostle's earnest warning against "the love of money" seems to be suggested by covetous religious teachers. S. Peter also exhorts the presbyters against base motives of action. "Tend the flock of God which is among you, exercising the oversight, not of constraint, but willingly, according unto God; nor yet for filthy lucre, but of a ready mind." (1 Peter v. 2.)

eternity, they yet were as the rest of men, whose business is directly with the things of this world. There is only one thing more repulsive than a coveteous, worldly clergyman, and that is the coveteous, worldly layman who denounces him, and glows with a spurious moral zeal in the performance. The clergyman's sacred profession neither alters his nature nor diminishes his temptations. It but adds immensely to his responsibilities, and enhances the gravity of his failures. The Church is bound to "maintain" the clergy in such wise that they are enabled to do their work efficiently, beyond that the precedent of the Apostolic Church does not advance.*

II. The duty of hospitality is frequently insisted on in the Epistles. "*In love of the brethren be tenderly affectioned one to another . . . communicating to the necessities of the saints; given to hospitality.*"† "*Let love of the brethren continue. Forget not to show love unto strangers: for thereby some have entertained angels unawares.*"‡ It is not hard to understand the reasons of this insistence. In a literal sense, which we, in these mild times, can with difficulty imagine, Christians were then "*pilgrims and strangers in the world.*" They were thrown back on themselves for the good offices of society which their pagan neigh-

---

* Let it be remembered that ministerial efficiency is not secured when the clergy are so poorly paid as to be unable to purchase books and sustain intellectual interests. At this moment, partly owing to poverty, partly to other causes, the Church of England is threatened with an ignorant clergy. In our case the mischief is particularly serious because the professional training of the English clergy is almost nil, and they therefore depend for most of their theological knowledge on their studies after Ordination.

† Rom. xii. 10, 13.   ‡ Heb. xiii. 1, 2.

bours either could not or would not render. The Christian "*strangers*" who, pursuing their errands of business or pleasure, passed to and fro between the great cities of antiquity, looked to the Church for friendly entertainment.

"Every one of those strangers who bore the Christian name had therein a claim to hospitality. For Christianity was, and grew because it was, a great fraternity. The name "*brother*," by which a Jew addressed his fellow-Jew, came to be the ordinary designation by which a Christian addressed his fellow-Christian. It vividly expressed a real fact. For, driven from city to city by persecution, or wandering from country to country an outcast or a refugee, a Christian found, wherever he went in the community of his fellow-Christians, a welcome and hospitality."* The generosity of the Church was speedily abused, and precautions against imposture had to be devised. The use of "*letters of commendation*"† was introduced. Of these we have a specimen in the Epistle to the Romans, "*I commend unto you Phœbe our sister, who is a servant of the Church that is at Cenchreæ, that ye receive her in the Lord, worthily of the saints, and that ye assist her in whatsoever matter she may have need of you; for she herself also hath been a succourer of many, and of mine own self.*"‡ The Bishop was in the early Church specially charged with the duty of organizing the hospitality of the community over which he presided, and the memory

---

* HATCH, *Bampton Lectures*, p. 44.

† 2 Cor. iii. 1. ἢ μὴ χρῄζομεν ὥς τινες συστατικῶν ἐπιστολῶν πρὸς ὑμᾶς ἢ ἐξ ὑμῶν.   ‡ Rom. xvi. 1-3.

of the fact is still perpetuated in the question addressed to the Bishop in the Consecration Service. "Will you show yourself gentle, and be merciful for Christ's sake to poor and needy people, and to all strangers destitute of help?" In the fourth century we find "guest-houses" among the institutions of the Church.

III. The maintenance of widows is proved by the regulations on the matter contained in the pastoral Epistles, and by the account of the institution of the Seven Deacons in the sixth chapter of the Acts, "*Let none be enrolled as a widow under threescore years old, having been the wife of one man, well-reported of for good works; if she hath brought up children, if she hath used hospitality to strangers, if she hath washed the saints' feet, if she hath relieved the afflicted, if she hath diligently followed every good work.*"*

IV. The relief of the poor, at all times a heavy charge, was at intervals rendered extremely burdensome by sudden and extensive calamities. Such an interval of special trial had necessitated the "*collection*" frequently referred to in the Corinthian Epistles. We must remember that poverty was at that time existing on a scale of which we now have no experience. "It was the crisis of the economical history of the Western world. There grew and multiplied a new class in Græco-Roman society—the class of paupers." At a slightly later period the Roman Government exerted itself with vigour to deal with this class. Private benevolence seems to have co-operated with

---

* 1 Tim. v. 9, 10.

the State; but the economic condition of the Roman Empire was incurably rotten, and all efforts were unavailing against the decay of society from within.

Christianity, then, was born into a world groaning under the problem of poverty, and it made special appeal to the poverty-stricken; the Church became their natural home. The famous "community of goods," of which we read in the Acts, and which exercises so powerful a fascination over men's minds still, at least testifies to the poverty of the earliest converts, and the strenuous efforts made to relieve it. In face of the silence of the Epistles, we should scarcely be justified in understanding the narrative in the Acts as meaning more than an extraordinary outburst of liberality. It was a literal carrying out by the richer Christians of Christ's counsel to the young man with great possessions. "*If thou wouldest be perfect, go, sell that thou hast, and give to the poor, and thou shalt have treasure in heaven; and come follow Me.*" Almsgiving became the most indispensable of Christian virtues. Both S. James and S. John propose it as the very test of genuine discipleship. "*If a brother or sister be naked*"— writes the former, and his words have a particular importance as emanating from the very scene of the so-called 'community of goods'—"*and in lack of daily food, and one of you say unto them, Go in peace, be ye warmed and filled; and yet ye give them not the things needful to the body: what doth it profit? Even so faith, if it have not works, is dead in itself.*"*
"*Whoso hath the world's goods*"—writes the latter—

* James ii. 15, 16.

"*and beholdeth his brother in need, and shutteth up his compassion from him, how doth the love of God abide in him?*"* The opinion of the sub-Apostolic Church is reflected in these words of an anonymous writer of the time, "Fasting is better than prayer, almsgiving is better than fasting; blessed is the man who is found perfect therein, for almsgiving lightens the weight of sin."†

V. Finally, there were the prisoners and other victims of persecution. To these reference is made in the Epistle to the Hebrews. "*Remember them that are in bonds, as bound with them; them that are evil-entreated, as being yourselves also in the body.*"‡ Within the period covered by the Epistles persecution on any general scale hardly existed; later, when the Imperial Power had thrown itself into the attempt to violently suppress the Christian religion, the care for the victims of persecution in the mines and in the prisons, as also of the wives and children deprived by the persecutor of their natural protectors, became a matter of the first importance.

If these were the normal needs, what were the normal sources of income? We may, I think, distinguish three. In the first place, were the donations of wealthy members of the Church. S. Timothy is specially bidden to stir up the richer Christians to the duty of munificent giving.

* 1 John iii. 17.
† *Vide* the so-called Second Epistle of Clement, c. 16. It may be regarded as "the earliest Christian homily extant." Bishop Lightfoot assigns it "with some confidence to the first half of the second century."
‡ xiii. 3.

T

"*Charge them that are rich in this present world, that they be not high-minded, nor have their hope set on the uncertainty of riches, but on God, who giveth us richly all things to enjoy: that they do good, that they be rich in good works, that they be ready to distribute, willing to communicate; laying up in store for themselves a good foundation against the time to come, that they may lay hold on the life which is life indeed.*"* Especially in the first beginnings of the Church the self-renouncing bounty of rich converts would be the main financial resource. The occurrences at Jerusalem were probably reproduced less conspicuously elsewhere. "*As many as were possessors of lands or houses sold them, and brought the prices of the things that were sold, and laid them at the Apostle's feet; and distribution was made unto each, according as anyone had need.*"† But in the nature of things this source of income could not permanently provide for the needs of the Church. Rich enthusiasts, once having resigned their property, could henceforth do but little to meet an expenditure which would be continually on the increase. The devotion of first beginnings does not commonly survive them. As the Church settled her organization on a normal basis, she had need for another and securer source of income. This she found in the regular offerings of her members. The collection, which originally was suggested by the distress of the famine-stricken brethren in Judæa, would almost inevitably develop into a permanent institution. "*Now concerning the collection* (λογίας) *for the saints*—writes S. Paul—

* 1 Tim. vi. 17-19. † Acts iv. 34, 35.

as I gave order (διέταξα) to the Churches of Galatia, so also do ye. Upon the first day of the week let each one of you lay by him (παρ' ἑαυτῷ τιθέτω) in store, as he may prosper, that no collections be made when I come. And when I arrive, whomsoever ye shall approve by letters, them will I send to carry your bounty unto Jerusalem; and if it be meet for me to go also, they shall go with me."* This passage deserves careful consideration. The object of the collection is first stated: it is "*for the saints*"; in the Roman Epistle, where the same matter is dealt with, it is more precisely stated to be "*for the poor among the saints that are at Jerusalem.*"† S. Paul characteristically places the collection on a basis of principle. The Jews had a special claim on the bounty of the Gentiles. "*For if the Gentiles have been made partakers of their spiritual things, they owe it to them also to minister unto them in carnal things.*" Perhaps we may again recognize the influence of his Rabbinic training. We are told that " collections were made among the Jews in foreign nations, for the poor Rabbins dwelling in Judæa, in the same manner as they were made among Christians in foreign nations for the poor Jews converted to Christianity in Judæa."‡ Then the method of making the collection is laid down. There is to be a weekly offering proportioned to income as reckoned by the Christian contributor in the sight of God. The gift must be honestly assessed, willingly given. "*Let each man do according as he hath

---

* 1 Cor. xvi. 1-4. † Rom. xv. 26.
‡ *Vide* J. LIGHTFOOT, *Works*, vol. xii. p. 556. London, 1825.

purposed in his heart, not grudgingly or of necessity, for God loveth a cheerful giver."* The Apostle insists on the religious solemnity of these weekly contributions. It does not seem clear whether the Corinthians were to bring their weekly offerings into the assembly, and there present them, or lay them by at home against the Apostle's arrival. In the next century the collection was, as it is still, publicly made at the Holy Communion. S. Justin describes it in these words, which will serve to illustrate what we have said as to the expenditure of the Church :—

"On the so-called day of the Sun there is a meeting of all of us who live in cities or the country, and the memoirs of the Apostles or the writings of the prophets are read, as long as time allows. Then when the reader has ceased, the president gives by word of mouth his admonition and exhortation to follow these excellent things. Afterwards we all rise at once and offer prayers; and, as I said, when we have ceased to pray, bread is brought, and wine and water, and the president likewise offers up prayers and thanksgivings to the best of his power, and the people assents with its Amen. Then follows the distribution to each and the partaking of that for which thanks were given, and to them that are absent a portion is sent by the hand of the deacons. Of those that are well-to-do and willing every one gives what he will according to his own purpose, and the collection is deposited with the president, and he it is that succours orphans and widows, and

* 2 Cor. ix. 7.

those that are in want through sickness or any other cause, and those that are in bonds, and the strangers that are sojourning, and in short he has the care of all that are in need." (*Apol.* i. c. 67.) This passage was written rather less than a century after S. Paul wrote the Corinthian Epistles, and it may be taken to represent fairly the practice of the sub-Apostolic Church.

It is eminently deserving notice how carefully the Apostle provides for the efficient administration of the money collected. The Corinthians are to elect persons in whom they had confidence, and to these the charge of the money is to be entrusted. S. Paul will not run any risks of suspicion which has even a semblance of justification. "*Whomsoever ye shall approve by letters, them will I send to carry your bounty to Jerusalem.*" He states the principle on which he acted in the second Epistle, "*avoiding this, that any man should blame us in the matter of this bounty which is ministered by us: for we take thought for things honourable, not only in the sight of the Lord, but also in the sight of men.*"[*] It had been well for the Church if this Apostolic principle had been allowed to govern her finance. Unhappily the precise contrary has been the case. Ecclesiastical finance is commonly a by-word among business men for incompetence, extravagance, and a species of unctuous dishonesty. That this impression rather represents the past than the present is, I think, certain; the system on which the special funds (for the rest is in chaos) of the Church are now

[*] 2 Cor. viii. 20, 21.

managed is framed on business models, and often administered by able men of business. But as much cannot be said for the countless semi-religious schemes of benevolence, which raise and expend immense sums of money. It is the duty of every man who cares for the good name of religion and the interest of philanthropy to withhold support from all financially unsatisfactory projects of piety or benevolence. The greatest possible publicity ought always to attach to the management of public funds. Unhappily the finance of the Church is still to the mass of men a veiled and suspected mystery. The most vigilant guard should be maintained against anything which can wound consciences or provoke contemptuous criticism. *Now* the clergy, in their efforts to raise funds for Church work, are everywhere emulating the arts of the cheap-jack and the advertising agent. We can imagine the indignant amazement with which S. Paul would have contemplated a modern bazaar. What words of strong scorn would have rushed from his lips! It may fairly be questioned whether the Church would not better fulfil her mission by worshipping again, as at the first, in private houses and beneath the open heaven, than by so degrading herself in order to raise money for costly fabrics. But the blame must not fall on the clergy alone. Let blame fall on them in the first place, but let some censure be reserved for the Christian laity, whose languid zeal for Christ will not be moved to action without the excitement of sham-commerce and the stimulus of real folly.

Finally, I think, it is not excessive to suppose that,

at least in Jewish circles, the resident ministry were held to succeed to the claim of the Mosaic priesthood in the matter of "*tithes and first-fruits.*" It is possible, perhaps probable, that this claim only obtained practical recognition after the destruction of Jerusalem, and the practical abolition of Judaism which that tremendous catastrophe involved. In any case *The Teaching of the Twelve Apostles* is evidence of the claim in the sub-Apostolic Church.

"But every true prophet who wishes to settle among you is worthy of his food.

"Likewise a true teacher is himself worthy, like the workman of his food.

"Therefore thou shalt take and give all the first fruit of the produce of the wine-press and threshing-floor, of oxen and sheep, to the prophets, for they are your chief priests.

"But if ye have no prophets, give to the poor."*

The financial aspect of ministerial claims is not the highest or noblest aspect of the subject, but it is an aspect which cannot be wholly ignored. I am not one of those who pitch the financial standard very high. Maintenance does not mean more than maintenance, though that must (unless the efficiency of the clergy is to diminish) include provision for intellectual as well as merely physical needs. I have ventured to urge in season, and (as some might say) out of season, the urgent need for more simplicity of life and self-restraint among the clergy. No one will accuse me of an excessive ardour for clerical privileges and clerical rights.

* Chap. xiii.

Therefore, perhaps, I may be permitted to point to the spiritual mischiefs which are plainly resulting from clerical poverty, and which must become worse as time advances. Is it nothing that the ambassadors of heaven are broken down with domestic anxieties, that teachers should be distracted by the menace of want, that Christ's witnesses should be too poor to be brave, too dependent to be faithful?

Let it be frankly admitted that the clergy at their Ordination ought to renounce, and ought to be understood to have renounced what, in common parlance, are called "professional prospects." I resent very strongly those comparisons between the Church and the "other professions," which imply the claim of the clergyman to regard his sacred calling as a means of money-making in the same sense as is legitimate and right in the case of the lawyer or the doctor. I think the clergyman should have as few domestic ties as possible. Improvident marriages are doubly blameworthy in a clergyman, and the laity who encourage or excuse such marriages offend against the best interests of the Church. Bearing this in mind, the case is yet stronger for the maintenance of the clergy in physical and mental efficiency. An inefficient clergy is manifestly a grave injury to religion. And an underbred, uneducated, I might even say in view of the facts which have come to light recently, an underfed and underclothed clergy, must be an inefficient clergy. The ultimate sufferer is the Church herself. It is surely a time when every Christian ought to examine his own conscience on the subject. Tithes and first-fruits are for most modern churchmen a name and nothing more. The dwindling rent-charge which endows some of the parishes takes nothing out of any man's pocket save in a sense that is true of every lawful due. But the duty to regularly contribute according to income rests on every disciple, and to neglect that duty must inflict on the negligent or niggardly Christian grave spiritual loss. The time has come in the Church of England for plain speaking on the subject. Unless there is a general and speedy awakening of the Christian conscience, and, as a result, a large increase in the regular contributions of churchmen to the income of the Church, it is as certain as any future event can be, that within the next generation the area of Christian work will be seriously contracted, and its quality gravely, if not irreparably injured.

CHAPTER IX.

CONCLUSIONS

THE first impression left on the mind by an inquiry into the Christianity of the Apostolic age is probably one of unpleasant surprise. Most men appeal to the New Testament in the interest either of their own system of faith and order or of their denunciation of all existing systems. The advocates of a system will hardly be satisfied with the witness of the Apostolic age; the advocates of individualism will hardly be satisfied either. There was a very vigorous Church system in the Apostolic age, but it was very unlike any system with which we are acquainted. This unlikeness of original Christianity to any modern counterpart is not wholly to the disadvantage of our own time. The Apostolic Church as revealed in the Corinthian Epistles was far indeed from perfection. Gross moral scandals existed; the members were by no means free from the spirit of rivalry and hatred; the "unity of the Body of Christ" was more apparent than real. There was much superstition even in those first days, and it would be difficult to find any sufficient parallel in subsequent ages to the shocking profanities which marked the Corinthian Eucharist.* Those who expect to find their ecclesiastical ideal in the Apostolic age will be rudely disappointed. It is, indeed, often the case that uninstructed students, reading the New Testament with little understanding of its contents, are apt to think of that period as a golden age, which provokes the envy while it rebukes the corruptions of all succeeding times. The intelligent student, however, will escape that error.

The habitual assumption of ecclesiastical advocates, that the Church of Christ started on its history with a complete equipment of organization, of which, forsooth, their own system—Papal, or Episcopalian, or Congregational or the like—is the sole existing representative, is disallowed by a serious study of Apostolic Christianity. We see a Church in the process of reaching an organization, and we mark the pressure of circumstances as the principal external agent in that process. We see that while most later polities can find their germs in the Apostolic Church, none can find their model. The authority of original Christianity cannot be unreservedly claimed on behalf of any existing Church

* The nearest parallel I can think of is the Test Act Communion of the last century, the evil effects of which are still perceptible. I attribute to the disgust provoked in pious minds by that official profanation of the Eucharist the powerful but unreasoning reluctance of many excellent and in all other respects Christian men to receive the Holy Sacrament. They unconsciously perpetuate the notion, which had but too much justification a century ago, that "going to the table" was the mark of the loose liver and the mere worldling; argued, in fact, a low level of spiritual sincerity.

order. It must suffice that that authority is friendly, or at least not adverse.

Of two opposing conceptions of the Church, I venture to affirm that they are condemned by the witness of Apostolic Christianity. The modern Roman theory, which bases unity on common obedience to a visible, earthly Head, is not merely ignored, but also positively contradicted by the New Testament. That S. Paul should denounce the schismatic tendencies of his Corinthian converts, that he should urge the sinfulness of division and dilate on the unity of the Church as Christ's Body, and should never so much as hint at the existence of any centre of unity, Divinely provided in the person of S. Peter and his successors, is sufficient proof that he himself had no knowledge that any such existed. This, however, is not all; his doctrine about the Church precludes the existence of any visible centre of unity. What room can be found for the Roman doctrine in such a passage as this, in which the Apostle specifically declares the constituents of the Church's unity, "*There is one body, and one Spirit, even as also ye were called in one hope of your calling: one Lord, one faith, one baptism, one God and Father of all, Who is over all, and through all, and in all.*"* It is no answer to my contention to adduce the verse in the Gospel in which our Saviour declared that He would build His Church on S. Peter, or on S. Peter's faith, or on S. Peter's confession (for the verse has never been unanimously understood, and probably never will be). My purpose

* Eph. iv. 4.

in this volume has been, apart from all prejudice, to see what the Apostolic Church was, and what it believed. The Gospels give place to the Epistles in that inquiry. You may make what you will of Christ's words to S. Peter, I point out to you that in the Apostolic age nobody suspected that they carried the modern Roman sense.*

Further, the notion of an invisible Church, which has no necessary Sacraments and no Divinely ordered ministry (which is essentially the doctrine of the Plymouth Brethren and the Quakers), finds no support in the Apostolic age. The ministry and the Sacraments evidently held a great place in the Christianity of the Apostles. To go no farther than the Corinthian Epistles, it is plain that a Christianity which dispenses with an ordained ministry, and despises visible Sacraments, would have seemed a strange thing both to the Corinthians and to the Apostle. The circumstances of the Corinthian Church led S. Paul to speak at some length on the character and claims of the Christian ministry, and on the awful dignity of the Sacraments. To this cause we owe the careful teachings on those subjects which mark his Epistles to the Corinthians. Thus

* Not long ago I attended a meeting at which Father Rivington ventured some courageous statements as to the Roman claims. Subsequently I was allowed to ask a question, and I asked "Whether he could name a single passage in the Epistles which even remotely suggested that the Apostolic Church recognized any supremacy in S. Peter, such as is assumed by modern Roman Catholics?" He replied, "The Gospels are quite sufficient for me." Of course, the whole issue is what the Petrine texts in the Gospels really mean; and in deciding that issue the silence of the Epistles is absolutely decisive so far as the Roman interpretation is concerned.

of the ministry, "*Let a man so account of us, as of ministers of Christ, and stewards of the mysteries of God.*" "*God hath set some in the Church, first Apostles, secondly prophets, thirdly teachers.*" "*Even so did the Lord ordain that they which preach the gospel should live of the Gospel.*" If S. Paul was right in thus maintaining that the regular Christian ministry had a Divine institution, was responsible to God alone, and by Christ's express commandment was maintained by the Church in order to confine itself to its sacred work, then it seems evident that the Plymouth Brother is wrong in rejecting that ministry.

So of the Sacraments, they are essential to the Christianity of S. Paul. "*In one Spirit were we all baptized into one body, whether Jews or Greeks, whether bond or free.*" Nor can the notion that the Apostle refers to some wholly inward experience be entertained for one moment. When he indignantly asks the Corinthians, "*Were ye baptized into the name of Paul?*" he is clearly referring to their public Baptism into the Divine Name. When he says to them, "*Ye were washed, ye were sanctified, ye were justified in the name of the Lord Jesus Christ, and in the Spirit of our God,*" he is plainly pointing them back to that solemn moment of their Baptism, when they were admitted into Christ's Church, and began their new life of discipleship. Of the Holy Communion S. Paul had to speak much, for the worst abuses of the Corinthians had gathered round that Sacrament. Their divisions and their sensuality argued a strange contempt of that which Christ instituted as the bond of unity and the means of purifying grace.

"*The cup of blessing which we bless, is it not a communion of the Blood of Christ? The bread which we break, is it not a communion of the Body of Christ? seeing that we, who are many, are one bread, one body; for we all partake of the one bread.*" S. Paul rehearses the institution of the Eucharist, and then declares the meaning of the Sacrament. "*For as often as ye eat this bread and drink the cup, ye proclaim the Lord's death till He come.*" It is, I think, manifest that those modern Christians—whether Quakers or Salvationists, or howsoever called—who reject the Sacraments are acting in direct opposition to the Apostolic Church.

Our inquiries will, on the whole, make us very tolerant of diversities of religious practice, so long as they do not involve any offence against essential Christianity. We shall hold somewhat lightly by ecclesiastical customs, however venerable and convenient; and certainly we shall be vigilant against claiming for them an authority which they do not really possess. But we shall take a very grave view of any conduct which tends to break up the unity of the Church. Especially shall we deprecate the notion that it is a matter of indifference whether or not Christians come together for common worship. We shall be very sceptical of a unity which can rest content with breaches of external communion; but we shall not exaggerate the real value of an external unity. The schismatical spirit within the Corinthian Church had not actually broken up the visible fellowship, but it had robbed that fellowship of meaning. The schismatical spirit, which at bottom is the spirit of mere self-assertion, the very opposite of that fraternal spirit which should inspire the family of God, may co-exist with a very strong sense of the importance of external unity. The only effectual remedy for that besetting malady is the cultivation of the Divine virtue of love or charity. We observe in the Apostolic Church that the tendency which we may call congregationalism was powerful, and that it was steadily resisted by S. Paul. The Church cannot be limited to a place or a nation; the general practice and belief of Christians constitute an authority which must not be ignored or lightly resisted.

Our inquiry will certainly have helped us to get a just perspective of Christianity. We can see that the essence of Christ's Religion was, in the first days, believed to consist pre-eminently in an honest service of a living Master and Lord. Doctrines which, in later times, have been made the tests of Christian fellowship were then unknown. It is not necessarily to be inferred that such doctrines are false. They may be, and in some cases plainly are, inevitably developed products of the earlier stage. But in some cases the attitude and spirit of the Apostolic Church are plainly incompatible with the later doctrines. To give but two sufficient examples: The Roman teaching about the Virgin Mary cannot be reconciled with the New Testament. The position of woman in the Church was a subject of urgent concern at Corinth. S. Paul was directly requested to deal with it; and he does so in the first Corinthian Epistle with great care. Is it conceivable that if he had held the modern Roman view of S. Mary he could have totally excluded her name from his argument? In the Epistles to the Romans and the Galatians S. Paul treats at length of the Redemption. He draws out the famous parallel between the first Adam and the second; but never once does he make any more specific reference to S. Mary than the general statement that Christ was "*born of a woman.*" Is it conceivable that the Apostle could have thus avoided all direct mention of the Blessed Virgin if he had believed her to be, as modern Roman preachers declare, the "second Eve," the sinless Mother of the new creation? The present Pope has recently informed us that to hope for salvation without praying for S. Mary's help is as reasonable as to seek to fly without wings. Is it not answer enough to point to these Epistles, wherein the whole subject of salvation is discussed by Apostles, and where S. Mary's name is never once mentioned? Apostolic Christianity was innocent of Mariolatry.

My other instance is of another kind. There are numerous Christians who maintain that a true believer can never fail of salvation; some would also say that he can never fall into sin. Such teaching is condemned by an appeal to Apostolic Christianity. What meaning could attach to the earnest and anxious warnings with which the Epistles are filled if they to whom those Epistles were addressed neither did sin, nor could sin? It is evident on the face of the New Testament, that the Christians whose spiritual state is therein displayed were men to whom discipleship meant no abrupt and easy passage from sin to holiness, but rather men who were committed to a sustained and difficult conflict with evil, who often failed, who sometimes failed scandalously and even irrecoverably, but who never lost the sense of conflict, as the very first consequence of their Christian profession. The student of Apostolic Christianity will have learned nothing if he has not learned this. To be a Christian before all things meant to live righteously, to bring life under the government of Christ's Law, to act with habitual reference to Christ's return to judgment.

The Apostolic age had its difficult problems; they were not precisely the same problems as those which face men now, but they were certainly not less grave and perplexing. They were solved—not easily, not without preliminary essays at solution which failed, never without much effort and anxiety. For the Apostolic age was pre-eminently the age of the Holy Spirit. Christians lived, and acted, and made decisions, and tried experiments, and started institutions, and shaped their whole religious polity under the overmastering conviction that the Spirit of God was living in the Church and governing it. Here is the real superiority of Apostolic Christianity. In spite of many faults and much scandal it was a genuinely spiritual thing. The very extravagances, which S. Paul rebukes, reveal the ardour of Christian enthusiasm and the strength of Christian conviction. To the Apostolic Church, perhaps, we may apply the

CONCLUSIONS

words which Christ spoke of the penitent woman in the Pharisee's house, "*Her sins, which are many, are forgiven: for she loved much.*" Love to Jesus Christ, necessarily expressing itself in love towards the brethren and towards all men, was the vital principle of Apostolic Christianity. "*If any man loveth not the Lord, let him be anathema.*" Those first Christians lived almost in the shadow of the Cross of Calvary, on which the measureless love of Christ had been displayed, and their Christianity drew its energy from the fact. S. Paul tells us that he found in the "*Word of the Cross*" the one prevailing argument. At Corinth especially he had proved its power. "*I determined not to know anything among you, save Jesus Christ, and Him crucified,*" so he summarizes his preaching to the Corinthians. He cannot, of course, mean that throughout his eighteen months' stay in Corinth he never spoke of anything save of Christ's death. We can gather from the Epistles that his teaching covered the whole field of faith and conduct, but he means that the inspiring motive which he always proposed, the basis of all his doctrine, the consideration which he always urged was this: Jesus Christ's love for sinners shown by the Crucifixion. He spoke with convincing force, for he spoke from a full heart. His own religion had had no other source; his own spiritual conflict was waged by no other inspiration. "*For the love of Christ constraineth us: because we thus judge, that one died for all, therefore all died: and He died for all, that they which live should no longer live unto themselves, but unto Him who for their sakes died and rose again.*"

He built his appeals on this foundation. Christian liberty must yield to a more pathetic claim. "*Through thy knowledge he that is weak perisheth, the brother for whose sake Christ died.*" Christian liberality must flow at the bidding of that August Example. "*For ye know the grace of our Lord Jesus Christ, that though He was rich, yet for your sakes He became poor, that ye through His poverty might become rich.*" The Church is venerable and sacred, for it is *Christ's Body;* the Holy Sacrament is awful, for it is *the Lord's Supper.* The clergy are clothed with authority, for they are "*ambassadors on behalf of Christ.*" The ordinary physical activities of human life are sacred, for the Christian's body is a "*member of Christ.*" The slave can cheerfully bear his bondage, for he is *the Lord's freedman.* Apparent failure need not discourage, for "*ye know that your labour is not vain in the Lord.*" Death has no terrors for the loyal disciple, for he would much rather "*be absent from the body, and at home with the Lord.*" But life with its duties, and opportunities, and claims, and problems is a solemn thing, for "*we must all be made manifest before the judgment-seat of Christ; that each one may receive the things done in the body, according to what He hath done, whether it be good or bad.*" Christ fills the whole horizon of Apostolic Christianity: therefore if love of Christ be absent, the very possibility of discipleship is lacking. "*If any man loveth not the Lord, let him be anathema.*"

Here I would find the moral of the history; I would make this the practical inference. If we would indeed vindicate our lineage from the Apostolic

CONCLUSIONS

Church, we too must fill our spiritual horizon with Jesus Christ. Hitherto we have been forcing before men other things, true, precious, even necessary in their place, but as we present them—torn out of their religious context, separated from their true connexions, stripped of their real justifications—both unintelligible and unprofitable. The Church, the Sacraments, the priesthood, the Bible, the preaching —these are paraded before the eyes of men, who, whether they know it or not, are longing for Jesus Christ. Cardinal Manning somewhere relates that he was deeply shocked by reading of a large public meeting in America where the Church was hissed and the name of Jesus received with cheers. I have myself heard a great assembly of self-styled Secularists in East London cheer our Saviour with obvious sincerity. There is a very deep truth, however discreditable to us Christians, revealed by this attitude. *Jesus Christ and Him crucified* must come first and remain first. On that foundation the rest can be builded; apart from that foundation the rest is positively mischievous.

And here also is our one hope of reunion. It is vain to put forward schemes of comprehension by which men are invited to compromise in the sphere of religion where compromise is treason. But let us all, whatever our religious preferences, whatever our denominational description, set *Jesus Christ and Him crucified* in the supreme place, and insist on everything being justified with reference to Him, and upon the darkness of our divisions the day-star of unity will begin to rise. For everything will find its true level and be seen in its true proportions. A mightier force than that of religious preferences, or than that of sectarian loyalty, will bear upon us, humbling our pride, enlightening our ignorance, abashing our prejudices, enkindling our affections— the force of Jesus crucified. When we bring all our mutual condemnations under this sufficient, Apostolic sentence, "*If any man loveth not the Lord let him be anathema*"—for him in our Church fellowship we have no place,—we shall not be far from uniting in the Apostolic salutation, "*Grace be with all them that love our Lord Jesus Christ in uncorruptness*"—of such, however ignorant and wrongheaded, we can spare none, for such, however we regard them, or they describe themselves, are disciples of Jesus, and members of His mystical body. "*No man can say, Jesus is Lord, but in the Holy Spirit.*"

APPENDICES

I. ST. PAUL'S TEACHING AT CORINTH
II. APOSTOLIC SUCCESSION
III. CONFESSION
IV. CELIBACY

APPENDIX I.

S. PAUL'S TEACHING AT CORINTH

IN the Acts (chap. xviii.) we learn that S. Paul's sojourn in Corinth lasted for no less than eighteen months, and that it fell into two distinct periods. In the first and shortest the Apostle "reasoned in the synagogue every Sabbath, and persuaded Jews and Greeks." Opposition was violent and unscrupulous, and it was met by an unusual vehemence on the part of S. Paul, which reached a climax on the arrival of Silas and Timothy from Macedonia, presumably with tidings of Jewish persecutions. "Paul was constrained ($συνείχετο$) by the Word, testifying to the Jews that Jesus was the Christ." His new vigour brought matters to the crisis which occasioned the public and formal separation of disciples from the synagogue, and their organization as a Christian Ecclesia, which met at the house of Titus Justus. Then the second and longest period of the Corinthian sojourn began. It is evident that the Apostle was convinced of the decisive importance of his own action at this time. The history of the independent Christian Ecclesia was inaugurated by a special Divine intervention, in which S. Paul was commanded to go forward with his undertaking, and assured of God's protection and assistance. Relying on this supernatural assurance he continued in Corinth for a long time, "teaching the Word of God." What was the range and character of that long course of teaching? That it was far more extensive and detailed than is commonly thought may perhaps be inferred from the contemptuous language of Gallio. The Jews brought a perplexing mass of complaints before the proconsul, which he could only describe as "questions about words and names, and your own law." The indirect evidence of the Epistles to the Corinthians confirms this inference. There is (with the exception of 1 Cor. xv., which stands quite by itself) very little deliberate theological instruction in these Epistles, but they assume a very considerable theological knowledge. It would seem that S. Paul's teaching had included the following :—

1. *The Evangelic Tradition*—the Life, Passion, Death, Resurrection, Ascension of Christ.

2. *Interpretation of the Old Testament in the light of Christian Belief.* See especially 1 Cor. x. 1–11 ; 2 Cor. iii.

3. *A detailed doctrine of the Person and Work of our Saviour.* It must be remembered that the great theological treatise, the Epistle to the Romans, and what may be almost described as its rough draft, the Epistle to the Galatians, belong to the same chronological group with the Corinthian Epistles, and may be taken to illustrate them. 1 Cor. i. 30 assumes a large background of theological knowledge. "But of Him (*i.e.*, God) are ye in Christ Jesus, Who was made unto us wisdom from God, and righteousness, and sanctification, and redemption." The great key words of the Pauline theology are here found in the least theological of his Epistles. δικαιοσύνη, ἁγιασμὸς, ἀπολύτρωσις.

4. *A very definite and rich teaching about the Holy Spirit.* S. Paul never thinks it necessary to explain his references to the Spirit, which are numerous, *e.g.*, 1 Cor. ii. 10–16 ; iii. 16 ; vi. 11, 19 ; xii. Necessarily resulting from

this we find that Trinitarian doctrine of a very positive kind was familiar to the Corinthians. The formula, 2 Cor. xiii. 14, implies a very definite and coherent Trinitarian belief.

5. *Eschatological doctrine*, *e.g.*, iii. 13–15; vi. 2, 3. The most probable explanation of this passage understands a reference to the final consummation. The point to be noticed is the quiet assumption that the Corinthians were quite familiar with the subject. "Know ye not that the saints shall judge the world? . . . Know ye not that we shall judge angels?" The Epistles to the Thessalonians were written during the Apostle's stay at Corinth, and they are very rich in eschatological suggestions.

6. *Careful moral teaching*, especially in connexion with the Sacrament of Holy Baptism.

7. *Ecclesiastical customs*, the παραδόσεις which the Apostle had delivered to the Corinthians. 1 Cor. xi. 1; cf. 2 Thess. iii. 6.

The formula "Know ye not?" occurs no less than ten times in the first Epistle to the Corinthians. It has been suggested that it ought to be understood as a specific reference to Apostolic teachings, but an examination of the passages in which it appears prohibits this. They are the following: iii. 16; v. 6; vi. 2, 3, 9, 15, 16, 19; ix. 13, 24.

APPENDIX II.

APOSTOLIC SUCCESSION

IT can hardly be disputed by any well-informed student that the conventional Anglican teaching about the Apostolic Succession is in many respects gravely objectionable.* It states boldly as a fact what is at best a probable supposition, and it is made to carry the burden of practical inferences so serious that nothing but the clearest and most convincing proofs could sufficiently commend them to the acceptance of thoughtful Christians. It ought to be admitted that in its crude traditional form the doctrine

* Such teaching as that given on "The Ministry of the Church," in a popular and in many respects excellent manual, by the Rev. VERNON STALEY, *The Catholic Religion.* What could be more arbitrary than this: "*The only possible meaning* of the saying, 'Lo I am with you always, even unto the end of the world,' is this. 'I will be *with the ministry* of which you are but the first members. I will be with you, and not only with you, but also with all who shall come after you *in the ministry.* You will die, but your office will live on, and I will be *with that office in the persons of your successors,* even unto the end of the world.' Thus we have the great promise on which the doctrine of the Apostolic Succession rests" (p. 20). It is held by many interpreters that the promise of Christ was addressed to the general company of the disciples, whose presence is hinted at in verse 17 ("some doubted"). It is simply not true that the passage admits of no other meaning than that stated. The words are not the commissioning of an order, but of a society. They are quite compatible with the view that the inspired society may develop organizations of teaching and government to match its necessities; and, in fact, this is the testimony of Church History.

of Apostolic Succession is subsequent to the Apostolic Age. Only with very large deductions can we allow the truth of the familiar Embertide hymn:—

> "His twelve Apostles first He made
> His ministers of grace,
> And they their hands on others laid
> To fill in turn their place."

For the Apostles, strictly speaking, had no successors. Their functions were unique and incommunicable. In a more general sense the Christian ministry, however designated or organized, stands in the Apostolic Succession. The crucial question is, Have we any sufficient grounds for pleading Apostolic authority in its extremest, most obligatory shape for that type of ecclesiastical order which we now call Episcopal? That the threefold ministry can be traced in a continuous line to Apostolic times is now generally admitted; that any other type of ecclesiastical order can be so traced may be securely denied; but, though these facts do undoubtedly confer on the Episcopal *régime* a prestige, a value, and an interest which are unique, can it be reasonably maintained that they justify the rigid and tremendous conclusion that non-Episcopal ministries are necessarily invalid? Since it is certain that the threefold ministry is not absolutely coeval with the Church, and since it is admittedly not based on any known commandment of Christ, can it be justly claimed that now the threefold ministry belongs to the "esse" of the Church?

These questions seem equally difficult and important. For the higher the theory of the Church the greater must be the authority of its permanent agreements, and the threefold ministry certainly represents one of the most permanent of all such agreements. The Divine Right of the ministry as certified by the Episcopal Succession from the Apostles was never questioned from the second century to the sixteenth. It would seem that to abandon a system so long-standing could hardly fail to involve the gravest spiritual consequences. But the commentary of nearly four centuries on the Reformation does not seem to correspond with the requirements of the rigid Episcopal theory. Christianity, it is contended, has been most Apostolic outside the Apostolic Succession, most Christian outside the sphere of Sacramental grace. This is an exaggeration of facts which, exaggeration apart, must be faced.

There is, of course, another side to the question. The witness of the last four centuries is by no means uniformly favourable to "Protestantism." Ecclesiastical anarchy is seen to have evils of its own scarcely less baleful than those of hierarchic absolutism. The decay of the Christian character through sectarian competition and conflict is hardly less ruinous than the debasement of the Christian life by ignorance and superstition. But this must be allowed. The evils of Protestant anarchy are very generally admitted, and are on the way to be overcome. The nineteenth century is more united and charitable than the seventeenth; but the evils of absolutism, at least so far as the Roman Church represents absolutism, seem to grow more inveterate and baleful. The Christianity of Southern Europe and Southern America is perhaps less intellectual and moral to-day than in the seventeenth century. On the whole view of the last four centuries I think it must be admitted that non-Episcopalian Christianity has proved its power to stand the moral test of discipleship proposed by our Lord at least as well as Episcopalian. Its "fruits," religious, social, political, intellectual, are indisputable. We are, then, driven to ask, How far shall all this affect our doctrine of Apostolic Succession? Is the "Witness of

History" valid up to the sixteenth century and not beyond? Is the development of the Christian Ecclesia to be arbitrarily arrested at the second century or the fourth? The Roman Church seems to stand for a truth when she answers in the negative these questions, though her arbitrary application of the truth she admits robs her admission of practical result. At all hazards it would seem that a living belief in the Church, as a Divinely Inspired Society, must require a willingness to revise past conclusions by present experience. It seems involved in the conviction that the Holy Spirit is continuously present in the Church, that we should give the greatest importance to the latest Christian experience. For that must be supposed to reflect His most recent guidance. Definitions must be adequate, if they are to be received as true. The strict conventional Episcopalian definition of the Church is ceasing to be adequate; the probability is that within a few generations it will become as patently inadequate as the kindred Roman definition. Probably, however, both definitions are rather lightly held. Men may be illogical, they are rarely in large numbers consciously absurd.

For the present, perhaps, the wisest course for the modest churchman is (1) to loyally adhere to the system of his own church; (2) to abstain from any positive condemnation of other ecclesiastical systems, except in so far as they advance exclusive claims; (3) to frankly recognize the "fruits of the Spirit" wherever manifested; (4) to discourage all proselytizing as between Christian denominations; (5) to gladly unite in combined action with other Christians wherever such union does not hurt consciences and involve insincerity.

Jeremy Taylor's contemptuous description of proselytizing might be usefully studied by the bustling zealots of our own day.

"... it is enough to weary the spirit of a disputer, that he shall argue till he hath lost his voice, and his time, and sometimes the question too; and yet no man shall be of his mind more than was before. How few turn Lutherans, or Calvinists, or Roman Catholics, from the religion either of their country or interest! Possibly two or three weak or interested, fantastic and easy, prejudicate and effeminate understandings, pass from church to church, upon grounds as weak as those, for which formerly they did dissent; and the same arguments are good or bad, as exterior accidents or interior appetites shall determine. I deny not but, for great causes, some opinions are to be quitted; but when I consider how few do forsake any, and when any do, oftentimes they choose the wrong side, and they that take the righter do it so by contingency, and the advantage is also so little, I believe that the triumphant persons have but small reason to please themselves in gaining proselytes, since their purchase is so small, and as inconsiderable to their triumph as it is unprofitable to them who change for the worse or for the better upon unworthy motives. In all this there is nothing certain, nothing noble. But he that follows the work of God, that is, labours to gain souls, not to a sect and a subdivision, but to the Christian Religion, that is, to the faith and obedience of the Lord Jesus, hath a promise to be assisted and rewarded; and all those that go to heaven are the purchase of such undertakings, the fruit of such culture and labours: for it is only a holy life that lands us there." — Dedication of the *Life of Christ; Works*, vol. ii. p. 12. London, 1828.

The conscience of Christendom is certainly being deeply moved on the subject of religious division. The desire for a worthier expression in the external sphere of that "unity of the Spirit" which all Christians profess is forcing all devout disciples to criticise with anxious severity the stumbling-blocks to fellowship. The exclusive claims of types of ecclesiastical order constitute, perhaps, the most obdurate and general of such stumbling-blocks. Most of those claims are certainly false, all are probably exaggerated, all may be ultimately found to be baseless. In any case, it must be a good thing that we should consider them with the grave consciousness of their practical effects, and an entire willingness to abandon them if the duty of Discipleship, that is, the Interest of Truth, so require.

APPENDIX III.

CONFESSION

IT is well known that in the earliest church the practice of private confession to the individual priest did not exist.* It was not until the fifth century that it received official recognition; it was not until the thirteenth that, in the West, it was made compulsory. The inference is very commonly drawn that any insistence on the practice must be regarded as an unwarrantable infringement of Christian liberty, and therefore to be firmly resisted.

It is not, however, sufficiently remembered that private confession to the Christian minister, though itself a comparatively modern practice, represents an important and indeed essential element of discipleship as conceived in the Apostolic age. The mode of confession, whether public or private, whether made in presence of the congregation or in that of the priest, is, after all, a matter of secondary importance. In some mode confession of sins is necessary, in some sense the Church is endowed with "the power of the keys," by some means the "ministry of reconciliation" must be fulfilled by the ordained ministry. The grave fact is that vast numbers of

* The history of the practice is traced in the article "Exomologesis" in *Dictionary of Christian Antiquity*, where references are given. See also Bishop Reichel's sermon on "Confession" in *Cathedral and University Sermons*, pp. 266-302, for a learned and fair statement of the case against the practice.

modern Christians have largely lost all real conception of repentance, that in repudiating (rightly enough) the exaggerated and mechanical procedure of the Mediæval Church, they have provided for themselves no alternative discipline. Moreover, it ought not to be forgotten that private confession to the Christian minister has the sanction of many centuries and many saints. It is not too much to say that it is commended by the *general* experience and the holiest examples of the Christian Society.

Yet it is very evident that much dislike exists among English churchmen to a religious practice which is allowed, and, under certain circumstances, recommended in the Prayer Book. I am not here concerned with the subject of private confession, save in so far as it represents an element of Apostolic Christianity.

Open acknowledgment of faults in the presence of others was certainly practised among the Jews, and adopted into the regular custom of the infant Church. Two passages seem to be conclusive on this point.

(1) S. James v. 14–16. "Is any among you sick? let him call for the elders (τοὺς πρεσβυτέρους) of the Church; and let them pray over him, anointing him with oil in the name of the Lord: and the prayer of faith shall save him that is sick, and the Lord shall raise him up; and if he have committed sins (ἁμαρτίας), it shall be forgiven him. Confess, therefore, your sins one to another, (ἐξομολογεῖσθε οὖν ἀλλήλοις τὰς ἁμαρτίας), and pray one for another, that ye may be healed (ἰαθῆτε)." It is to be specially noted that (α) the presbyters are present, and presumably the recipients of the sick man's confession; (β) forgiveness is apparently conditioned by confession, "Confess, *therefore*," etc.; (γ) the connexion between sin and bodily illness is assumed; the forgiveness of the one involves recovery from the other. We may compare the

narrative in the Gospel of S. Mark ii. 1-12. Christ forgives the sins of the man sick of the palsy. The association of physical distress and moral evil underlies S. Paul's words in 1 Cor. xi. 30.

(2) 1 John i. 9. "If we confess (ὁμολογῶμεν) our sins, He is faithful and righteous to forgive us our sins, and to cleanse us from all unrighteousness." The word ὁμολογεῖν, to confess, certainly indicates a public acknowledgment with the lips. Thus, to give but one example, S. Paul in Romans x. 10 distinguishes between inward faith and outward confession of faith, "with the heart man believeth unto righteousness; and with the mouth confession is made (ὁμολογεῖται) unto salvation."

Such open acknowledgment of sins was the recognized evidence of repentance. The multitudes who were converted by S. John the Baptist are said to have confessed their sins (S. Matt. iii. 6); and in Acts xix. 18 we read that many penitent Ephesians, dismayed by the fate of the sons of Sceva, "came, confessing and declaring their deeds."

It seems a reasonable inference that the undoubted practice* of the sub-Apostolic Church obtained from the first, that the normal preliminary to Baptism and Holy Communion was such open acknowledgment of sin. The penitential system of the early Church had its roots in Apostolic practice.

* The Didache contains two directions which sufficiently illustrate the sub-Apostolic practice, e.g.,

iv. 14. "In the congregation (ἐν ἐκκλησίᾳ) thou shalt confess thy transgressions, and thou shalt not come to thy prayer with an evil conscience."

xiv. 1. "And on the Lord's day of the Lord (κατὰ κυριακὴν δὲ Κυρίου) come together and break bread, and give thanks, having before confessed your transgressions [προ[σ]εξομολογησάμενοι τὰ παραπτώματα ὑμῶν], that your sacrifice may be pure.

The famous commission to the Apostles, S. John xx. 23, can hardly be altogether separated from the subject of confession.* The same writer records the words of Christ and gives the admonition to confession. He could hardly fail to connect the two. And if this be conceded, then the bold practice of the Church of England in including the famous words in the formula of ordination to the priesthood is not wholly destitute of justification.

Confession does not seem to necessarily involve a sacerdotal theory of the Christian ministry. I know no reason why confessions should not be heard and absolution pronounced by a layman, provided he be duly commissioned by the Church; there are obvious practical reasons why the clergy should normally hear confessions; it is not necessary to assume any other. There is an admirable sermon on "The Restoration of the Erring," by Robertson, of Brighton, which sets forth very impressively the deep truth which, with whatever admixture of irrelevant and erroneous ideas, is represented by "the confessional." He treats of the same subject also in his *Expository Lectures on the Epistles to the Corinthians.* Lecture XI., on "The Christian Idea of Absolution," is especially noteworthy. I do not see any vital discrepancy between the Catholic doctrine and the following :—

"Inasmuch as S. Paul absolved, let us learn the true

* But it must not be pressed too far. Bp. WESTCOTT's remarks (*S. John*, p. 295) are not always sufficiently remembered. "The commission must be regarded properly as the commission of the Christian Society, and not as that of the Christian ministry. . . . It is impossible to contemplate an absolute individual exercise of the power of 'retaining'; so far it is contrary to the scope of the passage to seek in it a direct authority for the absolute individual exercise of the 'remitting.'"

It is well known that the words of S. John xx. 23 are not found in any Ordinal earlier than the twelfth century.

principle of ministerial absolution. Humanity is the representative of Deity. The Church is the representative of Humanity, the ideal of Humanity. The minister is the representative of the Church. When, therefore, the minister reads the absolution, he declares a Fact. It does not depend on his character or his will. It is a true voice of man on earth echoing the Voice of God in heaven. But if the minister forgets his representative character; if he forgets that it is simply in the name of Humanity and God, 'in the person of Christ'; if by any mysterious language or priestly artifices he fixes men's attention on himself, or his office, as containing in it a supernatural power not shared by other men; then, just so far, he does not absolve or free the soul by declaring God. He binds it again by perplexed and awe-engendering falsehood, and, so far, is no priest at all; he has forfeited the priestly power of Christian Humanity, and claimed instead the spurious power of the priesthood of Superstition." Something must be allowed for the polemical atmosphere of 1851, when these words were spoken; they cannot in my opinion be accepted as an adequate statement of the Christian doctrine; but they do not seem to me necessarily incompatible with it, and they are certainly sufficient to justify the practice of private confession. Personally I am convinced—and experience deepens the conviction—that there are deep spiritual needs which by that practice alone can receive satisfaction; that those needs are far more widely distributed than is commonly supposed; that the Church of England fails to provide adequately for the spiritual necessities of the people, wherever the "ministry of reconciliation" is not so fulfilled as to bring frankly within the reach of penitents that "benefit of absolution" of which the Prayer Book speaks. I believe that one of the most urgent reforms needed in our Church is the regulation of the confessional. That the gravest risks are incurred by our present system, or no-system, seems to me too obvious to need argument. Confessions are being heard in ever-increasing numbers all over the country. This is, to my thinking, on the whole, a hopeful sign of our religious state. But the doctrine and procedure of confession are almost as various as the parishes. In one place the full Roman theory is insisted on, in another arbitrary rules are adopted, in others little or no teaching on the subject exists. Here confessions are heard in open Church, here in the vestry, here (a reprehensible practice) in the vicarage. All priests alike are supposed to be competent for the most delicate and difficult duty which any man can be called to perform. In all this I perceive almost infinite possibilities of danger. Two reforms are, to my thinking, imperative, both of which have the sanction of Christian experience: (1) The appointment of confessors, or, at least, the restriction of this ministry to priests of certain standing and position. No man ought ordinarily to be called upon to face this great duty without experience and without training. (2) The authorisation of public "confessionals." The publicity of private confession—if I may be allowed the paradox—is the best security against scandal. Unfortunately the silly clamour against "confessional boxes" raised by some fanatics gives little hope that this sensible arrangement can be adopted for a long while to come.

APPENDIX IV.

CELIBACY

THE reputation of S. Paul has suffered from his apparent preference for the celibate life. It may be useful to examine the passage which most clearly indicates that preference (1 Cor. vii. 1-9, 32-40). There seem to have been persons among the Corinthians who condemned the single life as in itself wrong; there were others who magnified it as the only worthy state. The one party followed the prevailing Rabbinic view; the other opposed to that view an extravagant asceticism. The Apostle, therefore, while asserting the legitimate and reasonable character of celibacy, is careful to point out the conditions under which the celibate life may rightly and wisely be adventured. "*It is good* [καλὸν] *for a man not to touch a woman*," *i.e.*, it is an honourable and excellent thing to lead the single life. This, however, does not altogether settle the practical question. So S. Paul immediately advances two limiting considerations. "*But, because of fornications* [διὰ δὲ τὰς πορνείας] *let each man have his own wife, and let each woman have her own husband.*" In view of the low moral standard which obtained among the Corinthian Christians, in view of the sensual habits in which many of them had grown up, in view of the prevailing licentiousness of Corinth, he could not advise celibacy. Marriage was a more prudent course. He stops to insist (against the ascetics) on an honest fulfilment of conjugal duty. He will not hear of that refusal to accept the obligations of marriage, which subsequently became very common in the Church.

S. Chrysostom, commenting on this passage, denounces the pseudo-chastity of Christian wives, which became the occasion of much misery and sin. Returning to the subject of celibacy, the Apostle avows his own preference for that state. "*Yet I would that all men were even as I myself.*" He recognizes, however, the equal honour of marriage. "*Howbeit each man hath his own gift* [χάρισμα] *from God, one after this manner, and another after that.*" This verse gives S. Paul's doctrine in a nutshell. Both marriage and celibacy are honourable and excellent states; both demand in the individual a distinctive "*gift from God.*" Men must be "called" to the one or the other. The essential thing for every man is to know and obey his own vocation.

"*But I say to unmarried and to the widows, It is good* [καλὸν] *for them if they abide even as I.*" He repeats his former proposition that the single life is honourable and excellent, and adds the second limiting consideration. "*But if they have not continency, let them marry: for it is better to marry than to burn*" [πυροῦσθαι]. By this forcible expression S. Paul describes the unhappy condition of the man who, without the χάρισμα of continence, endeavours to live the celibate life. He is consumed by the inward fires of an unceasing conflict between his will and his passions; if he escape the Charybdis of sensuality it is only to be wrecked on the Scylla of cynicism. There is a close parallel between this passage and 1 Cor. vi. 12. There also the Apostle first propounds the truth, and then states the qualifying considerations.

All things are lawful for me;	*It is good for a man not to touch a woman;*
but	*but*
not all things are expedient.	*because of fornications, let each man have his own wife, etc.*
All things are lawful for me;	*It is good for them if they abide even as I;*
but	*but*
I will not be brought under the power of any.	*if they have not continency, let them marry: for it is better to marry than to burn.*

Later in the chapter S. Paul advances two reasons for his preference for celibacy. The first is obsolete, the last is of permanent validity. "*I think therefore that this is good by reason of the present distress*" [διὰ τὴν ἐνεστῶσαν ἀνάγκην]. The reference is probably to the ending of the age which the whole Apostolic Church believed to be imminent. Experience has proved that this conviction was mistaken, and we may fairly cancel the argument built upon a demonstrable error. We cannot so easily dismiss the following reason: "*But I would have you to be free from cares. He that is unmarried is careful for the things of the Lord: but he that is married is careful for the things of the world, how he may please his wife. And there is a difference also between the wife and the virgin. She that is unmarried is careful for the things of the Lord, that she may be holy both in body and in spirit: but she that is married is careful for the things of the world, how she may please her husband. And this I say for your own profit; not that I may cast a snare upon you, but for that which is seemly, and that ye may attend upon the Lord without distraction.*"

It does not seem a fair inference from this teaching that S. Paul considered celibacy as intrinsically superior to marriage. He regarded both as honourable, but under existing circumstances and for certain purposes preferred celibacy.

It may be permitted to observe that the Pauline teaching demands the particular attention of the Church of England at this time. In our anxiety to escape the very obvious mischiefs of compulsory celibacy we have rushed into the opposite extreme of discouraging and suspecting all celibacy. The result has been disastrous. The extreme poverty of a married clergy threatens spiritual independence and official efficiency. The squalid distractions of domestic life on the border-land of actual want are equally unfavourable to parochial energy and intellectual exertion. Even the Rabbis made an exception in favour of students of the law. They were exempted from the obligation to marry. We have swept away the condition of celibacy, even from our fellowships, to the lasting injury of collegiate life, and the loss of sound learning. Surely the time has come when this domestic fanaticism may give place to a calmer temper. The Pauline doctrine of two states, celibacy and marriage, equally honourable, but not equally serviceable, may well command our attention. We may recognize at last that all men are not equally fitted for the same work, that all varieties of religious work cannot be equally performed by all men. We need an allocation of spheres. In the missionary field and in the great town parishes experience suggests that a celibate clergy working in companies would best serve the Church. In other places it may be that married men would be most useful.

TWO DISCOURSES

I. THE ADMINISTRATION OF HOLY BAPTISM IN LARGE URBAN PARISHES

Preached before the University of Oxford, in St. Mary's, on June 14th, 1896

II. THE SOCIAL INFLUENCE OF CHRISTIANITY

Preached in Westminster Abbey, on March 6th, 1898

THE
ADMINISTRATION OF HOLY BAPTISM IN LARGE URBAN PARISHES

S. MARK X. 14

PREACHED BEFORE THE UNIVERSITY OF OXFORD, IN S. MARY'S, ON JUNE 14TH, 1896

"But when Jesus saw it, He was moved with indignation, and said unto them, Suffer the little children to come unto Me: forbid them not, for of such is the Kingdom of heaven."—S. MARK x. 14.

THESE words are, perhaps, more familiar than any others to English Christians. They are incorporated in the Baptismal Service, where they provide the scriptural basis for the exhortation which the minister is charged to address to the congregation, which our Prayer Book assumes to be present when Holy Baptism is administered in the Church. I have, therefore, chosen them as the text of a sermon which proposes to treat of a matter of considerable and, I think, urgent practical importance, the administration of Holy Baptism in the Church of England.

There is a strong and suggestive contrast between the ancient and the modern practice of Christians in this matter. The protracted preparations and the elaborate ceremonial of former times have alike almost disappeared. The prevalence of the custom of baptizing infants necessarily annihilated the one; the Protestant reaction against all ceremony naturally affected the other. For centuries adult Baptism was the general rule in the Church; the famous Catechetical Lectures of S. Cyril of Jerusalem, delivered in the Lent of 347, clearly assume that the catechumens were adult; and, indeed, the Church was mainly a Missionary Church through those ages, which we call primitive, and which we have generally agreed to invest with special authority. It would seem sufficiently probable that the Baptism of infants was allowed in Apostolic times; it is clear that once allowed, it would speedily become prevalent; natural affection, not to say also the incorrigible superstition of mankind, would tend to erect an occasional indulgence into a universal rule. There are evidences, however, of misgivings in the Church on the subject, and it is certain that throughout the first four centuries infant Baptism was by no means considered obligatory on Christian parents.

In order to make clear the drift of my discourse I will submit three propositions as the heads or subjects of discussion :—

I. That the administration of Holy Baptism was anciently regarded as involving large risk to the Christian society, and was, therefore, conditioned by securities.

II. That under the circumstances of urban life these securities are now worthless.

III. That the modern practice of unconditioned, indiscriminate baptizing is indecent in itself, discreditable to the Church, and highly injurious to religion.

I shall conclude with hazarding a few suggestions for the reformation of the existing practice, which I shall hope to have shown to involve most serious scandal.

(1) The Church is a visible society, and Holy Baptism is the formal admission of a new member. No doubt this is very far from an adequate account of the Sacrament, but

it is, so far as it goes, a true account. My present purpose does not require me to approach what I will call the theology of Holy Baptism, I am mainly concerned with its ecclesiastical aspect. The first and not the least important effect of Baptism is admission into a visible society—the society of the Catholic Church. Every human society must be intimately interested in the character of those who seek admission into the number of its members; it will guard the avenues to membership with tests and inquisitions of every kind, designed to reduce to the narrowest limits the risk of admitting unsatisfactory, or scandalous, or treacherous persons. The Catholic Church also, following the self-protective policy of all human societies, took precautions against this risk. One, and that perhaps the most effectual security, was provided by the hostility of the world. There was comparatively slight inducement to false profession of discipleship when every profession conferred a title to oppression, imprisonment, and death. Yet (so native to man is imposture) there is no lack of evidences to show that even in the ages of persecution the Church was disturbed and degraded by hypocrites. These, however, became more numerous in prosperous times, and the Church had to depend for her defence against the intrusion of unworthy members upon such securities as she could herself devise. Careful instruction before Baptism, the greatest publicity and solemnity in the administration of the Sacrament, and the system of sponsors—about which we must speak immediately—were the principal of these securities. The elaborate and graduated system of instruction, which makes its appearance in the fourth century, had been gradually developed, and was, perhaps, at all times rather an ecclesiastical ideal than an actual practice; but we may at least deduce from it that a very careful and thorough course of teaching was in the theory of the Church the normal preliminary to Baptism. The Sacrament was administered but twice in the year, at the great Church Festivals; the Bishop himself presided, and every effort seems to have been made to invest the whole procedure with awful and expressive solemnity. Sponsors, in the case of adults, were primarily witnesses to character; they seem to have also been charged with the duty of preparing catechumens for the actual ceremonies of Baptism. So the office of sponsorship was of some importance, and was frequently held by members of the clerical order. *"The ancients excluded all catechumens, energumens, heretics, and penitents; that is, all persons who were never yet in full communion with the Church, as being themselves unbaptized; or else such as had forfeited the privileges of their Baptism by their errors, or crimes, or incapacity." It is obvious that when the practice of baptizing infants became general the sponsor became a more important functionary. The risk incurred by the Church in admitting to her membership those of whose character she could have no assurance was manifest, and the securities by which she endeavoured to protect herself were by no means as insignificant as we, judging the past by the present, are apt to suppose. †The children who were baptized were entitled to Baptism by the fact of their birth of Christian parents. The analogy of circumcision, which probably in the first instance determined the practice of the Church, would suggest the rigid limitation of the Sacrament to those who were "born within the covenant." In later times, under the influence of a developed doctrine of original sin, the limits of the

---

* *Dictionary of Christian Antiquities*, art. "Sponsors."
† *Vide* JEREMY TAYLOR, *Of Baptizing Infants*, vol. ii. p. 284.

covenant were less rigidly observed, but always in default of the Christian parent the Church required a sponsor, or sponsors, who could really fulfil the functions of the Christian parent.

*"It cometh sometime to pass," saith S. Augustine, "that the children of bond-slaves are brought to Baptism by their lord; sometime the parents being dead, the friends alive undertake that office; sometimes strangers or virgins consecrated unto God, which neither have nor can have children of their own, take up infants in the open streets, and so offer them unto Baptism, whom the cruelty of unnatural parents casteth out and leaveth to the adventure of uncertain pity, as therefore he which did the part of a neighbour was a neighbour to that wounded man whom the parable of the Gospel describeth; so they are fathers although strangers that bring infants to Him, which maketh them the sons of God." In the phrase of "some kind of men"—observes Hooker, commenting on this passage—"they used to be termed witnesses, as if they came but to see and testify what is done. It savoureth more of piety to give them their old accustomed name of fathers and mothers in God, whereby they are well put in mind what affection they ought to bear towards those innocents, for whose religious education the Church accepteth them as pledges." It would seem, indeed, that in ancient times the God-parent was held responsible for the physical maintenance as well as for the spiritual up-bringing of the baptized infant. Probably both responsibilities were largely transferred to the Church herself, regarded as "really and ultimately the spiritual mother" of all the baptized; but the danger of this would be comparatively slight, nay, there would be obvious counterbalancing advantages, so long as the physical and the spiritual responsibilities were conjoined;

---

* Quoted in *Hooker*, Book v. cl. 64, s. 5.

it was only when the physical was completely severed from the spiritual, as has been the almost universal fact in modern times, that the mischiefs with which we are so unhappily familiar have arisen. The spiritual responsibilities of sponsors have, indeed, been frequently asserted. The Synod of Chelsea in the year 787,* to give but one example from the annals of our own Church, enacted "that all who receive children from the font know that they are sureties to the Lord, according to their undertaking, for the renouncing of Satan, his works and pomps, and for the believing of the faith; that they teach them the Lord's Prayer and the Creed while they are coming to ripeness of age, for if they do not, what is promised to God on behalf of them that cannot speak shall be with rigour exacted of them."

The curious prohibition of parents from acting as sponsors for their own children—a prohibition which was only removed by the Convocation of Canterbury in 1865 by a canon which, I think, has never been ratified by the Crown, and therefore possesses no legal force—together with the still more curious applications of the doctrine of spiritual affinity in the matter of marriage, must be interpreted as indications of the great importance attached to the religious obligations of sponsorship. In the West, Confirmation, originally administered at the time of Baptism, and still so administered in the Churches of the East, came to be separated from it by an interval of years, and may, perhaps, have had the character of an official ratification by the Bishop of the action of his presbyters in baptizing infants. †A learned modern writer represents Confirmation as forming with Baptism but a

---

* HADDAN and STUBBS, *Councils*, iii. p. 448 (cf. the 11th can. of Council of Clovesho in 747.—*Ibid.* p. 366).

† Canon MASON, *The Relation of Confirmation to Baptism.*

single Sacrament, and, indeed, forming the principal part of that Sacrament; but the great neglect which has overtaken Confirmation, both in mediæval and in modern times, seems to suggest that this opinion was not generally admitted in the Church. This very brief review of the subject may, perhaps, justify the statement that the Church has always exacted securities for the Christian up-bringing of the infants she has received by Baptism into her membership, and that apart from such securities the baptism of infants can find no sufficient justification.

(2) I advance to show that under the circumstances of urban life there are no longer any adequate securities for the Christian up-bringing of a very large proportion of the children who are baptized. The law of the modern Church, expressed in the Rubrics of the Prayer Book, does, indeed, provide very careful regulations designed to secure the religious nurture of the baptized; but the law is largely obsolete, and, in many places, wholly unworkable. Baptism is no longer limited to the "children of the covenant"; probably the majority of English churchmen would endorse the language of Hooker (which I am bound to confess seems to me to go beyond the lines both of reason and piety), and would not be greatly averse to ignoring that limitation on the ground that it is "against both equity and duty to refuse the mother of believers herself, and not to take her in this case (*i.e.*, of parents who are unbelieving or 'accursed') for a faithful parent." But in this case Hooker supposes, what the primitive Church insisted upon, that adequate sponsors are present, prepared to take the place of the parents. This supposition, as we shall see, cannot any longer be made. The Rubric insists on the publicity of Baptism. It is to be administered "when the most number of people

come together: as well for that the congregation there present may testify the receiving of them that be newly baptized into the number of Christ's Church: as also because in the Baptism of Infants every man present may be put in remembrance of his own profession made to God in his Baptism." The service, indeed, assumes throughout the presence of a congregation. But the publicity which the Rubric was intended to secure no longer attaches to the administration of Holy Baptism in large parishes. The excessive (according to the modern standard) lengthening of the service, and (a still more formidable difficulty) the conduct of the infants (not rarely children above the age of two years) who, if they must be allowed to make no resistance to the grace of the Sacrament, do plainly and beyond all question resist the Sacrament itself, are practical obstacles to the carrying out of the Rubric, which cannot be surmounted.

Let me describe to you the actual method of administering Holy Baptism in a large urban parish. On a weeknight evening, or on Sunday afternoons, times when the absence of the congregation can be counted upon, the priest in a large town parish takes his stand at the font to administer the Sacrament of Holy Baptism to all who desire it. The candidates arrive in the arms of their mothers, who are sometimes assisted on these occasions by the monthly nurse, or a neighbour to whom baptisms and burials have an attraction not possessed by the other ordinances of religion, or a district visitor, or even, though this is almost unknown, by the father. No inquiries of any kind are addressed to them beyond the question with which the service begins, and the questions as to names and addresses necessary for the filling in of the register. The service proceeds; there are no sponsors save those whom I have mentioned. Often they cannot read; oftener they won't. They do not answer the questions, so solemn and so important, which are addressed to the sponsors; but with persistence the priest may, if he deem it worth his while, succeed in getting them to say after him the required responses. The service is over in half an hour, and the party retires to the pothouse and the slum. This is no exaggerated picture, not, thank God, of all, perhaps not of most, but certainly of very many baptisms as now administered in large parishes.

The sponsor-system has wholly broken down. I have been at some pains to ascertain the facts. For one great parish with a population of 15,000 souls, in which the average annual number of baptisms was about 500, I can speak with the authority of personal knowledge and the shame of personal responsibility. The majority of infants were really without sponsors, for the mother or friend who brought them to the font had no idea, not even the faintest, of spiritual responsibility as attaching to the act. "If the rule about godparents were enforced in this parish," writes the vicar of a great dock parish where more than 1000 infants are baptized every year, "the greater number of children would have to remain unbaptized." "The rule about sponsors," observes the vicar of a large East-end parish, "is wholly broken." He adds the following observations, which I make no apology for quoting: "The effect of enforcing the rule in all cases would *meâ sententiâ* stop all baptisms at any church where the rule was so enforced, or possibly cause a reversion to the old custom hereabouts of securing attendance of sponsors by standing 'a pot,' which came to be the recognized value of a sponsor." "The chief effect of insisting on the rule in all cases, I feel," writes a very well-known priest, whose opinion carries great weight, "would be that many children would die unbaptized." "The rule about sponsors," writes another, "is *fully* observed in about 20 per cent. There is always one sponsor, but sometimes only the mother." He calculates that the enforcement of the Rubric would reduce by 75 per cent. the number of baptisms, and he adds ;this observation, "I do not believe in a stringent rule for such parts as this. It would lead to paid sponsors, as in old days, or to the neglect of baptism." I will add but one more expression of opinion; it is from a well-known and highly-respected East-end clergyman. "If the rule were enforced in all cases it would cause a great grievance, as there is a strong feeling in favour of having the children baptized, and the monthly nurses seem to have it on their conscience to bring the mother and child before the month is up, and if the baptism is refused because there was no godfather or insufficient number of godparents it would cause a great scandal; on the other hand, if the male parent were enforced to attend in order that the child might be baptized, it would cause still greater scandal in the fact of an utterly irreligious being compelled to go through the form of sponsorship in order to obtain the baptism of his child. This, of course, would be aggravated were two male sponsors pressed for." The initial security of sponsors having been dispensed with, it is no matter for surprise that the careful instruction of the children, which sponsors were intended to ensure, has in very many cases shared the same fate. The common assumption that in a Christian country, equipped with large and detailed machinery of spiritual provision, there is a general probability reaching even to practical certainty that all children will come under Christian training cannot be rightly made. I desire to make very clear to you that in a large proportion of cases the baptized children were suffered to grow up without Christian instruction. Two facts may sufficiently authenticate this statement: the remarkably small proportion of the baptized who are presented for Confirmation, and the failure of the religious bodies to get the poorer children into Sunday-schools. I estimate that about one-fourth of the baptized (who reach the age of Confirmation) are actually confirmed. Without wearying you with statistics, I venture to submit that estimate with some confidence. That 75 per cent. of the baptized should fail of Confirmation gives the measure of the practical worth of the Rubrics and exhortations of the Prayer Book and Canons. In every parish with which I am acquainted, and I have taken great pains to reach the facts, a very large proportion of the children, and they the poorest and roughest children, do not attend the Sunday-schools, nor if they did would they be much benefited. Sunday-schools have enjoyed, and I believe do still enjoy in some quarters, a considerable reputation. This reputation, however, is largely factitious, arising less from the merits of the schools themselves than from their importance in current political controversy. It suits the interest of the Christian advocate for the de-christianizing of the elementary schools to make the most of this pretended substitute for doing the proper work of those schools. The fanatics of voluntaryism magnify a system which is sufficiently certified by its incompetence to be voluntary. But Sunday-schools are, as far as religious education is concerned, of little real worth. There is little teaching and no discipline; the teachers know neither what to teach, nor how to teach; a precarious and intermittent attendance is secured by periodical bribes to the children.* If any think that the

---

* The actual worth of the religious teaching of the Sunday-school may be gauged by the fact, to which representatives of all churches and denominations bear witness, that the vast majority of Sunday-school scholars abandon attendance at public worship as soon as they leave school. Personally I think Sunday-schools not rarely have a

Sunday-schools can take over from the elementary schools the task of teaching religion to the poor and rough children, he is labouring under a delusion which a slight acquaintance with the facts of urban life would speedily dispel. The home, the day-school, and the Church are the three agencies by which the baptized child must be taught the grace and the duty of that Christian membership conferred upon him (though often in such strange fashion) by the sacrament of Holy Baptism. But the home is commonly in no sense Christian; it is a breach of the law of England in most urban schools to teach a baptized child the doctrines of his religion: the Church, overweighted with duties, is wholly unable to supply the defects of home and school. Baptism in infancy in very many cases represents the entire contact with Christianity which our people receive, until with characters hardened into fixed types, with habits formed and dispositions developed, they pass out of school into the great life of the nation.

(3) I submit to you, and this is my final proposition, that the practice which works out to this miserable confusion, the modern practice of unconditioned, indiscriminate baptizing is indecent in itself, discreditable to the Church, and highly injurious to religion. That it is indecent will hardly be disputed by any who recognize the fidelity of the picture I have drawn (a picture drawn from life) of the existing method of administering this Sacrament in the crowded urban parishes. I am not preferring an indictment against my clerical brethren;

---

direct effect in creating that disgust of religious observance which is one of the most remarkable features of the present situation. But I admit that the parish priest is *almost compelled* to have a Sunday-school, thanks to the activity of the Dissenters, who are devoted to that institution, and the selfishness of the parents, who greatly value it as a means of taking their children off their hands for much of Sunday.

the description which I have given was certainly true of my own parish. I associate myself absolutely with them; they, I know, are much exercised in conscience on the subject. That it is discreditable to the Church will not, I think, be disputed. Certainly the scandalous laxity which presides over the admission of new members into the Divine society augurs ill for the future discipline of those members. It is notorious that the indiscriminate use of the Prayer Book services for marriage and for burial inflicts acute distress on many consciences; but so long as the mass of people, however morally and spiritually unworthy, are yet formally Christians, by title of their Baptism, it is extremely difficult to limit the use of these offices. It is not charity to indulge in the solemn mockery of their use in the cases where the assumption of Christianity cannot be reasonably made; it is grievous and baleful imposture. It strengthens in the general mind that insincerity of religious expression which is, perhaps, the besetting peril of those who worship by means of fixed formularies. Here are forms, beautiful, full of devotion, instinct with the pure ardours of discipleship, and they are used under circumstances which transform them into hideous satire. It is inevitable that the habit should grow of regarding the language as properly what it plainly is actually, unmeaning, a decent convention, a mere form, as destitute of significance as the plumes on the hearse and the staves in the hirelings' hands. The habit required by the *abuse* of one formulary readily extends to the *use* of another, and that lethargic acquiescence of unspiritual people in the use of devotional language (which is the bane of Anglicanism) becomes general. Our Church life draws a taint of hypocrisy from the laxity with which the Sacrament of the new birth is administered. There is a further mischief; the gravity of post-baptismal sin, so fearfully real to the mind of the primitive Church, has absolutely perished from the general mind. When no difference is perceptible between the baptized and the unbaptized; when, indeed, as is not rarely the case, the fact of Baptism is only discovered by an appeal to the register, the baptized child having been suffered to grow up in total ignorance of the circumstance, it is manifest that no distinction can be drawn between sin before and sin after Baptism; yet the authority of Holy Scripture unites with the consistent belief of the early Church, a belief wonderfully expressed in that elaborate penitential system, which at once amazes us by its detail and appals us by its severity, in drawing the distinction clearly and deeply. Is it any marvel that our people have come to think so meanly of the great Sacrament, which we ourselves dishonour by such amazing laxity? Is it any marvel that they easily acquiesce in the blasphemy of the modern Ana-baptist, or, as he prefers to call himself, perhaps to conceal the heinousness of his practice, the Baptist? How can we expect simple people to revere a Sacrament which is administered as we administer it? Our laxity lends a plausibility to the doctrines of heresy, which in themselves they do not possess. We are ourselves mainly responsible for that low estimate of Holy Baptism which we deplore in our people. Is it indeed to Christ that we bring these children, whom we so baptize that they never know they are Christ's? Have we any authority thus recklessly to bestow the Gift of the Regenerating Spirit? I say with Tertullian, though far indeed from endorsing his views, "There will be more caution used in worldly matters. Cautius agetur in secularibus ut cui substantia terrena non creditur, divina credatur."

It is easy to build up an indictment, it is not so easy to find the remedy even for admitted abuses. Yet I

HOLY BAPTISM

cannot accept the position that nothing can be done to rescue the Sacrament of Holy Baptism from the contempt into which it has been permitted to fall. We must undoubtedly be content to act slowly. The existing system has been gradually developed, and it is firmly rooted. It must be gradually reformed; at least, the attempt can be made and ought to be made to direct the mind of the Church to the subject. It is not, brethren, only among the very poor that the obligations of sponsorship are lightly regarded, and not rarely altogether ignored. If it were matter of conscience among the professed members of the Church to give meaning to the solemn language of the Prayer Book on this subject, I am very sure the effect for good would be felt widely. I plead for the enforcement of the twenty-ninth of the Canons of 1603, wherever reasonably practicable, at least for the general assertion of the principle which that Canon enshrines, when it enacts that no person "shall be admitted godfather or godmother to any child at Christening or Confirmation before the said person so undertaking hath received the Holy Communion." In the great urban parishes, at least, the practice of canvassing for Baptism might be stopped. District visitors have much to answer for in this matter. Much would be gained if it were made clear by those in authority, and especially by their Lordships the Bishops, that this urging of Baptism where there are no securities for Christian up-bringing is indefensible and mischievous. I think it ought to be possible to direct the devotion of Communicant Guilds to the subject. Why should not the pious zeal, which S. Augustine describes as marking the consecrated virgins of the primitive Church, be emulated by modern Christians who would undertake, always with the full consent of the parents, to stand as sponsors to the children of the very poor? The energies which are now wasted in Sunday-schools might be most happily employed in the instruction of god-children. Why should not sponsorship take its place among the recognized works of the Church? A guild of sponsors—all communicants—combined for mutual counsel and intercession might be a source of great blessing to a parish. The general standard of duty in the matter would be raised, and it might be possible to advance towards a real enforcement of the Rubrics. When all, however, is done that can be done, I cannot conceal from myself that we must face the necessity of greatly reducing the number of the baptized. It goes against the grain, I know, to even in appearance hedge round the Sacrament with restrictions. We dread calling forth against ourselves that "indignation" which was provoked in our Saviour by those officious disciples, who would have barred the babes from His presence, and if, indeed, the withholding of Baptism involved that consequence our anxiety would be well-founded; but who would adventure to affirm so much? I submit that our present laxity rather hinders than facilitates access to Christ. We degrade religion, we create stumbling-blocks, we hurt consciences, we endanger the Church. Can it be truly said that we help the children for whose sake we incur such losses? When at least seventy per cent. of the urban population is baptized and—as His Lordship of London has recently informed us—less than five per cent. receives the Holy Communion, it is evident that we have reached a state in which it is impossible to acquiesce and to retain the self-respect of our discipleship. The fact that the irreligious masses are baptized hinders the missionary action of the Church. The Christian preacher is deprived of his true objective, he cannot call sinners to the "*Washing of regeneration*," he has to persuade them that they are already washed. It would be interesting on this point to know the opinion of the mission-preachers of the Church, now a numerous body. I do not, however, think the practical convenience or inconvenience of any practice demonstrably indefensible ought to be admitted into the discussion of the Church's duty with regard to it. I submit that the existing method of administering Holy Baptism is as little consistent with the dignity of the Sacrament as it is congruous with the practice of the Church in past ages. I have shown that it violates the actual law of the Church, and I have endeavoured to show that it involves grave and extended scandal. If my contentions are as sound as they are sincere I have made out a case for immediate and thorough, though cautious and gradual reform.

THE SOCIAL INFLUENCE OF CHRISTIANITY.

S. MATTHEW v. 13.

PREACHED ON THE SECOND SUNDAY IN LENT, MARCH 6TH, 1898, IN WESTMINSTER ABBEY.

" *Ye are the salt of the earth.*"—S. MATTHEW v. 13.

THERE are no speculations at once more attractive and more precarious than those which attempt to estimate the social results of religions. The attractiveness is obvious and intelligible. Religion is the most deeply interesting thing in the world. Whether it attract or repel, this quality of interest is always present. Religion appeals to the deepest elements of human nature, and it raises every question into which it enters on to a higher platform. The conscience is directly concerned, the heart is directly affected, the imagination is powerfully stirred by every religious appeal. There is always the solemn charm of mystery; the chance, always moving in the background of the mind and disturbing the order of thought, that there may be truth in claims, apparently the most extravagant; validity in reasonings, apparently the most grotesque. In the religious sphere the spirit is oppressed by an ignorance so profound that a positive attitude seems an outrage on modesty. Where it is certain that all know so little, who shall be sure that he really knows anything at all? And yet there is no subject upon which men speak so confidently. The results of religion upon the characters and fortunes of nations are reckoned up and set down with amazing precision, and the estimates are as various as they are precise. Moreover, it is difficult to discover the principles of investigation which have been followed. Yet it would seem that no inquiries more plainly demand careful adhesion to sound principles. For none are more inherently difficult. The complexity of human life is such that no force works in isolation. There is a subtle and constant interplay of forces, out of which results emerge which may not rightly be ascribed to any single cause. Again, causes disguise themselves wonderfully, and the effects of one factor are easily mistaken for those of another. A large uncertainty must always attach to all conclusions as to the social results of religion.

"*Ye are the salt of the earth.*" Our Lord distinctly attributes to His Church the character of a social force. "*Salt*" is the familiar symbol of that which purifies and preserves. Among the Jews it was not merely, as among ourselves, an article of common domestic use, but also an important element in the sacrificial service of religion. Elsewhere our Lord directly refers to the religious use of salt. "*For everyone shall be salted with fire. Salt is good, but if the salt have lost its saltness, wherewith will ye season it? Have salt in yourselves, and be at peace one with another.*" An ancient reading, now by the revisers relegated to the margin, adds the words, "*and every sacrifice shall be salted with salt.*"

"*Ye are the salt of the earth.*" Our Lord avoids the abstract terms in which modern philosophers and reformers so freely indulge. We are apt to forget that "Christianity" is only a synonym for Christians themselves when we are discussing social questions. "*Ye, i.e. My disciples, are the salt of the earth.*" Perhaps the truest guide to a due

z

estimate of the social influence of Christianity is the study of individual discipleship. How does a Christian man's creed affect his social conduct? Evidently to a very large extent the behaviour and influence of the Christian in society have no relation whatever to his religion. The determining factors for the most part lie outside the range of his own choice. His place in society is prescribed for him; his powers of body and mind are not such as he might have chosen for himself; he acts under the authority of laws, traditions, customs, conventions, fashions, ideas which are, as the climate, wholly outside his control. Where is there any place for the action of his discipleship? How shall he be the "*salt of the earth*"? I do not think it sufficient to answer that he must be truthful, honest, just, industrious. So much is required of all good citizens; so much the general consent of reasonable men demands and approves. Without doubt the Christian will have motives for his civic virtue which his religion, and only his religion, could provide; but we are not now discussing motives. The social worth of virtue is independent of its motives. I suppose the social influence of the Christian citizen will reduce itself to the single category of character. How far does the Christian gain for himself "*the mind of Christ*"? How far does his social influence reflect the Christian character? The Sermon on the Mount opens with a description of the Christian character. This is the purpose of the Beatitudes. Christ shows the constituent elements of that character which should express discipleship, and constitute His followers the "*salt*" and the "*light*" of society.

"*Ye are the salt of the earth.*" Christians are to rebuke and disprove the wisdom of the world by setting before society the spectacle of lives governed by other principles, directed to other ends, and by that very fact bringing into the world's life a purifying influence which can restrain the action of the normal corruption, and quicken society with new moral energy. We know but too well that Christian lives are often strangely unworthy expositions of *the Mind of Christ*. We know also how prone men are to credit Christianity with the very faults which Christianity is unable to restrain. The ill-conduct of Christians is a great, nay, the very greatest stumbling-block in the way of Christianity—though in itself such ill-conduct argues nothing against the religion it disgraces. So in reviewing the history of civilization, or striving to interpret the enigma of contemporary society, the student must be on his guard against crediting Christianity with scandals which may indicate rather the defeat than the triumph of Christian principles. It is easy to build up a formidable case against the Church if you limit your inquiry and select your facts. Thus it has been argued with much plausibility that Christianity has favoured slavery, resisted political liberty, even degraded the female sex. It is obvious that for such contentions much may be said. There is a copious literature of social and political servility which professes to be Christian, and the doctrines of asceticism were certainly degrading to womankind; yet a very little reflection will demonstrate the paradoxical character of all such contentions. Slavery has perished throughout Christendom; political liberty is unknown outside that sphere; nowhere else is the position of woman so honourable and so secure. Such results carry the vindication of Christianity from the suspicions which are suggested by some facts of Christian history. The real drift of Christ's Religion shows itself on a broad view of the facts, and we should be mad reasoners if we interpreted the details without regard to the general effect.

Then, I think, we should always remember the extreme difficulty of the material upon which Christianity has to act. Human nature is a very intractable material from which to fashion the fair creations of social righteousness. It takes impressions very gradually; it learns very slowly and by definite stages. It would seem that the elements of right have to be beaten into the dull intelligence of the race one by one. Here, perhaps, is the explanation of some of the problems of Christian history. How can you reconcile, men ask, the severe, penitential system of the early Church with the compassion of the Gospel, or the extravagant exaltation of celibacy with the Christian doctrine of marriage, or the detailed legalism of the mediæval Church with the spirituality of Christ's teaching? Perhaps the answer must be found in the actual conditions of men's apprehension of the truth. Before the compassion of the Gospel can minister to righteousness the gravity of sin must have been grasped; and that lesson was effectually taught by the iron system of primitive penance. Before the true nobility of marriage can be understood men must learn the lesson of chastity; and that lesson was printed indelibly on the general mind by the ascetics. Before spiritual liberty can be securely proposed the majesty of the law must have been understood; and that, perhaps, was borne in on men's minds by the masterful government of the mediæval Church. There is advance in the religious education of mankind. The truth is not grasped at once, but gradually and fragmentarily, "*by divers portions and in divers manners.*" The partial teaching, regarded from the standpoint of complete knowledge, has a repulsive appearance; insisted on in the teeth of wider teachings it may be really mischievous; but in its own time it matched the urgent necessities of the race, and provided the indispensable condition of moral progress. The influence of the Church has ever been exerted upon actual society; it has, therefore, taken a myriad forms, addressing itself to the varying circumstances of human living, but always it has proved itself a purifying and preserving force, "*the salt of the earth.*"

Three things, perhaps, are always contributed by Christianity to the welfare of society. The Gospel brings to the world the gift of social hope. It upholds a social ideal, not as a mere aspiration, still less as a satire on the world's life, but as a practicable object, which can be gained and which will be gained. The Christian may not despair of society, however unpromising the social outlook may be. He believes that the Almighty has a purpose to fulfil in human history, and that the course of the world's life is not wholly independent of His will. Moreover, the Gospel brings to everyone who receives it the conviction that social service is a religious duty. The selfish withdrawal from the social task, whether in despair or in self-absorption, is the repudiation of a Divine Commission. Every Christian feels a certain responsibility for the world's sin, and for the sorrows which at once reflect and avenge it. Christ's example challenges every disciple. "*We must work the works of Him that sent Me, while it is day: the night cometh when no man can work.*" The world is saved from acquiescing in its scandals by the Divine indignation of Christ's disciples. There is no conspicuous evil of human society which has not provoked the resentment of the Christian conscience. In the background of every Christian's mind is the conviction that it is his duty to resist evil where it meets him, and to attack abuses when they cross his path. Finally, the Gospel brings to everyone who receives it the conviction that personal righteousness is a social duty and the condition of social service. Primarily the Christian's task is to illustrate in his own sphere *the mind of Christ.* The Christian conscience has always chafed against any severance of the disciple's practice from his profession. In the early centuries the custom obtained among persons who made pretensions to piety to adorn their garments with sacred pictures in place of those commonly adopted. "Bedizened with such figures they supposed—as Austerius, Bishop of Amasia in Pontus, in the last half of the fourth century, asserts—that their dress must be well-approved in the sight of God. This excellent churchman advises them rather to dispose of such garments, for as much as they would bring, and use the proceeds to honour the *living* images of God; instead of carrying about the sick of the palsy on their garments, rather to look up the actually sick and relieve them; instead of wearing on their bodies a kneeling penitent in embroidery, rather to mourn over their own sins with a penitent spirit."*

Such has always been the attitude of the Christian conscience towards the parade of piety. Translate your creed into conduct, give a social expression to discipleship, be yourself the illustration of your religion.

In so contributing to the world's life the elements of hope, of duty, and of personal discipline Christianity counteracts deep, normal tendencies making for corruption and decay, and literally fulfils the Word of the Divine Founder, "*Ye are the salt of the earth.*"

The civilization of antiquity broke down beneath the burden of its own pollutions; the machinery of government could not sustain the cynical wickedness of those who worked it. Philosophy had no message of hope, no power of moral restoration, no coercive motive of self-discipline. It sank into satire and despair. The civilizations of the East appear to contain no quickening principle,

* NEANDER, vol. iii. p. 388.

detecting abuses, waging war with them, always straining and striving after social advance—they petrify and pass.

The latest civilization of the West—if by so great a name we may describe the achievement of the century's labour to banish the Christian elements from a society which has grown from the depths of savagery to the heights of an unequalled culture, under the tutelary influence of the Church—seems to discover a fatal inability to secure uprightness of character. Prodigal of brave doctrines, of social duty, the secularist is doomed to see his hopes dashed to pieces on the sunken rocks of human selfishness. At the summit of material prosperity society threatens to collapse in a bankruptcy of character. Christianity in the social sphere stands for hope and the sense of duty, and the diffused leaven of personal righteousness; and let us lay it well to heart, Christianity is but the sum of the various moral impressions of individual Christian lives. Upon us all—who own ourselves the disciples of Christ, who in Holy Baptism were solemnly sealed as His "soldiers and servants"—lies the great obligation to be in our several spheres the exponents of the Gospel, not merely, if at all, in word of formal teaching, not often, if ever, by the violences of political action, but always and everywhere by the silent, ceaseless testimony of righteous lives—lives which visibly bear the Christian stamp, which are a continual rebuke to all the baseness of the world, a continual challenge to all the goodness in society—lives which, wherever lived, in cottage or in palace, in "*the strife of tongues and the tumult of the city*," or amid the solemn silences of immemorial hills, are great, and lofty, and fruitful, pouring into the general life unfailing streams of purity and hope, the "*salt*" and "*light*" of the earth.

PLYMOUTH
WILLIAM BRENDON AND SON
PRINTERS

A CATALOGUE OF BOOKS PUBLISHED BY METHUEN AND COMPANY: LONDON 36 ESSEX STREET W.C.

CONTENTS

	PAGE		PAGE
General Literature,	2-19	Little Blue Books,	27
Ancient Cities,	19	Little Books on Art,	27
Antiquary's Books,	20	Little Galleries,	28
Beginner's Books,	20	Little Guides,	28
Business Books,	20	Little Library,	28
Byzantine Texts,	21	Miniature Library,	30
Churchman's Bible,	21	Oxford Biographies,	30
Churchman's Library,	21	School Examination Series,	30
Classical Translations,	21	Social Questions of To-day,	31
Commercial Series,	22	Textbooks of Science,	31
Connoisseur's Library,	22	Textbooks of Technology	31
Library of Devotion,	23	Handbooks of Theology,	31
Standard Library,	23	Westminster Commentaries,	32
Half-Crown Library,	24		
Illustrated Pocket Library of Plain and Coloured Books,	24	Fiction,	32-36
		The Strand Novels,	37
Junior Examination Series,	26	Books for Boys and Girls,	38
Junior School-Books,	26	Novels of Alexandre Dumas,	38
Leaders of Religion,	27	Methuen's Sixpenny Books,	39

FEBRUARY 1906

A CATALOGUE OF

MESSRS. METHUEN'S PUBLICATIONS

Colonial Editions are published of all Messrs. METHUEN'S Novels issued at a price above 2s. 6d., and similar editions are published of some works of General Literature. These are marked in the Catalogue. Colonial editions are only for circulation in the British Colonies and India.

An asterisk denotes that a book is in the Press.
I.P.L. represents Illustrated Pocket Library.
S.Q.S. represents Social Questions Series.

PART I.—GENERAL LITERATURE

Abbot (Jacob). See Little Blue Books.
Abbott (J. H. M.). Author of 'Tommy Cornstalk.' AN OUTLANDER IN ENGLAND: BEING SOME IMPRESSIONS OF AN AUSTRALIAN ABROAD. *Second Edition.* Cr. 8vo. 6s.
A Colonial Edition is also published.
Acatos (M. J.). See Junior School Books.
Adams (Frank). JACK SPRATT. With 24 Coloured Pictures. *Super Royal 16mo.* 2s.
Adeney (W. F.), M.A. See Bennett and Adeney.
Æschylus. See Classical Translations.
Æsop. See I.P.L.
Ainsworth (W. Harrison). See I.P.L.
Alderson (J. P.). MR. ASQUITH. With Portraits and Illustrations. *Demy 8vo.* 7s. 6d. net.
A Colonial Edition is also published.
Aldis (Janet). MADAME GEOFFRIN, HER SALON, AND HER TIMES. With many Portraits and Illustrations. *Second Edition. Demy 8vo.* 10s. 6d. net.
A Colonial Edition is also published.
Alexander (William), D.D., Archbishop of Armagh. THOUGHTS AND COUNSELS OF MANY YEARS. *Demy 16mo.* 2s. 6d.
Aiken (Henry). THE NATIONAL SPORTS OF GREAT BRITAIN. With descriptions in English and French. With 51 Coloured Plates. *Royal Folio. Five Guineas net.* The Plates can be had separately in a Portfolio. £3, 3s. net.
See also I.P.L.
Allen (Jessie). See Little Books on Art.
Allen (J. Romilly), F.S.A. See Antiquary's Books.
Almack (E.). See Little Books on Art.
Amherst (Lady). A SKETCH OF EGYPTIAN HISTORY FROM THE EARLIEST TIMES TO THE PRESENT DAY. With many Illustrations. *Demy 8vo.* 10s. 6d. net.

Anderson (F. M.). THE STORY OF THE BRITISH EMPIRE FOR CHILDREN. With many Illustrations. *Cr. 8vo.* 2s.
Anderson (J. G.), B.A., Examiner to London University, NOUVELLE GRAMMAIRE FRANÇAISE. *Cr. 8vo.* 2s.
EXERCICES DE GRAMMAIRE FRANÇAISE. *Cr. 8vo.* 1s. 6d.
Andrewes (Bishop). PRECES PRIVATAE. Edited, with Notes, by F. E. BRIGHTMAN, M.A., of Pusey House, Oxford. *Cr. 8vo.* 6s.
Anglo-Australian. AFTER-GLOW MEMORIES. *Cr. 8vo.* 6s.
A Colonial Edition is also published.
Aristophanes. THE FROGS. Translated into English by E. W. HUNTINGFORD, M.A. *Cr. 8vo.* 2s. 6d.
Aristotle. THE NICOMACHEAN ETHICS. Edited, with an Introduction and Notes, by JOHN BURNET, M.A., Professor of Greek at St. Andrews. *Cheaper issue. Demy 8vo.* 10s. 6d. net.
Ashton (R.). See Little Blue Books.
Atkins (H. G.). See Oxford Biographies.
Atkinson (C. M.). JEREMY BENTHAM. *Demy 8vo.* 5s. net.
Atkinson (T. D.). A SHORT HISTORY OF ENGLISH ARCHITECTURE. With over 200 Illustrations. *Fcap. 8vo.* 3s. 6d. net.
*A GLOSSARY OF TERMS USED IN ENGLISH ARCHITECTURE. Illustrated. *Fcap. 8vo.* 3s. 6d. net.
Auden (T.), M.A., F.S.A. See Ancient Cities.
Aurelius (Marcus). See Standard Library and W. H. D. Rouse.
Austen (Jane). See Little Library and Standard Library.
Aves (Ernest). See Books on Business.
Bacon (Francis). See Little Library and Standard Library.

General Literature 3

Baden-Powell (R. S. S.), Major-General. THE DOWNFALL OF PREMPEH. A Diary of Life in Ashanti, 1895. Illustrated. *Third Edition. Large Cr. 8vo. 6s.*
A Colonial Edition is also published.
THE MATABELE CAMPAIGN, 1896. With nearly 100 Illustrations. *Fourth Edition. Large Cr. 8vo. 6s.*
A Colonial Edition is also published.
*Bagot (Richard). THE LAKE OF COMO. *Cr. 8vo. 3s. 6d. net.*
Bailey (J. C.), M.A. See Cowper.
Baker (W. G.), M.A. See Junior Examination Series.
Baker (Julian L.), F.I.C., F.C.S. See Books on Business.
Balfour (Graham). THE LIFE OF ROBERT LOUIS STEVENSON. *Second Edition. Two Volumes. Demy 8vo. 25s. net.*
A Colonial Edition is also published.
Bally (S. E.). See Commercial Series.
Banks (Elizabeth L.). THE AUTOBIOGRAPHY OF A 'NEWSPAPER GIRL.' *Second Edition. Cr. 8vo. 6s.*
A Colonial Edition is also published.
Barham (R. H.). See Little Library.
Baring (The Hon. Maurice). WITH THE RUSSIANS IN MANCHURIA. *Third Edition. Demy 8vo. 7s. 6d. net.*
A Colonial Edition is also published.
Baring-Gould (S.). THE LIFE OF NAPOLEON BONAPARTE. With over 450 Illustrations in the Text, and 12 Photogravure Plates. *Gilt top. Large quarto. 36s.*
THE TRAGEDY OF THE CÆSARS. With numerous Illustrations from Busts, Gems, Cameos, etc. *Fifth Edition. Royal 8vo. 10s. 6d. net.*
A BOOK OF FAIRY TALES. With numerous Illustrations by A. J. GASKIN. *Second Edition. Cr. 8vo. Buckram. 6s.*
OLD ENGLISH FAIRY TALES. With numerous Illustrations by F. D. BEDFORD. *Second Edition. Cr. 8vo. Buckram. 6s.*
A Colonial Edition is also published.
THE VICAR OF MORWENSTOW. Revised Edition. With a Portrait. *Cr. 8vo. 3s. 6d.*
DARTMOOR: A Descriptive and Historical Sketch. With Plans and numerous Illustrations. *Cr. 8vo. 6s.*
THE BOOK OF THE WEST. Illustrated. *Two volumes.* Vol. I. Devon. *Second Edition.* Vol. II. Cornwall. *Second Edition. Cr. 8vo. 6s. each.*
A BOOK OF NORTH WALES. Illustrated. *Cr. 8vo. 6s.*
A BOOK OF SOUTH WALES. Illustrated. *Cr. 8vo. 6s.*
A BOOK OF BRITTANY. Illustrated. *Cr. 8vo. 6s.*
A BOOK OF THE RIVIERA. Illustrated. *Cr. 8vo. 6s.*
A Colonial Edition is also published.

*THE RHINE. Illustrated. *Cr. 8vo. 6s.*
A BOOK OF GHOSTS. With 8 Illustrations by D. MURRAY SMITH, *Second Edition. Cr. 8vo. 6s.*
A Colonial Edition is also published.
OLD COUNTRY LIFE. With 67 Illustrations. *Fifth Edition. Large Cr. 8vo. 6s.*
A GARLAND OF COUNTRY SONG: English Folk Songs with their Traditional Melodies. Collected and arranged by S. BARING-GOULD and H. F. SHEPPARD. *Demy 4to. 6s.*
SONGS OF THE WEST: Folk Songs of Devon and Cornwall. Collected from the Mouths of the People. By S. BARING-GOULD, M.A., and H. FLEETWOOD SHEPPARD, M.A. New and Revised Edition, under the musical editorship of CECIL J. SHARP, Principal of the Hampstead Conservatoire. *Large Imperial 8vo. 5s. net.*
See also Little Guides and Half-Crown Library.
Barker (Aldred F.). See Textbooks of Technology.
Barnes (W. E.), D.D. See Churchman's Bible.
Barnett (Mrs. P. A.). See Little Library.
Baron (R. R. N.), M.A. FRENCH PROSE COMPOSITION. *Second Edition. Cr. 8vo. 2s. 6d. Key, 3s. net.* See also Junior School Books.
Barron (H. M.), M.A., Wadham College, Oxford. TEXTS FOR SERMONS. With a Preface by Canon SCOTT HOLLAND. *Cr. 8vo. 3s. 6d.*
Bartholomew (J. G.), F.R.S.E. See C. G. Robertson.
Bastable (C. F.), M.A. See S.Q.S.
Batson (Mrs. Stephen). A BOOK OF THE COUNTRY AND THE GARDEN. Illustrated by F. CARRUTHERS GOULD and A. C. GOULD. *Demy 8vo. 10s. 6d.*
A CONCISE HANDBOOK OF GARDEN FLOWERS. *Fcap. 8vo. 3s. 6d.*
Batten (Loring W.), Ph.D., S.T.D. THE HEBREW PROPHET. *Cr. 8vo. 3s. 6d. net.*
Beaman (A. Hulme). PONS ASINORUM; OR, A GUIDE TO BRIDGE. *Second Edition. Fcap. 8vo. 2s.*
Beard (W. S.). See Junior Examination Series and Beginner's Books.
Beckford (Peter). THOUGHTS ON HUNTING. Edited by J. OTHO PAGET, and Illustrated by G. H. JALLAND. *Second Edition. Demy 8vo. 6s.*
Beckford (William). See Little Library.
Beeching (H. C.), M.A., Canon of Westminster. See Library of Devotion.
Begbie (Harold). MASTER WORKERS. Illustrated. *Demy 8vo. 7s. 6d. net.*
Behmen (Jacob). DIALOGUES ON THE SUPERSENSUAL LIFE. Edited by BERNARD HOLLAND. *Fcap. 8vo. 3s. 6d.*

Belloc (Hilaire). PARIS. With Maps and Illustrations. *Cr. 8vo.* 6s.
*****MARIE ANTOINETTE.** With many Portraits and Illustrations. *Demy 8vo.* 12s. 6d. net.
A Colonial Edition is also published.
Bellot (H. H. L.), M.A. THE INNER AND MIDDLE TEMPLE. With numerous Illustrations. *Crown 8vo.* 6s. net.
See also L. A. A. Jones.
Bennett (W. H.), M.A. A PRIMER OF THE BIBLE. *Second Edition. Cr. 8vo.* 2s. 6d.
Bennett (W. H.) and Adeney (W. F.). A BIBLICAL INTRODUCTION. *Third Edition. Cr. 8vo.* 7s. 6d.
Benson (Archbishop) GOD'S BOARD: Communion Addresses. *Fcap. 8vo.* 3s. 6d. net.
Benson (A. C.), M.A. See Oxford Biographies.
Benson (R. M.). THE WAY OF HOLINESS: a Devotional Commentary on the 119th Psalm. *Cr. 8vo.* 5s.
Bernard (E. R.), M.A., Canon of Salisbury. THE ENGLISH SUNDAY. *Fcap. 8vo.* 1s. 6d.
Bertouch (Baroness de). THE LIFE OF FATHER IGNATIUS. Illustrated. *Demy 8vo.* 10s. 6d. net.
A Colonial Edition is also published.
Betham-Edwards (M.). HOME LIFE IN FRANCE. Illustrated. *Fourth Edition. Demy 8vo.* 7s. 6d. net.
A Colonial Edition is also published.
Bethune-Baker (J. F.), M.A. See Handbooks of Theology.
Bidez (M.). See Byzantine Texts.
Biggs (C. R. D.), D.D. See Churchman's Bible.
Bindley (T. Herbert), B.D. THE OECUMENICAL DOCUMENTS OF THE FAITH. With Introductions and Notes. *Cr. 8vo.* 6s.
Binns (H. B.). THE LIFE OF WALT WHITMAN. Illustrated. *Demy 8vo.* 10s. 6d. net.
A Colonial Edition is also published.
Binyon (Laurence). THE DEATH OF ADAM, AND OTHER POEMS. *Cr. 8vo.* 3s. 6d. net.
*****WILLIAM BLAKE.** In 2 volumes. *Quarto.* £1, 1s. each.
Vol. 1.—THE BOOK OF JOB.
Birnstingl (Ethel). See Little Books on Art.
Blackmantle (Bernard). See I.P.L.
Blair (Robert). See I.P.L.
Blake (William). See I.P.L. and Little Library.
Blaxland (B.), M.A. See Library of Devotion.
Bloom (T. Harvey), M.A. SHAKESPEARE'S GARDEN. *Fcap. 8vo.* 3s. 6d.; leather, 4s. 6d. net.
See also Antiquary's Books.

Blouet (Henri). See Beginner's Books.
Boardman (T. H.), M.A. See Textbooks of Science.
Bodley (J. E. C.), Author of 'France.' THE CORONATION OF EDWARD VII. *Demy 8vo.* 21s. net. By Command of the King.
Body (George), D.D. THE SOUL'S PILGRIMAGE: Devotional Readings from his writings. Selected by J. H. BURN, B.D., F.R.S.E. *Pott 8vo.* 2s. 6d.
Bona (Cardinal). See Library of Devotion.
Boon (F. C.). See Commercial Series.
Borrow (George). See Little Library.
Bos (J. Ritzema). AGRICULTURAL ZOOLOGY. Translated by J. R. AINSWORTH DAVIS, M.A. With 155 Illustrations. *Cr. 8vo. Third Edition.* 3s. 6d.
Botting (C. G.), B.A. EASY GREEK EXERCISES. *Cr. 8vo.* 2s. See also Junior Examination Series.
Boulton (E. S.), M.A. GEOMETRY ON MODERN LINES. *Cr. 8vo.* 2s.
Boulton (William B.). THOMAS GAINSBOROUGH. With 40 Illustrations. *Second Ed. Demy 8vo.* 7s. 6d. net.
SIR JOSHUA REYNOLDS, P.R.A. With 49 Illustrations. *Demy 8vo.* 7s. 6d. net.
Bowden (E. M.). THE IMITATION OF BUDDHA: Being Quotations from Buddhist Literature for each Day in the Year. *Fifth Edition. Cr. 16mo.* 2s. 6d.
Boyle (W.). CHRISTMAS AT THE ZOO. With Verses by W. BOYLE and 24 Coloured Pictures by H. B. NEILSON. *Super Royal 16mo.* 2s.
Brabant (F. G.), M.A. See Little Guides.
Bradley (J. W.). See Little Books on Art.
*****Brailsford (H. N.).** MACEDONIA. Illustrated. *Demy 8vo.* 12s. 6d. net.
Brodrick (Mary) and Morton (Anderson). A CONCISE HANDBOOK OF EGYPTIAN ARCHÆOLOGY. Illustrated. *Cr. 8vo.* 3s. 6d.
Brooke (A. S.), M.A. SLINGSBY AND SLINGSBY CASTLE. Illustrated. *Cr. 8vo.* 7s. 6d.
Brooks (E. W.). See Byzantine Texts.
Brown (P. H.), LL.D., Fraser Professor of Ancient (Scottish) History at the University of Edinburgh. SCOTLAND IN THE TIME OF QUEEN MARY. *Demy 8vo.* 7s. 6d. net.
Browne (Sir Thomas). See Standard Library.
Brownell (C. L.). THE HEART OF JAPAN. Illustrated. *Third Edition. Cr. 8vo.* 6s.; also *Demy 8vo.* 6d.
A Colonial Edition is also published.
Browning (Robert). See Little Library.
Buckland (Francis T.). CURIOSITIES OF NATURAL HISTORY. Illustrated by H. B. NEILSON. *Cr. 8vo.* 3s. 6d.

General Literature

Buckton (A. M.) THE BURDEN OF ENGELA: a Ballad-Epic. *Second Edition.* *Cr. 8vo.* 3s. 6d. *net.*

EAGER HEART: A Mystery Play. *Fourth Edition. Cr. 8vo.* 1s. *net.*

Budge (E. A. Wallis). THE GODS OF THE EGYPTIANS. With over 100 Coloured Plates and many Illustrations. *Two Volumes. Royal 8vo.* £3, 3s. *net.*

Bull (Paul), Army Chaplain. GOD AND OUR SOLDIERS. *Second Edition. Cr. 8vo.* 6s.
A Colonial Edition is also published.

Bulley (Miss). See S.Q.S.

Bunyan (John). THE PILGRIM'S PROGRESS. Edited, with an Introduction, by C. H. FIRTH, M.A. With 39 Illustrations by R. ANNING BELL. *Cr. 8vo.* 6s.
See also Library of Devotion and Standard Library.

Burch (G. J.), M.A., F.R.S. A MANUAL OF ELECTRICAL SCIENCE. Illustrated. *Cr. 8vo.* 3s.

Burgess (Gelett). GOOPS AND HOW TO BE THEM. Illustrated. *Small 4to.* 6s.

Burke (Edmund). See Standard Library.

Burn (A. E.), D.D., Prebendary of Lichfield. See Handbooks of Theology.

Burn (J. H.), B.D. See Library of Devotion.

Burnand (Sir F. C.). RECORDS AND REMINISCENCES. With a Portrait by H. v. HERKOMER. *Cr. 8vo. Fourth and Cheaper Edition.* 6s.
A Colonial Edition is also published.

Burns (Robert), THE POEMS OF. Edited by ANDREW LANG and W. A. CRAIGIE. With Portrait. *Third Edition. Demy 8vo, gilt top.* 6s.

Burnside (W. F.), M.A. OLD TESTAMENT HISTORY FOR USE IN SCHOOLS. *Cr. 8vo.* 3s. 6d.

Burton (Alfred). See I.P.L.

Butler (Joseph). See Standard Library.

Caldecott (Alfred), D.D. See Handbooks of Theology.

Calderwood (D. S.), Headmaster of the Normal School, Edinburgh. TEST CARDS IN EUCLID AND ALGEBRA. In three packets of 40, with Answers. 1s. each. Or in three Books, price 2d., 2d., and 3d.

Cambridge (Ada) [Mrs. Cross]. THIRTY YEARS IN AUSTRALIA. *Demy 8vo.* 7s. 6d.
A Colonial Edition is also published.

Canning (George). See Little Library.

Capey (E. F. H.). See Oxford Biographies.

Careless (John). See I.P.L.

Carlyle (Thomas). THE FRENCH REVOLUTION. Edited by C. R. L. FLETCHER, Fellow of Magdalen College, Oxford. *Three Volumes. Cr. 8vo.* 18s.

THE LIFE AND LETTERS OF OLIVER CROMWELL. With an Introduction by C. H. FIRTH, M.A., and Notes and Appendices by Mrs. S. C. LOMAS. *Three Volumes. Demy 8vo.* 18s. *net.*

Carlyle (R. M. and A. J.), M.A. See Leaders of Religion.

*Carpenter (Margaret). THE CHILD IN ART. Illustrated. *Cr. 8vo.* 6s.

Chamberlin (Wilbur B.). ORDERED TO CHINA. *Cr. 8vo.* 6s.
A Colonial Edition is also published.

Channer (C. C.) and Roberts (M. E.). LACEMAKING IN THE MIDLANDS, PAST AND PRESENT. With 16 full-page Illustrations. *Cr. 8vo.* 2s. 6d.

Chapman (S. J.). See Books on Business.

Chatterton (Thomas). See Standard Library.

Chesterfield (Lord), THE LETTERS OF, TO HIS SON. Edited, with an Introduction by C. STRACHEY, and Notes by A. CALTHROP. *Two Volumes. Cr. 8vo.* 12s.

*Chesterton (G. K.). DICKENS. With Portraits and Illustrations. *Demy 8vo.* 7s. 6d. *net.*
A Colonial Edition is also published.

Christian (F. W.). THE CAROLINE ISLANDS. With many Illustrations and Maps. *Demy 8vo.* 12s. 6d. *net.*

Cicero. See Classical Translations.

Clarke (F. A.), M.A. See Leaders of Religion.

Cleather (A. L.) and Crump (B.). RICHARD WAGNER'S MUSIC DRAMAS: Interpretations, embodying Wagner's own explanations. *In Four Volumes. Fcap 8vo.* 2s. 6d. *each.*
VOL. I.—THE RING OF THE NIBELUNG.
VOL. II.—PARSIFAL, LOHENGRIN, and THE HOLY GRAIL.
VOL. III.—TRISTAN AND ISOLDE.

Clinch (G.). See Little Guides.

Clough (W. T.). See Junior School Books.

Coast (W. G.), B.A. EXAMINATION PAPERS IN VERGIL. *Cr. 8vo.* 2s.

Cobb (T.). See Little Blue Books.

Cobb (W. F.), M.A. THE BOOK OF PSALMS: with a Commentary. *Demy 8vo.* 10s. 6d. *net.*

Coleridge (S. T.), SELECTIONS FROM. Edited by ARTHUR SYMONS. *Fcap. 8vo.* 2s. 6d. *net.*

Collingwood (W. G.). See Half-Crown Library.

Collins (W. E.), M.A. See Churchman's Library.

Colonna. HYPNEROTOMACHIA POLIPHILI UBI HUMANA OMNIA NON NISI SOMNIUM ESSE DOCET ATQUE OBITER PLURIMA SCITU SANE QUAM DIGNA COMMEMORAT. An edition limited to 350 copies on handmade paper. *Folio. Three Guineas net.*

Combe (William). See I.P.L.

Cook (A. M.), M.A. See E. C. Marchant.

Cooke-Taylor (R. W.). See S.Q.S.
Corelli (Marie). THE PASSING OF THE GREAT QUEEN : *Fcap. 4to. 1s.*
A CHRISTMAS GREETING. *Cr. 4to. 1s.*
Corkran (Alice). See Little Books on Art.
Cotes (Rosemary). DANTE'S GARDEN. With a Frontispiece. *Second Edition. Fcap. 8vo. 2s. 6d.; leather, 3s. 6d. net.*
BIBLE FLOWERS. With a Frontispiece and Plan. *Fcap. 8vo. 2s. 6d. net.*
Cowley (Abraham). See Little Library.
Cowper (William). THE POEMS OF. Edited with an Introduction and Notes by J. C. BAILEY, M.A. Illustrated, including two unpublished designs by WILLIAM BLAKE. *Demy 8vo. 10s. 6d. net.*
Cox (J. Charles), LL.D., F.S.A. See Little Guides, The Antiquary's Books, and Ancient Cities.
Cox (Harold), B.A. See S.Q.S.
Crabbe (George). See Little Library.
Craigie (W. A.). A PRIMER OF BURNS. *Cr. 8vo. 2s. 6d.*
Craik (Mrs.). See Little Library.
Crashaw (Richard). See Little Library.
Crawford (F. G.). See Mary C. Danson.
*Cross (J. A.). A LITTLE BOOK OF RELIGION. *Fcap. 8vo. 2s. 6d. net.*
Crouch (W.). BRYAN KING. With a Portrait. *Cr. 8vo. 3s. 6d. net.*
Cruikshank (G.). THE LOVING BALLAD OF LORD BATEMAN. With 11 Plates. *Cr. 16mo. 1s. 6d. net.*
Crump (B.). See A. L. Cleather.
Cunliffe (Sir F. H. E.), Fellow of All Souls' College, Oxford. THE HISTORY OF THE BOER WAR. With many Illustrations, Plans, and Portraits. *In 2 vols. Quarto. 15s. each.*
A Colonial Edition is also published.
Cunynghame (H.), C.B., See Connoisseur's Library.
Cutts (E. L.), D.D. See Leaders of Religion.
Daniell (G. W.), M.A. See Leaders of Religion.
Danson (Mary C.) and Crawford (F. G.). FATHERS IN THE FAITH. *Fcap. 8vo. 1s. 6d.*
Dante. LA COMMEDIA DI DANTE. The Italian Text edited by PAGET TOYNBEE, M.A., D.Litt. *Cr. 8vo. 6s.*
THE PURGATORIO OF DANTE. Translated into Spenserian Prose by C. GORDON WRIGHT. With the Italian text. *Fcap. 8vo. 2s. 6d. net.*
See also Paget Toynbee, Little Library and Standard Library.
Darley (George). See Little Library.
D'Arcy (R. F.), M.A. A NEW TRIGONOMETRY FOR BEGINNERS. *Cr. 8vo. 2s. 6d.*
Davenport (Cyril). See Connoisseur's Library and Little Books on Art.

*Davey (Richard). THE PAGEANT OF LONDON With 40 Illustrations in Colour by JOHN FULLEYLOVE, R. I. *In Two Volumes. Demy 8vo. 7s. 6d. net.*
Each volume may be purchased separately.
VOL. I.—TO A.D. 1500.
VOL. II.—A.D. 1500 TO 1900.
Davis (H. W. C.), M.A., Fellow and Tutor of Balliol College, Author of ' Charlemagne.' ENGLAND UNDER THE NORMANS AND ANGEVINS : 1066-1272. With Maps and Illustrations. *Demy 8vo. 10s. 6d. net.*
Dawson (A. J.). MOROCCO. Illustrated *Demy 8vo. 10s. 6d. net.*
Deane (A. C.). See Little Library.
Delbos (Leon). THE METRIC SYSTEM. *Cr. 8vo. 2s.*
Demosthenes. THE OLYNTHIACS AND PHILIPPICS. Translated by OTHO HOLLAND. *Cr. 8vo. 2s. 6d.*
Demosthenes. AGAINST CONON AND CALLICLES. Edited by F. DARWIN SWIFT, M.A. *Fcap. 8vo. 2s.*
Dickens (Charles). See Little Library and I.P.L.
Dickinson (Emily). POEMS. *Cr. 8vo. 4s. 6d. net.*
Dickinson (G. L.), M.A., Fellow of King's College, Cambridge. THE GREEK VIEW OF LIFE. *Fourth Edition. Cr. 8vo. 2s. 6d.*
Dickson (H. N.), F.R.Met. Soc METEOROLOGY. Illustrated. *Cr. 8vo. 2s. 6d.*
Dilke (Lady). See S.Q.S.
Dillon (Edward). See Connoisseur's Library and Little Books on Art.
Ditchfield (P. H.), M.A., F.S.A. THE STORY OF OUR ENGLISH TOWNS. With an Introduction by AUGUSTUS JESSOPP, D.D. *Second Edition. Cr. 8vo. 6s.*
OLD ENGLISH CUSTOMS: Extant at the Present Time. *Cr. 8vo. 6s.*
See also Half-crown Library.
Dixon (W. M.), M.A. A PRIMER OF TENNYSON. *Second Edition. Cr. 8vo. 2s. 6d.*
ENGLISH POETRY FROM BLAKE TO BROWNING. *Second Edition. Cr. 8vo. 2s. 6d.*
Dole (N. H.). FAMOUS COMPOSERS. With Portraits. *Two Volumes. Demy 8vo. 12s. net.*
Doney (May). SONGS OF THE REAL. *Cr. 8vo. 3s. 6d. net.*
A volume of poems.
Douglas (James). THE MAN IN THE PULPIT. *Cr. 8vo. 2s. 6d. net.*
Dowden (J.), D.D., Lord Bishop of Edinburgh. See Churchman's Library.
Drage (G.). See Books on Business.

General Literature

Driver (S. R.), D.D., D.C.L., Canon of Christ Church, Regius Professor of Hebrew in the University of Oxford. SERMONS ON SUBJECTS CONNECTED WITH THE OLD TESTAMENT. *Cr. 8vo.* 6s.
See also Westminster Commentaries.
Dry (Wakeling). See Little Guides.
Dryhurst (A. R.). See Little Books on Art.
Duguid (Charles). See Books on Business.
Dunn (J. T.), D.Sc., and Mundella (V. A.). GENERAL ELEMENTARY SCIENCE. With 114 Illustrations. *Second Edition. Cr. 8vo.* 3s. 6d.
Dunstan (A. E.), B.Sc. See Junior School Books and Textbooks of Science.
Durham (The Earl of). A REPORT ON CANADA. With an Introductory Note. *Demy 8vo.* 4s. 6d. net.
Dutt (W. A.). A POPULAR GUIDE TO NORFOLK. *Medium 8vo.* 6d. net.
THE NORFOLK BROADS. With coloured Illustrations by FRANK SOUTHGATE. *Cr. 8vo.* 6s. See also Little Guides.
Earle (John), Bishop of Salisbury. MICROCOSMOGRAPHIE, OR A PIECE OF THE WORLD DISCOVERED. *Post 16mo.* 2s net.
Edmonds (Major J. E.), R.E.; D.A.Q.-M.G. See W. Birkbeck Wood.
Edwards (Clement). See S.Q.S.
Edwards (W. Douglas). See Commercial Series.
Egan (Pierce). See I.P.L.
*****Egerton H. E.**, M.A. A HISTORY OF BRITISH COLONIAL POLICY. New and Cheaper Issue. *Demy 8vo.* 7s. 6d. net.
A Colonial Edition is also published.
Ellaby (C. G.). See The Little Guides.
Ellerton (F. G.). See S. J. Stone.
Ellwood (Thomas), THE HISTORY OF THE LIFE OF. Edited by C. G. CRUMP, M.A. *Cr. 8vo.* 6s.
Epictetus. See W. H. D. Rouse.
Erasmus. A Book called in Latin ENCHIRIDION MILITIS CHRISTIANI, and in English the Manual of the Christian Knight.
From the edition printed by Wynken de Worde, 1533. *Fcap. 8vo* 3s. 6d. net.
Fairbrother (W. H.), M.A. THE PHILOSOPHY OF T. H. GREEN. *Second Edition. Cr. 8vo.* 3s. 6d.
Farrer (Reginald). THE GARDEN OF ASIA. *Second Edition. Cr. 8vo.* 6s.
A Colonial Edition is also published.
*****Fea (Allan).** BEAUTIES OF THE SEVENTEENTH CENTURY. With 100 Illustrations. *Demy 8vo.* 12s. 6d. net.
FELISSA; OR, THE LIFE AND OPINIONS OF A KITTEN OF SENTIMENT. With 12 Coloured Plates. *Post 16mo.* 2s. 6d. net.
Ferrier (Susan). See Little Library.
Fidler (T. Claxton), M.Inst. C.E. See Books on Business.

Fielding (Henry). See Standard Library.
Finn (S. W.), M.A. See Junior Examination Series.
Firth (C. H.), M.A. CROMWELL'S ARMY: A History of the English Soldier during the Civil Wars, the Commonwealth, and the Protectorate. *Cr. 8vo.* 6s.
Fisher (G. W.), M.A. ANNALS OF SHREWSBURY SCHOOL. Illustrated. *Demy 8vo.* 10s. 6d.
FitzGerald (Edward). THE RUBAIYAT OF OMAR KHAYYÁM. Printed from the Fifth and last Edition. With a Commentary by Mrs. STEPHEN BATSON, and a Biography of Omar by E. D. ROSS. *Cr. 8vo.* 6s. See also Miniature Library.
*****FitzGerald (H. P.).** A CONCISE HANDBOOK OF CLIMBERS, TWINERS, AND WALL SHRUBS. Illustrated. *Fcap. 8vo.* 3s. 6d. net.
Flecker (W. H.), M.A., D.C.L., Headmaster of the Dean Close School, Cheltenham. THE STUDENT'S PRAYER BOOK. THE TEXT OF MORNING AND EVENING PRAYER AND LITANY. With an Introduction and Notes. *Cr. 8vo.* 2s. 6d.
Flux (A. W.), M.A., William Dow Professor of Political Economy in M'Gill University, Montreal. ECONOMIC PRINCIPLES. *Demy 8vo.* 7s. 6d. net.
Fortescue (Mrs. G.). See Little Books on Art.
Fraser (David). A MODERN CAMPAIGN; OR, WAR AND WIRELESS TELEGRAPHY IN THE FAR EAST. Illustrated. *Cr. 8vo.* 6s.
A Colonial Edition is also published.
Fraser (J. F.). ROUND THE WORLD ON A WHEEL. With 100 Illustrations. *Fourth Edition. Cr. 8vo.* 6s.
A Colonial Edition is also published.
French (W.), M.A. See Textbooks of Science.
Freudenreich (Ed. von). DAIRY BACTERIOLOGY. A Short Manual for the Use of Students. Translated by J. R. AINSWORTH DAVIS, M.A. *Second Edition. Revised. Cr. 8vo.* 2s. 6d.
Fulford (H. W.), M.A. See Churchman's Bible.
C., and F. C. G. JOHN BULL'S ADVENTURES IN THE FISCAL WONDERLAND. By CHARLES GEAKE. With 46 Illustrations by F. CARRUTHERS GOULD. *Second Edition. Cr. 8vo.* 1s. net.
*****Gallaher (D.) and Stead (D. W.).** THE COMPLETE RUGBY FOOTBALLER. With an Account of the Tour of the New Zealanders in England. With Illustrations. *Demy 8vo.* 10s. 6d. net.
Gallichan (W. M.). See Little Guides.
Gambado (Geoffrey, Esq.). See I.P.L.
Gaskell (Mrs.). See Little Library and Standard Library.
Gasquet, the Right Rev. Abbot, O.S.B. See Antiquary's Books.

MESSRS. METHUEN'S CATALOGUE

George (H. B.), M.A., Fellow of New College, Oxford. BATTLES OF ENGLISH HISTORY. With numerous Plans. *Fourth Edition.* Revised, with a new Chapter including the South African War. *Cr. 8vo.* 3s. 6d.
A HISTORICAL GEOGRAPHY OF THE BRITISH EMPIRE. *Second Edition. Cr. 8vo.* 3s. 6d.
Gibbins (H. de B.), Litt.D., M.A. INDUSTRY IN ENGLAND: HISTORICAL OUTLINES. With 5 Maps. *Fourth Edition. Demy 8vo.* 10s. 6d.
A COMPANION GERMAN GRAMMAR. *Cr. 8vo.* 1s. 6d.
THE INDUSTRIAL HISTORY OF ENGLAND. *Tenth Edition.* Revised. With Maps and Plans. *Cr. 8vo.* 3s.
ENGLISH SOCIAL REFORMERS. *Second Edition. Cr. 8vo.* 2s. 6d.
See also Commercial Series and S.Q.S.
Gibbon (Edward). THE DECLINE AND FALL OF THE ROMAN EMPIRE. A New Edition, edited with Notes, Appendices, and Maps, by J. B. Bury, M.A., Litt.D., Regius Professor of Greek at Cambridge. *In Seven Volumes. Demy 8vo. Gilt top,* 8s. 6d. *each. Also, Cr. 8vo.* 6s. *each.*
MEMOIRS OF MY LIFE AND WRITINGS. Edited by G. Birkbeck Hill, LL.D. *Demy 8vo, Gilt top.* 8s. 6d. *Also Cr. 8vo.* 6s.
See also Standard Library.
Gibson (E. C. S.), D.D., Lord Bishop of Gloucester. See Westminster Commentaries, Handbooks of Theology, and Oxford Biographies.
Gilbert (A. R.). See Little Books on Art.
Gloag (M.). See K. Wyatt.
Godfrey (Elizabeth). A BOOK OF REMEMBRANCE. Edited by. *Fcap. 8vo.* 2s. 6d. *net.*
Godley (A. D.), M.A., Fellow of Magdalen College, Oxford. LYRA FRIVOLA. *Third Edition. Fcap. 8vo.* 2s. 6d.
VERSES TO ORDER. *Second Edition. Fcap. 8vo.* 2s. 6d.
SECOND STRINGS. *Fcap. 8vo.* 2s. 6d.
Goldsmith (Oliver). THE VICAR OF WAKEFIELD. *Fcap. 32mo.* With 10 Plates in Photogravure by Tony Johannot. *Leather,* 2s. 6d. *net.* See also I.P.L. and Standard Library.
Goodrich-Freer (A.). IN A SYRIAN SADDLE. *Demy 8vo.* 7s. 6d. *net.*
A Colonial Edition is also published.
Goudge (H. L.), M.A., Principal of Wells Theological College. See Westminster Commentaries.
Graham (P. Anderson). See S.Q.S.
Granger (F. S.), M.A., Litt.D. PSYCHOLOGY. *Second Edition. Cr. 8vo.* 2s. 6d.
THE SOUL OF A CHRISTIAN. *Cr. 8vo.* 6s.

Gray (E. M'Queen). GERMAN PASSAGES FOR UNSEEN TRANSLATION. *Cr. 8vo.* 2s. 6d.
Gray (P. L.), B.Sc. THE PRINCIPLES OF MAGNETISM AND ELECTRICITY: an Elementary Text-Book. With 181 Diagrams. *Cr. 8vo.* 3s. 6d.
Green (G. Buckland), M.A., late Fellow of St. John's College, Oxon. NOTES ON GREEK AND LATIN SYNTAX. *Cr. 8vo.* 3s. 6d.
Green (E. T.), M.A. See Churchman's Library.
Greenidge (A. H. J.), M.A. A HISTORY OF ROME: During the Later Republic and the Early Principate. *In Six Volumes. Demy 8vo.* Vol. I. (133-104 B.C.). 10s. 6d. *net.*
Greenwell (Dora). See Miniature Library.
Gregory (R. A.). THE VAULT OF HEAVEN. A Popular Introduction to Astronomy. Illustrated. *Cr. 8vo.* 2s. 6d.
Gregory (Miss E. C.). See Library of Devotion.
Greville Minor. A MODERN JOURNAL. Edited by J. A. Spender. *Cr. 8vo* 3s. 6d. *net.*
Grubb (H. C.). See Textbooks of Technology.
Guiney (Louisa I.). HURRELL FROUDE; Memoranda and Comments. Illustrated. *Demy 8vo.* 10s. 6d. *net.*
Gwynn (M. L.). A BIRTHDAY BOOK. New and cheaper issue. *Royal 8vo.* 5s. *net.*
Hackett (John), B.D. A HISTORY OF THE ORTHODOX CHURCH OF CYPRUS. With Maps and Illustrations. *Demy 8vo.* 15s. *net.*
Haddon (A. C.), Sc.D., F.R.S. HEAD-HUNTERS BLACK, WHITE, AND BROWN. With many Illustrations and a Map. *Demy 8vo.* 15s.
Hadfield (R. A.). See S.Q.S.
Hall (R. N.) and Neal (W. G.). THE ANCIENT RUINS OF RHODESIA. Illustrated *Second Edition, revised. Demy 8vo.* 10s. 6d. *net.*
A Colonial Edition is also published.
Hall (R. N.). GREAT ZIMBABWE. With numerous Plans and Illustrations. *Second Edition. Royal 8vo.* 21s. *net.*
Hamilton (F. J.), D.D. See Byzantine Texts.
Hammond (J. L.). CHARLES JAMES FOX. *Demy 8vo.* 10s. 6d.
Hannay (D.). A SHORT HISTORY OF THE ROYAL NAVY, Illustrated. *Two Volumes. Demy 8vo.* 7s. 6d. *each.* Vol. I. 1200-1688.
Hannay (James O.), M.A. THE SPIRIT AND ORIGIN OF CHRISTIAN MONASTICISM. *Cr. 8vo.* 6s.
THE WISDOM OF THE DESERT. *Fcap. 8vo.* 3s. 6d. *net.*
Hare (A. T.), M.A. THE CONSTRUCTION OF LARGE INDUCTION COILS. With numerous Diagrams. *Demy 8vo.* 6s.

Harrison (Clifford). READING AND READERS. *Fcap. 8vo.* 2s. 6d.
Hawthorne (Nathaniel). See Little Library.
HEALTH, WEALTH AND WISDOM. *Cr. 8vo.* 1s. net.
Heath (Frank R.). See Little Guides.
Heath (Dudley). See Connoisseur's Library.
Hello (Ernest). STUDIES IN SAINT-SHIP. Translated from the French by V. M. CRAWFORD. *Fcap 8vo.* 3s. 6d.
Henderson (B. W.), Fellow of Exeter College, Oxford. THE LIFE AND PRINCIPATE OF THE EMPEROR NERO. Illustrated. *New and cheaper issue. Demy 8vo.* 7s. 6d. net.
AT INTERVALS. *Fcap 8vo.* 2s. 6d. net.
Henderson (T. F.). See Little Library and Oxford Biographies.
Henley (W. E.). See Half-Crown Library.
Henson (H. H.), B.D., Canon of Westminster. APOSTOLIC CHRISTIANITY: As Illustrated by the Epistles of St. Paul to the Corinthians. *Cr. 8vo.* 6s.
LIGHT AND LEAVEN: HISTORICAL AND SOCIAL SERMONS. *Cr. 8vo.* 6s.
DISCIPLINE AND LAW. *Fcap. 8vo.* 2s. 6d.
Herbert (George). See Library of Devotion.
Herbert of Cherbury (Lord). See Miniature Library.
Hewins (W. A. S.), B.A. ENGLISH TRADE AND FINANCE IN THE SEVENTEENTH CENTURY. *Cr. 8vo.* 2s. 6d.
Hewitt (Ethel M.) A GOLDEN DIAL. A Day Book of Prose and Verse. *Fcap. 8vo.* 2s. 6d. net.
Heywood (W.). PALIO AND PONTE: A Book of Tuscan Games. Illustrated. *Royal 8vo.* 21s. net.
Hilbert (T.). See Little Blue Books.
Hill (Clare). See Textbooks of Technology.
Hill (Henry), B.A., Headmaster of the Boy's High School, Worcester, Cape Colony. A SOUTH AFRICAN ARITHMETIC. *Cr. 8vo.* 3s. 6d.
Hillegas (Howard C.). WITH THE BOER FORCES. With 24 Illustrations. *Second Edition. Cr. 8vo.* 6s.
A Colonial Edition is also published.
Hirst (F. W.) See Books on Business.
Hobhouse (Emily). THE BRUNT OF THE WAR. With Map and Illustrations. *Cr. 8vo.* 6s.
A Colonial Edition is also published.
Hobhouse (L. T.), Fellow of C.C.C., Oxford. THE THEORY OF KNOWLEDGE. *Demy 8vo.* 10s. 6d. net.
Hobson (J. A.), M.A. INTERNATIONAL TRADE: A Study of Economic Principles. *Cr. 8vo.* 2s. 6d. net.
PROBLEMS OF POVERTY. *Fifth Edition. Cr. 8vo.* 2s. 6d.
Hodgkin (T.), D.C.L. See Leaders of Religion.

Hodgson (Mrs. W.) HOW TO IDENTIFY OLD CHINESE PORCELAIN. *Second Edition. Post 8vo.* 6s.
Hogg (Thomas Jefferson). SHELLEY AT OXFORD. With an Introduction by R. A. STREATFEILD. *Fcap. 8vo.* 2s. net.
Holden-Stone (G. de). See Books on Business.
Holdich (Sir T. H.), K.C.I.E. THE INDIAN BORDERLAND: being a Personal Record of Twenty Years. Illustrated. *Demy 8vo.* 10s. 6d. net.
A Colonial Edition is also published.
Holdsworth (W. S.), M.A. A HISTORY OF ENGLISH LAW. In Two Volumes. Vol. I. *Demy 8vo.* 10s. 6d. net.
Holland (Canon Scott). See Library of Devotion.
Holt (Emily). THE SECRET OF POPULARITY: How to Achieve Social Success. *Cr. 8vo.* 3s. 6d. net.
A Colonial Edition is also published.
Holyoake (G. J.). THE CO-OPERATIVE MOVEMENT TO-DAY. *Fourth Edition. Cr. 8vo.* 2s. 6d.
Hone (Nathaniel J.). See Antiquary's Books.
Hoppner. See Little Galleries.
Horace. See Classical Translations.
Horsburgh (E. L. S.), M.A. WATERLOO: A Narrative and Criticism. With Plans. *Second Edition. Cr. 8vo.* 5s. See also Oxford Biographies.
Horth (A. C.). See Textbooks of Technology.
Horton (R. F.), D.D. See Leaders of Religion.
Hosie (Alexander). MANCHURIA. With Illustrations and a Map. *Second Edition. Demy 8vo.* 7s. 6d. net.
A Colonial Edition is also published.
How (F. D.). SIX GREAT SCHOOLMASTERS. With Portraits and Illustrations *Second Edition. Demy 8vo.* 7s. 6d.
Howell (G.). See S. Q. S.
Hudson (Robert). MEMORIALS OF A WARWICKSHIRE PARISH. Illustrated. *Demy 8vo.* 15s. net.
Hughes (C. E.). THE PRAISE OF SHAKESPEARE. An English Anthology. With a Preface by SIDNEY LEE. *Demy 8vo.* 3s. 6d. net.
Hughes (Thomas). TOM BROWN'S SCHOOLDAYS. With an Introduction and Notes by VERNON RENDALL. Leather. *Royal 32mo.* 2s. 6d. net.
Hutchinson (Horace G.) THE NEW FOREST. Illustrated in colour with 50 Pictures by WALTER TYNDALE and 4 by Miss LUCY KEMP WELCH. *Large Demy 8vo.* 21s. net.
Hutton (A. W.), M.A. See Leaders of Religion and Library of Devotion.
Hutton (Edward). THE CITIES OF UMBRIA. With many Illustrations, of which 20 are in Colour, by A. PISA. *Second Edition. Cr. 8vo.* 6s.
A Colonial Edition is also published.

ENGLISH LOVE POEMS. Edited with an Introduction. *Fcap. 8vo.* 3s. 6d. *net.*
Hutton (R. H.). See Leaders of Religion.
Hutton (W. H.), M.A. THE LIFE OF SIR THOMAS MORE. With Portraits. *Second Edition. Cr. 8vo.* 5s. See also Leaders of Religion.
Hyett (F. A.). A SHORT HISTORY OF FLORENCE. *Demy 8vo.* 7s. 6d. *net.*
Ibsen (Henrik). BRAND. A Drama. Translated by WILLIAM WILSON. *Third Edition. Cr. 8vo.* 3s. 6d.
Inge (W. R.), M.A., Fellow and Tutor of Hertford College, Oxford. CHRISTIAN MYSTICISM. The Bampton Lectures for 1899. *Demy 8vo.* 12s. 6d. *net.* See also Library of Devotion.
Innes (A. D.), M.A. A HISTORY OF THE BRITISH IN INDIA. With Maps and Plans. *Cr. 8vo.* 6s.
ENGLAND UNDER THE TUDORS. With Maps. *Demy 8vo.* 10s. 6d. *net.*
Jackson (C. E.), B.A. See Textbooks of Science.
Jackson (S.), M.A. See Commercial Series.
Jackson (F. Hamilton). See Little Guides.
Jacob (F.), M.A. See Junior Examination Series.
Jeans (J. Stephen). See S. Q. S. and Business Books.
Jeffreys (D. Gwyn). DOLLY'S THEATRICALS. Described and Illustrated with 24 Coloured Pictures. *Super Royal 16mo.* 2s. 6d.
Jenks (E.), M.A., Reader of Law in the University of Oxford. ENGLISH LOCAL GOVERNMENT. *Cr. 8vo.* 2s. 6d.
Jenner (Mrs. H.). See Little Books on Art.
Jessopp (Augustus), D.D. See Leaders of Religion.
*Jevons (F. B.), M.A., Litt.D., Principal of Hatfield Hall, Durham. RELIGION IN EVOLUTION. *Cr. 8vo.* 3s. 6d. *net.* See also Churchman's Library and Handbooks of Theology.
Johnson (Mrs. Barham). WILLIAM BODHAM DONNE AND HIS FRIENDS. Illustrated. *Demy 8vo.* 10s. 6d. *net.*
Johnston (Sir H. H.), K.C.B. BRITISH CENTRAL AFRICA. With nearly 200 Illustrations and Six Maps. *Third Edition. Cr. 4to.* 18s. *net.*
A Colonial Edition is also published.
Jones (R. Crompton), M.A. POEMS OF THE INNER LIFE. Selected by. *Eleventh Edition. Fcap. 8vo.* 2s. 6d. *net.*
Jones (H.). See Commercial Series.
Jones (L. A. Atherley), K.C., M.P., and Bellot (Hugh H. L.). THE MINERS' GUIDE TO THE COAL MINES REGULATION ACTS. *Cr. 8vo.* 2s. 6d. *net.*
*COMMERCE IN WAR. *Demy 8vo.* 21s. *net.*
Jonson (Ben). See Standard Library.

Julian (Lady) of Norwich. REVELATIONS OF DIVINE LOVE. Edited by GRACE WARRACK. *Cr. 8vo.* 3s. 6d.
Juvenal. See Classical Translations.
'Kappa.' LET YOUTH BUT KNOW: A Plea for Reason in Education. *Cr. 8vo.* 3s. 6d. *net.*
Kaufmann (M.). See S. Q. S.
Keating (J. F.), D.D. THE AGAPE AND THE EUCHARIST. *Cr. 8vo.* 3s. 6d.
Keats (John). THE POEMS OF. Edited with Introduction and Notes by E. de Selincourt, M.A. *Demy 8vo.* 7s. 6d. *net.* See also Little Library, Standard Library, and E. de Selincourt.
Keble (John). THE CHRISTIAN YEAR. With an Introduction and Notes by W. LOCK, D.D., Warden of Keble College. Illustrated by R. ANNING BELL. *Third Edition. Fcap. 8vo.* 3s. 6d.; padded morocco, 5s. See also Library of Devotion.
Kempis (Thomas à). THE IMITATION OF CHRIST. With an Introduction by DEAN FARRAR. Illustrated by C. M. GERE. *Third Edition. Fcap. 8vo.* 3s. 6d.; padded morocco, 5s. See also Library of Devotion and Standard Library.
Also Translated by C. BIGG, D.D. *Cr. 8vo.* 3s. 6d.
Kennedy (Bart.). THE GREEN SPHINX. *Cr. 8vo.* 3s. 6d. *net.*
A Colonial Edition is also published.
Kennedy (James Houghton), D.D., Assistant Lecturer in Divinity in the University of Dublin. ST. PAUL'S SECOND AND THIRD EPISTLES TO THE CORINTHIANS. With Introduction, Dissertations and Notes. *Cr. 8vo.* 6s.
Kestell (J. D.). THROUGH SHOT AND FLAME: Being the Adventures and Experiences of J. D. KESTELL, Chaplain to General Christian de Wet. *Cr. 8vo.* 6s.
A Colonial Edition is also published.
Kimmins (C. W.), M.A. THE CHEMISTRY OF LIFE AND HEALTH. Illustrated. *Cr. 8vo.* 2s. 6d.
Kinglake (A. W.). See Little Library.
Kipling (Rudyard). BARRACK-ROOM BALLADS. *73rd Thousand. Twenty-first Edition. Cr. 8vo.* 6s.
A Colonial Edition is also published.
THE SEVEN SEAS. *62nd Thousand. Tenth Edition. Cr. 8vo.* 6s.
A Colonial Edition is also published.
THE FIVE NATIONS. *41st Thousand. Second Edition. Cr. 8vo.* 6s.
A Colonial Edition is also published.
DEPARTMENTAL DITTIES. *Sixteenth Edition. Cr. 8vo.* 6s.
A Colonial Edition is also published.
*Knight (Albert E.). THE COMPLETE CRICKETER. Illustrated. *Demy 8vo.* 7s. 6d. *net.*
A Colonial Edition is also published.

General Literature

Knowling (R. J.), M.A., Professor of New Testament Exegesis at King's College, London. See Westminster Commentaries.

Lamb (Charles and Mary), THE WORKS OF. Edited by E. V. Lucas. Illustrated. *In Seven Volumes. Demy 8vo. 7s. 6d. each.*

THE LIFE OF. See E. V. Lucas.
See also Little Library.

Lambert (F. A. H.). See Little Guides.

Lambros (Professor). See Byzantine Texts.

Lane-Poole (Stanley). A HISTORY OF EGYPT IN THE MIDDLE AGES. Fully Illustrated. *Cr. 8vo. 6s.*

Langbridge (F.), M.A. BALLADS OF THE BRAVE: Poems of Chivalry, Enterprise, Courage, and Constancy. *Second Edition. Cr. 8vo. 2s. 6d.*

Law (William). See Library of Devotion and Standard Library.

Leach (Henry). THE DUKE OF DEVONSHIRE. A Biography. With 12 Illustrations. *Demy 8vo. 12s. 6d. net.*
A Colonial Edition is also published.

*****Le Braz (Anatole).** THE LAND OF PARDONS. Translated by Frances M. Gostling. Illustrated in colour. *Crown 8vo. 6s.*

Lee (Captain L. Melville). A HISTORY OF POLICE IN ENGLAND. *Cr. 8vo. 3s. 6d. net.*

Leigh (Percival). THE COMIC ENGLISH GRAMMAR. Embellished with upwards of 50 characteristic Illustrations by John Leech. *Post 16mo. 2s. 6d. net.*

Lewes (V. B.), M.A. AIR AND WATER. Illustrated. *Cr. 8vo. 2s. 6d.*

*****Lewis (Mrs. Gwynn).** A CONCISE HANDBOOK OF GARDEN SHRUBS. Illustrated. *Fcap. 8vo. 3s. 6d. net.*

Lisle (Fortunée de). See Little Books on Art.

Littlehales (H.). See Antiquary's Books.

Lock (Walter), D.D., Warden of Keble College. ST. PAUL, THE MASTER-BUILDER. *Second Edition. Cr. 8vo. 3s. 6d.*
THE BIBLE AND CHRISTIAN LIFE. *Cr. 8vo. 6s.*
See also Leaders of Religion and Library of Devotion.

Locker (F.). See Little Library.

Longfellow (H. W.). See Little Library.

Lorimer (George Horace). LETTERS FROM A SELF-MADE MERCHANT TO HIS SON. *Fourteenth Edition. Cr. 8vo. 6s.*
A Colonial Edition is also published.
OLD GORGON GRAHAM. *Second Edition. Cr. 8vo. 6s.*
A Colonial Edition is also published.

Lover (Samuel). See I. P. L.

E. V. L. and C. L.|G. ENGLAND DAY BY DAY: Or, The Englishman's Handbook to Efficiency. Illustrated by George Morrow. *Fourth Edition. Fcap. 4to. 1s. net.*

Lucas (E. V.). THE LIFE OF CHARLES LAMB. With numerous Portraits and Illustrations. *Third Edition. Two Vols. Demy 8vo. 21s. net.*
A Colonial Edition is also published.
A WANDERER IN HOLLAND. With many Illustrations, of which 20 are in Colour by Herbert Marshall. *Fifth Edition. Cr. 8vo. 6s.*
A Colonial Edition is also published.
THE OPEN ROAD: a Little Book for Wayfarers. *Ninth Edition. Fcap. 8vo. 5s.; India Paper, 7s. 6d.*
THE FRIENDLY TOWN: a Little Book for the Urbane. *Second Edition. Fcap. 8vo. 5s.; India Paper, 7s. 6d.*

Lucian. See Classical Translations.

Lyde (L. W.), M.A. See Commercial Series.

Lydon (Noel S.). See Junior School Books.

Lyttelton (Hon. Mrs. A.). WOMEN AND THEIR WORK. *Cr. 8vo. 2s. 6d.*

M. M. HOW TO DRESS AND WHAT TO WEAR. *Cr. 8vo. 1s. net.*

Macaulay (Lord). CRITICAL AND HISTORICAL ESSAYS. Edited by F. C. Montague, M.A. *Three Volumes. Cr. 8vo. 18s.*
The only edition of this book completely annotated.

M'Allen (J. E. B.), M.A. See Commercial Series.

MacCulloch (J. A.). See Churchman's Library.

MacCunn (Florence A.). MARY STUART. With over 60 Illustrations, including a Frontispiece in Photogravure. *Demy 8vo. 10s. 6d. net.*
A Colonial Edition is also published. See also Leaders of Religion.

McDermott (E. R.). See Books on Business.

M'Dowall (A. S.). See Oxford Biographies.

Mackay (A. M.). See Churchman's Library.

Magnus (Laurie), M.A. A PRIMER OF WORDSWORTH. *Cr. 8vo. 2s. 6d.*

Mahaffy (J. P.), Litt.D. A HISTORY OF THE EGYPT OF THE PTOLEMIES. Fully Illustrated. *Cr. 8vo. 6s.*

Maitland (F. W.), LL.D., Downing Professor of the Laws of England in the University of Cambridge. CANON LAW IN ENGLAND. *Royal 8vo. 7s. 6d.*

Malden (H. E.), M.A. ENGLISH RECORDS. A Companion to the History of England. *Cr. 8vo. 3s. 6d.*
THE ENGLISH CITIZEN: HIS RIGHTS AND DUTIES. *Third Edition. Cr. 8vo. 1s. 6d.*
A SCHOOL HISTORY OF SURREY. Illustrated. *Cr. 8vo. 1s. 6d.*

Marchant (E. C.), M.A., Fellow of Peterhouse, Cambridge. A GREEK ANTHOLOGY. *Second Edition. Cr. 8vo. 3s. 6d.*

Marchant (C. E.), M.A., and **Cook (A. M.)**, M.A. PASSAGES FOR UNSEEN TRANSLATION. *Third Edition. Cr. 8vo. 3s. 6d.*

Marlowe (Christopher). See Standard Library.

Marr (J. E.), F.R.S., Fellow of St John's College, Cambridge. THE SCIENTIFIC STUDY OF SCENERY. *Second Edition.* Illustrated. *Cr. 8vo.* 6s.

AGRICULTURAL GEOLOGY. Illustrated. *Cr. 8vo.* 6s.

Marvell (Andrew). See Little Library.

Masefield (John). SEA LIFE IN NELSON'S TIME. Illustrated. *Cr. 8vo.* 3s. 6d. net.

*ON THE SPANISH MAIN. With Portraits and Illustrations. *Demy 8vo.* 10s. 6d. net.
A Colonial Edition is also published.

Maskell (A.). See Connoisseur's Library.

Mason (A. J.), D.D. See Leaders of Religion.

Massee (George). THE EVOLUTION OF PLANT LIFE: Lower Forms. Illustrated. *Cr. 8vo.* 2s. 6d.

Massinger (P.). See Standard Library.

Masterman (C. F. G.), M.A. TENNYSON AS A RELIGIOUS TEACHER. *Cr. 8vo.* 6s.

*Matheson (Hon. E. F.). COUNSELS OF LIFE. *Fcap. 8vo.* 3s. 6d. net.

May (Phil). THE PHIL MAY ALBUM. *Second Edition.* 4to. 1s. net.

Mellows (Emma S.). A SHORT STORY OF ENGLISH LITERATURE. *Cr. 8vo.* 3s. 6d.

Methuen (A. M. S.). THE TRAGEDY OF SOUTH AFRICA. *Cr. 8vo.* 2s. net. Also *Cr. 8vo.* 3d. net.
A revised and enlarged edition of the author's 'Peace or War in South Africa.'

ENGLAND'S RUIN: DISCUSSED IN SIXTEEN LETTERS TO THE RIGHT HON. JOSEPH CHAMBERLAIN, M.P. *Seventh Edition. Cr. 8vo.* 3d. net.

Michell (E. B.). THE ART AND PRACTICE OF HAWKING. With 3 Photogravures by G. E. LODGE, and other Illustrations. *Demy 8vo.* 10s. 6d.

Millais (J. G.). THE LIFE AND LETTERS OF SIR JOHN EVERETT MILLAIS, President of the Royal Academy. With many Illustrations, of which 2 are in Photogravure. *New Edition. Demy 8vo.* 7s. 6d. net.
A Colonial Edition is also published.

*Millin (G. P.). PICTORIAL GARDENING. Illustrated. *Cr. 8vo.* 3s. 6d. net.

Millis (C. T.), M.I.M.E. See Textbooks of Technology.

Milne (J. G.), M.A. A HISTORY OF ROMAN EGYPT. Fully Illustrated. *Cr. 8vo.* 6s.

Milton (John), THE POEMS OF, BOTH ENGLISH AND LATIN, Compos'd at several times. Printed by his true Copies. The Songs were set in Musick by Mr. HENRY LAWES, Gentleman of the Kings Chappel, and one of His Majesties Private Musick.
Printed and publish'd according to Order. Printed by RUTH RAWORTH for HUMPHREY MOSELEY, and are to be sold at the signe of the Princes Armes in Pauls Churchyard, 1645.
See also Little Library Standard Library, and R. F. Towndrow.

Minchin (H. C.), M.A. See R. Peel.

Mitchell (P. Chalmers), M.A. OUTLINES OF BIOLOGY. Illustrated. *Second Edition. Cr. 8vo.* 6s.

Mitton (G. E.). JANE AUSTEN AND HER TIMES. With many Portraits and Illustrations. *Second Edition. Demy 8vo.* 10s. 6d. net.
A Colonial Edition is also published.

'Moil (A.).' See Books on Business.

Moir (D. M.). See Little Library.

Money (L. G. Chiozza). RICHES AND POVERTY. *Second Edition. Demy 8vo.* 5s. net.

Montaigne. See C. F. Pond.

Moore (H. E.). See S. Q. S.

Moran (Clarence G.). See Books on Business.

More (Sir Thomas). See Standard Library.

Morfill (W. R.), Oriel College, Oxford. A HISTORY OF RUSSIA FROM PETER THE GREAT TO ALEXANDER II. With Maps and Plans. *Cr. 8vo.* 3s. 6d.

Morich (R. J.), late of Clifton College. See School Examination Series.

*Morris (J.). THE MAKERS OF JAPAN. With many portraits and Illustrations. *Demy 8vo.* 12s. 6d. net.
A Colonial Edition is also published.

Morris (J. E.). See Little Guides.

Morton (Miss Anderson). See Miss Brodrick.

THE MOTOR YEAR-BOOK FOR 1906. With many Illustrations and Diagrams. *Demy 8vo.* 7s. 6d. net.

Moule (H. C. G.), D.D., Lord Bishop of Durham. See Leaders of Religion.

Muir (M. M. Pattison), M.A. THE CHEMISTRY OF FIRE. Illustrated. *Cr. 8vo.* 2s. 6d.

Mundella (V. A.), M.A. See J. T. Dunn.

Munro (R.), LL.D. See Antiquary's Books.

Naval Officer (A). See I. P. L.

Neal (W. G.). See R. N. Hall.

Newman (J. H.) and others. See Library of Devotion.

Nichols (J. B. B.). See Little Library.

Nicklin (T.), M.A. EXAMINATION PAPERS IN THUCYDIDES. *Cr. 8vo.* 2s.

Nimrod. See I. P. L.

*Norgate (G. Le G.). SIR WALTER SCOTT. Illustrated. *Demy 8vo.* 7s. 6d. net.

General Literature 13

Norregaard (B. W.). THE GREAT SIEGE: The Investment and Fall of Port Arthur. Illustrated. *Demy 8vo.* 10s. 6d. net.

Northcote (James), R.A. THE CONVERSATIONS OF JAMES NORTHCOTE, R.A., AND JAMES WARD. Edited by ERNEST FLETCHER. With many Portraits. *Demy 8vo.* 10s. 6d.

Norway (A. H.). NAPLES. With 25 Coloured Illustrations by MAURICE GREIFFENHAGEN. A New Edition. *Cr. 8vo.* 6s.

Novalis. THE DISCIPLES AT SAÏS AND OTHER FRAGMENTS. Edited by Miss UNA BIRCH. *Fcap. 8vo.* 3s. 6d.

*****Oldfield (W. J.),** Canon of Lincoln. PRIMER OF RELIGION. *Fcap. 8vo.* 2s. 6d.

Oliphant (Mrs.). See Leaders of Religion.

Oman (C. W. C.), M.A., Fellow of All Souls', Oxford. A HISTORY OF THE ART OF WAR. Vol. II.: The Middle Ages, from the Fourth to the Fourteenth Century. Illustrated. *Demy 8vo.* 10s. 6d. net.

Ottley (R. L.), D.D. See Handbooks of Theology, and Leaders of Religion.

Overton (J. H.). See Leaders of Religion.

Owen (Douglas). See Books on Business.

Oxford (M. N.), of Guy's Hospital. A HANDBOOK OF NURSING. Third Edition. *Cr. 8vo.* 3s. 6d.

Pakes (W. C. C.). THE SCIENCE OF HYGIENE. Illustrated. *Demy 8vo.* 15s.

Palmer (Frederick). WITH KUROKI IN MANCHURIA. Illustrated. Third Edition. *Demy 8vo.* 7s. 6d. net.
A Colonial Edition is also published.

Parker (Gilbert). A LOVER'S DIARY. *Fcap. 8vo.* 5s.

*****Parkes (A. K.).** SMALL LESSONS ON GREAT TRUTHS. *Fcap. 8vo.* 1s. 6d.

Parkinson (John). PARADISI IN SOLE PARADISUS TERRESTRIS, OR A GARDEN OF ALL SORTS OF PLEASANT FLOWERS. *Folio.* £4, 4s. net.

Parmenter (John). HELIO-TROPES, OR NEW POSIES FOR SUNDIALS, 1625. Edited by PERCIVAL LANDON. *Quarto.* 3s. 6d. net.

Parmentier (Prof. Leon). See Byzantine Texts.

Pascal. See Library of Devotion.

Paston (George). SOCIAL CARICATURES IN THE EIGHTEENTH CENTURY. *Imperial Quarto.* £2, 12s. 6d. net. See also Little Books on Art and I.P.L.

Paterson (W. R.) (Benjamin Swift). LIFE'S QUESTIONINGS. *Cr. 8vo.* 3s. 6d. net.

Patterson (A. H.). NOTES OF AN EAST COAST NATURALIST. Illustrated in Colour by F. SOUTHGATE. Second Edition. *Cr. 8vo.* 6s.

NATURE IN EASTERN NORFOLK. A series of observations on the Birds, Fishes, Mammals, Reptiles, and stalk-eyed Crustaceans found in that neighbourhood, with a list of the species. With 12 Illustrations in colour, by FRANK SOUTHGATE. Second Edition. *Cr. 8vo.* 6s.

Peacock (N.). See Little Books on Art.

Pearce (E. H.), M.A. ANNALS OF CHRIST'S HOSPITAL. Illustrated. *Demy 8vo.* 7s. 6d.

Peel (Robert), and **Minchin (H. C.), M.A.** OXFORD. With 100 Illustrations in Colour. *Cr. 8vo.* 6s.

Peel (Sidney), late Fellow of Trinity College, Oxford, and Secretary to the Royal Commission on the Licensing Laws. PRACTICAL LICENSING REFORM. Second Edition. *Cr. 8vo.* 1s. 6d.

Peters (J. P.), D.D. See Churchman's Library.

Petrie (W. M. Flinders), D.C.L., LL.D., Professor of Egyptology at University College. A HISTORY OF EGYPT, FROM THE EARLIEST TIMES TO THE PRESENT DAY. Fully Illustrated. *In six volumes.* *Cr. 8vo.* 6s. each.

VOL. I. PREHISTORIC TIMES TO XVITH DYNASTY. *Fifth Edition.*
VOL. II. THE XVIITH AND XVIIITH DYNASTIES. *Fourth Edition.*
VOL. III. XIXTH TO XXXTH DYNASTIES.
VOL. IV. THE EGYPT OF THE PTOLEMIES. J. P. MAHAFFY, Litt.D.
VOL. V. ROMAN EGYPT. J. G. MILNE, M.A.
VOL. VI. EGYPT IN THE MIDDLE AGES. STANLEY LANE-POOLE, M.A.

RELIGION AND CONSCIENCE IN ANCIENT EGYPT. Illustrated. *Cr. 8vo.* 2s. 6d.

SYRIA AND EGYPT, FROM THE TELL EL AMARNA TABLETS. *Cr. 8vo.* 2s. 6d.

EGYPTIAN TALES. Illustrated by TRISTRAM ELLIS. *In Two Volumes.* *Cr. 8vo.* 3s. 6d. each.

EGYPTIAN DECORATIVE ART. With 120 Illustrations. *Cr. 8vo.* 3s. 6d.

Phillips (W. A.). See Oxford Biographies.

Phillpotts (Eden). MY DEVON YEAR. With 38 Illustrations by J. LEY PETHYBRIDGE. Second and Cheaper Edition. *Large Cr. 8vo.* 6s.

UP ALONG AND DOWN ALONG. Illustrated by CLAUDE SHEPPERSON. *Cr. 4to.* 5s. net.
A volume of poems.

Plonnar (Philip). WITH STEYN AND DE WET. Second Edition. *Cr. 8vo.* 3s. 6d.
A Colonial Edition is also published.

Plarr (Victor G.) and **Walton (C. W.).** A SCHOOL HISTORY OF MIDDLESEX. Illustrated. *Cr. 8vo.* 1s. 6d.

Plato. See Standard Library.

Plautus. THE CAPTIVI. Edited, with an Introduction, Textual Notes, and a Commentary, by W. M. LINDSAY, Fellow of Jesus College, Oxford. *Demy 8vo.* 10s. 6d. net.

Plowden-Wardlaw (J. T.), B.A., King's College, Cambridge. See School Examination Series.

Pocock (Roger). A FRONTIERSMAN. *Third Edition. Cr. 8vo.* 6s.
A Colonial Edition is also published.

Podmore (Frank). MODERN SPIRITUALISM. *Two Volumes. Demy 8vo.* 21s. net.
A History and a Criticism.

Poer (J. Patrick Le). A MODERN LEGIONARY. *Cr. 8vo.* 6s.
A Colonial Edition is also published.

Pollard (Alice). See Little Books on Art.

Pollard (A. W.). OLD PICTURE BOOKS. Illustrated. *Demy 8vo.* 7s. 6d. net.

Pollard (Eliza F.). See Little Books on Art.

Pollock (David), M.I.N.A. See Books on Business.

Pond (C. F.). A DAY BOOK OF MONTAIGNE. Edited by. *Fcap. 8vo.* 3s. 6d. net.

Potter (M. C.), M.A., F.L.S. A TEXTBOOK OF AGRICULTURAL BOTANY. Illustrated. *Second Edition. Cr. 8vo.* 4s. 6d.

Power (J. O'Connor). THE MAKING OF AN ORATOR. *Cr. 8vo.* 6s.

Pradeau (G.). A KEY TO THE TIME ALLUSIONS IN THE DIVINE COMEDY. With a Dial. *Small quarto.* 3s. 6d.

Prance (G.). See Half-Crown Library.

Prescott (O. L.). ABOUT MUSIC, AND WHAT IT IS MADE OF. *Cr. 8vo.* 3s. 6d. net.

Price (L. L.), M.A., Fellow of Oriel College, Oxon. A HISTORY OF ENGLISH POLITICAL ECONOMY. *Fourth Edition. Cr. 8vo.* 2s. 6d.

Primrose (Deborah). A MODERN BŒOTIA. *Cr. 8vo.* 6s.

Pugin and Rowlandson. THE MICROCOSM OF LONDON, OR LONDON IN MINIATURE. With 104 Illustrations in colour. *In Three Volumes. Small 4to.* £3, 3s. net.

'Q' (A. T. Quiller Couch). See Half-Crown Library.

Quevedo Villegas. See Miniature Library.

G. R. and E. S. THE WOODHOUSE CORRESPONDENCE. *Cr. 8vo.* 6s.
A Colonial Edition is also published.

Rackham (R. B.), M.A. See Westminster Commentaries.

Randolph (B. W.), D.D. See Library of Devotion.

Rannie (D. W.), M.A. A STUDENT'S HISTORY OF SCOTLAND. *Cr. 8vo.* 3s. 6d.

Rashdall (Hastings), M.A., Fellow and Tutor of New College, Oxford. DOCTRINE AND DEVELOPMENT. *Cr. 8vo.* 6s.

Rawstorne (Lawrence, Esq.). See I.P.L.

*Raymond (Walter). A SCHOOL HISTORY OF SOMERSETSHIRE. Illustrated. *Cr. 8vo.* 1s. 6d.

A Real Paddy. See I.P-L.

Reason (W.), M.A. See S.Q.S.

Redfern (W. B.), Author of 'Ancient Wood and Iron Work in Cambridge,' etc. ROYAL AND HISTORIC GLOVES AND ANCIENT SHOES. Profusely Illustrated in colour and half-tone. *Quarto.* £2, 2s. net.

Reynolds. See Little Galleries.

*Rhodes (W. E.). A SCHOOL HISTORY OF LANCASHIRE. Illustrated. *Cr. 8vo.* 1s. 6d.

Roberts (M. E.). See C. C. Channer.

Robertson (A.), D.D., Lord Bishop of Exeter. REGNUM DEI. The Bampton Lectures of 1901. *Demy 8vo.* 12s. 6d. net.

Robertson (C. Grant), M.A., Fellow of All Souls' College, Oxford, Examiner in the Honours School of Modern History, Oxford, 1901-1904. SELECT STATUTES, CASES, AND CONSTITUTIONAL DOCUMENTS, 1660-1832. *Demy 8vo.* 10s. 6d. net.

Robertson (C. Grant) and Bartholomew (J. G.), F.R.S.E., F.R.G.S. A HISTORICAL AND MODERN ATLAS OF THE BRITISH EMPIRE. *Quarto.* 4s. 6d. net.

Robertson (Sir G. S.), K.C.S.I. See Half-Crown Library.

Robinson (A. W.), M.A. See Churchman's Bible.

Robinson (Cecilia). THE MINISTRY OF DEACONESSES. With an Introduction by the late Archbishop of Canterbury. *Cr. 8vo.* 3s. 6d.

Robinson (F. S.). See Connoisseur's Library.

Rochefoucauld (La). See Little Library.

Rodwell (G.), B.A. NEW TESTAMENT GREEK. A Course for Beginners. With a Preface by WALTER LOCK, D.D., Warden of Keble College. *Fcap. 8vo.* 3s. 6d.

Roe (Fred). ANCIENT COFFERS AND CUPBOARDS: Their History and Description. Illustrated. *Quarto.* £3, 3s. net.

OLD OAK FURNITURE. With many Illustrations by the Author, including a frontispiece in colour. *Demy 8vo.* 10s. 6d. net.

Rogers (A. G. L.), M.A. See Books on Business.

Roscoe (E. S.). ROBERT HARLEY, EARL OF OXFORD. Illustrated. *Demy 8vo.* 7s. 6d.
This is the only life of Harley in existence.
See also Little Guides.

General Literature

Rose (Edward). THE ROSE READER. Illustrated. *Cr. 8vo. 2s. 6d. Also in 4 Parts. Parts I. and II. 6d. each; Part III. 8d.; Part IV. 10d.*

*Rouse (W. H.). WORDS OF THE ANCIENT WISE: Thoughts from Epictetus and Marcus Aurelius. Edited by. *Fcap. 8vo. 3s. 6d. net.*

Rowntree (Joshua). THE IMPERIAL DRUG TRADE. *Second Edition. Cr. 8vo. 5s. net.*

Ruble (A. E.), D.D. See Junior School ooks.

Russell (W. Clark). THE LIFE OF ADMIRAL LORD COLLINGWOOD. With Illustrations by F. BRANGWYN. *Fourth Edition. Cr. 8vo. 6s.*
A Colonial Edition is also published.

St. Anslem. See Library of Devotion.
St. Augustine. See Library of Devotion.
St. Cyres (Viscount). See Oxford Biographies.
St. Francis of Assisi. See Standard Library.

'Saki' (H. Munro). REGINALD. *Second Edition. Fcap. 8vo. 2s. 6d. net.*

Sales (St. Francis de). See Library of Devotion.

Salmon (A. L.). A POPULAR GUIDE TO DEVON. *Medium 8vo. 6d. net.* See also Little Guides.

Sargeant (J.), M.A. ANNALS OF WESTMINSTER SCHOOL. Illustrated. *Demy 8vo. 7s. 6d.*

Sathas (C.). See Byzantine Texts.
Schmitt (John). See Byzantine Texts.
Scott (A. M.). WINSTON SPENCER CHURCHILL. With Portraits and Illustrations. *Cr. 8vo. 3s. 6d.*
A Colonial Edition is also published.

Seeley (H. G.), F.R.S. DRAGONS OF THE AIR. Illustrated. *Cr. 8vo. 6s.*

*Selincourt (E. de). A DAY BOOK OF KEATS. Edited by. *Fcap. 8vo. 3s. 6d. net.*

Sells (V. P.), M.A. THE MECHANICS OF DAILY LIFE. Illustrated. *Cr. 8vo. 2s. 6d.*

Selous (Edmund). TOMMY SMITH'S ANIMALS. Illustrated by G. W. ORD. *Fourth Edition. Fcap. 8vo. 2s. 6d.*

Settle (J. H.). ANECDOTES OF SOLDIERS, in Peace and War. *Cr. 8vo. 3s. 6d. net.*
A Colonial Edition is also published.

Shakespeare (William).
THE FOUR FOLIOS, 1623; 1632; 1664; 1685. Each *Four Guineas net*, or a complete set, *Twelve Guineas net.*

The Arden Shakespeare.
Demy 8vo. 2s. 6d. net each volume.
General Editor, W. J. CRAIG. An Edition of Shakespeare in single Plays. Edited with a full Introduction, Textual Notes, and a Commentary at the foot of the page.

HAMLET. Edited by EDWARD DOWDEN, Litt.D.
ROMEO AND JULIET. Edited by EDWARD DOWDEN, Litt.D.
KING LEAR. Edited by W. J. CRAIG.
JULIUS CAESAR. Edited by M. MACMILLAN, M.A.
THE TEMPEST. Edited by MORETON LUCE.
OTHELLO. Edited by H. C. HART.
TITUS ANDRONICUS. Edited by H. B. BAILDON.
CYMBELINE. Edited by EDWARD DOWDEN.
THE MERRY WIVES OF WINDSOR. Edited by H. C. HART.
A MIDSUMMER NIGHT'S DREAM. Edited by H. CUNINGHAM.
KING HENRY V. Edited by H. A. EVANS.
ALL'S WELL THAT ENDS WELL. Edited by W. O. BRIGSTOCKE.
THE TAMING OF THE SHREW. Edited by R. WARWICK BOND.
TIMON OF ATHENS. Edited by K. DEIGHTON.
MEASURE FOR MEASURE. Edited by H. C. HART.
*TWELFTH NIGHT. Edited by MORETON LUCE.
THE MERCHANT OF VENICE. Edited by C. KNOX POOLER.
*TROILUS AND CRESSIDA. Edited by K. DEIGHTON.

The Little Quarto Shakespeare. Edited by W. J. CRAIG. With Introductions and Notes. *Pott 16mo. In 40 Volumes. Leather, price 1s. net each volume.* Mahogany Revolving Book Case. *10s. net.* See also Standard Library.

Sharp (A.). VICTORIAN POETS. *Cr. 8vo. 2s. 6d.*

Sharp (Cecil). See S. Baring-Gould.

Sharp (Mrs. E. A.). See Little Books on Art.

Shedlock (J. S.) THE PIANOFORTE SONATA. *Cr. 8vo. 5s.*

Shelley (Percy B.). ADONAIS; an Elegy on the death of John Keats, Author of 'Endymion,' etc. Pisa. From the types of Didot, 1821. *2s. net.*

Sheppard (H. F.), M.A. See S. Baring-Gould.

Sherwell (Arthur), M.A. See S.Q.S.

Shipley (Mary E.). AN ENGLISH CHURCH HISTORY FOR CHILDREN. With a Preface by the Bishop of Gibraltar. With Maps and Illustrations. Part I. *Cr. 8vo. 2s. 6d. net.*

Sichel (Walter). DISRAELI: A Study in Personality and Ideas. With 3 Portraits. *Demy 8vo. 12s. 6d. net.*
A Colonial Edition is also published.
See also Oxford Biographies.

Sime (J.). See Little Books on Art.

Simonson (G. A.). FRANCESCO GUARDI. With 41 Plates. *Imperial 4to. £2, 2s. net.*

Sketchley (R. E. D.). See Little Books on Art.

Skipton (H. P. K.). See Little Books on Art.

Sladen (Douglas). SICILY: The New Winter Resort. With over 200 Illustrations. *Second Edition. Cr. 8vo. 5s. net.*

Small (Evan), M.A. THE EARTH. An Introduction to Physiography. Illustrated. *Cr. 8vo. 2s. 6d.*

Smallwood (M. G.). See Little Books on Art.

Smedley (F. E.). See I.P.L.

Smith (Adam). THE WEALTH OF NATIONS. Edited with an Introduction and numerous Notes by EDWIN CANNAN, M.A. *Two volumes. Demy 8vo. 21s. net.*

See also English Library.

Smith (Horace and James). See Little Library.

Smith (H. Bompas), M.A. A NEW JUNIOR ARITHMETIC. *Crown 8vo. 2s. 6d.*

Smith (R. Mudie). THOUGHTS FOR THE DAY. Edited by. *Fcap. 8vo. 3s. 6d. net.*

Smith (Nowell C.). See W. Wordsworth.

Smith (John Thomas). A BOOK FOR A RAINY DAY: Or Recollections of the Events of the Years 1766-1833. Edited by WILFRED WHITTEN. Illustrated. *Demy 8vo. 12s. 6d. net.*

Snell (F. J.). A BOOK OF EXMOOR. Illustrated. *Cr. 8vo. 6s.*

Snowden (C. E.). A HANDY DIGEST OF BRITISH HISTORY. *Demy 8vo. 4s. 6d.*

Sophocles. See Classical Translations.

Sornet (L. A.). See Junior School Books.

South (Wilton E.), M.A. See Junior School Books.

Southey (R.). ENGLISH SEAMEN. Edited by DAVID HANNAY.
Vol. I. (Howard, Clifford, Hawkins, Drake, Cavendish). *Second Edition. Cr. 8vo. 6s.*
Vol. II. (Richard Hawkins, Grenville, Essex, and Raleigh). *Cr. 8vo. 6s.*
See also Standard Library.

Spence (C. H.), M.A. See School Examination Series.

Spooner (W. A.), M.A. See Leaders of Religion.

'Staley (Edgcumbe). THE GUILDS OF FLORENCE. Illustrated. *Royal 8vo. 21s. net.*

Stanbridge (J. W.), B.D. See Library of Devotion.

'Stancliffe.' GOLF DO'S AND DONT'S. *Second Edition. Fcap. 8vo. 1s.*

Stead (D. W.). See D. Gallaher.

Stedman (A. M. M.), M.A.
INITIA LATINA: Easy Lessons on Elementary Accidence. *Eighth Edition. Fcap. 8vo. 1s.*
FIRST LATIN LESSONS. *Ninth Edition. Cr. 8vo. 2s.*
FIRST LATIN READER. With Notes adapted to the Shorter Latin Primer and Vocabulary. *Sixth Edition revised. 18mo. 1s. 6d.*
EASY SELECTIONS FROM CÆSAR. The Helvetian War. *Second Edition. 18mo. 1s.*
EASY SELECTIONS FROM LIVY. The Kings of Rome. 18mo. *Second Edition. 1s. 6d.*
EASY LATIN PASSAGES FOR UNSEEN TRANSLATION. *Tenth Edition. Fcap. 8vo. 1s. 6d.*
EXEMPLA LATINA. First Exercises in Latin Accidence. With Vocabulary. *Third Edition. Cr. 8vo. 1s.*
EASY LATIN EXERCISES ON THE SYNTAX OF THE SHORTER AND REVISED LATIN PRIMER. With Vocabulary. *Tenth and Cheaper Edition, re-written. Cr. 8vo. 1s. 6d. Original Edition. 2s. 6d.* KEY, 3s. net.
THE LATIN COMPOUND SENTENCE: Rules and Exercises. *Second Edition. Cr. 8vo. 1s. 6d.* With Vocabulary. 2s.
NOTANDA QUAEDAM: Miscellaneous Latin Exercises on Common Rules and Idioms. *Fourth Edition. Fcap. 8vo. 1s. 6d.* With Vocabulary. 2s. Key, 2s. net.
LATIN VOCABULARIES FOR REPETITION: Arranged according to Subjects. *Thirteenth Edition. Fcap. 8vo. 1s. 6d.*
A VOCABULARY OF LATIN IDIOMS. *18mo. Second Edition. 1s.*
STEPS TO GREEK. *Second Edition, revised. 18mo. 1s.*
A SHORTER GREEK PRIMER. *Cr. 8vo. 1s. 6d.*
EASY GREEK PASSAGES FOR UNSEEN TRANSLATION. *Third Edition, revised. Fcap. 8vo. 1s. 6d.*
GREEK VOCABULARIES FOR REPETITION. Arranged according to Subjects. *Fourth Edition. Fcap. 8vo. 1s. 6d.*
GREEK TESTAMENT SELECTIONS. For the use of Schools. With Introduction, Notes, and Vocabulary. *Fourth Edition. Fcap. 8vo. 2s. 6d.*
STEPS TO FRENCH. *Seventh Edition. 18mo. 8d.*
FIRST FRENCH LESSONS. *Seventh Edition, revised. Cr. 8vo. 1s.*
EASY FRENCH PASSAGES FOR UNSEEN TRANSLATION. *Fifth Edition, revised. Fcap. 8vo. 1s. 6d.*

General Literature

EASY FRENCH EXERCISES ON ELEMENTARY SYNTAX. With Vocabulary. *Fourth Edition.* Cr. 8vo. 2s. 6d.
KEY. 3s. net.
FRENCH VOCABULARIES FOR REPETITION: Arranged according to Subjects. *Twelfth Edition.* Fcap. 8vo. 1s.
See also School Examination Series.
Steel (R. Elliott), M.A., F.C.S. THE WORLD OF SCIENCE. With 147 Illustrations. *Second Edition.* Cr. 8vo. 2s. 6d.
See also School Examination Series.
Stephenson (C.), of the Technical College, Bradford, and Suddards (F.) of the Yorkshire College, Leeds. ORNAMENTAL DESIGN FOR WOVEN FABRICS. Illustrated. *Demy 8vo. Third Edition.* 7s. 6d.
Stephenson (J.), M.A. THE CHIEF TRUTHS OF THE CHRISTIAN FAITH. *Crown 8vo.* 3s. 6d.
Sterne (Laurence). See Little Library.
Sterry (W.), M.A. ANNALS OF ETON COLLEGE. Illustrated. *Demy 8vo.* 7s. 6d.
Steuart (Katherine). BY ALLAN WATER. *Second Edition.* Cr. 8vo. 6s.
Stevenson (R. L.) THE LETTERS OF ROBERT LOUIS STEVENSON TO HIS FAMILY AND FRIENDS. Selected and Edited by SIDNEY COLVIN. *Sixth Edition.* Cr. 8vo. 12s.
LIBRARY EDITION. *Demy 8vo.* 2 vols. 25s. net.
A Colonial Edition is also published.
VAILIMA LETTERS. With an Etched Portrait by WILLIAM STRANG. *Fifth Edition.* Cr. 8vo. Buckram. 6s
A Colonial Edition is also published.
THE LIFE OF R. L. STEVENSON. See G. Balfour.
Stevenson (M. I.). FROM SARANAC TO THE MARQUESAS. Being Letters written by Mrs. M. I. STEVENSON during 1887-8. Cr. 8vo. 6s. net.
A Colonial Edition is also published.
LETTERS FROM SAMOA. Edited and arranged by M. C. BALFOUR. With many Illustrations. Cr. 8vo. 6s. net.
Stoddart (Anna M.). See Oxford Biographies.
Stokes (F. G.), B.A. HOURS WITH RABELAIS. From the translation of SIR T. URQUHART and P. A. MOTTEUX. With a Portrait in Photogravure. Cr. 8vo. 3s. 6d. net.
Stone (S. J.). POEMS AND HYMNS. With a Memoir by F. G. ELLERTON, M.A. With Portrait. Cr. 8vo. 6s.
*Storr (Vernon F.), M.A., Lecturer in the Philosophy of Religion in Cambridge University; Examining Chaplain to the Archbishop of Canterbury; formerly Fellow of University College, Oxford. DEVELOPMENT AND DIVINE PURPOSE Cr. 8vo. 5s. net.

Straker (F.). See Books on Business.
Streane (A. W.), D.D. See Churchman's Bible.
Stroud (H.), D.Sc., M.A. See Textbooks of Science.
Strutt (Joseph). THE SPORTS AND PASTIMES OF THE PEOPLE OF ENGLAND. Illustrated by many engravings. Revised by J. CHARLES COX, LL.D., F.S.A. *Quarto.* 21s. net.
Stuart (Capt. Donald). THE STRUGGLE FOR PERSIA. With a Map. Cr. 8vo. 6s.
*Sturch (F.), Staff Instructor to the Surrey County Council. SOLUTIONS TO THE CITY AND GUILDS QUESTIONS IN MANUAL INSTRUCTION DRAWING. *Imp. 4to.* 5s. net.
Suckling (Sir John). FRAGMENTA AUREA: a Collection of all the Incomparable Peeces, written by. And published by a friend to perpetuate his memory. Printed by his own copies.
Printed for HUMPHREY MOSELEY, and are to be sold at his shop, at the sign of the Princes Arms in St. Paul's Churchyard, 1646.
Suddards (F.). See C. Stephenson.
Surtees (R. S.). See I.P.L.
Swift (Jonathan). THE JOURNAL TO STELLA. Edited by G. A. AITKEN. Cr. 8vo. 6s.
Symes (J. E.), M.A. THE FRENCH REVOLUTION. *Second Edition.* Cr. 8vo. 2s. 6d.
Sympson (E. M.), M.A., M.D. See Ancient Cities.
Syrett (Netta). See Little Blue Books.
Tacitus. AGRICOLA. With Introduction Notes, Map, etc. By R. F. DAVIS, M.A., *Fcap. 8vo.* 2s.
GERMANIA. By the same Editor. *Fcap. 8vo.* 2s. See also Classical Translations.
Tallack (W.). HOWARD LETTERS AND MEMORIES. *Demy 8vo.* 10s. 6d. net.
Tauler (J.). See Library of Devotion.
Taunton (E. L.). A HISTORY OF THE JESUITS IN ENGLAND. Illustrated. *Demy 8vo.* 21s. net.
Taylor (A. E.). THE ELEMENTS OF METAPHYSICS. *Demy 8vo.* 10s. 6d. net.
Taylor (F. G.), M.A. See Commercial Series.
Taylor (I. A.). See Oxford Biographies.
Taylor (T. M.), M.A., Fellow of Gonville and Caius College, Cambridge. A CONSTITUTIONAL AND POLITICAL HISTORY OF ROME. Cr. 8vo. 7s. 6d.
Tennyson (Alfred, Lord). THE EARLY POEMS OF. Edited, with Notes and an Introduction, by J. CHURTON COLLINS, M.A. Cr. 8vo. 6s.
IN MEMORIAM, MAUD, AND THE PRINCESS. Edited by J. CHURTON COLLINS, M.A. Cr. 8vo. 6s. See also Little Library.

Terry (C. S.). See Oxford Biographies.
Terton (Alice). LIGHTS AND SHADOWS IN A HOSPITAL. *Cr. 8vo.* 3s. 6d.
Thackeray (W. M.). See Little Library.
Theobald (F. V.), M.A. INSECT LIFE. Illustrated. *Second Ed. Revised. Cr. 8vo.* 2s. 6d.
Thompson (A. H.). See Little Guides.
Tileston (Mary W.). DAILY STRENGTH FOR DAILY NEEDS. *Twelfth Edition. Medium 16mo.* 2s. 6d. net. Also an edition in superior binding, 6s.
Tompkins (H. W.), F.R.H.S. See Little Guides.
Towndrow (R. F.), A DAY BOOK OF MILTON. Edited by. *Fcap. 8vo.* 3s. 6d. net.
Townley (Lady Susan). MY CHINESE NOTE-BOOK. With 16 Illustrations and 2 Maps. *Third Edition. Demy 8vo.* 10s. 6d. net.
A Colonial Edition is also published.
*Toynbee (Paget), M.A., D.Litt. DANTE IN ENGLISH LITERATURE. *Demy 8vo.* 12s. 6d. net.
See also Oxford Biographies.
Trench (Herbert). DEIRDRE WED and Other Poems. *Cr. 8vo.* 5s.
Trevelyan (G. M.), Fellow of Trinity College, Cambridge. ENGLAND UNDER THE STUARTS. With Maps and Plans. *Second Edition. Demy 8vo.* 10s. 6d. net.
Troutbeck (G. E.). See Little Guides.
Tyler (E. A.), B.A., F.C.S. See Junior School Books.
Tyrell-Gill (Frances). See Little Books on Art.
Vardon (Harry). THE COMPLETE GOLFER. Illustrated. *Sixth Edition. Demy 8vo.* 10s. 6d. net.
A Colonial Edition is also published.
Vaughan (Henry). See Little Library.
Voegelin (A.), M.A. See Junior Examination Series.
Waddell (Col. L. A.), LL.D., C.B. LHASA AND ITS MYSTERIES. With a Record of the Expedition of 1903-1904. With 2000 Illustrations and Maps. *Demy 8vo.* 21s. net.
*Also Third and Cheaper Edition. With 155 Illustrations and Maps. *Demy 8vo.* 10s. 6d. net.
Wade (G. W.), D.D. OLD TESTAMENT HISTORY. With Maps. *Third Edition. Cr. 8vo.* 6s.
Wagner (Richard). See A. L. Cleather.
Wall (J. C.). DEVILS. Illustrated by the Author and from photographs. *Demy 8vo.* 4s. 6d. net. See also Antiquary's Books.
Walters (H. B.). See Little Books on Art.
Walton (F. W.). See Victor G. Plarr.
Walton (Izaac) and Cotton (Charles). See I.P.L., English Library, and Little Library.

Warmelo (D. S. Van). ON COMMANDO. With Portrait. *Cr. 8vo.* 3s. 6d.
A Colonial Edition is also published.
Warren-Vernon (Hon. William), M.A. READINGS ON THE INFERNO OF DANTE, chiefly based on the Commentary of BENVENUTO DA IMOLA. With an Introduction by the Rev. Dr. MOORE. In Two Volumes. *Second Edition. Cr. 8vo.* 15s. net.
Waterhouse (Mrs. Alfred). WITH THE SIMPLE-HEARTED: Little Homilies to Women in Country Places. *Second Edition. Small Pott 8vo.* 2s. net. See also Little Library.
Weatherhead (T. C.), M.A. EXAMINATION PAPERS IN HORACE. *Cr. 8vo.* 2s. See also Junior Examination Series.
Webb (W. T.). See Little Blue Books.
Webber (F. C.). See Textbooks of Technology.
Wells (Sidney H.). See Textbooks of Science.
Wells (J.), M.A., Fellow and Tutor of Wadham College. OXFORD AND OXFORD LIFE. *Third Edition. Cr. 8vo.* 3s. 6d.
A SHORT HISTORY OF ROME. *Sixth Edition.* With 3 Maps. *Cr. 8vo.* 3s. 6d.
See also Little Guides.
'Westminster Gazette' Office Boy (Francis Brown). THE DOINGS OF ARTHUR. *Cr. 4to.* 2s. 6d. net.
Wetmore (Helen C.). THE LAST OF THE GREAT SCOUTS ('Buffalo Bill') Illustrated. *Second Edition. Demy 8vo.* 6s.
A Colonial Edition is also published.
Whibley (C.). See Half-crown Library.
Whibley (L.), M.A., Fellow of Pembroke College, Cambridge. GREEK OLIGARCHIES: THEIR ORGANISATION AND CHARACTER. *Cr. 8vo.* 6s.
Whitaker (G. H.), M.A. See Churchman's Bible.
White (Gilbert). THE NATURAL HISTORY OF SELBORNE. Edited by L. C. MIALL, F.R.S., assisted by W. WARDE FOWLER, M.A. *Cr. 8vo.* 6s. See also Standard Library.
Whitfield (E. E.). See Commercial Series.
Whitehead (A. W.). GASPARD DE COLIGNY. Illustrated. *Demy 8vo.* 12s. 6d. net.
Whiteley (R. Lloyd), F.I.C., Principal of the Municipal Science School, West Bromwich. AN ELEMENTARY TEXTBOOK OF INORGANIC CHEMISTRY. *Cr. 8vo.* 2s. 6d.
Whitley (Miss). See S.Q.S.
Whitten (W.). See John Thomas Smith.
Whyte (A. G.), B.Sc. See Books on Business.
Wilberforce (Wilfrid). See Little Books on Art.
Wilde (Oscar). DE PROFUNDIS. *Sixth Edition. Cr. 8vo.* 5s. net.
A Colonial Edition is also published.

General Literature 19

Wilkins (W. H.), B.A. See S.Q.S.
Wilkinson (J. Frome). See S.Q.S.
*Williams (A.). PETROL PETER: or Mirth for Motorists. Illustrated in Colour by A. W. MILLS. *Demy 4to.* 3s. 6d. net.
Williamson (M. G.). See Ancient Cities.
Williamson (W.). THE BRITISH GARDENER. Illustrated. *Demy 8vo.* 10s. 6d.
Williamson (W.), B.A. See Junior Examination Series, Junior School Books, and Beginner's Books.
Willson (Beckles). LORD STRATHCONA: the Story of his Life. Illustrated. *Demy 8vo.* 7s. 6d.
A Colonial Edition is also published.
Wilmot-Buxton (E. M.). MAKERS OF EUROPE. *Cr. 8vo.* Fourth Ed. 3s. 6d.
A Text-book of European History for Middle Forms.
THE ANCIENT WORLD. With Maps and Illustrations. *Cr. 8vo.* 3s. 6d.
See also Beginner's Books.
Wilson (Bishop.). See Library of Devotion.
Wilson (A. J.). See Books on Business.
Wilson (H. A.). See Books on Business.
Wilton (Richard), M.A. LYRA PASTORALIS: Songs of Nature, Church, and Home. *Pott 8vo.* 2s. 6d.
Winbolt (S. E.), M.A. EXERCISES IN LATIN ACCIDENCE. *Cr. 8vo.* 1s. 6d.
LATIN HEXAMETER VERSE: An Aid to Composition. *Cr. 8vo.* 3s. 6d. KEY, 5s. net.
Windle (B. C. A.), D.Sc., F.R.S. See Antiquary's Books, Little Guides and Ancient Cities.
Winterbotham (Canon), M.A., B.Sc., LL.B. See Churchman's Library.
Wood (J. A. E.). See Textbooks of Technology.
Wood (J. Hickory). DAN LENO. Illustrated. *Third Edition. Cr. 8vo.* 6s.
A Colonial Edition is also published.
Wood (W. Birkbeck), M.A., late Scholar of Worcester College, Oxford, and **Edmonds (Major J. E.), R.E., D.A.Q.-M.G.** A HISTORY OF THE CIVIL WAR IN THE UNITED STATES. With an Introduction by H. SPENSER WILKINSON. With 24 Maps and Plans. *Demy 8vo.* 12s. 6d. net.

Wordsworth (Christopher). See Antiquary's Books.
*Wordsworth (W.). THE POEMS OF. With Introduction and Notes by NOWELL C. SMITH, Fellow of New College, Oxford. *In Four Volumes. Demy 8vo.* 5s. net each. See also Little Library.
Wordsworth (W.) and Coleridge (S. T.). See Little Library.
Wright (Arthur), M.A., Fellow of Queen's College, Cambridge. See Churchman's Library.
Wright (C. Gordon). See Dante.
Wright (J. C.). TO-DAY. *Fcap. 16mo.* 1s. net.
Wright (Sophie). GERMAN VOCABULARIES FOR REPETITION. *Fcap. 8vo.* 1s. 6d.
Wrong (George M.), Professor of History in the University of Toronto. THE EARL OF ELGIN. Illustrated. *Demy 8vo.* 7s. 6d. net.
A Colonial Edition is also published.
Wyatt (Kate) and Gloag (M.). A BOOK OF ENGLISH GARDENS. With 24 Illustrations in Colour. *Cr. 8vo.* 10s. 6s. net.
Wylde (A. B.). MODERN ABYSSINIA. With a Map and a Portrait. *Demy 8vo.* 15s. net.
A Colonial Edition is also published.
Wyndham (George). THE POEMS OF WILLIAM SHAKESPEARE. With an Introduction and Notes. *Demy 8vo. Buckram, gilt top.* 10s. 6d.
Wyon (R.). See Half-crown Library.
Yeats (W. B.). AN ANTHOLOGY OF IRISH VERSE. *Revised and Enlarged Edition. Cr. 8vo.* 3s. 6d.
Young (Filson). THE COMPLETE MOTORIST. With 138 Illustrations. *Fifth Edition. Demy 8vo.* 12s. 6d. net.
A Colonial Edition is also published.
Young (T. M.). THE AMERICAN COTTON INDUSTRY: A Study of Work and Workers. *Cr. 8vo. Cloth,* 2s. 6d.; *paper boards,* 1s. 6d.
Zimmern (Antonia). WHAT DO WE KNOW CONCERNING ELECTRICITY? *Fcap. 8vo.* 1s. 6d. net.

Ancient Cities

General Editor, B. C. A. WINDLE, D.Sc., F.R.S.

Cr. 8vo. 4s. 6d. net.

CHESTER. By B. C. A. Windle, D.Sc. F.R.S. Illustrated by E. H. New.
SHREWSBURY. By T. Auden, M.A., F.S.A. Illustrated.
CANTERBURY. By J. C. Cox, LL.D., F.S.A. Illustrated.

*EDINBURGH. By M. G. Williamson. Illustrated by Herbert Railton.
*LINCOLN. By E. Mansel Sympson, M.A., M.D. Illustrated by E. H. New.

MESSRS. METHUEN'S CATALOGUE

Antiquary's Books, The
General Editor, J. CHARLES COX, LL.D., F.S.A.

A series of volumes dealing with various branches of English Antiquities; comprehensive and popular, as well as accurate and scholarly.

Demy 8vo.   7s. 6d. net.

ENGLISH MONASTIC LIFE. By the Right Rev. Abbot Gasquet, O.S B. Illustrated. *Third Edition.*

REMAINS OF THE PREHISTORIC AGE IN ENGLAND. By B. C. A. Windle, D.Sc., F.R.S. With numerous Illustrations and Plans.

OLD SERVICE BOOKS OF THE ENGLISH CHURCH. By Christopher Wordsworth, M.A., and Henry Littlehales. With Coloured and other Illustrations.

CELTIC ART. By J. Romilly Allen, F.S.A. With numerous Illustrations and Plans.

ARCHÆOLOGY AND FALSE ANTIQUITIES. By R. Munro, LL.D. Illustrated.

SHRINES OF BRITISH SAINTS. By J. C. Wall. With numerous Illustrations and Plans.

THE ROYAL FORESTS OF ENGLAND. By J. C. Cox, LL.D., F.S.A. Illustrated.

*THE MANOR AND MANORIAL RECORDS. By Nathaniel J. Hone. Illustrated.

*SEALS. By J. Harvey Bloom. Illustrated.

Beginner's Books, The
Edited by W. WILLIAMSON, B.A.

EASY FRENCH RHYMES. By Henri Blouet. Illustrated. *Fcap. 8vo.   1s.*

EASY STORIES FROM ENGLISH HISTORY. By E. M. Wilmot-Buxton, Author of 'Makers of Europe.' *Cr. 8vo.   1s.*

EASY EXERCISES IN ARITHMETIC. Arranged by W. S. Beard. *Fcap. 8vo.* Without Answers, *1s.* With Answers, *1s. 3d.*

EASY DICTATION AND SPELLING. By W Williamson, B.A. *Fourth Edition. Fcap 8vo.   1s.*

Business, Books on
Cr. 8vo.   2s. 6d. net.

A series of volumes dealing with all the most important aspects of commercial and financial activity. The volumes are intended to treat separately all the considerable industries and forms of business, and to explain accurately and clearly what they do and how they do it. Some are Illustrated. The first volumes are—

PORTS AND DOCKS. By Douglas Owen.

RAILWAYS. By E. R. McDermott.

THE STOCK EXCHANGE. By Chas. Duguid. *Second Edition.*

THE BUSINESS OF INSURANCE. By A. J. Wilson.

THE ELECTRICAL INDUSTRY: LIGHTING, TRACTION, AND POWER. By A. G. Whyte, B.Sc.

THE SHIPBUILDING INDUSTRY: Its History, Science, Practice, and Finance. By David Pollock, M.I.N.A.

THE MONEY MARKET. By F. Straker.

THE BUSINESS SIDE OF AGRICULTURE. By A. G. L. Rogers, M.A.

LAW IN BUSINESS. By H. A. Wilson.

THE BREWING INDUSTRY. By Julian L. Baker, F.I.C., F.C.S.

THE AUTOMOBILE INDUSTRY. By G. de H. Stone.

MINING AND MINING INVESTMENTS. By 'A. Moil.'

THE BUSINESS OF ADVERTISING. By Clarence G. Moran, Barrister-at-Law. Illustrated.

TRADE UNIONS. By G. Drage.

CIVIL ENGINEERING. By T. Claxton Fidler, M.Inst. C.E. Illustrated.

THE IRON TRADE. By J. Stephen Jeans. Illustrated.

MONOPOLIES, TRUSTS, AND KARTELLS. By F. W. Hirst.

THE COTTON INDUSTRY AND TRADE. By Prof. S. J. Chapman, Dean of the Faculty of Commerce in the University of Manchester. Illustrated.

*THE COAL INDUSTRY. By Ernest Aves. Illustrated.

Byzantine Texts

Edited by J. B. BURY, M.A., Litt.D.

A series of texts of Byzantine Historians, edited by English and foreign scholars.

ZACHARIAH OF MITYLENE. Translated by F. J. Hamilton, D.D., and E. W. Brooks. *Demy 8vo.* 12s. 6d. net.

EVAGRIUS. Edited by Léon Parmentier and M. Bidez. *Demy 8vo.* 10s. 6d. net.

THE HISTORY OF PSELLUS. Edited by C. Sathas. *Demy 8vo.* 15s. net.

ECTHESIS CHRONICA. Edited by Professor Lambros. *Demy 8vo.* 7s. 6d. net.

THE CHRONICLE OF MOREA. Edited by John Schmitt. *Demy 8vo.* 15s. net.

Churchman's Bible, The

General Editor, J. H. BURN, B.D., F.R.S.E.

A series of Expositions on the Books of the Bible, which will be of service to the general reader in the practical and devotional study of the Sacred Text.

Each Book is provided with a full and clear Introductory Section, in which is stated what is known or conjectured respecting the date and occasion of the composition of the Book, and any other particulars that may help to elucidate its meaning as a whole. The Exposition is divided into sections of a convenient length, corresponding as far as possible with the divisions of the Church Lectionary. The Translation of the Authorised Version is printed in full, such corrections as are deemed necessary being placed in footnotes.

THE EPISTLE OF ST. PAUL THE APOSTLE TO THE GALATIANS. Edited by A. W. Robinson, M.A. *Second Edition. Fcap. 8vo.* 1s. 6d. net.

ECCLESIASTES. Edited by A. W. Streane, D.D. *Fcap. 8vo.* 1s. 6d. net.

THE EPISTLE OF ST. PAUL THE APOSTLE TO THE PHILIPPIANS. Edited by C. R. D. Biggs, D.D. *Second Edition. Fcap 8vo.* 1s. 6d. net.

THE EPISTLE OF ST. JAMES. Edited by H. W. Fulford, M.A. *Fcap. 8vo.* 1s. 6d. net.

ISAIAH. Edited by W. E. Barnes, D.D. Two Volumes. *Fcap. 8vo.* 2s. net each. With Map.

THE EPISTLE OF ST. PAUL THE APOSTLE TO THE EPHESIANS. Edited by G. H. Whitaker, M.A. *Fcap. 8vo.* 1s. 6d. net.

Churchman's Library, The

General Editor, J. H. BURN, B.D., F.R.S.E.

THE BEGINNINGS OF ENGLISH CHRISTIANITY. By W. E. Collins, M.A. With Map. *Cr. 8vo.* 3s. 6d.

SOME NEW TESTAMENT PROBLEMS. By Arthur Wright, M.A. *Cr. 8vo.* 6s.

THE KINGDOM OF HEAVEN HERE AND HEREAFTER. By Canon Winterbotham, M.A., B.Sc., LL.B. *Cr. 8vo.* 3s. 6d.

THE WORKMANSHIP OF THE PRAYER BOOK: Its Literary and Liturgical Aspects. By J. Dowden, D.D. *Second Edition. Cr. 8vo.* 3s. 6d.

EVOLUTION. By F. B. Jevons, M.A., Litt.D. *Cr. 8vo.* 3s. 6d.

THE OLD TESTAMENT AND THE NEW SCHOLARSHIP. By J. W. Peters, D.D. *Cr. 8vo.* 6s.

THE CHURCHMAN'S INTRODUCTION TO THE OLD TESTAMENT. By A. M. Mackay, B.A. *Cr. 8vo.* 3s. 6d.

THE CHURCH OF CHRIST. By E. T. Green, M.A. *Cr. 8vo.* 6s.

COMPARATIVE THEOLOGY. By J. A. MacCulloch. *Cr. 8vo.* 6s.

Classical Translations

Edited by H. F. FOX, M.A., Fellow and Tutor of Brasenose College, Oxford.

Crown 8vo.

A series of Translations from the Greek and Latin Classics, distinguished by literary excellence as well as by scholarly accuracy.

ÆSCHYLUS—Agamemnon, Choephoroe, Eumenides. Translated by Lewis Campbell, LL.D. 5s.

CICERO—De Oratore I. Translated by E. N. P. Moor, M.A. 3s. 6d.

CICERO—Select Orations (Pro Milone, Pro Mureno, Philippic II., in Catilinam). Translated by H. E. D. Blakiston, M.A. 5s.

CICERO—De Natura Deorum. Translated by F. Brooks, M.A. 3s. 6d.

[*Continued.*

MESSRS. METHUEN'S CATALOGUE

CLASSICAL TRANSLATIONS—*continued.*

CICERO—De Officiis. Translated by G. B. Gardiner, M.A. 2s. 6d.
HORACE—The Odes and Epodes. Translated by A. D. Godley, M.A. 2s.
LUCIAN—Six Dialogues (Nigrinus, Icaro-Menippus, The Cock, The Ship, The Parasite, The Lover of Falsehood) Translated by S.

T. Irwin, M.A. 3s. 6d.
SOPHOCLES—Electra and Ajax. Translated by E. D. A. Morshead, M.A. 2s. 6d.
TACITUS—Agricola and Germania. Translated by R. B. Townshend. 2s. 6d.
THE SATIRES OF JUVENAL. Translated by S. G. Owen. 2s. 6d.

Commercial Series

Edited by H. DE B. GIBBINS, Litt.D., M.A.

Crown 8vo.

A series intended to assist students and young men preparing for a commercial career, by supplying useful handbooks of a clear and practical character, dealing with those subjects which are absolutely essential in the business life.

COMMERCIAL EDUCATION IN THEORY AND PRACTICE. By E. E. Whitfield, M.A. 5s.
An introduction to Methuen's Commercial Series treating the question of Commercial Education fully from both the point of view of the teacher and of the parent.
BRITISH COMMERCE AND COLONIES FROM ELIZABETH TO VICTORIA. By H. de B. Gibbins, Litt.D., M.A. *Third Edition.* 2s.
COMMERCIAL EXAMINATION PAPERS. By H. de B. Gibbins, Litt.D., M.A. 1s. 6d.
THE ECONOMICS OF COMMERCE. By H. de B. Gibbins, Litt.D., M.A. *Second Edition.* 1s. 6d.
A GERMAN COMMERCIAL READER. By S. E. Bally. With Vocabulary. 2s.
A COMMERCIAL GEOGRAPHY OF THE BRITISH EMPIRE. By L. W. Lyde, M.A. *Fourth Edition.* 2s.
A COMMERCIAL GEOGRAPHY OF FOREIGN NATIONS. By F. C. Boon, B.A. 2s.

A PRIMER OF BUSINESS. By S. Jackson, M.A. *Third Edition.* 1s. 6d.
COMMERCIAL ARITHMETIC. By F. G. Taylor, M.A. *Fourth Edition.* 1s. 6d.
FRENCH COMMERCIAL CORRESPONDENCE. By S. E. Bally. With Vocabulary. *Third Edition.* 2s.
GERMAN COMMERCIAL CORRESPONDENCE. By S. E. Bally. With Vocabulary. *Second Edition.* 2s. 6d.
A FRENCH COMMERCIAL READER. By S. E. Bally. With Vocabulary. *Second Edition.* 2s.
PRECIS WRITING AND OFFICE CORRESPONDENCE. By E. E. Whitfield, M.A. *Second Edition.* 2s.
A GUIDE TO PROFESSIONS AND BUSINESS. By H. Jones. 1s. 6d.
THE PRINCIPLES OF BOOK-KEEPING BY DOUBLE ENTRY. By J. E. B. M'Allen, M.A. 2s.
COMMERCIAL LAW. By W. Douglas Edwards. *Second Edition.* 2s.

Connoisseur's Library, The

Wide Royal 8vo. 25s. *net.*

A sumptuous series of 20 books on art, written by experts for collectors, superbly illustrated in photogravure, collotype, and colour. The technical side of the art is duly treated. The first volumes are—

MEZZOTINTS. By Cyril Davenport. With 40 Plates in Photogravure.
PORCELAIN. By Edward Dillon. With 19 Plates in Colour, 20 in Collotype, and 5 in Photogravure.
MINIATURES. By Dudley Heath. With 9 Plates in Colour, 15 in Collotype, and 15 in Photogravure.

IVORIES. By A. Maskell. With 80 Plates in Collotype and Photogravure.
ENGLISH FURNITURE. By F. S. Robinson. With 160 Plates in Collotype and one in Photogravure. *Second Edition.*
'EUROPEAN ENAMELS. By H. CUNYNGHAME, C.B. With many Plates in Collotype and a Frontispiece in Photogravure.

General Literature 23

Devotion, The Library of

With Introductions and (where necessary) Notes.

Small **Pott** *8vo, cloth,* 2s. ; *leather,* 2s. 6d. *net.*

These masterpieces of devotional literature are furnished with such Introductions and Notes as may be necessary to explain the standpoint of the author and the obvious difficulties of the text, without unnecessary intrusion between the author and the devout mind.

THE CONFESSIONS OF ST. AUGUSTINE. Edited by C. Bigg, D.D. *Fifth Edition.*
THE CHRISTIAN YEAR. Edited by Walter Lock, D.D. *Third Edition.*
THE IMITATION OF CHRIST. Edited by C. Bigg, D.D. *Fourth Edition.*
A BOOK OF DEVOTIONS. Edited by J. W. Stanbridge. B.D. *Second Edition.*
LYRA INNOCENTIUM. Edited by Walter Lock, D.D.
A SERIOUS CALL TO A DEVOUT AND HOLY LIFE. Edited by C. Bigg, D.D. *Second Edition.*
THE TEMPLE. Edited by E. C. S. Gibson, D.D. *Second Edition.*
A GUIDE TO ETERNITY. Edited by J. W. Stanbridge, B.D.
THE PSALMS OF DAVID. Edited by B. W. Randolph, D.D.
LYRA APOSTOLICA. By Cardinal Newman and others. Edited by Canon Scott Holland and Canon H. C. Beeching, M.A.
THE INNER WAY. By J Tauler. Edited by A. W. Hutton, M.A.
THE THOUGHTS OF PASCAL. Edited by C. S. Jerram, M.A.

ON THE LOVE OF GOD. By St. Francis de Sales. Edited by W. J. Knox-Little, M.A.
A MANUAL OF CONSOLATION FROM THE SAINTS AND FATHERS. Edited by J. H. Burn, B.D.
THE SONG OF SONGS. Edited by B. Blaxland, M.A.
THE DEVOTIONS OF ST. ANSELM. Edited by C. C. J. Webb, M.A.
GRACE ABOUNDING. By John Bunyan. Edited by S. C. Freer, M.A.
BISHOP WILSON'S SACRA PRIVATA. Edited by A. E. Burn, B.D.
LYRA SACRA : A Book of Sacred Verse. Edited by H. C. Beeching, M.A., Canon of Westminster.
A DAY BOOK FROM THE SAINTS AND FATHERS. Edited by J. H. Burn, B.D.
HEAVENLY WISDOM. A Selection from the English Mystics. Edited by E. C. Gregory.
LIGHT, LIFE, and LOVE. A Selection from the German Mystics. Edited by W. R. Inge, M.A.
'AN INTRODUCTION TO THE DEVOUT LIFE. By St. Francis de Sales. Translated and Edited by T. Barns, M.A.

Standard Library, The

In Sixpenny Volumes.

THE STANDARD LIBRARY is a new series of volumes containing the great classics of the world, and particularly the finest works of English literature. All the great masters will be represented, either in complete works or in selections. It is the ambition of the publishers to place the best books of the Anglo-Saxon race within the reach of every reader, so that the series may represent something of the diversity and splendour of our English tongue. The characteristics of THE STANDARD LIBRARY are four :—1. SOUNDNESS OF TEXT. 2. CHEAPNESS. 3. CLEARNESS OF TYPE. 4. SIMPLICITY. The books are well printed on good paper at a price which on the whole is without parallel in the history of publishing. Each volume contains from 100 to 250 pages, and is issued in paper covers, Crown 8vo, at Sixpence net, or in cloth gilt at One Shilling net. In a few cases long books are issued as Double Volumes or as Treble Volumes.

The following books are ready with the exception of those marked with a †, which denotes that the book is nearly ready :—

THE MEDITATIONS OF MARCUS AURELIUS. The translation is by R. Graves.
THE NOVELS OF JANE AUSTEN. In 5 volumes. VOL. I.—Sense and Sensibility.
ESSAYS AND COUNSELS and THE NEW ATLANTIS. By Francis Bacon, Lord Verulam.

†RELIGIO MEDICI and URN BURIAL. By Sir Thomas Browne. The text has been collated by A. R. Waller.
THE PILGRIM'S PROGRESS. By John Bunyan.
REFLECTIONS ON THE FRENCH REVOLUTION. By Edmund Burke.
†THE ANALOGY OF RELIGION, NATURAL AND REVEALED. By Joseph Butler, D.D.

[*Continued.*

The Standard Library—*continued.*

The Poems of Thomas Chatterton. In 2 volumes.
†Vol. I.—Miscellaneous Poems.
†Vol. II.—The Rowley Poems.
†Vita Nuova. By Dante. Translated into English by D. G. Rossetti.
Tom Jones. By Henry Fielding. Treble Vol.
†Cranford. By Mrs. Gaskell.
The History of the Decline and Fall of the Roman Empire. By Edward Gibbon. In 7 volumes.
Vol. V. is nearly ready.
The Text and Notes have been revised by J. B. Bury, Litt.D., but the Appendices of the more expensive edition are not given.
†The Vicar of Wakefield. By Oliver Goldsmith.
The Poems and Plays of Oliver Goldsmith.
The Works of Ben Jonson.
†Vol. I.—The Case is Altered. Every Man in His Humour. Every Man out of His Humour.
The text has been collated by H. C. Hart.
The Poems of John Keats. Double volume. The Text has been collated by E. de Selincourt.
On the Imitation of Christ. By Thomas à Kempis.
The translation is by C. Bigg, D.D., Canon of Christ Church.
†A Serious Call to a Devout and Holy Life. By William Law.
The Plays of Christopher Marlowe.
†Vol. I.—Tamburlane the Great.
The Plays of Philip Massinger.
†Vol. I.—The Duke of Milan.

The Poems of John Milton. In 2 volumes.
†Vol. I.—Paradise Lost.
The Prose Works of John Milton.
†Vol. I.—Eikonoklastes and The Tenure of Kings and Magistrates.
Select Works of Sir Thomas More.
†Vol. I.—Utopia and Poems.
†The Republic of Plato. Translated by Sydenham and Taylor. Double Volume. The translation has been revised by W. H. D. Rouse.
†The Little Flowers of St. Francis. Translated by W. Heywood.
The Works of William Shakespeare. In 10 volumes.
Vol. I.—The Tempest; The Two Gentlemen of Verona; The Merry Wives of Windsor; Measure for Measure; The Comedy of Errors.
Vol. II.—Much Ado About Nothing; Love's Labour's Lost; A Midsummer Night's Dream; The Merchant of Venice; As You Like It.
Vol. III.—The Taming of the Shrew; All's Well that Ends Well; Twelfth Night; The Winter's Tale.
Vol. IV.—The Life and Death of King John; The Tragedy of King Richard the Second; The First Part of King Henry IV.; The Second Part of King Henry IV.
†Vol. V.—The Life of King Henry V.; The First Part of King Henry VI.; The Second Part of King Henry VI.
The Life of Nelson. By Robert Southey.
†The Natural History and Antiquities of Selborne. By Gilbert White.

Half-Crown Library
Crown 8vo. 2s. 6d. net.

The Life of John Ruskin. By W. G. Collingwood, M.A. With Portraits. *Sixth Edition.*
English Lyrics. By W. E. Henley. *Second Edition.*
The Golden Pomp. A Procession of English Lyrics. Arranged by A. T. Quiller Couch. *Second Edition.*
Chitral: The Story of a Minor Siege. By Sir G. S. Robertson, K.C.S.I. *Third Edition.* Illustrated.

Strange Survivals and Superstitions. By S. Baring-Gould. *Third Edition.*
Yorkshire Oddities and Strange Events. By S. Baring-Gould. *Fourth Edition.*
English Villages. By P. H. Ditchfield, M.A., F.S.A. Illustrated.
A Book of English Prose. By W. E. Henley and C. Whibley.
The Land of the Black Mountain. Being a Description of Montenegro. By R. Wyon and G. Prance. With 40 Illustrations.

Illustrated Pocket Library of Plain and Coloured Books, The
Fcap 8vo. 3s. 6d. net each volume.

A series, in small form, of some of the famous illustrated books of fiction and general literature. These are faithfully reprinted from the first or best editions without introduction or notes. The Illustrations are chiefly in colour.

COLOURED BOOKS

Old Coloured Books. By George Paston. With 16 Coloured Plates. *Fcap. 8vo. 2s. net.*
The Life and Death of John Mytton, Esq.

By Nimrod. With 18 Coloured Plates by Henry Alken and T. J. Rawlins. *Third Edition.*

[*Continued.*

General Literature 25

Illustrated Pocket Library of Plain and Coloured Books—*continued.*

The Life of a Sportsman. By Nimrod. With 35 Coloured Plates by Henry Alken.
Handley Cross. By R. S. Surtees. With 17 Coloured Plates and 100 Woodcuts in the Text by John Leech.
Mr. Sponge's Sporting Tour. By R. S. Surtees. With 13 Coloured Plates and 90 Woodcuts in the Text by John Leech.
Jorrocks' Jaunts and Jollities. By R. S. Surtees. With 15 Coloured Plates by H. Alken.
    This volume is reprinted from the extremely rare and costly edition of 1843, which contains Alken's very fine illustrations instead of the usual ones by Phiz.
Ask Mamma. By R. S. Surtees. With 13 Coloured Plates and 70 Woodcuts in the Text by John Leech.
The Analysis of the Hunting Field. By R. S. Surtees. With 7 Coloured Plates by Henry Alken, and 43 Illustrations on Wood.
The Tour of Dr. Syntax in Search of the Picturesque. By William Combe. With 30 Coloured Plates by T. Rowlandson.
The Tour of Doctor Syntax in Search of Consolation. By William Combe. With 24 Coloured Plates by T. Rowlandson.
The Third Tour of Doctor Syntax in Search of a Wife. By William Combe. With 24 Coloured Plates by T. Rowlandson.
The History of Johnny Quae Genus: the Little Foundling of the late Dr. Syntax. By the Author of 'The Three Tours.' With 24 Coloured Plates by Rowlandson.
The English Dance of Death, from the Designs of T. Rowlandson, with Metrical Illustrations by the Author of 'Doctor Syntax.' *Two Volumes.*
    This book contains 76 Coloured Plates.
The Dance of Life: A Poem. By the Author of 'Doctor Syntax.' Illustrated with 26 Coloured Engravings by T. Rowlandson.
Life in London: or, the Day and Night Scenes of Jerry Hawthorn, Esq., and his Elegant Friend, Corinthian Tom. By Pierce Egan. With 36 Coloured Plates by I. R. and G. Cruikshank. With numerous Designs on Wood.
Real Life in London: or, the Rambles and Adventures of Bob Tallyho, Esq., and his Cousin, The Hon. Tom Dashall. By an Amateur (Pierce Egan). With 31 Coloured Plates by Alken and Rowlandson, etc. *Two Volumes.*
The Life of an Actor. By Pierce Egan. With 27 Coloured Plates by Theodore Lane, and several Designs on Wood.
The Vicar of Wakefield. By Oliver Goldsmith. With 24 Coloured Plates by T. Rowlandson.
The Military Adventures of Johnny Newcome. By an Officer. With 15 Coloured Plates by T. Rowlandson.
The National Sports of Great Britain. With Descriptions and 51 Coloured Plates by Henry Alken.
    This book is completely different from the large folio edition of 'National Sports' by the same artist, and none of the plates are similar.
The Adventures of a Post Captain. By A Naval Officer. With 24 Coloured Plates by Mr. Williams.
Gamonia: or, the Art of Preserving Game; and an Improved Method of making Plantations and Covers, explained and illustrated by Lawrence Rawstorne, Esq. With 15 Coloured Plates by T. Rawlins.
An Academy for Grown Horsemen: Containing the completest Instructions for Walking, Trotting, Cantering, Galloping, Stumbling, and Tumbling. Illustrated with 27 Coloured Plates, and adorned with a Portrait of the Author. By Geoffrey Gambado, Esq.
Real Life in Ireland, or, the Day and Night Scenes of Brian Boru, Esq., and his Elegant Friend, Sir Shawn O'Dogherty. By a Real Paddy. With 19 Coloured Plates by Heath, Marks, etc.
The Adventures of Johnny Newcome in the Navy. By Alfred Burton. With 16 Coloured Plates by T. Rowlandson.
The Old English Squire: A Poem. By John Careless, Esq. With 20 Coloured Plates after the style of T. Rowlandson.
*The English Spy. By Bernard Blackmantle. With 72 Coloured Plates by R. Cruikshank, and many Illustrations on wood. *Two Volumes.*

PLAIN BOOKS

The Grave: A Poem. By Robert Blair. Illustrated by 12 Etchings executed by Louis Schiavonetti from the original Inventions of William Blake. With an Engraved Title Page and a Portrait of Blake by T. Phillips, R.A.
    The illustrations are reproduced in photogravure.
Illustrations of the Book of Job. Invented and engraved by William Blake.
    These famous Illustrations—21 in number—are reproduced in photogravure.
Æsop's Fables. With 380 Woodcuts by Thomas Bewick.

[*Continued.*

ILLUSTRATED POCKET LIBRARY OF PLAIN AND COLOURED BOOKS—*continued*.

WINDSOR CASTLE. By W. Harrison Ainsworth. With 22 Plates and 87 Woodcuts in the Text by George Cruikshank.

THE TOWER OF LONDON. By W. Harrison Ainsworth. With 40 Plates and 58 Woodcuts in the Text by George Cruikshank.

FRANK FAIRLEGH. By F. E. Smedley. With 30 Plates by George Cruikshank.

HANDY ANDY. By Samuel Lover. With 24 Illustrations by the Author.

THE COMPLEAT ANGLER. By Izaak Walton and Charles Cotton. With 14 Plates and 77 Woodcuts in the Text.
 This volume is reproduced from the beautiful edition of John Major of 1824.

THE PICKWICK PAPERS. By Charles Dickens. With the 43 Illustrations by Seymour and Phiz, the two Buss Plates, and the 32 Contemporary Onwhyn Plates.

Junior Examination Series

Edited by A. M. M. STEDMAN, M.A. *Fcap. 8vo.* 1s.

This series is intended to lead up to the School Examination Series, and is intended for the use of teachers and students, to supply material for the former and practice for the latter. The papers are carefully graduated, cover the whole of the subject usually taught, and are intended to form part of the ordinary class work. They may be used *vivâ voce* or as a written examination.

JUNIOR FRENCH EXAMINATION PAPERS. By F. Jacob, M.A.

JUNIOR LATIN EXAMINATION PAPERS. By C. G. Botting, M.A. *Third Edition.*

JUNIOR ENGLISH EXAMINATION PAPERS. By W. Williamson, B.A.

JUNIOR ARITHMETIC EXAMINATION PAPERS. By W. S. Beard. *Second Edition.*

JUNIOR ALGEBRA EXAMINATION PAPERS. By S. W. Finn, M.A.

JUNIOR GREEK EXAMINATION PAPERS. By T. C. Weatherhead, M.A.

JUNIOR GENERAL INFORMATION EXAMINATION PAPERS. By W. S. Beard.
 A KEY TO THE ABOVE. Crown 8vo. 3s. 6d.

JUNIOR GEOGRAPHY EXAMINATION PAPERS. By W. G. Baker, M.A.

JUNIOR GERMAN EXAMINATION PAPERS. By A. Voegelin, M.A.

Junior School-Books

Edited by O. D. INSKIP, LL.D., and W. WILLIAMSON, B.A.

A series of elementary books for pupils in lower forms, simply written by teachers of experience.

A CLASS-BOOK OF DICTATION PASSAGES. By W. Williamson, B.A. *Eleventh Edition. Cr. 8vo.* 1s. 6d.

THE GOSPEL ACCORDING TO ST. MATTHEW. Edited by E. Wilton South, M.A. With Three Maps. *Cr. 8vo.* 1s. 6d.

THE GOSPEL ACCORDING TO ST. MARK. Edited by A. E. Rubie, D.D. With Three Maps. *Cr. 8vo.* 1s. 6d.

A JUNIOR ENGLISH GRAMMAR. By W. Williamson, B.A. With numerous passages for parsing and analysis, and a chapter on Essay Writing. *Third Edition. Cr. 8vo.* 2s.

A JUNIOR CHEMISTRY. By E. A. Tyler, B.A., F.C.S. With 78 Illustrations. *Second Edition. Cr. 8vo.* 2s. 6d.

THE ACTS OF THE APOSTLES. Edited by A. E. Rubie, D.D. *Cr. 8vo.* 2s.

A JUNIOR FRENCH GRAMMAR. By L. A. Sornet and M. J. Acatos. *Cr. 8vo.* 2s.

ELEMENTARY EXPERIMENTAL SCIENCE. PHYSICS by W. T. Clough, A.R.C.S. CHEMISTRY by A. E. Dunstan B.Sc. With 2 Plates and 154 Diagrams. *Third Edition. Cr. 8vo.* 2s. 6d.

A JUNIOR GEOMETRY. By Noel S. Lydon. With 239 Diagrams. *Second Edition. Cr. 8vo.* 2s.

*A JUNIOR MAGNETISM AND ELECTRICITY. By W. T. Clough. Illustrated. *Cr. 8vo.* 2s. 6d.

ELEMENTARY EXPERIMENTAL CHEMISTRY. By A. E. Dunstan, B.Sc. With 4 Plates and 109 Diagrams. *Cr. 8vo.* 2s.

A JUNIOR FRENCH PROSE COMPOSITION. By R. R. N. Baron, M.A. *Cr. 8vo.* 2s.

*THE GOSPEL ACCORDING TO ST. LUKE. With an Introduction and Notes by William Williamson, B.A. With Three Maps. *Cr. 8vo.* 2s.

Leaders of Religion

Edited by H. C. BEECHING, M.A., Canon of Westminster. *With Portraits.* Cr. 8vo. 2s. net.

A series of short biographies of the most prominent leaders of religious life and thought of all ages and countries.

CARDINAL NEWMAN. By R. H. Hutton.
JOHN WESLEY. By J. H. Overton, M.A.
BISHOP WILBERFORCE. By G. W. Daniell, M.A.
CARDINAL MANNING. By A. W. Hutton, M.A.
CHARLES SIMEON. By H. C. G. Moule, D.D.
JOHN KEBLE. By Walter Lock, D.D.
THOMAS CHALMERS. By Mrs. Oliphant.
LANCELOT ANDREWES. By R. L. Ottley, D.D. *Second Edition.*
AUGUSTINE OF CANTERBURY. By E. L. Cutts, D.D.

WILLIAM LAUD. By W. H. Hutton, M.A. *Third Edition.*
JOHN KNOX. By F. MacCunn. *Second Edition.*
JOHN HOWE. By R. F. Horton, D.D.
BISHOP KEN. By F. A. Clarke, M.A.
GEORGE FOX, THE QUAKER. By T. Hodgkin, D.C.L.
JOHN DONNE. By Augustus Jessopp, D.D.
THOMAS CRANMER. By A. J. Mason, D.D.
BISHOP LATIMER. By R. M. Carlyle and A. J. Carlyle, M.A.
BISHOP BUTLER. By W. A. Spooner, M.A.

Little Blue Books, The

General Editor, E. V. LUCAS.

Illustrated. Demy 16mo. 2s. 6d.

A series of books for children. The aim of the editor is to get entertaining or exciting stories about normal children, the moral of which is implied rather than expressed.

1. THE CASTAWAYS OF MEADOWBANK. By Thomas Cobb.
2. THE BEECHNUT BOOK. By Jacob Abbott. Edited by E. V. Lucas.
3. THE AIR GUN. By T. Hilbert.
4. A SCHOOL YEAR. By Netta Syrett.
5. THE PEELES AT THE CAPITAL. By Roger Ashton.
6. THE TREASURE OF PRINCEGATE PRIORY. By T. Cobb.
7. MRS. BARBERRY'S GENERAL SHOP. By Roger Ashton.
8. A BOOK OF BAD CHILDREN. By W. T. Webb.
9. THE LOST BALL. By Thomas Cobb.

Little Books on Art

With many Illustrations. Demy 16mo. 2s. 6d. net.

A series of monographs in miniature, containing the complete outline of the subject under treatment and rejecting minute details. These books are produced with the greatest care. Each volume consists of about 200 pages, and contains from 30 to 40 illustrations, including a frontispiece in photogravure.

GREEK ART. H. B. Walters. *Second Edition.*
BOOKPLATES. E. Almack.
REYNOLDS. J. Sime. *Second Edition.*
ROMNEY. George Paston.
WATTS. R. E. D. Sketchley.
LEIGHTON. Alice Corkran.
VELASQUEZ. Wilfrid Wilberforce and A. R. Gilbert.
GREUZE AND BOUCHER. Eliza F. Pollard.
VANDYCK. M. G. Smallwood.
TURNER. Frances Tyrell-Gill.
DÜRER. Jessie Allen.
HOPPNER. H. P. K. Skipton.

HOLBEIN. Mrs. G. Fortescue.
BURNE-JONES. Fortunée de Lisle. *Second Edition.*
REMBRANDT. Mrs. E. A. Sharp
COROT. Alice Pollard and Ethel Birnstingl.
RAPHAEL. A. R. Dryhurst.
MILLET. Netta Peacock.
ILLUMINATED MSS. J. W. Bradley.
*CHRIST IN ART. Mrs. Henry Jenner.
JEWELLERY. Cyril Davenport.
CLAUDE. Edward Dillon.
*THE ARTS OF JAPAN. Edward Dillon.

Little Galleries, The

Demy 16mo. 2s. 6d. net.

A series of little books containing examples of the best work of the great painters. Each volume contains 20 plates in photogravure, together with a short outline of the life and work of the master to whom the book is devoted.

A LITTLE GALLERY OF REYNOLDS.
A LITTLE GALLERY OF ROMNEY.
A LITTLE GALLERY OF HOPPNER.
A LITTLE GALLERY OF MILLAIS.
A LITTLE GALLERY OF ENGLISH POETS.

Little Guides, The

Small Pott 8vo, cloth, 2s. 6d. net.; leather, 3s. 6d. net.

OXFORD AND ITS COLLEGES. By J. Wells, M.A. Illustrated by E. H. New. *Sixth Edition*.

CAMBRIDGE AND ITS COLLEGES. By A. Hamilton Thompson. *Second Edition*. Illustrated by E. H. New.

THE MALVERN COUNTRY. By B. C. A. Windle, D.Sc., F.R.S. Illustrated by E. H. New.

SHAKESPEARE'S COUNTRY. By B. C. A. Windle, D.Sc., F.R.S. Illustrated by E. H. New. *Second Edition*.

SUSSEX. By F. G. Brabant, M.A. Illustrated by E. H. New.

WESTMINSTER ABBEY. By G. E. Troutbeck. Illustrated by F. D. Bedford.

NORFOLK. By W. A. Dutt. Illustrated by B. C. Boulter.

CORNWALL. By A. L. Salmon. Illustrated by B. C. Boulter.

BRITTANY. By S. Baring-Gould. Illustrated by J. Wylie.

HERTFORDSHIRE. By H. W. Tompkins, F.R.H.S. Illustrated by E. H. New.

THE ENGLISH LAKES. By F. G. Brabant, M.A. Illustrated by E. H. New.

KENT. By G. Clinch. Illustrated by F. D. Bedford.

ROME By C. G. Ellaby. Illustrated by B. C. Boulter.

THE ISLE OF WIGHT. By G. Clinch. Illustrated by F. D. Bedford.

SURREY. By F. A. H. Lambert. Illustrated by E. H. New.

BUCKINGHAMSHIRE. By E. S. Roscoe. Illustrated by F. D. Bedford.

SUFFOLK. By W. A. Dutt. Illustrated by J. Wylie.

DERBYSHIRE. By J. C. Cox, LL.D., F.S.A. Illustrated by J. C. Wall.

THE NORTH RIDING OF YORKSHIRE. By J. E. Morris. Illustrated by R. J. S. Bertram.

HAMPSHIRE. By J. C. Cox. Illustrated by M. E. Purser.

SICILY. By F. H. Jackson. With many Illustrations by the Author.

DORSET. By Frank R. Heath. Illustrated.

CHESHIRE. By W. M. Gallichan. Illustrated by Elizabeth Hartley.

*NORTHAMPTONSHIRE. By Wakeling Dry. Illustrated.

*THE EAST RIDING OF YORKSHIRE. By J. E. Morris. Illustrated.

*OXFORDSHIRE. By F. G. Brabant. Illustrated by E. H. New.

*ST. PAUL'S CATHEDRAL. By George Clinch. Illustrated by Beatrice Alcock.

Little Library, The

With Introductions, Notes, and Photogravure Frontispieces.

Small Pott 8vo. Each Volume, cloth, 1s. 6d. net; leather, 2s. 6d. net.

A series of small books under the above title, containing some of the famous works in English and other literatures, in the domains of fiction, poetry, and belles lettres. The series also contains volumes of selections in prose and verse. The books are edited with the most scholarly care. Each one contains an introduction which gives (1) a short biography of the author; (2) a critical estimate of the book. Where they are necessary, short notes are added at the foot of the page.

Each volume has a photogravure frontispiece, and the books are produced with great care.

Anon. ENGLISH LYRICS, A LITTLE BOOK OF.

Austen (Jane). PRIDE AND PREJUDICE. Edited by E. V. Lucas. *Two Volumes*.

NORTHANGER ABBEY. Edited by E. V. Lucas.

Bacon (Francis). THE ESSAYS OF LORD BACON. Edited by EDWARD WRIGHT.

General Literature

Barham (R. H.). THE INGOLDSBY LEGENDS. Edited by J. B. ATLAY. *Two Volumes.*

Barnett (Mrs. P. A.). A LITTLE BOOK OF ENGLISH PROSE.

Beckford (William). THE HISTORY OF THE CALIPH VATHEK. Edited by E. DENISON ROSS.

Blake (William). SELECTIONS FROM WILLIAM BLAKE. Edited by M. PERUGINI.

Borrow (George). LAVENGRO. Edited by F. HINDES GROOME. *Two Volumes.*
THE ROMANY RYE. Edited by JOHN SAMPSON.

Browning (Robert). SELECTIONS FROM THE EARLY POEMS OF ROBERT BROWNING. Edited by W. HALL GRIFFIN, M.A.

Canning (George). SELECTIONS FROM THE ANTI-JACOBIN: with GEORGE CANNING'S additional Poems. Edited by LLOYD SANDERS.

Cowley (Abraham). THE ESSAYS OF ABRAHAM COWLEY. Edited by H. C. MINCHIN.

Crabbe (George). SELECTIONS FROM GEORGE CRABBE. Edited by A. C. DEANE.

Craik (Mrs.). JOHN HALIFAX, GENTLEMAN. Edited by ANNE MATHESON. *Two Volumes.*

Crashaw (Richard). THE ENGLISH POEMS OF RICHARD CRASHAW. Edited by EDWARD HUTTON.

Dante (Alighieri). THE INFERNO OF DANTE. Translated by H. F. CARY. Edited by PAGET TOYNBEE, M.A., D.Litt.
THE PURGATORIO OF DANTE. Translated by H. F. CARY. Edited by PAGET TOYNBEE, M.A., D.Litt.
THE PARADISO OF DANTE. Translated by H. F. CARY. Edited by PAGET TOYNBEE, M.A., D.Litt.

Darley (George). SELECTIONS FROM THE POEMS OF GEORGE DARLEY. Edited by R. A. STREATFEILD.

Deane (A. C.). A LITTLE BOOK OF LIGHT VERSE.

Dickens (Charles). CHRISTMAS BOOKS. *Two Volumes.*

Ferrier (Susan). MARRIAGE. Edited by A. GOODRICH-FREER and LORD IDDESLEIGH. *Two Volumes.*
THE INHERITANCE. *Two Volumes.*

Gaskell (Mrs.). CRANFORD. Edited by E. V. LUCAS. *Second Edition.*

Hawthorne (Nathaniel). THE SCARLET LETTER. Edited by PERCY DEARMER.

Henderson (T. F.). A LITTLE BOOK OF SCOTTISH VERSE.

Keats (John). POEMS. With an Introduction by L. BINYON, and Notes by J. MASEFIELD.

Kinglake (A. W.). EOTHEN. With an Introduction and Notes. *Second Edition.*

Lamb (Charles). ELIA, AND THE LAST ESSAYS OF ELIA. Edited by E. V. LUCAS.

Locker (F.). LONDON LYRICS. Edited by A. D. GODLEY, M.A. A reprint of the First Edition.

Longfellow (H. W.). SELECTIONS FROM LONGFELLOW. Edited by L. M. FAITHFULL.

Marvell (Andrew). THE POEMS OF ANDREW MARVELL. Edited by E. WRIGHT.

Milton (John). THE MINOR POEMS OF JOHN MILTON. Edited by H. C. BEECHING, M.A., Canon of Westminster.

Moir (D. M.). MANSIE WAUCH. Edited by T. F. HENDERSON.

Nichols (J. B. B.). A LITTLE BOOK OF ENGLISH SONNETS.

Rochefoucauld (La). THE MAXIMS OF LA ROCHEFOUCAULD. Translated by Dean STANHOPE. Edited by G. H. POWELL.

Smith (Horace and James). REJECTED ADDRESSES. Edited by A. D. GODLEY, M.A.

Sterne (Laurence). A SENTIMENTAL JOURNEY. Edited by H. W. PAUL.

Tennyson (Alfred, Lord). THE EARLY POEMS OF ALFRED, LORD TENNYSON. Edited by J. CHURTON COLLINS, M.A.
IN MEMORIAM. Edited by H. C. BEECHING, M.A.
THE PRINCESS. Edited by ELIZABETH WORDSWORTH.
MAUD. Edited by ELIZABETH WORDSWORTH.

Thackeray (W. M.). VANITY FAIR. Edited by S. GWYNN. *Three Volumes.*
PENDENNIS. Edited by S. GWYNN. *Three Volumes.*
ESMOND. Edited by S. GWYNN.
CHRISTMAS BOOKS. Edited by S. GWYNN.

Vaughan (Henry). THE POEMS OF HENRY VAUGHAN. Edited by EDWARD HUTTON.

Walton (Izaak). THE COMPLEAT ANGLER. Edited by J. BUCHAN.

Waterhouse (Mrs. Alfred). A LITTLE BOOK OF LIFE AND DEATH. Edited by. *Eighth Edition.*

Wordsworth (W.). SELECTIONS FROM WORDSWORTH. Edited by NOWELL C. SMITH.

Wordsworth (W.) and Coleridge (S. T.). LYRICAL BALLADS. Edited by GEORGE SAMPSON.

Miniature Library

Reprints in miniature of a few interesting books which have qualities of humanity, devotion, or literary genius.

EUPHRANOR: A Dialogue on Youth. By Edward FitzGerald. From the edition published by W. Pickering in 1851. *Demy 32mo. Leather, 2s. net.*

POLONIUS: or Wise Saws and Modern Instances. By Edward FitzGerald. From the edition published by W. Pickering in 1852. *Demy 32mo. Leather, 2s. net.*

THE RUBÁIYÁT OF OMAR KHAYYÁM. By Edward FitzGerald. From the 1st edition of 1859, *Third Edition. Leather, 1s. net.*

THE LIFE OF EDWARD, LORD HERBERT OF CHERBURY. Written by himself. From the edition printed at Strawberry Hill in the year 1764. *Medium 32mo. Leather, 2s. net.*

THE VISIONS OF DOM FRANCISCO QUEVEDO VILLEGAS, Knight of the Order of St James. Made English by R. L. From the edition printed for H. Herringman, 1668 *Leather. 2s. net.*

POEMS. By Dora Greenwell. From the edition of 1848. *Leather, 2s. net.*

Oxford Biographies

Fcap. 8vo. Each volume, cloth, 2s. 6d. net; leather, 3s. 6d. net.

These books are written by scholars of repute, who combine knowledge and literary skill with the power of popular presentation. They are illustrated from authentic material.

DANTE ALIGHIERI. By Paget Toynbee, M.A., D.Litt. With 12 Illustrations. *Second Edition.*

SAVONAROLA. By E. L. S. Horsburgh, M.A. With 12 Illustrations. *Second Edition.*

JOHN HOWARD. By E. C. S. Gibson, D.D., Bishop of Gloucester. With 12 Illustrations.

TENNYSON. By A. C. BENSON, M.A. With 9 Illustrations.

WALTER RALEIGH. By I. A. Taylor. With 12 Illustrations.

ERASMUS. By E. F. H. Capey. With 12 Illustrations.

THE YOUNG PRETENDER. By C. S. Terry. With 12 Illustrations.

ROBERT BURNS. By T. F. Henderson. With 12 Illustrations.

CHATHAM. By A. S. M'Dowall. With 12 Illustrations.

ST. FRANCIS OF ASSISI. By Anna M. Stoddart. With 16 Illustrations.

CANNING. By W. Alison Phillips. With 12 Illustrations.

BEACONSFIELD. By Walter Sichel. With 12 Illustrations.

GOETHE. By H. G. Atkins. With 12 Illustrations.

*FENELON. By Viscount St. Cyres. With 12 Illustrations.

School Examination Series

Edited by A. M. M. STEDMAN, M.A. *Cr. 8vo. 2s. 6d.*

FRENCH EXAMINATION PAPERS. By A. M. M. Stedman, M.A. *Thirteenth Edition.*
A KEY, issued to Tutors and Private Students only to be had on application to the Publishers. *Fifth Edition. Crown 8vo. 6s. net.*

LATIN EXAMINATION PAPERS. By A. M. M. Stedman, M.A. *Thirteenth Edition.*
KEY (*Fourth Edition*) issued as above. 6s. net.

GREEK EXAMINATION PAPERS. By A. M. M. Stedman, M.A. *Eighth Edition.*
KEY (*Third Edition*) issued as above. 6s. net.

GERMAN EXAMINATION PAPERS. By R. J. Morich. *Sixth Edition.*

KEY (*Third Edition*) issued as above. 6s. net.

HISTORY AND GEOGRAPHY EXAMINATION PAPERS. By C. H. Spence, M.A. *Second Edition.*

PHYSICS EXAMINATION PAPERS. By R. E. Steel, M.A., F.C.S.

GENERAL KNOWLEDGE EXAMINATION PAPERS. By A. M. M. Stedman, M.A. *Fifth Edition.*
KEY (*Third Edition*) issued as above. 7s. net.

EXAMINATION PAPERS IN ENGLISH HISTORY. By J. Tait Plowden-Wardlaw, B.A.

Social Questions of To-day

Edited by H. DE B. GIBBINS, Litt.D., M.A. *Crown 8vo. 2s. 6d.*

A series of volumes upon those topics of social, economic, and industrial interest that are foremost in the public mind.

TRADE UNIONISM—NEW AND OLD. By G. Howell. *Third Edition.*
THE COMMERCE OF NATIONS. By C. F. Bastable, M.A. *Third Edition.*
THE ALIEN INVASION. By W. H. Wilkins, B.A.
THE RURAL EXODUS. By P. Anderson Graham.
LAND NATIONALIZATION. By Harold Cox, B.A. *Second Edition.*
A SHORTER WORKING DAY. By H. de B. Gibbins and R. A. Hadfield.
BACK TO THE LAND. An Inquiry into Rural Depopulation. By H. E. Moore.
TRUSTS, POOLS, AND CORNERS. By J. Stephen Jeans.
THE FACTORY SYSTEM. By R. W. Cooke Taylor.
WOMEN'S WORK. By Lady Dilke, Miss Bulley, and Miss Whitley.
SOCIALISM AND MODERN THOUGHT. By M. Kauffmann.
THE PROBLEM OF THE UNEMPLOYED. By J. A. Hobson, M.A.
LIFE IN WEST LONDON. By Arthur Sherwell, M.A. *Third Edition.*
RAILWAY NATIONALIZATION. By Clement Edwards.
UNIVERSITY AND SOCIAL SETTLEMENTS. By W. Reason, M.A.

Textbooks of Science.

PRACTICAL MECHANICS. By Sidney H. Wells. *Third Edition. Cr. 8vo.* 3s. 6d.
PRACTICAL PHYSICS. By H. Stroud, D.Sc., M.A. *Cr. 8vo.* 3s. 6d.
PRACTICAL CHEMISTRY. Part I. By W. French, M.A. *Cr.8vo. Third Edition.* 1s.6d.
PRACTICAL CHEMISTRY. Part II. By W. French, M.A., and T. H. Boardman, M.A.
Cr. 8vo. 1s. 6d.
EXAMPLES IN PHYSICS. By C. E. Jackson, B.A., Science Master at Bradford Grammar School. *Cr. 8vo.* 2s. 6d.
ELEMENTARY ORGANIC CHEMISTRY. By A. E. Dunstan, B.Sc., Head of Chemical Department, East Ham Technical College. Illustrated. *Cr. 8vo.* 2s. 6d.

Technology, Textbooks of

Edited by G. F. GOODCHILD, B.A., B.Sc., and G. R. MILLS, M.A.
Fully Illustrated.

HOW TO MAKE A DRESS. By J. A. E. Wood. *Third Edition. Cr. 8vo.* 1s. 6d.
CARPENTRY AND JOINERY. By F. C. Webber. *Fourth Edition. Cr. 8vo.* 3s. 6d.
MILLINERY, THEORETICAL AND PRACTICAL. By Clare Hill. *Second Edition. Cr. 8vo.* 2s.
TECHNICAL ARITHMETIC AND GEOMETRY. By C. T. Millis, M.I.M.E. *Cr. 8vo.* 3s. 6d.
AN INTRODUCTION TO THE STUDY OF TEXTILE DESIGN. By Aldred F. Barker. *Demy 8vo.* 7s. 6d.
BUILDERS' QUANTITIES. By H. C. Grubb. *Cr. 8vo.* 4s. 6d.
RÉPOUSSÉ METAL WORK. By A. C. Horth. *Cr. 8vo.* 2s. 6d.

Theology, Handbooks of

Edited by R. L. OTTLEY, D.D., Professor of Pastoral Theology at Oxford, and Canon of Christ Church, Oxford.

The series is intended, in part, to furnish the clergy and teachers or students of Theology with trustworthy Textbooks, adequately representing the present position of the questions dealt with; in part, to make accessible to the reading public an accurate and concise statement of facts and principles in all questions bearing on Theology and Religion.

THE XXXIX. ARTICLES OF THE CHURCH OF ENGLAND. Edited by E. C. S. Gibson, D.D. *Third and Cheaper Edition in one Volume. Demy 8vo.* 12s. 6d.
AN INTRODUCTION TO THE HISTORY OF RELIGION. By F. B. Jevons. M.A., Litt.D. *Third Edition. Demy 8vo.* 10s. 6d.
THE DOCTRINE OF THE INCARNATION. By R. L. Ottley, D.D. *Second and Cheaper Edition. Demy 8vo.* 12s. 6d.
AN INTRODUCTION TO THE HISTORY OF THE CREEDS. By A. E. Burn, B.D. *Demy 8vo.* 10s. 6d.
THE PHILOSOPHY OF RELIGION IN ENGLAND AND AMERICA. By Alfred Caldecott, D.D. *Demy 8vo.* 10s. 6d.
A HISTORY OF EARLY CHRISTIAN DOCTRINE. By J. F. Bethune Baker, M.A. *Demy 8vo.* 10s. 6d.

MESSRS. METHUEN'S CATALOGUE

Westminster Commentaries, The

General Editor, WALTER LOCK, D.D., Warden of Keble College, Dean Ireland's Professor of Exegesis in the University of Oxford.

The object of each commentary is primarily exegetical, to interpret the author's meaning to the present generation. The editors will not deal, except very subordinately, with questions of textual criticism or philology; but, taking the English text in the Revised Version as their basis, they will try to combine a hearty acceptance of critical principles with loyalty to the Catholic Faith.

THE BOOK OF GENESIS. Edited with Introduction and Notes by S. R. Driver, D.D. *Fourth Edition* *Demy 8vo.* 10s. 6d.
THE BOOK OF JOB. Edited by E. C. S. Gibson, D.D. *Second Edition.* *Demy 8vo.* 6s.
THE ACTS OF THE APOSTLES. Edited by R. B. Rackham, M.A. *Demy 8vo. Second and Cheaper Edition.* 10s. 6d.

THE FIRST EPISTLE OF PAUL THE APOSTLE TO THE CORINTHIANS. Edited by H. L. Goudge, M.A. *Demy 8vo.* 6s.

THE EPISTLE OF ST. JAMES. Edited with Introduction and Notes by R. J. Knowling, M.A. *Demy 8vo.* 6s.

PART II.—FICTION

Albanesi (E. Maria). SUSANNAH AND ONE OTHER. *Fourth Edition.* *Cr. 8vo.* 6s.
THE BLUNDER OF AN INNOCENT. *Second Edition. Cr. 8vo.* 6s.
CAPRICIOUS CAROLINE. *Second Edition. Cr. 8vo.* 6s.
LOVE AND LOUISA. *Second Edition. Cr. 8vo.* 6s.
PETER, A PARASITE. *Cr. 8vo.* 6s.
THE BROWN EYES OF MARY. *Third Edition. Cr. 8vo.* 6s.

Anstey (F.), Author of 'Vice Versâ.' A BAYARD FROM BENGAL. Illustrated by Bernard Partridge. *Third Edition. Cr. 8vo.* 3s. 6d.

Bacheller (Irving), Author of 'Eben Holden.' DARREL OF THE BLESSED ISLES. *Third Edition. Cr. 8vo.* 6s.

Bagot (Richard). A ROMAN MYSTERY. *Third Edition. Cr. 8vo.* 6s.
THE PASSPORT. *Fourth Ed. Cr. 8vo.* 6s.

Baring-Gould (S.). ARMINELL. *Fifth Edition. Cr. 8vo.* 6s.
URITH. *Fifth Edition. Cr. 8vo.* 6s.
IN THE ROAR OF THE SEA. *Seventh Edition. Cr. 8vo.* 6s.
CHEAP JACK ZITA. *Fourth Edition. Cr. 8vo.* 6s.
MARGERY OF QUETHER. *Third Edition. Cr. 8vo.* 6s.
THE QUEEN OF LOVE. *Fifth Edition. Cr. 8vo.* 6s.
JACQUETTA. *Third Edition. Cr. 8vo.* 6s.
KITTY ALONE. *Fifth Edition. Cr. 8vo.* 6s.
NOÉMI. Illustrated. *Fourth Edition. Cr. 8vo.* 6s.
THE BROOM-SQUIRE. Illustrated. *Fifth Edition. Cr. 8vo.* 6s.

DARTMOOR IDYLLS. *Cr. 8vo.* 6s.
THE PENNYCOMEQUICKS. *Third Edition. Cr. 8vo.* 6s.
GUAVAS THE TINNER. Illustrated. *Second Edition. Cr. 8vo.* 6s.
BLADYS. Illustrated. *Second Edition. Cr. 8vo.* 6s.
PABO THE PRIEST. *Cr. 8vo.* 6s.
WINEFRED. Illustrated. *Second Edition. Cr. 8vo.* 6s.
ROYAL GEORGIE. Illustrated. *Cr. 8vo.* 6s.
MISS QUILLET. Illustrated. *Cr. 8vo.* 6s.
CHRIS OF ALL SORTS. *Cr. 8vo.* 6s.
IN DEWISLAND. *Second Edition. Cr. 8vo.* 6s.
LITTLE TU'PENNY. *A New Edition.* 6d.
See also Strand Novels and Books for Boys and Girls.

Barlow (Jane). THE LAND OF THE SHAMROCK. *Cr. 8vo.* 6s. See also Strand Novels.

Barr (Robert). IN THE MIDST OF ALARMS. *Third Edition. Cr. 8vo.* 6s.
THE MUTABLE MANY. *Third Edition. Cr. 8vo.* 6s.
THE COUNTESS TEKLA. *Third Edition. Cr. 8vo.* 6s.
THE LADY ELECTRA. *Second Edition. Cr. 8vo.* 6s.
THE TEMPESTUOUS PETTICOAT. Illustrated. *Third Edition. Cr. 8vo.* 6s.
See also Strand Novels and S. Crane.

Begbie (Harold). THE ADVENTURES OF SIR JOHN SPARROW. *Cr. 8vo.* 6s.

Belloc (Hilaire). EMMANUEL BURDEN MERCHANT. With 36 Illustrations by G. K. Chesterton. *Second Edition. Cr. 8vo.* 6s.

FICTION

Benson (E. F.) DODO. *Fourth Edition.* *Cr. 8vo.* 6s. See also Strand Novels.
Benson (Margaret). SUBJECT TO VANITY. *Cr. 8vo.* 3s. 6d.
Bourne (Harold C.). See V. Langbridge.
Burton (J. Bloundelle). THE YEAR ONE: A Page of the French Revolution. Illustrated. *Cr. 8vo.* 6s.
THE FATE OF VALSEC. *Cr. 8vo.* 6s.
A BRANDED NAME. *Cr. 8vo.* 6s. See also Strand Novels.
Capes (Bernard), Author of 'The Lake of Wine.' THE EXTRAORDINARY CONFESSIONS OF DIANA PLEASE. *Third Edition. Cr. 8vo.* 6s.
A JAY OF ITALY. *Fourth Ed. Cr. 8vo.* 6s.
*LOAVES AND FISHES. *Cr. 8vo.* 6s.
Chesney (Weatherby). THE TRAGEDY OF THE GREAT EMERALD. *Cr. 8vo.* 6s.
THE MYSTERY OF A BUNGALOW. *Second Edition. Cr. 8vo.* 6s. See also Strand Novels.
Clifford (Hugh). A FREE LANCE OF TO-DAY, *Cr. 8vo.* 6s.
Clifford (Mrs. W. K.). See Strand Novels and Books for Boys and Girls.
Cobb (Thomas). A CHANGE OF FACE. *Cr. 8vo.* 6s.
Corelli (Marie). A ROMANCE OF TWO WORLDS. *Twenty-Sixth Edition. Cr. 8vo.* 6s.
VENDETTA. *Twenty-Second Edition. Cr. 8vo.* 6s.
THELMA. *Thirty-Third Edition. Cr. 8vo.* 6s.
ARDATH: THE STORY OF A DEAD SELF. *Sixteenth Edition. Cr. 8vo.* 6s.
THE SOUL OF LILITH. *Thirteenth Edition. Cr. 8vo.* 6s.
WORMWOOD. *Fourteenth Edition. Cr. 8vo.* 6s.
BARABBAS: A DREAM OF THE WORLD'S TRAGEDY. *Fortieth Edition. Cr. 8vo.* 6s.
THE SORROWS OF SATAN. *Fiftieth Edition. Cr. 8vo.* 6s.
THE MASTER CHRISTIAN. 167th *Thousand. Cr. 8vo.* 6s.
TEMPORAL POWER: A STUDY IN SUPREMACY. 130th *Thousand. Cr. 8vo.* 6s.
GOD'S GOOD MAN: A SIMPLE LOVE STORY. 134th *Thousand. Cr. 8vo.* 6s.
THE MIGHTY ATOM. *A New Edition. Cr. 8vo.* 6s.
BOY. *A New Edition. Cr. 8vo.* 6s.
JANE. *A New Edition. Cr. 8vo.* 6s.
Crockett (S. R.), Author of 'The Raiders,' etc. LOCHINVAR. Illustrated. *Third Edition. Cr. 8vo.* 6s.
THE STANDARD BEARER. *Cr. 8vo.* 6s.
Croker (B. M.). THE OLD CANTONMENT. *Cr. 8vo.* 6s.
JOHANNA. *Second Edition. Cr. 8vo.* 6s.

THE HAPPY VALLEY. *Third Edition. Cr. 8vo.* 6s.
A NINE DAYS' WONDER. *Third Edition. Cr. 8vo.* 6s.
PEGGY OF THE BARTONS. *Sixth Edition. Cr. 8vo.* 6s.
ANGEL. *Fourth Edition. Cr. 8vo.* 6s.
A STATE SECRET. *Third Edition. Cr. 8vo.* 3s. 6d.
Dawson (Francis W.). THE SCAR. *Cr. 8vo.* 6s.
Dawson (A. J). DANIEL WHYTE. *Cr. 8vo.* 3s. 6d.
Doyle (A. Conan), Author of 'Sherlock Holmes,' 'The White Company,' etc. ROUND THE RED LAMP. *Ninth Edition. Cr. 8vo.* 6s.
Duncan (Sara Jeannette) (Mrs. Everard Cotes). THOSE DELIGHTFUL AMERICANS. Illustrated. *Third Edition. Cr. 8vo.* 6s. See also Strand Novels.
Findlater (J. H.). THE GREEN GRAVES OF BALGOWRIE. *Fifth Edition. Cr. 8vo.* 6s. See also Strand Novels.
Findlater (Mary). A NARROW WAY. *Third Edition. Cr. 8vo.* 6s.
THE ROSE OF JOY. *Third Edition. Cr. 8vo.* 6s. See also Strand Novels.
Fitzpatrick (K.) THE WEANS AT ROWALLAN. Illustrated. *Second Edition. Cr. 8vo.* 6s.
Fitzstephen (Gerald). MORE KIN THAN KIND. *Cr. 8vo.* 6s.
Fletcher (J. S.). LUCIAN THE DREAMER. *Cr. 8vo.* 6s.
Fraser (Mrs. Hugh), Author of 'The Stolen Emperor.' THE SLAKING OF THE SWORD. *Cr. 8vo.* 6s.
*THE SHADOW OF THE LORD. *Cr. 8vo.* 6s.
*Fuller-Maitland (Mrs.), Author of 'The Day Book of Bethia Hardacre.' BLANCHE ESMEAD. *Cr. 8vo.* 6s.
Gerard (Dorothea), Author of 'Lady Baby.' THE CONQUEST OF LONDON. *Second Edition. Cr. 8vo.* 6s.
HOLY MATRIMONY. *Second Edition. Cr. 8vo.* 6s.
MADE OF MONEY. *Cr. 8vo.* 6s.
THE BRIDGE OF LIFE. *Cr. 8vo.* 6s.
THE IMPROBABLE IDYL. *Third Edition. Cr. 8vo.* 6s. See also Strand Novels.
Gerard (Emily). THE HERONS' TOWER. *Cr. 8vo.* 6s.
Gissing (George), Author of 'Demos,' 'In the Year of Jubilee,' etc. THE TOWN TRAVELLER. *Second Ed. Cr. 8vo.* 6s.
THE CROWN OF LIFE. *Cr. 8vo.* 6s.
Gleig (Charles). BUNTER'S CRUISE. Illustrated. *Cr. 8vo.* 3s. 6d.
Harraden (Beatrice). IN VARYING MOODS. *A New Edition. Cr. 8vo.* 6s.

*THE SCHOLAR'S DAUGHTER. Cr. 8vo. 6s.
Harrod (F.) (Frances Forbes Robertson). THE TAMING OF THE BRUTE. Cr. 8vo. 6s.
Herbertson (Agnes G.). PATIENCE DEAN. Cr. 8vo. 6s.
Hichens (Robert). THE PROPHET OF BERKELEY SQUARE. Second Edition. Cr. 8vo. 6s.
TONGUES OF CONSCIENCE. Second Edition. Cr. 8vo. 6s.
FELIX. Fifth Edition. Cr. 8vo. 6s.
THE WOMAN WITH THE FAN. Sixth Edition. Cr. 8vo. 6s.
BYEWAYS. Cr. 8vo. 3s. 6d.
THE GARDEN OF ALLAH. Twelfth Edition. Cr. 8vo. 6s.
THE BLACK SPANIEL. Cr. 8vo. 6s.
Hobbes (John Oliver), Author of 'Robert Orange.' THE SERIOUS WOOING. Cr. 8vo. 6s.
Hope (Anthony). THE GOD IN THE CAR. Tenth Edition. Cr. 8vo. 6s.
A CHANGE OF AIR. Sixth Edition. Cr. 8vo. 6s.
A MAN OF MARK. Fifth Edition. Cr. 8vo. 6s.
THE CHRONICLES OF COUNT ANTONIO. Sixth Edition. Cr. 8vo. 6s.
PHROSO. Illustrated by H. R. Millar. Sixth Edition. Cr. 8vo. 6s.
SIMON DALE. Illustrated. Sixth Edition. Cr. 8vo. 6s.
THE KING'S MIRROR. Fourth Edition. Cr. 8vo. 6s.
QUISANTE. Fourth Edition. Cr. 8vo. 6s.
THE DOLLY DIALOGUES. Cr. 8vo. 6s.
A SERVANT OF THE PUBLIC. Illustrated. Fourth Edition. Cr. 8vo. 6s.
Hope (Graham), Author of 'A Cardinal and his Conscience,' etc., etc. THE LADY OF LYTE. Second Ed. Cr. 8vo. 6s.
Hough (Emerson). THE MISSISSIPPI BUBBLE. Illustrated. Cr. 8vo. 6s.
Housman (Clemence). THE LIFE OF SIR AGLOVALE DE GALIS. Cr. 8vo. 6s.
Hyne (C. J. Cutcliffe), Author of 'Captain Kettle.' MR. HORROCKS, PURSER. Third Edition. Cr. 8vo. 6s.
Jacobs (W. W.). MANY CARGOES. Twenty-Eighth Edition. Cr. 8vo. 3s. 6d.
SEA URCHINS. Twelfth Edition. Cr. 8vo. 3s. 6d.
A MASTER OF CRAFT. Illustrated. Sixth Edition. Cr. 8vo. 3s. 6d.
LIGHT FREIGHTS. Illustrated. Fifth Edition. Cr. 8vo. 3s. 6d.
James (Henry). THE SOFT SIDE. Second Edition. Cr. 8vo. 6s.
THE BETTER SORT. Cr. 8vo. 6s.
THE AMBASSADORS. Second Edition. Cr. 8vo. 6s.
THE GOLDEN BOWL. Third Edition. Cr. 8vo. 6s.

Janson (Gustaf). ABRAHAM'S SACRIFICE. Cr. 8vo. 6s.
Keays (H. A. Mitchell). HE THAT EATETH BREAD WITH ME. Cr. 8vo. 6s.
Langbridge (V.) and Bourne (C. Harold.). THE VALLEY OF INHERITANCE. Cr. 8vo. 6s.
Lawless (Hon. Emily). WITH ESSEX IN IRELAND. Cr. 8vo. 6s.
See also Strand Novels.
Lawson (Harry), Author of 'When the Billy Boils.' CHILDREN OF THE BUSH. Cr. 8vo. 6s.
Le Queux (W.). THE HUNCHBACK OF WESTMINSTER. Third Edition. Cr. 8vo. 6s.
THE CLOSED BOOK. Third Edition. Cr. 8vo. 6s.
THE VALLEY OF THE SHADOW. Illustrated. Third Edition. Cr. 8vo. 6s.
BEHIND THE THRONE. Third Edition. Cr. 8vo. 6s.
Levett-Yeats (S.). ORRAIN. Second Edition. Cr. 8vo. 6s.
Long (J. Luther), Co-Author of 'The Darling of the Gods.' MADAM BUTTERFLY. Cr. 8vo. 3s. 6d.
SIXTY JANE. Cr. 8vo. 6s.
Lowis (Cecil). THE MACHINATIONS OF THE MYO-OK. Cr. 8vo. 6s.
Lyall (Edna). DERRICK VAUGHAN, NOVELIST. 42nd Thousand. Cr. 8vo. 3s. 6d.
M'Carthy (Justin H.), Author of 'If I wer King.' THE LADY OF LOYALTY HOUSE. Illustrated. Third Edition. Cr. 8vo. 6s.
THE DRYAD. Second Edition. Cr. 8vo. 6s.
Macdonald (Ronald). THE SEA MAID. Cr. 8vo. 6s.
Macnaughtan (S.). THE FORTUNE OF CHRISTINA MACNAB. Third Edition. Cr. 8vo. 6s.
Malet (Lucas). COLONEL ENDERBY'S WIFE. Fourth Edition. Cr. 8vo. 6s.
A COUNSEL OF PERFECTION. New Edition. Cr. 8vo. 6s.
THE WAGES OF SIN. Fourteenth Edition. Cr. 8vo. 6s.
THE CARISSIMA. Fourth Edition. Cr. 8vo. 6s.
THE GATELESS BARRIER. Fourth Edition. Cr. 8vo. 6s.
THE HISTORY OF SIR RICHARD CALMADY. Seventh Edition. Cr. 8vo. 6s.
See also Books for Boys and Girls.
Mann (Mrs. M. E.). OLIVIA'S SUMMER. Second Edition. Cr. 8vo. 6s.
A LOST ESTATE. A New Edition. Cr. 8vo. 6s.
THE PARISH OF HILBY. A New Edition. Cr. 8vo. 6s.
THE PARISH NURSE. Fourth Edition. Cr. 8vo. 6s.

Fiction

GRAN'MA'S JANE. *Cr. 8vo. 6s.*
MRS. PETER HOWARD. *Cr. 8vo. 6s.*
A WINTER'S TALE. *A New Edition. Cr. 8vo. 6s.*
ONE ANOTHER'S BURDENS. *A New Edition. Cr. 8vo. 6s.*
ROSE AT HONEYPOT. *Second Ed. Cr. 8vo. 6s.* See also Books for Boys and Girls.
Marriott (Charles), Author of 'The Column.' GENEVRA. *Second Edition. Cr. 8vo. 6s.*
Marsh (Richard). THE TWICKENHAM PEERAGE. *Second Edition. Cr. 8vo. 6s.*
A DUEL. *Cr. 8vo. 6s.*
THE MARQUIS OF PUTNEY. *Second Edition. Cr. 8vo. 6s.*
See also Strand Novels.
Mason (A. E. W.), Author of 'The Four Feathers,' etc. CLEMENTINA. Illustrated. *Second Edition. Cr. 8vo. 6s.*
Mathers (Helen), Author of 'Comin' thro' the Rye.' HONEY. *Fourth Edition. Cr. 8vo. 6s.*
GRIFF OF GRIFFITHSCOURT. *Cr. 8vo. 6s.*
THE FERRYMAN. *Second Edition. Cr. 8vo. 6s.*
Maxwell (W. B.), Author of 'The Ragged Messenger.' VIVIEN. *Seventh Edition. Cr. 8vo. 6s.*
THE RAGGED MESSENGER. *Third Edition. Cr. 8vo. 6s.*
FABULOUS FANCIES. *Cr. 8vo. 6s.*
Meade (L. T.). DRIFT. *Second Edition. Cr. 8vo. 6s.*
RESURGAM. *Cr. 8vo. 6s.*
VICTORY. *Cr. 8vo. 6s.*
See also Books for Girls and Boys.
Meredith (Ellis). HEART OF MY HEART. *Cr. 8vo. 6s.*
'Miss Molly' (The Author of). THE GREAT RECONCILER. *Cr. 8vo. 6s.*
Mitford (Bertram). THE SIGN OF THE SPIDER. Illustrated. *Sixth Edition. Cr. 8vo. 3s. 6d.*
IN THE WHIRL OF THE RISING. *Third Edition. Cr. 8vo. 6s.*
THE RED DERELICT. *Second Edition. Cr. 8vo. 6s.*
Montresor (F. F.), Author of 'Into the Highways and Hedges.' THE ALIEN. *Third Edition. Cr. 8vo. 6s.*
Morrison (Arthur). TALES OF MEAN STREETS. *Sixth Edition. Cr. 8vo. 6s.*
A CHILD OF THE JAGO. *Fourth Edition. Cr. 8vo. 6s.*
TO LONDON TOWN. *Second Edition. Cr. 8vo. 6s.*
CUNNING MURRELL. *Cr. 8vo. 6s.*
THE HOLE IN THE WALL. *Fourth Edition. Cr. 8vo. 6s.*
DIVERS VANITIES. *Cr. 8vo. 6s.*

Nesbit (E.). (Mrs. E. Bland). THE RED HOUSE. Illustrated. *Fourth Edition. Cr. 8vo. 6s.*
See also Strand Novels.
Norris (W. E.). THE CREDIT OF THE COUNTY. Illustrated. *Second Edition. Cr. 8vo. 6s.*
THE EMBARRASSING ORPHAN. *Cr. 8vo. 6s.*
NIGEL'S VOCATION. *Cr. 8vo. 6s.*
BARHAM OF BELTANA. *Second Edition. Cr. 8vo. 6s.*
See also Strand Novels.
Ollivant (Alfred). OWD BOB, THE GREY DOG OF KENMUIR. *Eighth Edition. Cr. 8vo. 6s.*
Oppenheim (E. Phillips). MASTER OF MEN. *Third Edition. Cr. 8vo. 6s.*
Oxenham (John), Author of 'Barbe of Grand Bayou.' A WEAVER OF WEBS. *Second Edition. Cr. 8vo. 6s.*
THE GATE OF THE DESERT. *Fourth Edition. Cr. 8vo. 6s.*
Pain (Barry). THREE FANTASIES. *Cr. 8vo. 1s.*
LINDLEY KAYS. *Third Edition. Cr. 8vo. 6s.*
Parker (Gilbert). PIERRE AND HIS PEOPLE. *Sixth Edition.*
MRS. FALCHION. *Fifth Edition. Cr. 8vo. 6s.*
THE TRANSLATION OF A SAVAGE. *Second Edition. Cr. 8vo. 6s.*
THE TRAIL OF THE SWORD. Illustrated. *Ninth Edition. Cr. 8vo. 6s.*
WHEN VALMOND CAME TO PONTIAC: The Story of a Lost Napoleon. *Fifth Edition. Cr. 8vo. 6s.*
AN ADVENTURER OF THE NORTH: The Last Adventures of 'Pretty Pierre.' *Third Edition. Cr. 8vo. 6s.*
THE SEATS OF THE MIGHTY. Illustrated. *Fourteenth Edition. Cr. 8vo.*
THE BATTLE OF THE STRONG: a Romance of Two Kingdoms. Illustrated. *Fifth Edition. Cr. 8vo. 6s.*
THE POMP OF THE LAVILETTES. *Second Edition. Cr. 8vo. 3s. 6d.*
Pemberton (Max). THE FOOTSTEPS OF A THRONE. Illustrated. *Third Edition. Cr. 8vo. 6s.*
I CROWN THEE KING. With Illustrations by Frank Dadd and A. Forrestier. *Cr. 8vo. 6s.*
Phillpotts (Eden). LYING PROPHETS. *Cr. 8vo. 6s.*
CHILDREN OF THE MIST. *Fifth Edition. Cr. 8vo. 6s.*
THE HUMAN BOY. With a Frontispiece. *Fourth Edition. Cr. 8vo. 6s.*
SONS OF THE MORNING. *Second Edition. Cr. 8vo. 6s.*

THE RIVER. *Third Edition. Cr. 8vo. 6s.*
THE AMERICAN PRISONER. *Third Edition. Cr. 8vo. 6s.*
THE SECRET WOMAN. *Fourth Edition. Cr. 8vo. 6s.*
KNOCK AT A VENTURE. With a Frontispiece. *Third Edition. Cr. 8vo. 6s.*
*THE PORTREEVE. *Cr. 8vo. 6s.*
See also Strand Novels.
Pickthall (Marmaduke). SAÏD THE FISHERMAN. *Fifth Edition. Cr. 8vo. 6s.*
BRENDLE. *Second Edition. Cr. 8vo. 6s.*
'Q,' Author of 'Dead Man's Rock.' THE WHITE WOLF. *Second Edition. Cr. 8vo. 6s.*
THE MAYOR OF TROY. *Cr. 8vo. 6s.*
Rhys (Grace). THE WOOING OF SHEILA. *Second Edition. Cr. 8vo. 6s.*
THE PRINCE OF LISNOVER. *Cr. 8vo. 6s.*
Rhys (Grace) and Another. THE DIVERTED VILLAGE. Illustrated by DOROTHY GWYN JEFFREYS. *Cr. 8vo. 6s.*
Ridge (W. Pett). LOST PROPERTY. *Second Edition. Cr. 8vo. 6s.*
'ERB. *Second Edition. Cr. 8vo. 6s.*
A SON OF THE STATE. *A New Edition. Cr. 8vo. 3s. 6d.*
A BREAKER OF LAWS. *A New Edition. Cr. 8vo. 3s. 6d.*
MRS. GALER'S BUSINESS. Illustrated. *Second Edition. Cr. 8vo. 6s.*
SECRETARY TO BAYNE, M.P. *Cr. 8vo. 3s. 6d.*
Ritchie (Mrs. David G.). THE TRUTHFUL LIAR. *Cr. 8vo. 6s.*
Roberts (C. G. D.). THE HEART OF THE ANCIENT WOOD. *Cr. 8vo. 3s. 6d.*
Russell (W. Clark). MY DANISH SWEETHEART. Illustrated. *Fifth Edition. Cr. 8vo. 6s.*
HIS ISLAND PRINCESS. Illustrated. *Second Edition. Cr. 6vo. 6s.*
ABANDONED. *Cr. 8vo. 6s.*
See also Books for Boys and Girls.
Sergeant (Adeline). ANTHEA'S WAY. *Cr. 8vo. 6s.*
THE PROGRESS OF RACHAEL. *Cr. 8vo. 6s.*
THE MYSTERY OF THE MOAT. *Second Edition. Cr. 8vo. 6s.*
MRS. LYGON'S HUSBAND. *Cr. 8vo. 6s.*
THE COMING OF THE RANDOLPHS. *Cr. 8vo. 6s.*
See also Strand Novels.
Shannon (W. F.). THE MESS DECK. *Cr. 8vo. 3s. 6d.*
See also Strand Novels.

Sonnichsen (Albert). DEEP-SEA VAGABONDS. *Cr. 8vo. 6s.*
Thompson (Vance). SPINNERS OF LIFE. *Cr. 8vo. 6s.*
Urquhart (M.), A TRAGEDY IN COMMONPLACE. *Second Ed. Cr. 8vo. 6s.*
Waineman (Paul). BY A FINNISH LAKE. *Cr. 8vo. 6s.*
THE SONG OF THE FOREST. *Cr. 8vo. 6s.* See also Strand Novels.
Waltz (E. C.). THE ANCIENT LANDMARK: A Kentucky Romance. *Cr. 8vo. 6s.*
Watson (H. B. Marriott). ALARUMS AND EXCURSIONS. *Cr. 8vo. 6s.*
CAPTAIN FORTUNE. *Third Edition. Cr. 8vo. 6s.*
TWISTED EGLANTINE. With 8 Illustrations by FRANK CRAIG. *Second Edition. Cr. 8vo. 6s.*
'THE HIGH TOBY. With a Frontispiece. *Cr. 8vo. 6s.* See also Strand Novels.
Wells (H. G.). THE SEA LADY. *Cr. 8vo. 6s.*
Weyman (Stanley), Author of 'A Gentleman of France.' UNDER THE RED ROBE. With Illustrations by R. C. WOODVILLE. *Nineteenth Edition. Cr. 8vo. 6s.*
White (Stewart E.), Author of 'The Blaze Trail.' CONJUROR'S HOUSE. A Romance of the Free Trail. *Second Edition. Cr. 8vo. 6s.*
White (Percy). THE SYSTEM. *Third Edition. Cr. 8vo. 6s.*
THE PATIENT MAN. *Second Edition. Cr. 8vo. 6s.*
Williamson (Mrs. C. N.), Author of 'The Barnstormers.' THE ADVENTURE OF PRINCESS SYLVIA. *Cr. 8vo. 3s. 6d.*
THE WOMAN WHO DARED. *Cr. 8vo. 6s.*
THE SEA COULD TELL. *Second Edition. Cr. 8vo. 6s.*
THE CASTLE OF THE SHADOWS. *Third Edition. Cr. 8vo. 6s.*
PAPA. *Cr. 8vo. 6s.*
*LADY BETTY ACROSS THE WATER. *Cr. 8vo. 6s.*
Williamson (C. N. and A. M.). THE LIGHTNING CONDUCTOR: Being the Romance of a Motor Car. Illustrated. *Thirteenth Edition. Cr. 8vo. 6s.*
THE PRINCESS PASSES. Illustrated. *Sixth Edition. Cr. 8vo. 6s.*
MY FRIEND THE CHAUFFEUR. With 16 Illustrations. *Sixth Edition. Cr. 8vo. 6s.*
*Wyllarde (Dolf), Author of 'Uriah the Hittite.' THE PATHWAY OF THE PIONEER. *Cr. 8vo. 6s.*

FICTION

The Strand Novels
Cr. 8vo. Cloth, 1s. net.

ENCOURAGED by the great and steady sale of their Sixpenny Novels, Messrs. Methuen have determined to issue a new series of fiction at a low price under the title of 'THE STRAND NOVELS.' These books are well printed and well bound in *cloth*, and the excellence of their quality may be gauged from the names of those authors who contribute the early volumes of the series.

Messrs. Methuen would point out that the books are as good and as long as a six shilling novel, that they are bound in cloth and not in paper, and that their price is One Shilling *net*. They feel sure that the public will appreciate such good and cheap literature, and the books can be seen at all good booksellers.

The first volumes are:—

Balfour (Andrew). VENGEANCE IS MINE.
TO ARMS.
Baring-Gould (S.). MRS. CURGENVEN OF CURGENVEN.
*DOMITIA.
*THE FROBISHERS.
Barlow (Jane), Author of 'Irish Idylls. FROM THE EAST UNTO THE WEST
A CREEL OF IRISH STORIES.
*THE FOUNDING OF FORTUNES.
Barr (Robert). THE VICTORS.
Bartram (George). THIRTEEN EVENINGS.
Benson (E. F.), Author of 'Dodo.' THE CAPSINA.
Bowles (G. Stewart). A STRETCH OFF THE LAND.
Brooke (Emma). THE POET'S CHILD.
Bullock (Shan F.). THE BARRYS.
THE CHARMER.
THE SQUIREEN.
THE RED LEAGUERS.
Burton (J. Bloundelle). ACROSS THE SALT SEAS.
THE CLASH OF ARMS.
DENOUNCED.
*FORTUNE'S MY FOE.
Capes (Bernard). AT A WINTER'S FIRE.
Chesney (Weatherby). THE BAPTIST RING.
THE BRANDED PRINCE.
THE FOUNDERED GALLEON.
JOHN TOPP.
Clifford (Mrs. W. K.). A FLASH OF SUMMER.
Collingwood (Harry). THE DOCTOR OF THE 'JULIET.'
Cornford (L. Cope). SONS OF ADVERSITY.
Crane (Stephen). WOUNDS IN THE RAIN.
Denny (C. E.). THE ROMANCE OF UPFOLD MANOR.
Dickson (Harris). THE BLACK WOLF'S BREED.
Dickinson (Evelyn). THE SIN OF ANGELS.

*Duncan (Sara J.). THE POOL IN THE DESERT.
*A VOYAGE OF CONSOLATION.
Embree (C. F.). A HEART OF FLAME.
Fenn (G. Manville). AN ELECTRIC SPARK.
Findlater (Jane H.). THE DAUGHTER OF STRIFE.
*Findlater (Mary). OVER THE HILLS.
Forrest (R. E.). THE SWORD OF AZRAEL.
Francis (M. E.). MISS ERIN.
Gallon (Tom). RICKERBY'S FOLLY.
Gerard (Dorothea). THINGS THAT HAVE HAPPENED.
Glanville (Ernest). THE DESPATCH RIDER.
THE LOST REGIMENT.
THE KLOOF BRIDE.
THE INCA'S TREASURE.
Gordon (Julien). MRS. CLYDE.
WORLD'S PEOPLE.
Goss (C. F.). THE REDEMPTION OF DAVID CORSON.
*Gray (E. M'Queen). MY STEWARDSHIP.
Hales (A. G.). JAIR THE APOSTATE.
Hamilton (Lord Ernest). MARY HAMILTON.
Harrison (Mrs. Burton). A PRINCESS OF THE HILLS. Illustrated.
Hooper (I.). THE SINGER OF MARLY.
Hough (Emerson). THE MISSISSIPPI BUBBLE.
'Iota' (Mrs. Caffyn). ANNE MAULEVERER.
*Jepson (Edgar). KEEPERS OF THE PEOPLE.
Kelly (Florence Finch). WITH HOOPS OF STEEL.
Lawless (Hon. Emily). MAELCHO.
Linden (Annie). A WOMAN OF SENTIMENT.
*Lorimer (Norma). JOSIAH'S WIFE.
Lush (Charles K.). THE AUTOCRATS.
Macdonnell (A.). THE STORY OF TERESA.
Macgrath (Harold). THE PUPPET CROWN.

MESSRS. METHUEN'S CATALOGUE

Mackie (Pauline Bradford). THE VOICE IN THE DESERT.
Marsh (Richard). THE SEEN AND THE UNSEEN.
*GARNERED.
*A METAMORPHOSIS.
MARVELS AND MYSTERIES.
BOTH SIDES OF THE VEIL.
Mayall (J. W.). THE CYNIC AND THE SYREN.
Monkhouse (Allan). LOVE IN A LIFE.
Moore (Arthur). THE KNIGHT PUNCTILIOUS.
Nesbit (Mrs. Bland). THE LITERARY SENSE.
Norris (W. E.). AN OCTAVE.
Oliphant (Mrs.). THE LADY'S WALK.
SIR ROBERT'S FORTUNE.
THE TWO MARY'S.
Penny (Mrs. F. A.). A MIXED MARRIAGE.
Phillpotts (Eden). THE STRIKING HOURS.
FANCY FREE.
Randall (J.). AUNT BETHIA'S BUTTON.
*Raymond (Walter). FORTUNE'S DARLING.
*Rayner (Olive Pratt). ROSALBA.
Rhys (Grace). THE DIVERTED VILLAGE.

Rickert (Edith). OUT OF THE CYPRESS SWAMP.
Roberton (M. H.). A GALLANT QUAKER.
Saunders (Marshall). ROSE A CHARLITTE.
Sergeant (Adeline). ACCUSED AND ACCUSER.
BARBARA'S MONEY.
THE ENTHUSIAST.
A GREAT LADY.
*THE LOVE THAT OVERCAME.
THE MASTER OF BEECHWOOD.
UNDER SUSPICION.
*THE YELLOW DIAMOND.
Shannon (W. F.). JIM TWELVES.
*Strain (E. H.). ELMSLIE'S DRAG NET.
Stringer (Arthur). THE SILVER POPPY.
Stuart (Esmè). CHRISTALLA.
Sutherland (Duchess of). ONE HOUR AND THE NEXT.
Swan (Annie). LOVE GROWN COLD.
Swift (Benjamin). SORDON.
Tanqueray (Mrs. B. M.). THE ROYAL QUAKER.
Trafford-Taunton (Mrs. E. W.). SILENT DOMINION.
*Upward (Allen). ATHELSTANE FORD
Waineman (Paul). A HEROINE FROM FINLAND.
Watson (H. B. Marriott). THE SKIRTS OF HAPPY CHANCE.

Books for Boys and Girls

Illustrated. Crown 8vo. 3s. 6d.

THE GETTING WELL OF DOROTHY. By Mrs. W. K. Clifford. *Second Edition.*
THE ICELANDER'S SWORD. By S. Baring-Gould.
ONLY A GUARD-ROOM DOG. By Edith E. Cuthell.
THE DOCTOR OF THE JULIET. By Harry Collingwood.
LITTLE PETER. By Lucas Malet. *Second Edition.*
MASTER ROCKAFELLAR'S VOYAGE. By W. Clark Russell.

THE SECRET OF MADAME DE MONLUC. By the Author of "Mdlle. Mori."
SYD BELTON: Or, the Boy who would not go to Sea. By G. Manville Fenn.
THE RED GRANGE. By Mrs. Molesworth.
A GIRL OF THE PEOPLE. By L. T. Meade. *Second Edition.*
HEPSY GIPSY. By L. T. Meade. 2s. 6d.
THE HONOURABLE MISS. By L. T. Meade.
THERE WAS ONCE A PRINCE. By Mrs. M. E. Mann.
WHEN ARNOLD COMES HOME. By Mrs. M. E. Mann.

The Novels of Alexandre Dumas

Price 6d. Double Volumes, 1s.

THE THREE MUSKETEERS. With a long Introduction by Andrew Lang. Double volume.
THE PRINCE OF THIEVES. *Second Edition.*
ROBIN HOOD. A Sequel to the above.
THE CORSICAN BROTHERS.
GEORGES.

CROP-EARED JACQUOT; JANE; Etc.
TWENTY YEARS AFTER. Double volume.
AMAURY.
THE CASTLE OF EPPSTEIN.
THE SNOWBALL, and SULTANETTA.
CECILE; OR, THE WEDDING GOWN.
ACTÉ.

FICTION

THE BLACK TULIP.
THE VICOMTE DE BRAGELONNE.
  Part I. Louise de la Vallière. Double Volume.
  Part II. The Man in the Iron Mask. Double Volume.
THE CONVICT'S SON.
THE WOLF-LEADER.
NANON; OR, THE WOMEN' WAR. Double volume.
PAULINE; MURAT; AND PASCAL BRUNO.
THE ADVENTURES OF CAPTAIN PAMPHILE.
FERNANDE.
GABRIEL LAMBERT.
CATHERINE BLUM.
THE CHEVALIER D'HARMENTAL. Double volume.
SYLVANDIRE.
THE FENCING MASTER.
THE REMINISCENCES OF ANTONY.
CONSCIENCE.
PERE LA RUINE.
*THE GREAT MASSACRE. The first part of Queen Margot.
*HENRI OF NAVARRE. The second part of Queen Margot.
*THE WILD DUCK SHOOTER.

Illustrated Edition.

Demy 8vo. Cloth.

THE THREE MUSKETEERS. Illustrated in Colour by Frank Adams. 2s. 6d.

THE PRINCE OF THIEVES. Illustrated in Colour by Frank Adams. 2s.
ROBIN HOOD THE OUTLAW. Illustrated in Colour by Frank Adams. 2s.
THE CORSICAN BROTHERS. Illustrated in Colour by A. M. M'Lellan. 1s. 6d.
THE WOLF-LEADER. Illustrated in Colour by Frank Adams. 1s. 6d.
GEORGES. Illustrated in Colour by Munro Orr. 2s.
TWENTY YEARS AFTER. Illustrated in Colour by Frank Adams. 3s.
AMAURY. Illustrated in Colour by Gordon Browne. 2s.
THE SNOWBALL, and SULTANETTA. Illustrated in Colour by Frank Adams. 2s.
THE VICOMTE DE BRAGELONNE. Illustrated in Colour by Frank Adams.
  Part I. Louise de la Vallière. 3s.
  Part II. The Man in the Iron Mask. 3s.
*CROP-EARED JACQUOT; JANE; Etc. Illustrated in Colour by Gordon Browne. 2s.
THE CASTLE OF EPPSTEIN. Illustrated in Colour by Stewart Orr. 1s. 6d.
ACTÉ. Illustrated in Colour by Gordon Browne. 1s. 6d.
*CECILE; OR, THE WEDDING GOWN. Illustrated in Colour by D. Murray Smith. 1s. 6d.
*THE ADVENTURES OF CAPTAIN PAMPHILE. Illustrated in Colour by Frank Adams. 1s. 6d.

Methuen's Sixpenny Books

Austen (Jane). PRIDE AND PREJUDICE.
Bagot (Richard). A ROMAN MYSTERY.
Balfour (Andrew). BY STROKE OF SWORD.
Baring-Gould (S.). FURZE BLOOM.
CHEAP JACK ZITA.
KITTY ALONE.
URITH.
THE BROOM SQUIRE.
IN THE ROAR OF THE SEA.
NOÉMI.
A BOOK OF FAIRY TALES. Illustrated.
LITTLE TU'PENNY.
THE FROBISHERS.
Barr (Robert). JENNIE BAXTER, JOURNALIST.
IN THE MIDST OF ALARMS.
THE COUNTESS TEKLA.
THE MUTABLE MANY.
Benson (E. F.). DODO.
Brontë (Charlotte). SHIRLEY.
Brownell (C. L.). THE HEART OF JAPAN.

Burton (J. Bloundelle). ACROSS THE SALT SEAS.
Caffyn (Mrs.), ('Iota'). ANNE MAULEVERER.
Capes (Bernard). THE LAKE OF WINE.
Clifford (Mrs. W. K.). A FLASH OF SUMMER.
MRS. KEITH'S CRIME.
Connell (F. Norreys). THE NIGGER KNIGHTS.
Corbett (Julian). A BUSINESS IN GREAT WATERS.
Croker (Mrs. B. M.). PEGGY OF THE BARTONS.
A STATE SECRET.
ANGEL.
JOHANNA.
Dante (Alighieri). THE VISION OF DANTE (CARY).
Doyle (A. Conan). ROUND THE RED LAMP.
Duncan (Sara Jeannette). A VOYAGE OF CONSOLATION.
THOSE DELIGHTFUL AMERICANS.

Eliot (George). THE MILL ON THE FLOSS.
Findlater (Jane H.). THE GREEN GRAVES OF BALGOWRIE.
Gallon (Tom). RICKERBY'S FOLLY.
Gaskell (Mrs.). CRANFORD.
MARY BARTON.
NORTH AND SOUTH.
Gerard (Dorothea). HOLY MATRIMONY.
THE CONQUEST OF LONDON.
MADE OF MONEY.
Gissing (George). THE TOWN TRAVELLER.
THE CROWN OF LIFE.
Glanville (Ernest). THE INCA'S TREASURE.
THE KLOOF BRIDE.
Gleig (Charles). BUNTER'S CRUISE.
Grimm (The Brothers). GRIMM'S FAIRY TALES. Illustrated.
Hope (Anthony). A MAN OF MARK.
A CHANGE OF AIR.
THE CHRONICLES OF COUNT ANTONIO.
PHROSO.
THE DOLLY DIALOGUES.
Hornung (E. W.). DEAD MEN TELL NO TALES.
Ingraham (J. H.). THE THRONE OF DAVID.
Le Queux (W.). THE HUNCHBACK OF WESTMINSTER.
*Levett-Yeats (S. K.). THE TRAITOR'S WAY.
Linton (E. Lynn). THE TRUE HISTORY OF JOSHUA DAVIDSON.
Lyall (Edna). DERRICK VAUGHAN.
Malet (Lucas). THE CARISSIMA.
A COUNSEL OF PERFECTION.
Mann (Mrs. M. E.). MRS. PETER HOWARD.
A LOST ESTATE.
THE CEDAR STAR.
Marchmont (A. W.). MISER HOADLEY'S SECRET.
A MOMENT'S ERROR.
Marryat (Captain). PETER SIMPLE.
JACOB FAITHFUL.
Marsh (Richard). THE TWICKENHAM PEERAGE.
THE GODDESS.
THE JOSS.
Mason (A. E. W.). CLEMENTINA.
Mathers (Helen). HONEY.
GRIFF OF GRIFFITHSCOURT.
SAM'S SWEETHEART
Meade (Mrs. L. T.). DRIFT.
Mitford (Bertram). THE SIGN OF THE SPIDER.
Montresor (F. F.). THE ALIEN.
Moore (Arthur). THE GAY DECEIVERS.
Morrison (Arthur). THE HOLE IN THE WALL.
Nesbit (E.). THE RED HOUSE.
Norris (W. E.). HIS GRACE.
GILES INGILBY.
THE CREDIT OF THE COUNTY.
LORD LEONARD.
MATTHEW AUSTIN.
CLARISSA FURIOSA.
Oliphant (Mrs.). THE LADY'S WALK.
SIR ROBERT'S FORTUNE.
THE PRODIGALS.
Oppenheim (E. Phillips). MASTER O.' MEN.
Parker (Gilbert). THE POMP OF THE LAVILETTES.
WHEN VALMOND CAME TO PONTIAC.
THE TRAIL OF THE SWORD.
Pemberton (Max). THE FOOTSTEPS OF A THRONE.
I CROWN THEE KING.
Phillpotts (Eden). THE HUMAN BOY
CHILDREN OF THE MIST.
Ridge (W. Pett). A SON OF THE STATE.
LOST PROPERTY.
GEORGE AND THE GENERAL.
Russell (W. Clark). A MARRIAGE AT SEA.
ABANDONED.
MY DANISH SWEETHEART.
Sergeant (Adeline). THE MASTER OF BEECHWOOD.
BARBARA'S MONEY.
THE YELLOW DIAMOND.
Surtees (R. S.). HANDLEY CROSS. Illustrated.
MR. SPONGE'S SPORTING TOUR. Illustrated.
ASK MAMMA. Illustrated.
Valentine (Major E. S.). VELDT AND LAAGER.
Walford (Mrs. L. B.). MR. SMITH.
THE BABY'S GRANDMOTHER.
Wallace (General Lew). BEN-HUR.
THE FAIR GOD.
Watson (H. B. Marriot). THE ADVENTURERS.
Weekes (A. B.). PRISONERS OF WAR.
Wells (H. G.). THE STOLEN BACILLUS.
*White (Percy). A PASSIONATE PILGRIM.

www.ingramcontent.com/pod-product-compliance
Lightning Source LLC
Chambersburg PA
CBHW051243300426
44114CB00011B/869